HOW TO MAKE TROUBLE AND INFLUENCE PEOPLE.

PRANKS, PROTESTS, GRAFFITI & POLITICAL MISCHIEF-MAKING

from across **AUSTRALIA**

1788 until 2012

bomb the Patriarchy
Feminist Action Collective 2003

Mass Demonstration

BATTERY HENS LIVE IN HELL

CONSUME, BE SILENT DIE. WE RELY ON YOUR APATHY

Yellow cute a heavy addiction

HOMLESS? Here's a home

Freedom of speech means Nothing when Nothing is being said

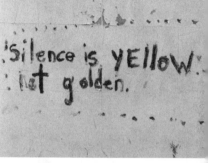

Silence is YELLOW not golden.

HANSON = MUTOID SUPREMACY.

1990's THE AGE OF DENIAL

JOY

STAGE 2 NOW SELLING STRONACH Advance Australia where?

LOCAL TRAFFIC ONLY

NO DAMS

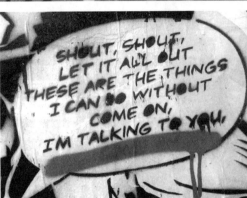

STOP THE KILLING
END THE U.S ALLIANCE

DEMOCRACY
—WE
DELIVER

We recognise and pay respect to the Indigenous nations and traditional custodians of Australia. We express solidarity with the ongoing struggles for land rights, self-determination, sovereignty and the recognition of past injustices.

AUTHOR AND EDITOR
IAIN MᶜINTYRE

BOOK DESIGN AND GRAPHIC EDITOR
TOM SEVIL (AKA CIVIL)

EDITOR AND ADDITIONAL RESEARCH
LOU SMITH

PROOF READING: PETER CAHILL, SHANE MCGRATH AND GREGORY NIPPER

Second Edition
Co-Published in 2013 by:

PM PRESS

PO BOX 23912, OAKLAND, CA 94623 USA
WWW.PMPRESS.ORG

BREAKDOWN PRESS

PO BOX 1283 CARLTON, MELBOURNE, VIC 3053 AUS
WWW.BREAKDOWNPRESS.ORG

First Published in 2009 by Breakdown Press.

FOR MORE INFORMATION
WWW.HOWTOMAKETROUBLEANDINFLUENCEPEOPLE.ORG

This book is an expanded compilation of the zines:
How To Make Trouble And Influence People, 1996
How To Stop Whining And Start Living, 1999
Revenge Of The Troublemaker, 2003.

Dedicated to Ned Sevil (1980-2010), Pete Gray (1981-2011) and Dara Greenwald (1971-2012).

Aboriginal and Torres Strait Islander peoples are advised that this book contains images of deceased persons.

ISBN: 978-1-60486-595-0
LCCN: 2012913624

Printed in the USA on recycled paper by the Employee Owners of Thomson-Shore in Dexter, Michigan. www.thomsonshore.com

"Let no one say the past is dead.
The past is all about us and within."

Oodgeroo Noonuccal, 1970

"Australia has progressed by a series of little rebellions."

L. Haylen, 1948

CHECKPOINT FOR
WEAPONS OF MASS
DISTRACTION

INTRODUCTORY PAGES
PHOTO CREDITS

PAGE 2: Anonymous graffiti captured while wandering the streets of Melbourne, 2008-09. Photographer: Andrew J. Cosgriff. **PAGE 3:** 1990s graffiti – Hobart, Adelaide, Sydney, Newcastle. Photographer: Ian Sweeney. **PAGE 4: Top to bottom, left to right:** Masked-up protester stencil by Sixten, Ned Kelly stencil by HA HA, character by Phibs, Inner Melbourne, 2007. Photographer: Tom Sevil • Anonymous stencil, Melbourne 2006. Photographer Tom Sevil • Supermarket sculpture. Sydney, 2003. Photographer: Ned Sevil • "Shout, Shout," street stencil by Meggs. Photographer: Plasmo • Hunter Street Mall, Newcastle, 1997. Photographer: Ian Sweeney • Woman diving stencil by Leroy Black, King Street Newcastle 2003, Photographer: Lou Smith • Tagged door, Brunswick, Melbourne 2012. Photographer: Tom Sevil. **PAGE 5: Clockwise from top left:** Woman with bike paste-up, Gertrude Street, Melbourne, 2008 {now gone} by Miso • Sunflower bike stencil, Anon. Photographer: Lonely Radio • Bike rider with friends stencil by Ghostpatrol. Photographer: Peter Chen • Aerial bike stencil, Anon. Photographer: Peter Chen • DIY Bike Lane, Reclaim the Streets. Sydney, 1997. Photographer: Ian Sweeney. **PAGE 6:** Climate Clowns at Hazelwood coal-fired power station protest. Victoria, September, 2009. Photographer: Rodney Dekker (www.switchoffhazelwood.org). **PAGE 7:** Members of the Australian Workers' Union Bicycle Squad assembled at Coonamble, NSW during the 1902 Shearers strike. Photographer: Andrew Barton "Banjo" Paterson. • The Bundaberg Bicycle Squad used to to seek out non-unionised workers during the The Sugar Strike of 1911. Photographer unknown • Anti-Uranium Bike Ride, Canberra, 1977. Photographs courtesy of Friends of the Earth, Melbourne. **PAGES 8-9:** Longstanding creative activist Benny Zable as Greedozer. Climate Summit, Canberra. 2009. Photographer: Kristy Henderson. • Anti-war protest, Perth 1984. Photograph courtesy People for Nuclear Disarmament. • Graffiti reading "No jobs on a dead planet" along with anti-logging slogans adorn the disused Lonsdale Street power station's smokestack. Melbourne, 2003. Photographer: Tom Sevil. **PAGE 10:** Yulanji Bardon and Emily Nielson camped for 11 days during joint US-Australian military exercises to reclaim Shoalwater Bay for peace, Northern Queensland, 2009. Photograph taken on mobile phone by Mark Palmer • Tranny Cops, this Sydney-based drag dance troupe have lampooned and infuriated riot police across the country by performing at events such as the G20 and APEC protests. This photograph is from Reclaim The Streets. Sydney, April 2006. Photographer: moz.net.nz • Billboard Graffiti in action, New England Highway near Tamworth. 2002. • **PAGE 11:** Australia Day Real Estate billboard revision pointing out whose country it really is via the use of the black, red and yellow Aboriginal Flag. Newcastle, 2008. Courtesy of Cooks Hill Massive. • Goolengook anti-logging action, Victoria 1993. Photographer: Sarojini Krishnapillai. **PAGE 12:** Patches, collection courtesy of Tom Sevil. **PAGE 13:** 750 women take part in the Disrobe to Disarm action spelling No War with their naked bodies. Byron Bay, 2003. The action sent a strong message to PM Howard and the world about opposition to the war. At the time this photo was downloaded by 4,500 media outlets across the globe. • Hobart Graffiti, late 1990s. Photographer: Ian Sweeney. **PAGE 14:** Phuc It Up billboard revision. Melbourne, 1999. Photograph courtesy of Phuc It Up. **PAGE 15:** Stanmore pedestrian tunnel stencil based on an image from a government "anti-terrorism" booklet. Sydney, 2004. Photographer: Dean Sewell. **PAGES 16-17: Top Left:** Lizards Revenge, Roxby Downs SA. 2012. **Bottom left:** Smoke bombs hurled by anti-apartheid protesters disrupt play at the SCG during the Springbok rugby tour. Sydney, 1971. Courtesy of Meredith Burgmann. **Main image:** Anti-World Trade Organisation (WTO) protest. Sydney, 2002. Photographer: Dean Sewell. **Opposite:** In November 2004, Zanny Begg created an art project for the Blacktown Arts Centre that involved installing life-size stencils around the area reading "Checkpoint For Weapons Of Mass Distraction". While in the process of doing so, she was approached by a Community Law Enforcement Officer who told her to remove the work as it was "illegal" and "inappropriate in the climate of terrorism". After suggesting the officer contact the curator of the installation, she received a phone call informing her that her work had been withdrawn. Following much publicity concerning this act of censorship, Zanny exhibited the work again at Mori Gallery in early 2005 alongside works by other anti-war artists. To further spread comment on the ongoing "War On Terror", 100 of the stencils were distributed, and subsequently appeared all over Sydney on September 11th 2006. Photograph courtesy of Zanny Begg. **Background to this page and pages 18-19:** Sydney, Early 1970s. Courtesy of Pat Fiske, from her film *Rocking The Foundations*, www.roninfilms.com.au.

Contents

MAKING TROUBLE AND INFLUENCING PEOPLE
PRANKS, PROTESTS, GRAFFITI & POLITICAL MISCHIEF-MAKING
FROM ACROSS AUSTRALIA

CONVERSATIONS

The Jack-in-the-Box

JOSH MACPHEE

Organiser of CELEBRATE PEOPLE'S HISTORY POSTER SERIES
and member of JUSTSEEDS ARTISTS' COOPERATIVE (Justseeds.org)   / USA

I can't articulate how much glee I felt in 2003 when I first saw the photos of the Sydney Opera House inscribed with the giant red letters "NO WAR". Who did that? How? In this 21st century of surveillance cameras, retina scans, and completely militarised police forces, a couple of guys got to the top of Australia's most well known national landmark and did a giant roller piece on it? No shit! Two friends, Dave Burgess and Will Saunders, just scaled up the side of the building with a can of red paint. It was that simple. And Iain McIntyre had the good sense to interview Dave about how and why they did it. And it's right here, in this book!

Well, at least it looks like a book and feels like a book, but it's actually a mischievous jack-in-the-box. Well, not exactly. It's the box, and once you've read it, you become the jack. This box is so crammed with tricks, treats, and creative protest techniques that you can't help but get wound up. It's not simply a compendium of pranks done for their own sake, nor a giant pile of protest photos we've seen before, *How to Make Trouble and Influence People* maps the intersections of popular creativity, humour, and political rage: all three mixing up into a powerful molotov of past, present, and potential action.

What kind of action? Graffiti, street performances, puppetry, stencilling, billboard alterations, tree sits, protest signs, flyers, wheatpasting, banner drops, boating actions, occupations, un-permissioned public sculptures, electoral stunts, parties in the street, protest camps, light projections, drag routines, viral songs, posters, and on and on and on. And we're just talking about Australia! Yup, this book sticks to what's been going on within the boundaries of this big island in the Pacific. But before you worry about provincialism, all this national frame does is show those of us elsewhere how desperately we need a *How To Make Trouble and Influence People* for our own backyards.

While reading through the time(less) line of seemingly infinite anecdotes of creative resistance multiple things begin to emerge. First, this is an overflowing toolbox that should be within reach of every activist and organiser. It is also an anecdotal history of Australia from below. The over 200 years of stories and 100 years of photographs in this book give us a peek into the strange brew of wily workers and militant Indigenous peoples that define a true people's history. This flow of information makes it hard to read cover to cover, but also ensures that every time you pick it up something new pops out. The design is flawless, bringing our eyes from one incredible nugget to the next.

Part handbook, part art book, part reference book, part history, part how-to — I'm not sure even Iain knows what this thing is, but I know I'm glad I've got my hands on a copy!

The Prank Paradox

ANDREW HANSEN from *THE CHASER*

IN *THE CHASER'S* EARLY DAYS, before anyone realised we were making TV shows, public figures got pretty stroppy when we pranked them. Which, in comedy, was the ideal reaction.

Whenever Craig Reucassel wore a ridiculous bishop's outfit to confront politician Tony Abbott (which seemed to happen about twice a week), it was much funnier back when the baffled Abbott would scowl and grouch. Later on, once Abbott realised home viewers were judging how smoothly he'd handle the prank, he would chuckle like a good-natured mule.

Which was also funny, but less so.

The irony is, pranks are always funniest and most effective when there are people who find them neither funny nor effective.

Whenever I edit footage for a *Chaser* stunt, I look out for people in the shot who are unamused. They are where the comedy lies. It's hardly a prank if everyone's being a bloody good sport about it.

I've heard Aussies boast about this invisible, mysterious guy they know – he's called our "national character". This "guy" is said to be open-minded, suspicious of authority, and he enjoys a laugh at his own expense. Yet my experience in *The Chaser* proves there are countless Australians who don't fit that description at all.

Even our most harmless segment, "If Life Were a Musical", which involved traipsing into places to sing whimsical songs, was typically met with abject fury and calls to the police. Where was the invisible guy then? Nowhere to be seen, that's where. As might be expected of someone lacking visibility.

To be fair, the world's not divided into wowsers and good sports. There's a prank paradox within each and every one of us. On the one hand, we delight in watching extroverted people make trouble. It's wonderful entertainment. On the other hand, we love to disapprove of such behaviour. Think for a moment how satisfying it is to lodge official complaints. Mmm, lodging complaints is one of life's great pleasures. Especially for people who use words like "inappropriate" and "unintelligent", they adore lodging complaints about anything fun or spontaneous taking place.

Of course, being serious doesn't necessarily make you a bad person. A staunch Christian once chastised me for a sketch that satirised religious miracles, and when I put it to him that Jesus would have a sense of humour he said, "No, he doesn't."

Who's to define what's funny, what's clever, what's offensive? Politicians, talkback presenters and current affairs reporters seem to think the job's up to them. But the truth is, the job's up to all of us. Just

The Chaser, posing as Osama Bin Laden and motorcade, manage to enter the APEC restricted zone in one of the most memorable hoaxes of the decade. Sydney, 2007. Dressed as Bin Laden, Chas Licciardello makes his exit near the InterContinental Hotel where US President George W. Bush was staying. Photograph courtesy of *The Chaser.*

don't expect us to agree. It'd be great if everyone on earth could take a joke in a jolly spirit, but what if someone's idea of a joke is glassing you in the face?

Much of the troublemaking described in this book was done as a form of protest. I reckon protesters who scream and write swear words on placards and chuck rocks and smash stuff and punch police officers will have a hard time changing the average person's mind. That's where imaginative, inspiring troublemaking can help. The sort of stuff this book is about. When Saunders and Burgess painted "No War" on the Sydney Opera House, they created a never-before-seen image that penetrated the drooping eyelids of the Publics, even if Joe and Jo Public might have tut-tutted a little. "No War" was original, simple, didn't hurt anyone. At just two words, it could hardly have been more tightly scripted. Well done, I say.

I'm a comedian/writer/performer type of guy. I'm not an activist. I'm not trying to improve the world. And I don't feel any shame about that, any more than I do about not being a dentist or a plumber or a veterinarian.

But thank that sourpuss Christ, someone's doing it.

ADVERTISEMENT

APEC LEADERS FORUM, 7 - 9 SEPTEMBER 2007, SYDNEY.

21 world leaders.
1 great city.
100s of reasons to protest.

Help us by planning for APEC.
Visit www.apec2007.org

APEC
AUSTRALIA 2007

Bus shelter graffiti. Sydney, 2007. Anonymous

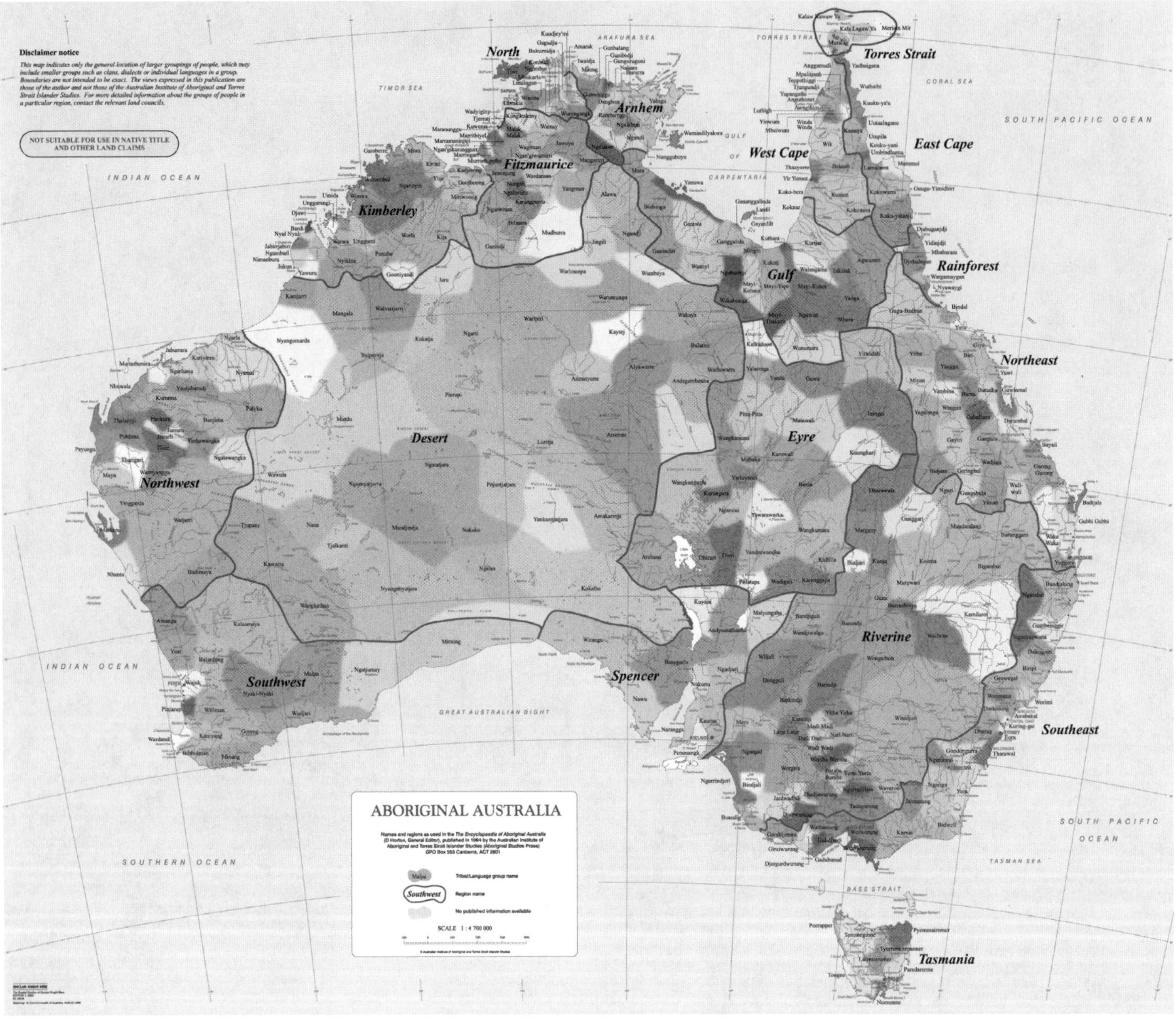

Disclaimer notice

This map indicates only the general location of larger groupings of people, which may include smaller groups such as clans, dialects or individual languages in a group. Boundaries are not intended to be exact. The views expressed in this publication are those of the author and not those of the Australian Institute of Aboriginal and Torres Strait Islander Studies. For more detailed information about the groups of people in a particular region, contact the relevant land councils.

NOT SUITABLE FOR USE IN NATIVE TITLE AND OTHER LAND CLAIMS

ABORIGINAL AUSTRALIA

Names and regions as used in the The Encyclopaedia of Aboriginal Australia (D Horton, General Editor), published in 1994 by the Australian Institute of Aboriginal and Torres Strait Islander Studies (Aboriginal Studies Press) GPO Box 553 Canberra, ACT 2601

Malya — Tribal/Language group name

Southwest — Region name

— No published information available

SCALE 1 : 4 700 000

© Australian Institute of Aboriginal and Torres Strait Islander Studies

Indigenous Australia

This map is just one representation of many other map sources that are available for Aboriginal Australia. Using published resources available between 1988–1994, this map attempts to represent all the language, social or nation groups of the Indigenous people of Australia. It indicates only the general location of larger groupings of people which may include smaller groups such as clans, dialects or individual languages in a group. Boundaries are not intended to be exact.

This map is NOT SUITABLE FOR USE IN NATIVE TITLE AND OTHER LAND CLAIMS. David R Horton, creator, © Aboriginal Studies Press, AIATSIS and Auslig/Sinclair, Knight, Merz, 1996. No reproduction allowed without permission.

To view map at larger scale go to www.howtomaketroubleandinfluencepeople.org

Australian States and Cities

Post-colonisation cartography of Australia.

Only Dead Fish Go with the Flow

IAIN MCINTYRE, 2013

Welcome to the collected and expanded edition of *How To Make Trouble And Influence People*. For over 15 years this series of books and pamphlets has focused on how generations of Australian troublemakers have moved beyond political inertia to push the boundaries of "acceptable" protest. As a result, the publications have not only included tales of pranks and hoaxes designed to humiliate the rich and powerful and illuminate the rest of us, but also creative and comedic graffiti, posters, placards and other protest ephemera. Similarly tactics and strategies, like strikes, that may have been relatively common for one group of Australians at a particular time and place have been shown to be creatively subversive when used in a different context, say by high-school students or in solidarity with those struggling against apartheid in South Africa.

The first volume of this series came out in 1996 as an 80-page, self-published zine documenting and celebrating Australian political pranking and creative direct action. *How To Make Trouble And Influence People* proved to be a modest success and in 1998 ABC radio produced a documentary and website using the title. The zine was reprinted a number of times by anarchist collective Scam Publications before spawning two sequels, *How To Stop Whining And Start Living* in 1999 and *Revenge Of The Troublemaker* in 2003. A collection of more in-depth essays, *Disturbing The Peace: Tales From Australia's Rebel History*, was also published in 2005 as an adjunct to the original series.

With material for a fourth volume piling up Tom Sevil and Lou Smith from Breakdown Press came on board in 2008, agreeing to assist not only with design, publication and editing, but also with sourcing new contributions, mainly photographs and images, via their own networks. Since all of the earlier publications were long out of print we decided to

bring together the best material from the first three books along with hundreds of new listings and graphics into one volume. The material on Aotearoa/New Zealand which appeared in the original volumes, as well as the chapters from *Disturbing The Peace*, were put aside for future publication. A US volume focusing on creative political action in that country since the 1960s is currently being written.

The 2009 version of *How To Make Trouble And Influence People* sold out within a year, after which PM Press kindly offered to republish it. Previously the material in the book had been arranged non-chronologically. However, as this new edition will be available to overseas audiences we decided to restructure it along chronological lines and to add icons and events, such as Ned Kelly and the Eureka Stockade, that would be familiar to Australians. To further situate the events described within their historical context, brief introductions focusing on the macro-economic, social and political trends of the times have been added to each section.

Covering a wide gamut of seditious political acts, from Indigenous guerrilla resistance to anti-uranium blockades and Critical Mass bike rides, this collected and expanded edition provides a potted, although far from detailed, history of Australian radical politics from the colonial era onwards. It is informed by a commonly held belief on the Left that social progress does not emanate from the pronouncements of "enlightened" politicians, but instead derives from grassroots resistance to inequality and discrimination. Today's troublemakers may understandably feel isolated and overwhelmed, but they are not the first to find themselves in such a position. History is filled with individuals and organisations who were totally out of step with the mainstream of their time, but whose ideas around racism, gender, sexuality and workers' rights eventually found some level of acceptance, if not success.

In learning about the deeds of rebels past, we are provided with a memory bank of ideas and tactics from which to draw. These tales and images also serve to remind us that political activity need not be a predictable and grim slog. As well-resourced as our opponents may be, they are vulnerable to the use of creativity, solidarity and humour. Indeed, these are often the only tools we have.

Another major factor originally pushing me towards researching and writing about Australian radical history was a cultural cringe that I encountered when I first got involved in a variety of activist scenes during the late 1980s and early 1990s. Many of us seemed to know more about the revolutionary history of Spain or Russia than we knew

NSW Builders Labourers Federation members and supporters march to defend the union's green bans on environmentally sensitive sites. Sydney, early 1970s. Courtesy of *Changing Australia – The Union Story*.

about Australia, and our strategies and ideas, and even our fashion sense, were often based on movements that were happening tens of thousands of kilometres from where we were. Now there is nothing wrong with showing solidarity and taking a broad view, but I believe that it is vital that we understand our own history and traditions if we are to make a difference in the country where we live. I'm hardly the first person to assert this and there are plenty of great books about Australia's radical history, but the fact that many important struggles remain largely forgotten continues to spur me on.

To more widely disseminate knowledge that would otherwise have remained buried within the realms of academia, and in the memories of those who lived it, the summaries and quotes in the original books, and this new one, have deliberately been presented in what I hope is an accessible, yet thought-provoking format. Much of the material contained in this collection and its predecessors has been gleaned from interviews and stories passed on by friends and acquaintances, as well as from publications found in radical collections such as those located at the Collective of Self Help Groups, Jura Books, Barricade Infoshop, Melbourne Resistance Centre, Perth Anarchist Library and Loophole Community Centre. Many hours have also been spent in more formal state, university and local libraries poring over activist publications and the work of labour historians. Websites such as the Indymedia family

and EngageMedia.org, and the occasional anonymous submission by email, have further assisted the research process.

Although a myriad of Australian researchers and writers have helped inform and inspire this series (many of whom can be found in the bibliography) two overseas influences deserve special mention — the late UK situationist Larry Law and his *Buffo* booklet and the original San Franciscan RE/Search group with their *Pranks* tomes. Like the former, I have compiled a number of accounts covering a wide range of incendiary activities. As with the latter a series of dialogues with well-known, and not so well-known, creative activists have been included. These interviews cover the history and modus operandi of a variety of campaigns, groups and individuals in greater depth than a simple summary would otherwise allow. They also include dialogues with popular entertainers Chris Taylor (from *The Chaser*) and John Safran, both of whom, while not activists themselves, have demonstrated how a critical and mischievous approach to issues and public figures can be thought-provoking and subversive.

In the end, of course, the main inspiration for a book like this remains the people documented within it, those who continue to work (and play) towards a more sustainable, ethical and fulfilling society. As the old saying goes, "Keep on swimming against the stream, only dead fish go with the flow."

MAKING TROUBLE

AND INFLUENCING PEOPLE

Pranks, Protests, Graffiti & Political Mischief-Making from across Australia

1788 – 2012

MAURICE MARGAROT Sentenced to Fourteen Years Transportation for Sedition.

REV.d THOMAS FISHE PALMER Sentenced to Seven Years Transportation for Sedition.

TRANSPORTED FOR SEDITION.

THOMAS MUIR Esq.r of Huntershill Sentenced by the HIGH COURT of Justiciary at EDINBURGH the 31.st of August 1793 To fourteen Year's Transportation for SEDITION

WILLIAM SKIRVING Sentenced to Fourteen Years Transportation for Sedition

JOSEPH GERRALD Sentenced to Fourteen Years Transportation for Sedition

A View of Botany Bay

OPPOSITE: Graphic depicting the Scottish Martyrs who were exiled to Australia for their part in advocating democratic reform. Artist unknown.

THIS PAGE: Gweagal people opposing the arrival of Captain James Cook in 1770. Engraving from *Australia: The First Hundred Years*, by Andrew Garran, 1886

1788–1849

Prior to the British invasion of 1788 the Australian continent had been occupied by Indigenous peoples for at least 42,000, if not 150,000 years. Living a largely nomadic lifestyle, involving gradual modification of their eco-systems through fire and selective hunting and gathering, Indigenous Australians' cultural forms and customs varied widely. Regardless of this divergence all emphasised a deep connection to the land and the intrinsic place of humans within it.

Outside of the Torres Strait Islands, which are situated between Cape York Peninsula, QLD and Papua New Guinea, most of the hundreds of Indigenous language groups and nations were organised in relatively non-hierarchal ways with power decentralised rather than centred in the hands of a few. Conflict between different communities occurred, but permanent standing armies were unknown and the annihilation of rival populations did not occur.

The first contacts with Europeans occurred from the Seventeenth Century as firstly Dutch, and then French and British, explorers and traders sought new territories to document and conquer. Most of these interactions ended in conflict, or with the local population fleeing their intruders.

Following Captain Cook's mapping of the Northern and Eastern coastlines in 1770, the British decided to set up a colony at Botany Bay in 1788. This decision was motivated by a number of factors, the most commonly cited of which was the need to establish a new penal colony in the wake of the American Revolution. The increasing urbanisation of the British populace and the impoverishment that followed the enclosure of lands, as society moved from feudalism to industrialisation, had generated major social dislocation. Minor property crimes, let alone political agitation, were dealt with harshly and, with many courts becoming less inclined to dish out the death penalty, Britain's jails and prison hulks were overflowing.

During the first eight decades of their existence the Australian colonies played host to around 160,000 convicts, 26,500 imported directly from Ireland. The decision to occupy Australia was, however, driven by more than the need to dump excess proletarians. Britain was engaged in fierce competition with the other European powers and felt the need to get in first, not least because a new colony at the bottom of the Pacific would provide a base for trade routes and naval supplies.

British law stipulated that negotiations should be entered into with the Indigenous owners of the lands they planned to annexe, but in the case of Australia the fiction of *"terra nullius"* was employed to void such obligations. Under this concept it was decreed that Australia was an "empty" land populated by people whose lack of European-style agriculture meant they lived only on the coast and lacked ties to any particular place. This falsehood was adhered to for the following 204 years, even though once invasion had taken place it became rapidly apparent that Indigenous groups lived in every part of the country and exerted strong claims to it. As a result Indigenous sovereignty has never been ceded and Australia remains without a treaty.

Due to the size of the continent, the colonisation of Australia took quite some time with some Indigenous peoples maintaining their traditional lifestyle into the 1960s. The initial invasion of new territories generally began with coastal enclaves. Although friction was evident, these small settlements, such as the first set up at Port Jackson (Botany

Bay having proved unsuitable), were generally able to live in peace with Indigenous locals as the colonists engaged in trade and had a limited impact on the ecosystem.

Once these outposts began to expand conflict became inevitable, as Indigenous people were denied access to their lands, and the native plants and animals they relied upon were displaced by farms and stock runs. Many settlers on the frontier, some of which were dubbed "squatters" as they seized land before colonial permission had been granted, also engaged in raids of extermination and the use of poison. The occupation of sacred sites and disruption to traditional travel and customs further strained relations.

The level of Indigenous resistance which met British expansion varied according to factors such as the degree to which resident populations had been decimated by newly introduced diseases, the ability of colonial powers to deploy troopers and police in support of settlers, and the level of unity amongst Indigenous locals. The existing knowledge and capability of groups to engage in warfare and the nature of the country being fought in were also important.

Indigenous opposition creatively adapted customary forms of battle to suit new situations. As semi-nomadic peoples lacking a permanent military caste Indigenous Australians were unable to unite into large scale armies capable of carrying out conventional warfare, as had occurred in other British dominions. As a result resistance took place reactively region by region with guerrilla attacks focused upon individual farms and colonists. These involved the killing of some settlers, but primarily focused on the destruction and capture of tools, crops and stock to sustain Indigenous populations and bankrupt their opponents.

Reprisals by British authorities and settlers were sometimes limited to the warriors involved, but were generally indiscriminate. As Britain had annexed the island, Indigenous Australians were technically British citizens, but legal protections were rarely extended to them. Generally charges brought against those carrying out massacres were dismissed, either for lack of anyone left or willing to provide evidence or because, unable to swear an oath on the Bible, Indigenous people were not allowed to act as witnesses. Following the occasional case where settlers or soldiers were punished their fellow colonists became careful to ensure that no documentation or proof of their actions remained.

As the colonies became more established, and police forces were founded, the use of soldiers was phased out. From the 1840s onwards frontier police were increasingly backed by the use of "Native Troopers". These Indigenous collaborators were generally recruited from groups who had no connection, or were hostile, to those being suppressed. The use of these people's knowledge of the bush and language became invaluable with Indigenous police carrying out most of the punitive operations in parts of Queensland.

The ability of Britain to project its military power had seen it defeat Indigenous peoples almost everywhere it had invaded and Australia proved to no exception. In some cases resistance limited expansion for decades and massacres carried out by Europeans continued into the 1920s. However by the 1850s significant coastal areas had already come under colonial control. As military resistance was progressively broken Indigenous opposition took more covert forms, primarily involving a simple willingness to survive physically and culturally.

A second main source of resistance to British authority came from those the colony was ostensibly founded to imprison. The quality of convict life over the decades varied greatly depending on broad factors such as trends in British policy, the attitude of local authorities and the state of the colonial economy. At an individual level, influences included where and to whom a convict was assigned, their possession of marketable skills, and their ability to abide by the law (or bend it successfully). As a result, whilst many transportees were brutally mistreated, particularly in places of secondary punishment such as Moreton Bay, others enjoyed opportunities they could never have dreamed of back in Britain. Once paroled, enterprising ex-convicts set themselves up as merchants or joined free settlers in stealing land from the locals, some founding dynasties that dominated colonial politics for decades.

Such opportunities did not exist for all however, and exploitation and maltreatment inevitably led to conflict. Other than generating resistance by dint of their position as bottom dogs in colonial society, a number of convicts were predisposed to rebellion due to their involvement in Irish uprisings as well as trade union and democratic movements. Most chose to resist furtively by feigning stupidity, pilfering, "losing" tools, and working slowly and inefficiently. Many asserted their humanity by engaging in relationships, same-sex and otherwise, proscribed by law. Occasionally opposition became more overt with strikes, rebellions and escapes. From the 1820s onwards, when Britain instituted a harsher regime for convicts, some also engaged in social banditry as increasing numbers of prisoners "bolted" to become bushranging outlaws.

A boom in the price of wool, tied to the Industrial Revolution, saw a major expansion in the colonies with new settlements founded in the 1820s and 1830s. WA and Queensland began as outposts, Victoria came about through largely unplanned and often illegal land grabs, and SA was set up as a convict-free planned settlement. Van Diemen's Land, known as Tasmania from the 1850s onwards, had first been invaded in 1803 and became a separate colony in 1825.

As this expansion took place a number of non-convict immigrants, freed convicts and Australian-born colonists involved in "free labour" began to agitate around the issues affecting them. Coming up against draconian laws and exploitation by employers, skilled workers – including shipwrights, cabinet makers, and typographers – combined into small societies from the late 1820s onwards. These attempts at organisation, and the occasional strike action they undertook, were often undermined by the authorities' use of convicts. When this was coupled with an economic depression during the 1840s, caused by what would become a familiar pattern of a speculation bubble centred on land and commodities giving way to financial collapse and austerity, anti-transportation leagues ballooned. Following protests, lobbying and the circulation of petitions within Australia, one of which was signed by two thirds of NSW's population, as well as campaigns by British evangelicals and humanitarians overseas, Britain ended the convict system in the eastern colonies in 1853. In WA, which had only imported convicts from 1850, due to its failure to attract immigrants, the system continued until 1868.

"A more wicked, abandoned and irreligious set of people have never been brought together in any place in the world."

Governor Hunter on colonial Australians, 1798

SYDNEY, 1770

The first landing of British explorers upon Australia sets a precedent of resistance, colonial arrogance and dispossession that will continue for centuries. When Captain Cook's party attempt to come ashore at Botany Bay they are warned off by two warriors from the Eora nation who are the custodians of the area that will eventually become Sydney. Following attempts to entreat the men with gifts of beads and nails, Cook surmises that the pair will allow him to land, but when they continue to oppose his entry he fires upon them with his musket, wounding one. Following some stone and spear throwing and further shots from Cook the warriors eventually retreat.

Cook unsurprisingly later notes that regardless of further offerings of gifts, of the Aboriginal people he had met so far "all they seem'd to want was for us to be gone", as further trips ashore result in Indigenous people either fleeing from the explorers or throwing spears at them.

SYDNEY, 1790

Two years after the invasion of Australia the colony's first Governor, Arthur Phillip, is speared in the collarbone at Manly by an Indigenous elder, Willemering. Some accounts hold that this came about through a misunderstanding, whilst others believe the action was meted out as a traditional punishment for him having allowed those under his command to take the Eora's lives, land, livelihood and property.

SYDNEY, 1791

A group of 21 convicts escape from Port Jackson into the bush. All apparently die from hunger and exposure or are recaptured. Some of the escapees are reported to have thought that they could make it to China by foot. Historians later quibble over whether the convicts' lack of education led them to believe that this was actually possible, or whether it was a story that was concocted in the hope of receiving lighter sentences. Either way, despite the knowledge that death in the bush or following recapture may await them, convicts continued to opt out of the colony with 53 missing muster in January 1792 alone.

The first escape by sea also takes place in 1791 with Mary and William Bryant, their two children and a group of other convicts requisitioning a small boat from Governor Phillip to head for Timor. All survive the 5,000 kilometre journey to arrive in Coupang, where they pose as shipwreck survivors. The local Dutch Governor soon sees through their story sending them on to Batavia (Jakarta) where a number die in prison from disease, including William and one of the children. The couple's other child dies during the journey to England where Mary's trial becomes a cause célèbre. Following a wave of popular support and sympathy she is pardoned in 1793.

NSW, 1795

With British settlers establishing farms beyond Botany Bay and displacing the Darug people, as well as kidnapping their children to serve as slave labour, Australia's first full-scale frontier war erupts along the Hawkesbury River. Five colonists are killed in the first half of 1795 leading to reprisals from soldiers who kill and capture a number of Darug. One of these prisoners later escapes by diving into Sydney Harbour and swimming away.

Generally avoiding open warfare against the better-armed and militarily organised British, the Darug concentrate on guerrilla attacks. Up to 150 Darug at a time converge on isolated farms to strip them of their corn crops, tools and stock. This not only bankrupts settlers, but also generates enough supplies to enable the resistance to continue uninterrupted by the need to gather food. Smaller parties of warriors carry out raids on British boats and farmhouses whilst houses and wheat crops (which the Darug do not requisition due to the need for processing) are torched by fire.

A rare conventional battle in 1797 sees up to 100 warriors, under the leadership of Pemulwuy, storm the town of Parramatta. This attempt to overrun the settlement is defeated when the resistance fighters are cut down by gunfire and their leader captured. Despite being wounded, Pemulwuy breaks his chains and escapes into the night a few weeks later giving rise to an aura of invincibility.

Carrying out raids at Lane Cove and Kissing

Point, the Darug begin to recruit discontented whites, with Governor Hunter complaining in a letter that convicts have been supporting actions designed to "annoy and distress the settlers, who have many of them been murder'd by them, their houses burnt, and their stock destroyed. They have threatened to burn and destroy our crops upon the ground, and to kill our cattle wherever they can find them."

Although Pemulwuy is killed in 1802, and his head removed and souvenired, resistance continues. Able to only deploy troops intermittently, due to the small size of the colony and the fear and reality of Irish convict rebellion elsewhere, Hunter's successor Governor King attempts to cut a deal with three Darug men in 1804. Although his promise to end further settlement in the lower Hawkesbury is never truly honoured, Darug resistance, combined with flooding, permits only a few farms to be established until 1810.

SYDNEY, 1796

Having been arrested for sedition and transported to Australia in 1793, Scottish republican democrat Thomas Muir, along with a group of convicts and mutinying sailors, escapes the colony aboard the American ship *Otter*.

SYDNEY, 1798

An Irish convict is given 100 lashes at Toongabbie for throwing down his hoe and giving three cheers for liberty.

SYDNEY, 1798

Australia's first "work to rule" action takes place after convicts are reprimanded for not taking their hats off to officers whenever they pass by. Shortly after the order is given a work gang rolling a boulder uphill doffs their hats appropriately with the result that the rock rolls away, knocking an overseer down and breaking his leg.

SYDNEY, 1798

Governor Hunter condemns the colony's convicts after the first church in Australia is burnt down, reputedly in response to mandatory Sunday attendance.

NSW, 1799

Sydney's public gaol is torched. In the same year the main gaol at NSW's second colony of Parramatta is burnt out by convicts.

NSW, 1802

Colonial authorities report that escaped convict George Clarke, alias The Barber, has teamed up with Aboriginal people in the Liverpool Plains area. Scarifying and painting his body, he helps to set up slaughter yards to speed up the killing of sheep.

VICTORIA, 1803

With the first attempt to colonise Victoria about to be abandoned several convicts seize a boat and escape. While most head in the direction of NSW one, William Buckley, remains, going to live with the Wathaurong people for 32 years.

NSW, 1804

With 600 former Irish rebels under their guard, colonial authorities decide to form a series of Loyal Associations in Sydney and Parramatta as well as a homegrown military unit, the New South Wales Corps, to provide extra muscle should it be required. In February, Governor King bolsters the numbers of guards at Castle Hill in an attempt to quash rumblings of dissent there, but this move only serves to further antagonise the prisoners, 200 of whom leave their barracks on March 4th to begin a revolt. Over the next day the rebels wreck settlers' homes, flog the local flogger and begin raising an army to march on Parramatta with the goal of capturing the entire colony before sailing home.

These ambitious plans, however, fail to take into account the superior resources and cunning of the colonial authorities, who muster the NSW Corps, the militia and any sailor or marine they can find. Declaring martial law, Governor King proclaims "the districts of Parramatta, Castle Hill, Toongabbie, Prospect, Seven and Baulkham Hills, Hawkesbury and Nepean to be in a state of rebellion ... I do therefore strictly charge and command all His Majesty's liege subjects to be assisting in apprehending and giving up to the nearest officer or magistrate every person they may stop who is unprovided with a pass, under pain of being tried by Court Martial. And

every person who is seen in a state of rebellious opposition to the peace and tranquillity of this colony, and does not give himself or themselves up within 24 hours, will be tried by Court Martial and suffer the sentence to be passed on him or them. And if they or any of them give up the ringleaders to justice it may be an effectual means of procuring them that amnesty which it is so much my wish to grant."

Thanks to an escaping militiaman, the authorities are tipped off to the rebels' movements, leading them to secure the jail at Parramatta and send out troopers to attack two columns of rebels who have become lost. The remaining 400 convicts regroup and march to the Hawkesbury to incite rebellion. There they are met at what becomes known as Vinegar Hill (after the site of a revolt in Ireland) by the bulk of British forces.

With both sides gathered in the area the NSW Corps second-in-command Major Johnston flies a white flag and attempts to buy time by parlaying with the rebels. His first emissary is sent back with the flints removed from his pistol and a message that the convicts will not surrender. A Catholic priest is then sent forth, but returns with the same answer before Johnston challenges one of the rebel leaders, Philip Cunningham, to meet him under truce, stating, "You have very little spirit if you don't come and speak to me."

Following a series of discussions in which Johnston promises to avoid bloodshed if the men surrender, Cunningham replies that they will only choose "Death or Liberty". Breaking the truce, Johnston and his Quartermaster Laycock then draw their pistols, taking the rebel leader and his second-in-command prisoner. The Major orders his men to attack and with their superior arms and training they soon scatter the convicts. Whilst the majority of the rebels escape, 26 are immediately captured, 9 killed on the road and many more in the bush. Cunningham is hanged without delay.

Over the next week settlers, emboldened by the appearance of the soldiers, assist in the capture of more than 300 convicts, 8 of whom are executed, 50 sent to the Newcastle penal colony and 9 given 500 lashes. Following the revolt, convict anger at injustice continues to simmer, but takes a less confrontational appearance in the form of work avoidance and sabotage.

Detail from Convict uprising at Castle Hill, 1804. Image portrays the NSW Corps firing upon Irish convict rebels. Artist unknown

SYDNEY, 1810

50 convicts seize the fully provisioned brig *Harrington* in Farm Cove. The fugitives make it as far as the coast of Indonesia where their ship is captured by the British Phoenix. When the ships dock in Sarawak, however, a number of the prisoners once more escape.

PORT JACKSON, 1816

Convicts building a lighthouse seize the *Trial*, which they later shipwreck further up the coast.

SYDNEY, 1817

The primary overseer of convict labourers, Major George Druitt, sparks industrial action by sawyers at Pennant Hills when he orders them to increase their workload by more than a third. In a report to a commission into the use of convicts he notes that the men:

> in a body refused to do [the work]; This continued for two or three weeks when His Excellency The Governor requested me to visit the Settlement and to speak to the people to represent to them that they were only asked to perform the same work as their fellow prisoners did in the Lumber Yard. I did so and there was a general murmur throughout the whole body; and two men stepped forward close to me and said if all the men were of their way of thinking, that nothing more than the old task should be done, as they considered the ration of a pound and a half of beef and a pound and a half of flour not near sufficient for a man to work hard on. They were extremely insolent and I have no doubt would have made an attack on me had not a resolute overseer been near me and ready to offer assistance.

Sadly the striking convicts are forced to capitulate a day later after their two spokesmen receive 100 lashes each for their efforts.

PORT MACQUARIE, 1817

Aboriginal people spear William Blake, a member of Surveyor-General John Oxley's expedition, when the explorers intrude upon their lands.

SYDNEY, 1822

Convict James Straiter is sentenced to 500 lashes and one month's solitary confinement on bread and water with the remainder of his sentence to be served in a penal colony for the crime of "exciting his Master's servants to raise their wages and increase their rations or otherwise destroy their master's property, in sheep entrusted to their care; and with violently resisting [their] orders and setting at defiance all those in authority on the establishment."

BATHURST, 1822

After seven years of relative peace, a three-fold increase in the number of sheep in the Bathurst area leads to conflict with local Wiradjuri people. Guerrilla attacks on stock and settlers soon brings colonial expansion to a halt leading Governor Brisbane to declare martial law west of the Blue Mountains in 1824. Despite massacres and the introduction of mounted troops, whose horses allow them to deploy more quickly and launch surprise attacks in the bush, it takes another two years for the resistance to be broken.

NSW, 1822

Royal Commissioner J T Bigge reports to British officials that, "At Windsor [in the Hawkesbury region], and in the adjoining regions, the offense termed bushranging, or absconding in the woods, and living on plunder and the robbing of orchards are most prevalent."

NORTHERN TERRITORY, 1823

When Fort Dundas is first established on Melville Island, few problems are encountered with the Indigenous locals beyond the disappearance of a few axes and utensils. However, when sheep and cattle are introduced to the area resistance begins in earnest, and within four years troopers and settlers find themselves unable to leave the confines of the fort. Well aware of the superior ability of cannons and rifles, the Aboriginal guerrillas stay out of the range of fire, mocking the denizens of the fort in English and attacking the few work teams who dare to venture outside. By 1829, with guards now being picked off the walls of the fortress itself, the settlement is abandoned.

MORETON BAY, 1824

Established with the aim of creating a prison within a prison, as well as a beachhead in Northern Australia, the Moreton Bay Penal Settlement soon serves as a living hell for recalcitrant transportees. Malnourished, beset by dysentery and trachoma, and flogged mercilessly, the convict death rate peaks at 115 per 1,000 in 1829 alone.

In response to this treatment, prisoners carry out small-scale riots, engage in work refusal, deride their captors and sabotage property. Despite brutal punishments, including hundreds of lashes and public hanging, roughly a quarter of the 2,202 convicts who pass through the settlement carry out more than 700 escape attempts over 15 years. Lacking bushcraft and facing starvation, most fugitives soon return, but a minority make it as far south as Port Macquarie. Encounters with the Indigenous people of the area often leads to death or capture and return, but a handful of escapees manage to settle in and live with the locals.

SYDNEY, 1824

Coopers set up Australia's first recorded picket line to close down their workplace. They are later arrested and tried under English anti-union laws.

TASMANIA, 1824

In response to Lieutenant Governor Arthur's offer of a reward for his capture, Matthew Brady, bushranger at large, posts his own public notice reading, "It has caused Matthew Brady much concern that such a person known as Sir George Arthur is still at large. Twenty gallons of rum will be given to any person that can deliver his person to me." Sadly no one takes him up on his offer.

PARRAMATTA, 1827

Women convicts from the Female Factory break out and march on Government House, seizing its stores to breakfast on bread and cold meats. By the time the authorities arrive the feasting has ended and the women march back to jail jeering and hooting their captors along the way.

Detail from *Aborigines with spears attacking Europeans in a rowing boat* by convict artist Joseph Lycett. Tasmania, c. 1830. Courtesy of National Library of Australia.

TASMANIA, 1828

Following a series of attacks on farms by Indigenous Tasmanians angry at the theft of their lands, colonial authorities ban Aboriginal people from entering European settlements. The decree restricts Aboriginal people to the far North East, far West and the forests of the South West, but fails to prevent Indigenous Tasmanians from visiting their traditional lands. As a result the colonial authorities resolve to "inspire them with terror" by putting settled districts under Martial Law in November 1829. This too fails to stymie Indigenous resistance, with the result that Governor Arthur sets up group of "five-pound catchers" who are paid five quid for every adult and two pounds for every child they take into custody.

This new strategy also proves to be of negligible value, but rather than negotiating with the original occupants, Arthur decides to go all out in 1830 by extending Martial Law to the entire colony. With this in place, he mobilises 5,000 men to march three metres apart across the whole of the island with the aim of driving the Indigenous population into the South Eastern peninsula. Despite "beating the bush" and carrying 1,000 muskets, 300 handcuffs and 30,000 rounds of ammunition, the Black Line operation proves an abject failure, capturing only one man and a boy while enduring regular attacks and harassment from those it was meant to scare away. Having spent £36,000 (a fortune for the time), Arthur calls the whole thing off after two months with the loss of five men to accidents and two to Aboriginal resistance.

Despite cannily avoiding their pursuers, Indigenous Tasmanians continue to suffer as the spread of disease, loss of land, use of poisoned flour and massacres of men, women and children decimate their numbers over the next four years. By 1832 those left alive largely surrender, and Arthur, with the help of Aboriginal "Protector" G.A. Robinson, exiles them to Flinders Island. In spite of this ethnic cleansing Indigenous Tasmanians survive into the 21st Century fighting for recognition, land rights and the return of their ancestors' remains.

BATHURST, 1829

After two convicts are given 50 lashes for skinny-dipping at work, one of them, Ralph Entwhistle, decides he can no longer live under the tyranny of colonial rule. Gathering a small band of fellow prisoners together, Entwhistle fails to find the man who ordered the flogging, Lieutenant Thomas Evernden, but the group kills one of his overseers during a visit to his property. Hooking up with a similar crew of runaways who had been chased out of the Hunter Valley, the number of rebels soon rises to 124, threatening Bathurst and prompting Governor Darling to strengthen the chains of the 1,500 prisoners held there.

After the rebels humiliate a local squatters' militia, during a battle at Captain Cook Lookout, the commander of the Bathurst garrison sends out a detachment of hardened troopers, but these too are repelled by the convicts, suffering many casualties in the process. A third battle sees troops from Goulburn scattered at Barona Plains and their commander wounded, but after weeks of fighting, and having run low on provisions and ammunition, the guerrilla band are eventually massacred by Sydney's 39th regiment. Entwhistle and ten others are spared, only to be hanged in public following a show trial a few weeks later.

NSW, 1829

Convicts being transported to Moreton Bay mutiny on the City Of Edinburgh. Troopers are only able to bring them to heel by firing into the hold, killing one and wounding seven.

TASMANIA, 1829

18 convicts, under the leadership of serial escapee William Swallow, seize the government brig *Cyprus*. Sailing out of Recherche Bay they take the vessel across the Pacific before heading on to Japan and China. After switching ships and posing as shipwreck survivors five of the men eventually make it to London. Their freedom is short lived and they are later put on trial for piracy after one of their group, John Pobjoy, betrays them.

SYDNEY, 1829

In the first case of its kind to land before a NSW court the editor of *The Australian*, Atwell Hayes, is charged with seditious libel for criticising the placing of an iron collar on a convict named Sudds. Hayes is eventually found guilty and serves three months in prison for the crime of publishing an article "calculated to bring the Governor into disesteem and disrespect, and to create an offensive feeling in the public."

PARRAMATTA, 1829

Dishing out the punishment they usually receive, female convicts shave the head of the Superintendent of the Female Factory before absconding from prison.

NSW, 1829

12 convicts at Stonequarry are flogged for refusing to work on Christmas Day.

SYDNEY, 1829

Typographers from The Australian newspaper successfully strike, with solidarity from carpenters and sailors, against currency reforms which would have cut their wages.

TASMANIA, 1830s

A young convict writes to his parents of a recent rebellion and the authorities response to it:

> We have to work from 14 to 18 hours a day, sometimes up to our knees in cold water, 'til we are ready to sink with fatigue.
>
> [After four went on strike] the inhuman driver struck one, John Smith, with a heavy thong, which caused the gang to rise and dreadfully beat the drivers, by which one of them died the same day.
>
> The soldiers were immediately sent for, and 47 of us taken into custody.
>
> Nine were sentenced to die, and 18 were sentenced to go to the mercury mines to work underground.
>
> On Saturday, July 2, at 7 a.m., we were all paraded in front of the scaffold. The nine unfortunate men came on with a firm step, the chaplain taking leave of them. The executioner commenced tying them up to the beam, by which they hang 16 at a time... The men seemed to cry out with one voice, "We die happy."

TASMANIA, 1830

Clarence River settler John Sherwin's property is attacked for the fourth time before being razed by fire. During the raid Indigenous warriors remain out of the range of musket fire whilst crying out to the settlers in English, "Go away you white buggers – what business have you here?"

MORETON BAY, 1832

11 convicts seize the schooner *Caledonia* at Amity Point putting its crew ashore and compelling its Master to navigate them out to sea.

PERTH, 1831

The British invasion of the area now known as Perth initially sees good relations with the various Nyungar peoples of the area as the colonial authorities distribute goods and rations in compensation for the use of Indigenous land. However, when the settlers begin to threaten traditional ways of life the Nyungar begin to oppose encroachment, with one man, Yagan, emerging as a key leader.

Yagan's first recorded act of rebellion comes in June when he spears a white servant and destroys a mud brick home in response to the killing of another Nyungar man for "stealing" from a settler's garden. Following this, he takes part in a number of reprisal attacks before being arrested. Speaking through a white interpreter Yagan avoids the death penalty by successfully claiming he is a prisoner of war. He also confronts the court with its complicity in sparking the guerrilla war by stating, "You came to our country. You have driven us from our haunts and disturbed us in our occupations. As we walk in our own country we are fired upon by white men. Why should he mistreat us so?"

After being exiled to Carnac Island, Yagan and another man soon make their escape to the mainland. With trigger happy settlers continuing to relocate and murder Nyungars, including Yagan's father Midgegooroo, the warrior soon finds himself leading resistance activities once more.

Ranged against the indiscriminate use of firearms the number of Nyungar deaths is unsurprisingly much higher than the 25 Europeans killed in the first quarter century of colonisation. Yagan himself is killed, along with a companion, in 1833, after being shot in the back by teenage bounty hunters who had lured the pair in with false promises of friendship. Not content with his execution, the West Australian authorities remove his skin for its traditional markings and send his head to Britain where it is falsely and ghoulishly displayed as belonging to the "Chief of the Swan River." Following a long campaign by Indigenous activists the head is finally returned 163 years later, in 1997, where it is buried in an undisclosed location.

The death of one leader however does not end the resistance, with houses and haystacks continuing to be set alight and crops and stock destroyed by fire. One letter written by settler Robert Lyon in 1833 reports, "[they] carry on the war against us in the heart of the settlement, after their own manner, not only with spear, but the torch; that most dangerous of all weapons in a country so full of combustibles." Parties of up to 30 Nyungars also keep their people supplied with food by seizing hundreds of kilograms of potatoes and flour from farms and outposts, including the iconic Shenton windmill. Following a battle at Pinjarra in 1834, in which Nyungar warriors are lured into open battle and their families massacred, the bulk of opposition is broken, although new conflicts soon erupt as the colony expands along the Avon River.

NORTHERN TERRITORY, 1832

The Northern Territory's first cattle station at Avon Downs is abandoned due to Aboriginal resistance.

HOBART, 1832

Following the arrest of Martin Cash's wife the bushranger and his gang send the following letter to the Governor: "Messrs. Cash and Co, beg to notify his Excellency Sir John Franklin and his satellites that a very respectable person named Mrs Cash is now falsely imprisoned in Hobart Town, and if the said Mrs Cash is not released forthwith, and properly remunerated, we will, in the first instance visit Government House, and beginning with Sir John administer a wholesome lesson in the shape of a sound flogging; after which we will pay the same currency to his followers."

SYDNEY, 1832

In a troublesome year for Masters a number of convicts are flogged for attempting to set their own work hours as well as for striking over the quality of rations.

PORT MACQUARIE, 1834

Bullock driver John Norman is flogged for being one of a party of convicts who refused to work with informers.

TASMANIA, 1834

Having worked with "great propriety" in executing the orders of Master Shipwright David Hoy with "promptitude and alacrity", the convicts who built the *Frederick* at Sarah Island promptly requisition the fruit of their labours and sail it to South America. Claiming to be shipwrecked sailors four of the men settle in Chile, but are eventually recaptured and sent back to Australia, while another six move on to America and Jamaica, where they remain at large.

SYDNEY, 1834

John Jenkins, an ex-convict and bushranger, is sentenced to death for the killing of a Doctor Wardell. Before he is executed he gives an incendiary speech that is reputedly responsible for the ending of public executions. "Well, goodbye lads, I have not much time to say much to you; I acknowledge that I shot the Doctor, but it was not for gain, it was for the sake of my fellow prisoners because he was a tyrant, and I have one thing to recommend you as a friend, if any of you take to the bush, shoot every tyrant you come across, and there are several now in the yard who ought to be served so."

TASMANIA, 1836

Convict Eleanor Redding is charged for turning her boss's shirts into "pasteboard" after he complains of her using insufficient starch. She is far from the only woman taking action as the Principal Superintendent of Convicts publicly complains that the women under his charge are in "continual warfare" with their Masters.

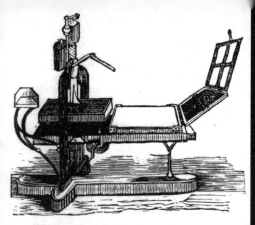

ONCE ENSLAVED FAREWELL !

This is The Thing
    That in spite of new Acts,
And attempts to restrain it,
    By Soldiers or Tax,
Will POISON the vermin that plunder the wealth,
    That lay in the house that Jack built.

COLONEL ARTHUR'S LEECHES, SUCKING THE BLOOD OF A FREE COLONIST.

Business (generally speaking) is shocking DEAD—very little money down on the NAIL now—GRAVE & MOURNFUL times make people look as BLACK as a FUNERAL in a snow storm—but, notwithstanding, I, myself, have no particular reason to grumble, tho' I like to be at something in my usual way—I think this job is a safe spec—for, I understand, from my friend in black, (DEATH and the DEVIL are constant cronies) that his particular friend, * * * * has had symptoms of a COFFIN fit for some time past, and in his opinion, (which is always worth something) he can't stand out very long —however, I'll make a FINISH of this job, and in a few weeks give him A CALL.

DESECRATED
/TO THE MEMORY OF
*
BORN in sin, and died
in PUBIC HATRED !
Beloved by all foes to
FREEDOM, and
detested by all foes to
DESPOTISM.

THE NEVER FAILING UNDERTAKER.

CORNWALL CHRONICLE,
1836-1837

One of Australia's earliest political cartoonists, William Lushington Goodwin, ran the newspaper the *Cornwell Chronicle* in Launceston, Van Diemen's Land (now Tasmania). It regularly featured his illustrations demanding a free press and criticising the tyrannical Governor Arthur

WATCH-HOUSE BREAKOUT
MELBOURNE, 1838

Despite acting upon their own lands and being unable to speak English, a group of Aboriginal men are charged with cattle theft and imprisoned in the Port Phillip watch-house. Before the night is through, the men start a fire by poking long reeds of grass through the prison window into a torch hanging in the gaolers' room. Using the reeds to light up the watch-house roof, they soon have the entire building ablaze. Panicking, the guards free their captives before going off to get help. By the time they return, both the prison and the prisoners are long gone.

Artist unknown

NSW, 1836

Turning class relations on their head, bushrangers flog station owner George Barting for mistreating his servants.

MORETON BAY, 1837

Convict Thomas Barton is scourged after he parodies guards by parading with a broom propped, musket style, upon his shoulder.

SYDNEY, 1837

Transportee William Gordon torches his master's haystack after being cheated out of rations and wages.

QUEENSLAND, 1838

An attempt to convert Aboriginal people at Moreton Bay meets an unseemly end when locals drive off Lutheran missionaries, gravely wounding one pastor and closing the state's first mission in the process. Despite being condemned by the authorities as thoughtless and ungrateful, Queensland's Indigenous people continue to repudiate Christianity,

evicting another mission from Noonga Creek in 1846. A further attempt by Catholic missionaries to convert locals at Stradbroke Island similarly ends in ignominious failure the following year.

VICTORIA, 1838

With settlers seizing their land and destroying the local ecosystem through the introduction of cattle and sheep, Aboriginal people from around the Murray and Ovens River areas embark on a campaign aimed at driving out squatters. The Faithfull brothers are just two of many settlers affected when their attempt to expand their run into the Benalla area sees them lose 14 shepherds, 200 pounds of supplies and most of their stock. Reeling from this they withdraw to an area near the present town of Wangaratta, but here too they find little peace with William Faithfull noting "my cattle were destroyed in numbers within the short distance of only six miles from my hut ... Thus my men and I were kept in a constant

state of alarm. We dared not move to supply our huts with wood and water without a gun and many of my men absconded from my service, throwing away their firelocks, and in some cases destroying their firelocks and making them wholly useless from sheer terror of the blacks." Within six months local Aboriginal people have incorporated the use of firearms, going on to harass the overland route to NSW for the best part of a decade.

SYDNEY, 1838

Having already escaped prison once, a Bushranger only known as Hall (not the infamous Ben) is recaptured and sentenced to death. When dragged from the courthouse he calls out to the crowds gathered outside, "I've been all over the country in my time without taking the life of any one. I've been baited like a bulldog and I'm only sorry now that I didn't shoot every _____ tyrant in New South Wales. I've never had a thing to say against prisoners, but I've a grudge against every head swell in the country. I'll

Detail from a flyer opposing the
transportation of convicts, 1841.
Unknown

go the gallows and die as comfortably as a
biddy and be glad of the chance."

NSW, 1839

Multiple escapee and onetime bushranger
Francis "Frank the Poet" MacNamara, an
Irish convict from Tipperary, becomes
famous for composing several satirical
pieces that are memorised and recited by
his peers for decades. His most famous
composition proves to be "A Convict's Tour
of Hell", written in 1839 whilst working as
a shepherd. Over its 218 lines MacNamara
dreams he dies and travels to Hell. Upon his
entrance to the fiery depths he discovers
they have been set aside for the "grandees
of the land", including a variety of well-
known guards, informers and officers as
well as notables such as Captain Cook.
Whilst these suffer all manner of torments,
a trip to Heaven reveals it plays host to those
bushrangers and convicts who suffered at
the hands of their earthly "betters".

VICTORIA, 1840s

The Kirrae, Gunditjmara and Tjapwurong

peoples turn back colonial invasion for a
number of years in the Hamilton, Grampians
and Glenelg River areas by killing stock and
destroying crops before retreating to the
Stoney Rises, a region impossible to access on
horseback. At one point a white accountant,
Peter Codd, is killed for raping and beating
black women.

SYDNEY, 1840

When seamen on leave from the *Druid* hit the
poverty stricken, but hard partying, Rocks area
they soon find themselves involved in a punch-up
with locals. As soon as police arrive to break
up the disturbance the hatred of both sides for
the law sees them join forces. Despite the use
of cutlasses, the constabulary fail to clear the
streets due to, according to a Captain Innes,
"the ruffianly conduct of a large body of three to
four hundred of the lowest canaille [lower class
rabble] in Sydney, who opposed the police in
every possible manner and excited to outrage the
seamen..." Within days of making this statement
the lawman is almost killed when he is toppled
from his horse after riding into a clothes line
strung across the street in The Rocks.

NSW, 1840

Indigenous people in the Clarence River district
resort to reprisals after settler Thomas Coults
survives an attempt to bring charges against
him for the murder of Indigenous people by
poisoning. Over an eight-year period Coults
loses three of his men and his stock run of
5,000 is cut in half. Attempting to escape, the
squatter moves his stock to a new run, but he is
followed there and forced to move to Dawson
River, Queensland. His ongoing occupation of
Aboriginal land continues to bring him into
conflict with the locals, however, and within a
few years he is forced into bankruptcy after his
entire run is slaughtered.

MILDURA, 1841

In one of more than 100 recorded engagements
in the Victorian Aboriginal guerrilla war against
colonial invasion, 400 members of Maraura clan
cut the Adelaide to Sydney stock route, turning
back 5,000 sheep and 11 stockmen.

SYDNEY, 1841

Seamen and Sydney's underclass once more
act in concert after police attack sailors who
have been "bonneting" (knocking the hats
off) wealthy patrons outside of the Victoria
Theatre. Hundreds soon gather and fighting
ranges up and down the streets as rioters
battle police and smash windows and lamps.

With seven of their number arrested,
seamen meet once more outside the theatre
the following night. Thousand gather in
support and take part in chanting before
moving on to the Harrington St watch-house
in The Rocks. Using stones and poles the
crowd overruns the prison freeing its inmates
before moving onto the St James watch-
house. Finding it abandoned by the police
they trash the property.

After a return visit to the Victoria Theatre
the remaining 500-600 rioters move on the
main police station and court in the centre of the
city. After they rain rocks down on police their
opponents open fire with blanks and, when these
are greeted with derision, live ammunition. One
man later dies and 21 are arrested as the riotous
crowd is driven from the area.

VICTORIA, 1842

Over a two-month period alone, Aboriginal resistance in the Portland area sees 12 settlers killed or wounded, 3,500 sheep scattered, numerous shotguns captured, 102 tons of potatoes impounded and cattle and horses speared. In the wake of the poisonings and massacres that follow, C. Hall, a Clunes squatter notes, "The diplomatists of their tribes may have pleaded justifications — that their kangaroos and emus were driven away by the flocks and herds of the settlers — for reprisals upon an invading enemy stimulating a sort of guerilla warfare ..."

QUEENSLAND, 1842

Aboriginal resistance escalates after the opening of a new road between Moreton Bay and Westbrook with one settler reporting, "A black fellow came to see me in Brisbane and warned me not to go to the Darling Downs ... that it was now to be war in earnest ...that their intention was first to spear all the commandants, then to fence up the road and stop the drays from travelling and to starve the jackeroos." True to their word the local Indigenous people force a number of squatters into bankruptcy over the following year by killing shepherds and scattering their sheep in the process.

SOUTHERN QUEENSLAND, 1843

Aboriginal clans cut off all communication between squatters in the Darling Downs and Moreton Bay by blocking the main road from Ipswich with a barricade of timber and upturned drays. When a British commander is sent in to break up the blockade he finds the opposition tougher than expected, with guerrilla attacks continuing for the next three years.

PARRAMATTA, 1843

Troops are called in to quell riots by prisoners at the Female Factory.

SYDNEY, 1844

A difficult New Year's Day for the authorities begins when a crowd surrounds Governor Gipps demanding democratic rights and action over poverty, convictism and unemployment. In the late afternoon, following pitch invasions and clashes with constables at a cricket match, rioting breaks out as crowds march to watch-houses and convict barracks to cheer inmates (who respond in kind) and free any arrestees they come across.

When Gipps confronts the crowd, ordering it to disperse, they reply with a torrent of abuse stating, "What should we go to our homes for? We've got nothing to eat." The crown's representative then orders mounted police and troopers to clear Queen's Square after Edward Phelan exhorts the crowd to "go further and do as the Canadians did [in 1837]" by opting for all-out rebellion. The would-be revolutionary later receives 12 months in irons for his efforts.

QUEENSLAND, 1844

Pastoralists abandon sheep runs en masse in the Goondiwindi district of South-West Queensland after Indigenous resistance claims the lives of 14 settlers and thousands of sheep and cattle.

HOBART, 1845

Despite the imposition of harsh punishments and the use of extra guards, separate mattresses and screens between beds, attempts to prevent same sex relationships between convicts fail dismally. The following letter, confiscated from one of 12 men condemned to death for his part in a revolt, demonstrates how love was able to overcome such barriers:

Dear Lover,

I hope you won't forget me when I am far away and all my bones is mouldered away I have not closed an eye since I have lost sight of you your precious sight was always a welcome and loving charming spectacle. Dear Jack I value Death nothing but it is in leaving you my dear behind and no one to look after you But I hope you will be aware of the delusive of man. the only thing that grieves me love is when I think of the pleasant nights we had together. I hope you wont fall in love with no other man when I am dead I remain your True and loving affectionate Lover.

NORFOLK ISLAND, 1846

After constables confiscate their homemade billy cans, one of the few personal items they own, prisoners break into the penal settlement's stores. After retrieving their possessions most opt to avoid further conflict by heading off to breakfast. One party led by William Westwood, who is heard to say, "I'm going to the gallows, I'll bear this oppression no longer", decide to up the ante. Killing an overseer and three guards they trigger an all-out rebellion involving over 1,000 prisoners.

After the island's garrison subdues the rioters with bayonets, Westwood and 10 others are sentenced to hang. As with many others executed at the brutal penal settlement the former bushranger greets his sentence with relief stating, "I welcome death as a friend; the world, or what I have seen of it, has no allurements for me... Out of the bitter cup of misery I have drunk from my sixteenth year – ten long years – and the sweetest draught is that which takes away the misery of living death."

NORTHAMPTON, 1848

Whilst visiting the region to inspect a recent find of lead ore the West Australian Governor, Charles Fitzgerald, and his party come under attack by a group of 50 Indigenous people. During the melee, the Crown's representative is speared, and lives, whilst at least one Aboriginal woman and two men are shot, and perish.

AUSTRALIA, 1849

Attempts to land convicts from the *Randolph* and *Hashemy* at Port Phillip (later Melbourne) fail after a major protest is held. With the *Argus* newspaper calling for armed resistance the ships move on to Sydney where they are met by a mass meeting at Circular Quay. Fearing the anger of his fellow colonists Governor Fitzroy surrounds his residence with police and soldiers before sending the vessels onto Moreton Bay in Queensland, where the convicts finally disembark.

December 1st 1854

1850 – 1899

OPPOSITE: Rebel miners swearing Allegiance to the 'Southern Cross' during the Eureka revolt, 1854. Watercolour by Charles Doudiet.

ABOVE: The original eight-hour day banner made by the daughters of T. W. Vine, 1856. Photographer unknown.

The 1850s saw marked changes in the Australian polity. Firstly, the new states of Victoria, in 1851, and Queensland, in 1859, were created out of parts of NSW. Secondly, self-government was granted to SA, Tasmania, NSW and Victoria in 1852 with Queensland and WA following in later decades. Key decisions concerning diplomacy and the military remained in the hands of London, but individual colonies were now able to pass laws concerning infrastructure, revenue, public services and land distribution.

Initially, as had been the case with pre-existing legislative councils, voting rights were limited to wealthy landowners. However, the gold rush, which kicked off in 1851, shook up the colonial order and triggered a long boom which lasted until the 1880s. A swathe of new immigrants brought democratic ideals with them and the healthy economy, despite occasional fluctuations, generally saw increased wages and good employment opportunities. Working class confidence, a low tolerance for traditional deference towards "betters", and the influence of Chartism built pressure to the point where suffrage was increasingly extended to all male British subjects, including some Indigenous people, from the late 1850s onwards (although Tasmania would hold out until 1896). Immigrants and women would have to wait some time, with female suffrage and civil rights becoming a major issue towards the end of the century.

Widening suffrage brought about parliamentary alliances between sections of the working class and middle class liberals who favoured land reform and government intervention in markets and some aspects of daily life. This brought them into conflict with the large landholders and bankers who continued to dominate the economy and wielded, via upper houses whom only the wealthy could vote for, the ability to block legislation.

The 1850s to 1880s saw legislation to improve workers' legal rights, introduce compulsory secular schooling, and encourage local industry via import tariffs. Attempts at land reform, largely driven by the vast number of newcomers who failed to find their fortune on the goldfields, were cruelled. Whilst Land Selection Acts did allow some immigrants and workers to begin farming, resistance from large landowners, and the use of rorts and loopholes, meant that they hung onto their wealth and privileges.

A sizeable percentage of new land holders, or "selectors", became mired in poverty due to their small holdings and a lack of capital. As a result of this, and the increased transport of gold and other valuables, armed robbery by mounted outlaws flourished in rural areas during the 1850s and 1860s. Continuing until the late 1870s bushranging, despite its often indiscriminate nature, came to be celebrated for its defiance of authority and humiliation of the police.

Conflict over the control of land and wealth was of course predicated on the continuing dispossession of Australia's original owners. With European explorers mapping out new areas, and state investment establishing a wide network of telegraphs and railways, the frontier continued to widen at great pace. By the end of the century all but the most remote inland and northern areas had come under European control. Indigenous resistance continued to meet this growth with warfare in northern Queensland and WA's Kimberley region slowing expansion for a decade or more.

The difficulties of getting anyone else to work in remote areas saw the widespread, and often forced, integration of Aboriginal labour into the rural economies in Northern Australia. For the most part policies of "protection", which had been initially employed in Tasmania in the 1830s with disastrous results, were implemented across the rest of Australia. Segregated on small rural missions and reserves, often far from their traditional lands, and holding the legal status of children, Indigenous survivors lived in overcrowded conditions and were subject to dictatorial rule by state appointed managers. From the 1880s onwards children of mixed Aboriginal and European descent began being removed from their parents and reserves to be "assimilated" into white society. Resistance to poverty, the theft of their children, and attacks on what little cultural and economic autonomy Indigenous people were able to carve out for themselves, occasionally took the form of protests and petitions sent to British and local authorities. Generally more covert means were employed such as the, often secret, maintenance of language and cultural customs.

By the second half of the nineteenth century, colonial Australia was a primarily urban society. As it increasingly modernised the majority of the population, city and rural dwellers alike, became involved in wage work. Employment in railways, the pastoral industry and construction expanded for men and women increasingly moved out of domestic labour to join their male counterparts in shops and factories.

The numerical rise of the working class brought with it struggles around wages and conditions as well as the right to organise. A 58-hour working week was common in the 1850s, with some working longer, and the use of child labour was widespread. Those in skilled niches were best positioned to exert pressure upon employers. The craft unions they formed came and went according to fluctuations in the economy and resistance from employers. Over time they were able to strengthen and began coordinating their activities through Trades Hall councils and other bodies. They also began to nominate members for political office.

The 1856 success of Melbourne and Sydney's stonemasons in becoming some of the first workers in the world to gain the 8 hour day sparked a nationwide movement which held annual parades attracting crowds of supporters. Although a 40 hour working week would not be established as a national norm until the 1940s, the campaign for it, and similar efforts to reduce retail working hours via Early Closing legislation, saw union membership grow over the decades.

By the 1880s this movement took a radical turn as the concept of "New Unionism" emerged. Catering to the majority of people working outside of skilled crafts a wave of new organisations emerged favouring militant tactics and mass membership over respectability and the maintenance of closed numbers in select trades. Rejecting the defensive nature of their forebears unions representing shearers, miners, factory hands, transport workers and others spoke the language of class warfare and published radical papers such as the *Hummer* and *Worker*.

The practice of solidarity and equality that these new organisations advocated had strict limits. In some industries the organisation of women was encouraged, but the movement as a whole was racist and patriarchal. Support for the burgeoning movement for women's property, voting and civil rights was splintered, and the entry of women into male dominated industries hotly contested. Chinese immigrants, who had come in large numbers during the gold rush and continually suffered prejudice and violence, were vilified as were the large number of Pacific Islanders who had been tricked, or forced, into labouring on plantations. Although a minority of socialists, anarchists and liberals spoke out against the divisive and extreme racism of their peers the union movement as a whole barred non-Europeans from membership and campaigned for their deportation.

Having made major gains in recent years the workers' movement was met by a concerted employer offensive in the early 1890s. With a major depression generating mass unemployment and causing the banking sector to fail, the middle and upper classes closed ranks to demand the lower orders bear the pain. As a result, a series of massive strikes took place along the Eastern seaboard, each creating great social tumult.

Defeated by a combination of unfavourable economic conditions and martial force, union coverage spiralled downwards, and with it the average wage. In response sections of the union movement took a conservative turn and, via amalgamation and centralisation, a union bureaucracy loyal to capitalism increasingly solidified its position. In the midst of continuing industrial turmoil, which would rise as the economy improved in the late 1890s, these elements joined liberal politicians in advocating for, and in some cases creating, arbitration boards to rule on solutions to disputes.

Mindful of the state power that had recently been levelled against them unionists of all stripes increased their involvement in electoral politics. Labor parties increased their share of the vote in the final decade of the nineteenth century and even took power in Queensland for 6 days in 1899. Although they would successfully extract some concessions familiar splits within these parties soon emerged over the degree to which they were willing to compromise with their liberal and conservative opponents. Sensing, and in some cases witnessing, that electoral strategies would abrogate socialist ideals, a minority of activists continued to focus wholly on industrial and community level struggles as well as the creation of anti-capitalist parties and organisations.

"He's punished less who roundly robs the nation, Than he who steals a jumbuck from a station."

Anon, 1891

SOUTH-WEST QUEENSLAND, 1850

Over a two-year period Indigenous resisters destroy 6,000 cattle and 2,000 sheep in defence of the Maranoa River ecosystem.

SYDNEY, 1851

After a sailor dressed in women's clothing is arrested for disrupting church services and fighting with a policeman, his fellow sailors and Sydney locals go on a rampage. A number of lock-ups are attacked and their prisoners freed before the riots culminate in a pitched battle down George Street.

MELBOURNE, 1851

28 prisoners go on strike refusing to operate the Old Melbourne Gaol's exhausting and agonising treadmill. When a chaplain is sent to convince them to relent he is told to "delay his [unknown expletive] clapper, and keep his [unknown expletive] preachments for Sunday."

BRISBANE, 1854

Having eluded the authorities for 14 years Indigenous leader Dundalli is captured and sent to trial for his part in resistance in and around the Brisbane area. Before being sentenced to death, he cheekily offers to row the judge to Sydney in return for his freedom. Defiant to the last he calls out to his supporters to kill his captors "so they never come back", before he is hanged outside the Brisbane Gaol.

MELBOURNE, 1856

Having seen a small number of their Sydney peers win the eight-hour day the previous year, Melbourne's stonemasons accelerate their campaign for all across the industry to enjoy "Eight Hours Labour, Eight Hours Rest and Eight Hours Recreation". With the contractor for Parliament House holding up negotiations, unionist James Stephens calls a stop-work at his Melbourne University worksite. Insisting, "that the resolution of our society should be carried by physical force if necessary" he calls, "upon the men to follow me, to which they immediately consented..." Marching to various building sites the workers shut down work across the city. Following this display of clout the stonemasons' employers free up the deadlock granting the men a working day beginning at 7am and finishing at 5pm, with two hours for meals.

MELBOURNE, 1857

Having run the penal colony of Norfolk Island with such brutality that several Church leaders, and even his superiors, began to publicly question his rule, Commandant John Price moves onto a new job in 1854, that of Inspector-General of Penal Establishments for the fledgling colony of Victoria.

Three years later, whilst visiting Williamstown, Price is addressed by a number of convicts who have stopped work over the quality of their rations. After one, frustrated at what he sees as the Inspector-General's stalling, cries out "You bloody tyrant, your race will soon be run", Price attempts to have the man returned to the hulk ship *Success* for punishment. His orders are not carried out as further groups of convicts down tools, blocking the removal of the man and issuing their own complaints. After Price orders all of them to return to the *Success* some begin hurling rocks at him, causing injuries which will claim his life the following afternoon.

Although the killing is looked upon with shock and dismay in some quarters of the colony, in others it is celebrated. Following attempts by convicts to break out of the *President* and *Success* all are locked below decks with further warders and troops brought in to subdue them. Four groups of convicts are later tried for their part in the murder and, despite key witnesses being unable to identify the assailants, seven are executed.

VICTORIA, 1859

After enduring racist attacks for the best part of a decade, Chinese immigrants decide enough is enough when the Victorian Government attempts to introduce a resident tax that affects them alone. Castlemaine sees a protest of 3,000 who call for a boycott of European businesses amidst speeches declaring, "We have feelings like other men, we want to be brothers with the Englishmen – why not let it be so?" Attempts to collect the tax in Bendigo

EUREKA REBELLION
BALLARAT, 1854

The discovery of gold in the 1850s saw people from all over the world head to Australia in search of fortune. With a large number of local workers doing the same wages quickly rose. In response the government attempted to coerce people back to wage labour and raise capital by levying onerous licence fees upon individual miners. With police sent in to hound prospectors a protest movement soon emerged. Whilst racism against Chinese immigrants was rife on the goldfields democratic, though not anti-racist, elements were also strong and the struggle soon widened beyond simple tax refusal.

After a hotel owner was acquitted by a corrupt magistrate for the murder of miner James Scobie a mass rally was held in the Victorian town of Ballarat on October 17 1854. This soon turned to rioting. Following arrests related to this event and other grievances further rallies were held culminating in a meeting of 10,000 at Bakery Hill on November 1. With veterans of overseas democratic struggles present the rally formed the Ballarat Reform League and adopted the Chartist principle, "That it is the inalienable right of every citizen to have a voice in making the laws he is called on to obey, that taxation without representation is tyranny".

Following negotiations with the government and an attack on police reinforcements en-route to Ballarat a meeting was held on November 12 which saw licences burnt and a policy of non-compliance adopted. With police stepping up action further violent clashes occurred. Under a new leadership of militants the Ballarat Reform League formed armed sections and called for open rebellion at a meeting on November 30. Beneath a republican flag they pledged an oath of allegiance stating "We swear by the Southern Cross to stand truly by each other and fight to defend our rights and liberties." An improvised and largely symbolic stockade was built with up to 2000 armed miners prepared to defend it.

In the early hours of Sunday December 3 the numbers assembled at the Eureka Stockade were less than 200. One section of the miners had left to confront a rumoured and non-existent detachment of troopers coming from Melbourne whilst others had not returned from regular Saturday festivities. An assumption that the authorities would not mount an attack on the Sabbath was proved incorrect as a force of 276 police and troops moved in at 3am smashing all resistance within 20 minutes. Many casualties ensued with police and troops continuing to assault the vanquished rebels after the battle had ended. Whilst six on the government side died at least 27 rebels lost their lives, although the exact number is unknown as some of those badly wounded fled the site.

Following the crushing of the rebellion martial law was declared in Ballarat. Although the region was now ruled with an iron fist there was widespread sympathy for the miners. 13 out of the 120 arrested during the uprising went to trial for high treason in 1855. All were acquitted by a jury with African-American John Joseph and others being carried around the streets of Melbourne in a celebration involving thousands of supporters. In the period following a Royal Commission condemned the military response, miners licenses were replaced with a milder form of taxation and the Legislative Council was expanded to cover the goldfields.

In subsequent years the Stockade and it's flag have been embraced by various political movements with many on the Left seeing it as an expression of anti colonialism and civil rights. Most recently there has been resistance to attempts by conservative governments and employers to ban the flag from construction sites where it is proudly flown as a sign of union representation and independence.

Top: Poster for meeting on Bakery Hill. This Poster was tendered as evidence for the prosecution of the 'digger-rebels' at the treason trials held before Judge Redmond Barry in 1855. • **Middle:** Acquittal of Ballarat Rioters in 1855, Engraving published in Illustrated Australian News 25 June 1887 • **Bottom:** 'Rebels' in the dock', Wood engraving by Samuel Calvert, published in the Age, 10 March 1855.

see 700 Chinese people defy police, toppling them from their horses and freeing arrestees, before going on to hold an all-night protest outside the constabulary's camp. Although the wealthy merchants comprising the official leadership of the campaign soon cave in, the grassroots continue with civil disobedience. Out of 20,000 Chinese miners in the colony, 4,000 are fined and 2,000 gaoled within months for non-payment.

MELBOURNE, 1860

A crowd of unemployed people demanding land, march on Parliament and stone the building during a legislative session.

NORTHERN TERRITORY, 1860

John Stuart's exploration party are attacked and turned away from the area now known as Attack Creek by Warramunga people opposed to the intrusion upon their lands.

MINMI, 1861

After mine owners bring in scabs to break a strike in this NSW coal town, locals respond by tin kettling, which involves women beating kettles and pots day and night at a deafening volume. When police move in to arrest the women they are forced back by coal throwers.

BENDIGO, 1863

200 to 300 railway labourers, marching four abreast and carrying a ragged black flag upon a pole, travel to a worksite where workers are constructing the Echuca railway line for wages that undercut the average by 2 shillings a day. After compelling the scabs to "knock off" the marchers then proceed to smash and throw wheelbarrows, picks and shovels "down old holes in the vicinity of the works." Trailed by three policeman and offering cheers for themselves, as well as groans for the railway contractor Mr Higgins, the group moves onto a second worksite. This is similarly disrupted and equipment totalling hundreds of pounds destroyed, causing work to be halted for a week. Confronted by a party of hastily mobilised police the men chant "8 Shillings and No Surrender" and march on Higgins' lodgings

at the Metropolitan Hotel before dispersing.

Despite police reinforcements being brought in, a few weeks later more trouble breaks out when 300 men lured to the area with false promises of work storm a railway site after they are refused employment. Shutting work down they proceed to destroy a dray and tools worth 50 pounds before returning to their tents.

NSW, 1863

The bushranger Ben Hall and his gang take over Canowindra rounding up the small town's citizenry and single constable to join in a party at Robinson's Inn. Placing sentries at each end of the town's lone street the bandits waylay 14 drays forcing their passengers to join in festivities, which include all the food, drink and cigars they can consume. Over three days no one, other than the wealthy hotel keeper, is robbed and locals wishing to visit their homes are provided with "leave of absence" passes signed by members of the gang. Despite their ability to come and go, none of the attendees attempt to alert the authorities, and proceedings only come to an end when a rising river threatens to confine everyone to the area.

BRISBANE, 1866

After cuts to Government spending and work projects during July leads to mass unemployment, 2,000 rally in the city with speakers calling for Governor Bowen to be stoned and Government House torched. A month later unemployed labourers at Helidon requisition a train and force it to take them to Ipswich where local supporters provide them with food.

As the lay-offs continue, a mass rally at Green Hills is held on 31 August. Ten days later 135 men march into the city centre carrying spades with placards attached reading "No Work To Do." Concerned at developments, the Government swears in volunteers as "special" constables. It also offers concessions by proposing to release funds for relief work as well as to transport 200 to work in Rockhampton and 30 married couples to Gayndah.

This placates some, but protests continue, and on September 11 a rally of over 500 takes up the slogan "Bread or Blood" before attempting to raid a food warehouse. Battering its doors they

fail to gain entry before police arrive armed with bayonets. When a protest leader is arrested and the Police Magistrate orders the Riot Act to be read, the crowd respond with a shower of stones. Although the protesters are pushed out of the area they continue to battle police for three hours. At one point the sign windows of the Dunmore Arms Hotel are put in after its owner comes to the aid of the constabulary.

MELBOURNE, 1867

In honour of a visit by His Royal Highness Prince Edward, a committee decides to lay on a lavish banquet. So that all his subjects may be included it is decided that the poor will be admitted, with free food being donated by a variety of tradespeople and merchants. In the centre of the banquet a wine fountain is constructed with an enormous cask capable of satisfying 8,000 diners.

Unfortunately the organisers fail to correctly estimate the number of Melbourne's poor. Come the night 90,000 hungry proles pour into the Zoological Gardens, quickly demolishing all edibles laid before them. The fountain fails to provide its bounty quickly enough and its jets are cut so that mugs, billies and open mouths can be filled more rapidly. Storage tents are torn apart and looted of their contents. Faced with a still-hungry mob the organisers flee to warn the Duke, who wisely elects to spend the night at Government House.

FREMANTLE, 1869

Exiled Irish Republican poet John Boyle O'Reilly escapes the colony of Western Australia on board the whaler *Gazette*. Arriving in the US he becomes the editor of Boston newspaper *The Pilot* and begins organising the rescue of other Fenian convicts.

VICTORIA, 1867

Aboriginal people living on a reserve at Framlingham resist attempts by authorities to forcibly remove them to Lake Condah by refusing to leave and, if compelled to do so, by returning as quickly as possible. Sending a deputation to the Chief Secretary they convince the colonial government to officially reopen the reserve two years later.

CATALPA ESCAPE FROM FREMANTLE, 1876

After years of agitation John Boyle O'Reilly and other US-based Irish republicans raise enough money to send the *Catalpa* to WA to rescue six Fenian revolutionaries transported to Australia for militarily opposing the British occupation of Ireland. The conspiracy to free the men first places an undercover agent, James Breslin, in the West Australian colony. Discovering that there are two other groups plotting to free the convicts he takes on the role of coordinating the efforts of all Irish sympathisers in the area. Posing as an American investor he also tours the prison where the Fenians are held.

Before the *Catalpa* arrives the prisoners manage to convince their gaolers to allow them to work outside the

have nowhere to go. Come Easter Monday, when most the colony is attending an annual boat regatta, the six a picked up by Breslin and rushed by horse and buggy nearby Rockingham where the *Catalpa* awaits.

With telegraph wires cut by supporters, some whom are later arrested, much time passes before th authorities in Perth are informed of the escape. Eluding number of pursuers the rebel ship is eventually caught by British steamer, which fires across its bow and demands surrender. The *Catalpa*'s captain responds by unfurling th ship's American flag, daring the British to fire again. Fearf of creating an international incident the steamer withdraw allowing the escapees to travel to New York where they a

QUEENSLAND, 1868

Indentured Pacific Islanders forced to work at Booval are brought before the Ipswich court after they attempt to escape. The following year further groups of bonded men are dragged before magistrates, who threaten to gaol them, after they abscond from sugar plantations.

NEW SOUTH WALES, 1870

Swagmen are reported to be letting loose the "red steer" (aka bushfires) after being refused rations by station owners.

NEW SOUTH WALES, 1870s

French ships transporting members of the French Commune into exile decide to bypass Australia after Port Phillip dockworkers stage a protest demanding better treatment for the revolutionaries. This attempt to keep the Communards away from Australian shores fails in 1874, when, after being whisked away by the captain of the *Peace, Comfort & Ease*, five prominent escapees are greeted by large crowds in Newcastle and Sydney.

NORTH WEST QUEENSLAND, 1874

Having already encountered stiff resistance from the Indigenous owners of what is now known as Queensland, leading eventually to the death of more than 1,500 colonists and 30,000 locals, pastoralists face their biggest challenge when they move into lands belonging to the Kalkadoon people. Initially relations are relatively cordial, but after cattle begin polluting waterholes and locals are shot the Kalkadoons begin a decade-long guerrilla war that sees drays ambushed, settlers killed and stock driven off.

Able to disappear into hill country and access hidden weapons caches, the Indigenous locals taunt pastoralists by roasting cattle within view of their homesteads, but out of the range of their guns, as well as by issuing insults and challenges to the authorities. Following the killing of a Sub-Inspector and four of his Native Troopers in 1883, and the subsequent destruction of all horses belonging to the Mounted Police, the area is flooded with colonial reinforcements. Lured into an open confrontation at Battle Mountain in 1884, Kalkadoon warriors find themselves unable to match the rifle fire of Native Troopers with rocks and spears. As a result hundreds are killed and, in the raids of extermination that follow, their resistance broken.

VICTORIA, 1874

Under threat of being dispersed to new areas Indigenous people at Coranderrk campaign against moves by locals and the government to carve up their reserve. After carrying out a much publicised walk to Parliament, William Barak convinces the Chief Secretary to allow his people to stay. However a cut in funding to the reserve sees its residents slip into extreme poverty with the result that a second walk is launched in 1881 to demand better conditions and an end to further threats of closure. Although Barak's demand that the Government, "Give us the ground and let us manage here and get all the money" fails to lead to autonomy the residents manage to remain on site until 1924. Even then attempts to remove all of them to Lake Tyers fail when nine refuse to leave.

SOUTH AUSTRALIA, 1874

Strikes at Wallaroo and Moonta mines see women armed with brooms chase off scabs, occupy the pits and shut down production.

MELBOURNE, 1880

Despite having seen his compadres killed and his dreams of a republican uprising scuttled Ned Kelly remains defiant until the end. After receiving 28 bullet wounds during his capture at Glenrowan he struggles to recover in time to face trial for the killing of Constable Lonigan. During the hearing the bushranger does his best to convince the public that he was "hunted and hounded from step to step. They will see that I am not the monster I have been made out. What I have done has been under severe provocation."

Poorly represented by his lawyer and facing the same judge, conservative Protestant Sir Redmond Barry who had previously sentenced his uncle to death and imprisoned his mother, Kelly receives little opportunity to state his case. Between Barry's support for the prosecution and his ban on a verdict of manslaughter Ned's fate is quickly sealed, but not before he gets to shoot a few well aimed barbs. Informing Barry that, "I declare before you and my God that my mind is as easy and clear as it can be," Kelly turns the tables on the hanging judge, affirming, "I do not fear death and I am the last man in the world to take another's life away ... I am not a murderer, but if there is innocent life at stake, then I say I must take some action."

Unused to being spoken to out of turn, Barry condemns the accused as a liar, to which Kelly coolly replies, "I dare say the day will come when we all shall have to go to a bigger court than this. Then we shall see who is right and wrong." Upon receiving the death sentence with the words, "May the Lord have mercy on your soul," Kelly assures Barry that, "Yes, I will meet you there."

Despite being doomed by colonial law Ned comes out on top in the court of public opinion, with up to 60,000 (out of a total population of 300,000) Melburnians signing a petition demanding he be offered clemency. Having snuck the wounded outlaw past waiting crowds upon his arrival from Glenrowan, the authorities are unable to prevent thousands from taking part in protests at the Hippodrome and outside Melbourne Gaol, where Kelly is finally hanged on November 11.

MELBOURNE, 1882

After employers attempt to cut the rates paid for piece work women workers strike and form the first all-female union in Australia, the Victorian Tailoresses' Union.

NORTHERN QUEENSLAND, 1883

Eleven Pacific Islanders escape slave-like conditions on a sugar plantation only to be recaptured following a "desperate struggle" with police. In the same year another group attending a race day in MacKay stone a racist refreshment stand owner after they are refused drinks.

SYDNEY, 1887

Atheist William Symes flouts a ban on non-religious Sabbath meetings by holding a mock sermon parodying elements of the Bible.

THE AUSTRALASIAN SKETCHER

Nᵒ· 101.—VOL. VIII.   MELBOURNE, SATURDAY, JULY 3, 1880.   PRICE 6d.

NED KELLY AT BAY.
FROM A SKETCH DRAWN ON THE SPOT BY MR. T. CARRINGTON.

THE KELLY GANG, 1878-1880, VICTORIA

To alleviate tensions in the city and country over unemployment and poverty, state authorities during the 1840s and 1850s sold off small rural plots of land to members of the working class. These "free selection" schemes were destined to fail from the beginning as the plots were too small to enable land holders to repay their debt to the state. Because of their habitual bankruptcy and class background the selectors also attracted police harassment. This only increased as a number of them took to cattle duffing and bushranging as a means of survival.

The Kelly Gang were amongst those who turned to crime. Having already had various brushes with the law, Ned, his brother Dan and their friends Steve Hart and Joe Byrne, took to robbing banks and staging raids in and around the Greta area after a policeman harassed and abused their family during an attempt to arrest Dan. The gang soon attracted much notoriety for their use of bullet-proof armour and ability to defeat and elude police. During their reign they attracted much support from locals, with around 20 arrested for refusing to collaborate with the authorities.

At one point the gang took over the township of Jerilderie for a number of days. Whilst there, Ned drafted a 56 page letter declaring war on all squatters who did not contribute a portion of their profits to the poor of the district. The letter also betrayed his Irish Republican sympathies and vehemently attacked the Victorian police labelling them, "A parcel of big ugly fat necked wombat-headed, big bellied, magpie-legged narrow hipped splay footed sons of Irish bailiffs or English landlords..."

The gang was eventually defeated in a shoot-out at Glenrowan in 1880 with Ned, the only survivor, later hanged following a trial in which he defied and taunted his captors. A legend soon grew around Kelly with rebels and misfits from Maoists through to Bikers claiming him as a hero over the years.

Anti-clockwise from top left: Photograph of The Kelly Gang, from left: Steve Hart, Dan Kelly and Ned Kelly. • Engraving of the Bushrangers from *Australasian Sketcher* • The armour made from tractor sheet metal worn by the men during their last stand. • Ned Kelly the day before his execution, 10 November 1880.

BULLI, 1887

The arrival of strikebreakers in this NSW coal town is met by miners' wives who place themselves in front of a train, halting its journey. Some women lie down on the railway line while others take off their red petticoats and wave them. 36 of the scabs decide to return home voluntarily with the remaining four forced to follow suit by a column of angry women.

SYDNEY, 1887

Over a series of weeks, Sydney's radicals disrupt plans by the elite to commemorate Queen Victoria's Jubilee. Turning up to pro-monarchy Town Hall meetings militants stack proceedings passing their own motions, such as one reading "In the opinion of this meeting the proposal to impress upon the children of the colony the value of the jubilee year of a sovereign is unwise and calculated to injure the democratic spirit of the colony."

Seeing these disturbances as a reflection of the growing influence of secularists and democrats, the authorities turn to draconian measures by banning Sunday night meetings. 6,000 rally in defiance of the measure, but it continues to stand until 1915.

Meanwhile, determined to overturn their previous humiliations, the "cream" of NSW society mobilises 3,000 supporters in support of the Queen at a public meeting held in the Exhibition Buildings. With similar numbers of republicans ranged against them, numerous fights break out during proceedings, before the monarchists are able to clear the hall and ram through motions of support for their beloved ruler.

SYDNEY, 1888

The first Australian women's newspaper, *The Dawn*, is founded by Louisa Lawson. Defying a boycott campaign against its advertisers and physical harassment from the NSW Typographical Association, which refuses women membership, the newspaper successfully employs an all-female staff.

MELBOURNE, 1889

As part of ongoing industrial action that has hit the city's construction trade, work on Paliamentary buildings is halted when masons successfully strike to begin working at seven, rather than six, a.m.

BROKEN HILL, 1889

Fed up with the dangerous conditions their mining families face, via pollution and poor living and working conditions, women overcome the resistance of male union officials to set up a Women's Brigade. Taking part in Broken Hill's first major strike they set upon scabs and shift bosses who are "tarred and whitewashed" in the process. Before the week-long strike is over the *Adelaide Advertiser* reports that of the Brigade's 400 members, "two hundred spent the night in the mines and two of them have been locked up for trespassing."

BRISBANE, 1890

Queensland trade unionist Peter Airey, writing under the nom de plume of Peter Luftig, characterises union opposition to Australian involvement in the Boer War with a poem published in *The Bulletin*:

Rub-a-dub-dub says the loud beating drum,

Country's in danger, so come along, come.

Rifle on shoulder, the brave boys and tall,

Bushman and farmer and miner come all.

But where is Sir Fat Paunch? Oh where does he stay?

Can the first at the feast, be the last in the fray?

Grip what you get and get what you can,

Is the battle cry of the businessman!

QUEENSLAND, 1890

An attempt by employers to introduce non-unionists into shearing sheds in Jondaryan is defeated when waterside workers refuse to load scab wool onto ships. After the "Darling Downs" agreement is settled, allowing for union-only sheds, the goods are finally shipped. Further headaches ensue for the pastoralists as when their goods reach London local dockers, unaware of the settlement, initially refuse to unload them.

MELBOURNE, 1890

Feisty unemployed crash the Eight Hour Day procession calling for revolution over reform and unfurling a banner reading "Feed On Our Flesh And Blood You Capitalist Hyenas: It Is Your Funeral Feast."

QUEENSLAND, 1890

After their flour ration is cut Pacific Islander workers at the Woodlands Sugar Plantation at Marburg strike. After a number decide to opt out altogether and run away the police are brought in leading to their capture and an appearance before the magistrates' court.

AUSTRALIA, 1890

In the first of a series of major strikes to rock the country, maritime workers hit back at employer attempts to prevent their union from affiliating to Melbourne Trades Hall. The strike quickly spreads from the wharfs and ships to mines and shearing sheds eventually drawing in 50,000 Australian workers and 10,000 New Zealanders.

Determined to break the growing trend of solidarity strikes, and desperate to curb union power, employers and authorities draft in scabs and deploy police and the military to protect them. In reply, huge rallies are held and ships stormed across the Eastern seaboard. A riot breaks out in Adelaide after three workers are arrested for confronting a strikebreaker who had drawn a gun. Women from the Mt Kembla community in NSW attack scabs working in a mine and five of their number are charged with assault after they "tried to get a rope around [a strikebreaker] and had some tar, feathers, flour and pepper handy." In Sydney crowds stone a parade of business leaders when they attempt to triumphantly drive carts of scab-sheared wool through the city. After two ships manned by scabs in Brisbane break out of the harbour, 400 strikers storm and occupy the Port office.

Defying the racist stereotypes heaped upon them Chinese labourers from a plantation in Queensland refuse to load a strike-breaking ship at Goondi. Monies raised by Chinese workers for strike funds are initially, albeit reluctantly, accepted by the Melbourne Committee of Finance and Control before pressure from racist furnishing unions see further donations rejected.

During various clashes the Riot Act is read and troops brought into towns and cities. Most notoriously Colonel Tom Price, on the eve of a rally of 40,000 strike supporters in Melbourne, instructs the Victorian Mounted Rifles that, "To do your work faintly would be a grave mistake. If it has to be done effectively you will each be supplied with 40 rounds of ammunition, leaden bullets, and if the order to fire is given, don't let me see any rifle pointed in the air; fire low and lay them out so that the duty will not have be performed again." Luckily this particular rally goes off peacefully, but the combination of state violence, arrests and the unwillingness of strike leaders to push on towards a General Strike eventually sees the last of the resistance collapse after 5 months.

As ever, humour often sees strikers through hard times. During one case in Melbourne, in which five strikers are sent to gaol for attacking scabs, a police magistrate denounces such behaviour as, "absolutely un-English ... I begin to think that the race has died out." In response, one of those in the dock replies, "Thanks be to the Lord ... I'm Irish."

QUEENSLAND, 1891

Just as the Maritime strike is petering out mass industrial action breaks out in Queensland where shearers strike against attempts to cut their pay and break their organisations. Typically for the time, rather than attempt to bring migrant workers into their unions they also demand that employers exclude Chinese labour, thereby cutting off potential supporters and condemning non Anglo-Australian shearers to scabbery.

The strike swiftly intensifies to near civil war levels with thousands of shearers, some armed, gathering in more than 40 camps. Similar numbers of troops, police and recently sworn in "special" constables are sent into the countryside to oppose them. Over five months workers raid, and, in a small number of cases, torch woolsheds, outstations, huts, wagons and other properties.

Numerous strikers are arrested, with some receiving sentences of two years hard

labour. Whilst imprisoned unionists find their letters censored and reading materials impounded. In response one smuggles out messages written on toilet paper. Another, whilst in hospital, memorises William Lane's *The Workingman's Paradise* in order to later recite it to his fellow inmates.

Railway workers, many of whom are donating a day's pay per month to strike funds, are harassed by the government and sacked if they take part in support rallies and meetings. Fearing derailment all trains bearing government forces are preceded by a pilot engine to test the track.

In the midst of the strike one of the world's first May Day marches is held in Barcaldine where over 1,300 men, 618 on horseback, parade bearing Eureka Flags. A number of songs, poems, and books are also written, during and after the strike, by notables such as Henry Lawson and William Lane. Some are also composed by anonymous strikers, including the one who penned the following prayer:

> "May the Lord above send a dove,
> With wings as sharp as razors,
> To cut the throats of bloody scabs,
> Who cut down poor men's wages."

Although the strike eventually collapses the spirit of rebellion rolls on. When politicians meet to pass a resolution thanking infantry chiefs for their role in the dispute 3,000 Brisbanites disrupt Parliament with a noisy demonstration.

BRISBANE, 1891

A group of waitresses sue their employer for failing to comply with the Factory and Shops Act. Despite being fined he continues to flaunt regulations with the result that his employees walk off the job at a critical time leaving him with no one to serve the lunch hour rush.

MELBOURNE, 1891

Feminists present Parliament with a "Monster Petition" containing 30,000 signatures in support of women's suffrage. Measuring 260 metres the document takes over three hours to

fully unroll. Despite its impressive size women fail to gain the vote at a state level in Victoria for another 18 years.

BROKEN HILL, 1892

During the latest of many strikes to be carried out in this remote mining town unionist Dick Sleath buys a single share in the BHP mining company in order to gain entrance to the company's meeting in Melbourne. Facing down the hostility of 600 shareholders he puts forth the Australian Miners' Association's opposition to the company's attempts to remove unionists and drive down wages and conditions.

Back in Broken Hill defence groups staff picket lines and hound scabs. The 500 member Women's Brigade once more sees action, holding daily rallies and setting upon strikebreakers with sticks and broom handles.

In one instance of mass action thousands rally to "greet" 18 scabs and a number of armed police as they enter town. When their train arrives police attempt to elude the gathered unionists by not stopping at the expected station, instead sending the vehicle straight through to the mines. Undaunted, the crowd still manage to shower it with stones as it passes them by.

When the strike enters its third month 30 police, armed with fixed bayonets and supported by mounted officers, arrest strike leaders during a meeting in their Defence Committee rooms. Fearing they will not get the outcome they desire the government has the unionists sent to the conservative town of Deniliquin for trial. As the defendants are transported through the countryside crowds line the track at various points to cheer them on. True to their employers' wishes they all receive sentences of up to two years in jail for conspiracy and inciting riots.

With strike funds drying up and unemployed replacements pouring in from the cities the strike collapses after 16 weeks. Further rematches however are not too far away.

MELBOURNE, 1892

Andrade's Bookery, an Anarchist centre that includes a library, coffee shop and vegetarian restaurant, defies local laws, Victorian era values and the social control of women's reproductive rights by making contraception and information about birth control available to its customers.

MELBOURNE, 1892

400 unemployed people demand admittance to jail in order to access food and shelter.

MINMI, 1893

During a coal strike a barracks used to house scabs comes under fire from a homemade cannon. 14 women are also arrested and jailed for two weeks when they refuse to stop tin kettling strike breakers.

MELBOURNE, 1893

Having formed a union eight years previously 300 to 400 Chinese cabinet makers strike for weeks against attempts by their employers to lower their wages to rates less than those paid to Europeans. Sadly the Trades Hall Council and other union bodies fail to come to their aid, instead preferring to ignorantly spread the falsehood that non-white workers are incapable of organisation and committed to undercutting the earnings of others. Four years later hundreds of Chinese unionists strike again, this time seeking to ban piece work in favour of a minimum wage.

SYDNEY, 1893

Militant socialists and anarchists form the Active Service Brigade. The organisation rents a building in Castlereagh Street in order to host lectures and a reading room as well as provide accommodation, bathing facilities and a soup kitchen for the unemployed. In actions designed to confront their "betters" with the anger of the unemployed, ASB members raid church services and disrupt conservative meetings and a parliamentary session. One event sees 250 parade through the city toting a huge crucifix bearing the effigy of a poverty stricken man clothed in rags, covered with red paint and adorned with placards reading "Murdered by the rich" and "Humanity crucified".

QUEENSLAND, 1894

Following an offensive against wages and conditions another mass shearer's strike breaks out in Queensland involving, once more, thousands on each side of the employment divide. Even more bitter than the previous clash, this one sees eleven woolsheds burnt down, gunfire exchanged and the river steamer *Rodney* burnt to the water line at Pooncarie after it is used to ship scabs.

Echoing the rancorous tone of the dispute, anarchists respond to the use of military force against picket lines by releasing a leaflet reminding bushmen that, "It is better to belt one squatter than half a dozen scabs. Go to the fountainhead, the head of the police, the head of the military, the leading men of the employers' union, the head of the Government. Strike to the earth all who illegally use their authority, position or wealth to enslave you."

After the strike is broken many workers respond to continuing attacks via the formation of Labor parties. In response, another anarchist missive appears which denounces electoral politics as an "almighty swindle", declaring that, "the tree of liberty bears fruit only when manured with the bones of fat usurers, insolent despots, perfidious politicians and blacklegs generally."

KIMBERLEY, 1894

Born around 1873 Indigenous resistance leader Jandamarra spends his formative years learning the ways of the Bunuba people before receiving training as a stockman for white settlers at Lennard River Station, one of the first outposts of colonial rule in Western Australia's Kimberley region. Having learnt English, horse riding and the use of guns he returns to the Bunuba only to be later cast out for breaking rules regarding sexual relationships.

After being captured by the police and jailed for "stealing" sheep he returns to his country, initially to work as a stockman before joining the police as a tracker under the command of his friend Constable Bill Richardson. During this time he assists in the capture of other Banuba, many of whom are killed or sent into exile in faraway areas.

This period of collaboration comes to an end when a raiding party he is a member of captures a group of senior elders, including his uncle (whom it is believed Jandamarra had previously freed from an earlier seizure). Following entreaties from the captives Jandamarra breaks with white society, killing Richardson and setting his countrymen free.

Within weeks Jandamarra has come to lead a guerrilla campaign against European domination which, most chillingly for the invaders, includes the use of firearms. During the battle of Windjana Gorge, in which 30 armed troopers clash with Bunuba warriors, Jandamarra is badly injured, but survives, giving rise to a reputation for invincibility.

With indiscriminate reprisals following this melee the Banuba withdraw into the hill country and switch to guerrilla tactics. Occasionally entering into firefights, but generally avoiding taking their opponents lives they focus on destroying property, crops and stock, thereby hindering pastoralist expansion for three years.

Resistance only comes to an end after an Aboriginal tracker named Micki, who hails from a different region and whose children are being held hostage by the police, hunts Jandamarra down and kills him on April 1, 1897. In keeping with colonial customs of the time, the resistance leader's head is removed and sent as a trophy to England whilst another Banuba's head is falsely displayed in Perth as Jandamarra's.

NSW, 1894

Indentured Pacific Islanders working at Robb sugar mill at Cudgen strike demanding an end to piece rates and the introduction of a weekly wage. In a situation that turns racist stereotypes on their head white workers are brought in as scabs. Despite this being reported through the media, Anglo-Australian unionists fail to lend solidarity, instead focusing their efforts on lobbying for a White Australia Policy.

FREMANTLE, 1899

Labourers at Western Australia's major port strike for 5 weeks in response to cuts in wages and conditions. After strikers confront police and invade ships carrying scabs their employers agree to settle the dispute via arbitration.

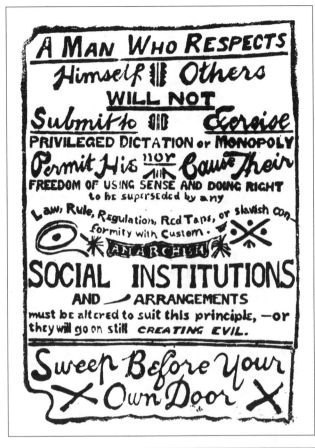

ANARCHY.

Neither GOD nor LAW nor PROPERTY:

—BUT—

LIBERTY—EQUALITY—FRATERNITY.

No. 2.   January, 1892.   Monthly, 1d.

AUTHORITY.

There are 2 kinds of authority; 1 which rules by TERROR, & 1 which rules by ERROR. One is based directly on brute force; the other rests on the voluntary submission of those who are subject to it—a submission which is voluntary only through their ignorance. But as soon as any of them cease to be willing slaves, the authority of force is quickly resorted to.

Anyone can understand & hate the tyranny which rests on simple aggressive violence. Yet it is far the less dangerous. Men only submit to it while they have to. The other they submit to, to their own & each others' harm, when they need not, because they think it is their "duty."

If there are duties. The first duty of every man is to be true to himself. True to himself in his own welfare—true to himself in sacrificing his common welfare, even, for the higher welfare he feels in making others happy. But that he may so be true to himself he must be independent; his will must be free. He cannot be true to his own nature when he is the mere obedient puppet of another. In giving up his conduct to outside dictation, he becomes a mere machine—an idiotic body, move at the command of another's brain, or of brainless blind custom—a voluntary lunatic.

The man who does so, is false to himself; & false, too, to his fellow-men: because he has ceased to move in touch with his and their needs, & has become a weapon against them, ready to hand for all who can profit by the control

JOHN ARTHUR ANDREWS, 1890s

Pioneering anarchist activist J.A. Andrews travelled the East Coast of Australia during the 1880s and 1890s opposing racism and agitating for revolution, personal freedoms, and workers' rights. Living in penury and jailed twice, his propaganda work took in a variety of forms including graffiti, newspaper articles and public speaking as well as prints, manifestoes and journals created on a hand-made cut-out wooden fount and tobacco-tin press.

Opposite: Detail from Anti-conscription leaflet by Claude Marquet featuring a caricature of PM Billy Hughes, Australia, 1917.

1900–1945

In 1901 Australia became a federated nation with a Commonwealth government. Following a series of consultations, conventions and referenda, as well as a great deal of haggling between the states, a constitution was agreed upon by the political classes and a central government formed. In keeping with the existing set-up in the states there were to be two elected houses (one to legislate and one to review), a High Court to adjudicate on constitutional issues and differences between states and the Commonwealth government, and a Governor-General to serve as the representative of the British Monarchy. Electoral attendance was initially on a voluntary basis, but after 1911 Federal enrolment was made compulsory with voting joining it in 1924 as the states increasingly adopted similar laws.

Central government would come to encroach on many of the states' responsibilities as time went by, but its initial role was to facilitate national economic development, coordinate between the states and govern on matters affecting the entire continent. As a result its powers concerned communications, customs and excise taxes, diplomacy, foreign trade, immigration, military matters, and the arbitration of industrial disputes that crossed state borders. In 1911 it also came to govern the Northern Territory, once it was separated from SA, as well as the tiny Australian Capital Territory (ACT), where the nation's Parliament would be housed after Canberra was declared the nation's capital two years later.

The new Federal order was formed around what has been termed the "Deakinite consensus", and this paradigm would remain dominant until the 1980s. Although there were to be vast policy differences on a number of issues, broad agreement between elected representatives was retained around the right of governments to interfere in the market economy. This primarily occurred via protectionist tariffs, industrial arbitration boards and the setting of minimum wages and conditions. Loyalty and subservience to a great Imperial power, initially Britain and later the US, also remained paramount with Australia's economic, defence and foreign policies heavily shaped by the dictates of foreign allies and customers.

Political unanimity was further found concerning the introduction of the White Australia Policy. Many people of colour were deported and future immigration tightly restricted to (primarily British) Caucasians, who came to make up 98% of the population by the 1940s. Although people of Chinese, Japanese, Afghan and Pacific Islander descent remained in Australia after 1901, they were denied voting and other civil rights.

Indigenous people were denied Federal suffrage and continued to suffer under a variety of "protection" policies giving government bodies complete power over their lives. With control of their movements and earnings resting in the hand of others they remained exiled on reserves and missions and exploited as rural workers. People of mixed descent were increasingly forced to separate from their families and the practice of removing children widened. Such "assimilation" practices only led to further marginalisation

and pain. Although overt resistance was initially muted, Indigenous activists became increasingly emboldened as the decades passed, organising protests and campaigns that peaked with the 1938 Day of Mourning and 1939 Cummeragunja Walk-off.

The Australian economy continued to modernise during the first few decades of the twentieth century. Following the defeats of the 1890s union membership rose to a third of the working population by 1914, drawing in large numbers of white-collar workers and women. Although union leaderships became increasingly enmeshed in court activity and electoral politics, employer attacks and pressure from below saw disputes at the industrial level persist, including a general strike in Brisbane in 1912.

Anarchists, socialists, feminists and other militants carried on with agitation around civil and workplace rights whilst calling for a radically restructured society. Although this was not achieved, a series of progressive reforms were gained. Despite retaining their second-class status legally and economically, women won the vote Federally and achieved it in all states by 1909. Some welfare payments for whites were introduced, including maternity allowances and pensions for widows and the elderly, and a government bank, with limited protections for ordinary people's savings, established.

When Britain entered the war against the Central Powers in 1914, the federal Labor Government was quick to declare its loyalty to the Empire. Although a small number of Australians had previously served in the Boer War, this was to be the country's first official overseas sortie. To prove that the new nation's young men were the equal of any in killing and dying, an army was rapidly recruited. Out of a population of five million, 60,000 Australians would lose their lives and 150,000 return injured.

Despite the emergence of an ANZAC blood myth in later decades, the massacre of Australians at Gallipoli during the invasion of Turkey would not have appeared to be a nation-forging event at the time. Indeed, far from uniting, Australian society increasingly fractured as the war dragged on. A sizeable proportion of Australians were of Irish descent and a disinclination to support Imperial designs turned to opposition following Britain's crushing of the Easter Uprising in 1916. This feeling intensified amongst the broader population and coalitions of unionists, feminists, pacifists and others formed when the Federal Government attempted to introduce conscription later that same year.

Many young Australians had initially been recruited through marketing that portrayed the conflict in Europe as an adventurous holiday. As casualties mounted, and the reality of war became more apparent, enlistment dried up and the Army was unable to meet British demands. Forced to put the issue to a national vote via a referendum, which was narrowly defeated, conscription split the Australian Labor Party (ALP). Expelled from the party PM Billy Hughes, a former union radical, formed a Nationalist coalition and forced the country back to the ballot box for a second referendum in 1917. Despite the draconian suppression of his opponents, which saw the syndicalist Industrial Workers of the World (IWW) banned and a number of its members jailed, Hughes was once more defeated.

In the context of political crisis, diminished patriotism, and war-related inflation, the government's problems rolled on. Workers mounted industrial battles from the grassroots, including a general strike centred on NSW. Socialists and feminists led food riots and protests in Melbourne and elsewhere. At the war's end dissension trailed on with Northern Territorians ousting their Federally appointed Administrator in 1918 and fighting on Perth's wharfs leading to the killing of a striker in 1919.

Although the economy improved by the mid-1920s, industrial disputes continued and, in the face of attacks from employers and the government, the Australian Council of Trade Unions (ACTU) was formed to coordinate activity across the country. The ACTU would often play a conservative role in stifling action and prioritising electoral solutions, but as workplace militancy peaked the ALP itself was pushed to the Left and many of its sections, including the Federal party, adopted socialism as a goal. In power though, MPs, as in the decades before, preached the path of moderate reform and, holding back radicals in the union movement, prioritised the health and survival of the market economy over worker's needs.

During these years, inspired by the Russian revolution, various groupings came together to form a party modelled along Leninist lines. By the late 1920s, when class struggle sharpened, the increasingly Stalinist Communist party of Australia (CPA) gained enough traction to become a dominant force on Australia's Left.

Life in the late 1920s, with the defeat of a series of strikes and the national unemployment figure hovering around 10%, was economically difficult for many Australians. Reliant on primary exports, and heavily indebted to European and American banks, Australia proved particularly vulnerable to the collapse of world markets in 1929.

Elected in 1929 the Federal ALP government failed to react adequately to the onset of the Great Depression. Initially continuing to borrow heavily, Federal and State governments later imposed deep spending cuts after British lenders called in their debts. Sections of the ALP resisted austerity, most notably the NSW Lang ALP government. Dismissed by the state's Governor in 1932, it held that no interest be paid on loans until the economy improved.

With up to a third of Australians out of work, whilst others continued to live lives of wealth and sloth, it was clear that the labouring classes would bear the brunt of the global downturn. The Federal ALP split twice over the issue of repayments, but its conservative wing prevailed with PM Scullin vowing to "tax Australians to the last penny." When Labor collapsed, and the right-wing United Australia Party took power, little changed.

During the first years of the Depression there were few handouts and a minimal level of welfare available to unwaged families, with little or no assistance provided to unmarried men, women and Indigenous Australians. In response, a number of unemployed people began to organise. Targeting the council bodies and charities primarily responsible for dispensing relief, suburban unemployed groups emerged, many of them organised out of branches of the ALP and CPA. The most radical of these was the Unemployed Workers Movement (UWM). Dominated by Communists, although far from wholly controlled by them, the UWM claimed a membership of more than 30,000 in 1932, whilst the CPA went from 300 members in 1930 to around 2,000 four years later.

Campaigning militantly, unemployed groups organised protests, hunger marches, "dole strikes" and occupations. Poverty continued to be pervasive, but from 1932 onwards such activism successfully forced governments to widen relief payments and schemes, provide rental subsidies and implement other forms of welfare. Fiercely repressed by the police, as well as by middle class based quasi-fascist paramilitaries, a number of militants spent time before the courts and in jail.

Although unemployed activists of all political stripes tended to work together at the local level much of the CPA's work had been marked by attacks on other groupings. This ended in the mid-1930s after the party, in line with the Comintern policy, adopted a "Popular Front" strategy and sent its members into the ALP. With the rise of Fascism and dictatorships in Europe and Japan a variety of religious, and left-wing groups, with the support of some unions, came together with the CPA to oppose the Australian Government's policy of appeasement and campaign against militarism at home.

Unemployed activists reentered industry as the economy gradually picked up. Along with other radicals they set about rebuilding union membership, injecting militancy and creating the conditions for Communists and other radicals to take leading positions in transport, maritime, mining and other unions. As they did so, Left-leaning unions helped foster working class culture through the promotion of literature, theatre, art and education.

Although the conservative PM Menzies, who came to power in 1939, had previously spoken admiringly of aspects of Nazi Germany, and refused to place an embargo on supplies to Japan, his government did not hesitate to follow Britain in declaring war on the Axis Powers. Initially supporting the war the CPA soon followed Moscow's line, and joined small groups of religious pacifists, Trotskyists and pro-fascists, in opposing it. Declared illegal the party lost a number of key members as well as its foothold in the ALP. Following Germany's invasion of Russia in 1942 CPA policy abruptly reversed once more, to the point of suppressing wartime strikes in the industries where it held influence. Thanks to its position in the unions and Red Army victories in Europe, party membership and influence rose to new heights with the CPA winning a seat in Northern Queensland during the 1944 state elections.

War converted the economy as military requirements, and the need to cover gaps in imports, saw a massive boost in manufacturing. With over 800,000 women entering the labour force, gender roles were temporarily transformed. Campaigns and strikes, with and without the support of union bureaucrats, sought, semi-successfully, to establish equal pay whilst low unemployment and grassroots militancy saw wages and conditions improve across the board.

Traditionally the Australian state, with only a small population to draw upon, had relied on the UK to uphold its military interests, and the conservatives maintained this policy in following the dictates of London. After the British were decimated in Singapore the Japanese military captured territory as far south as Papua New Guinea (PNG), a country which Australia had run part of as a colony in all but name since 1904 before taking the rest of it from Germany during WW1.

Looking to the US as a new protector the Curtin ALP government, elected in 1941, struck deals that saw Australia serve as a major military and supply base for the Pacific war. In the midst of bombing raids upon Darwin, and other parts of the Northern coastline, Australian troops, augmented by local conscript labour, fought in Timor and PNG. As the Japanese military retreated, the Australian Government semi-successfully moved to position itself to fill the vacuum as a major post-war force in the region. Following the war, Australian foreign policy and military strategy, as well as cultural traits, would become increasingly Americanised as the country shifted from a colonial relationship with Britain to a neo-colonial one with the US.

"Those who make the quarrel should be the only ones to fight."

Anti-conscriptionist Emma Miller, 1916.

MELBOURNE, 1901

Pioneering anarchist Chummy Fleming disrupts the opening of Federal Parliament by leading an unemployed demonstration against a State visit by the Duke and Duchess of York. According to *The Age*, just as the Mayor is about to begin the opening ceremonies, "Fleming remarks that he is very sorry that in the circumstances he cannot, on behalf of his party, extend a welcome to their Royal Highnesses, in view of the fact that he believes thousands of people here are out of work, and many in the colonies are consequently suffering the miseries of starvation." When a Detective Stokes runs down the steps to the Yarra Bank to order Fleming to cease speaking, the anarchist replies that he is just addressing a few friends. In response to what Fleming labels "this outrage on the right of free speech" he and his supporters burst into singing *La Marseillaise*.

MELBOURNE, 1908

A deputation of several hundred unemployed people demanding relief brawls with police after being barred from entering the public gallery of the Federal Parliament. After the fighting spills onto the floor of the House Parliament is adjourned. A number of unemployed arrested on the day are later barred from the Parliamentary precinct for life.

In the same year a demonstration of 300 unemployed people occupies the Stock Exchange, bringing trade to a sudden halt. Traders are denounced as "a body of parasites which are fattened upon labour".

SYDNEY, 1909

Having defeated white heavyweight boxing champion Tom Burns, African-American boxer Jack Johnson comes under a welter of racist abuse from white Australians, many of whom accuse him of being a "barbarian". In response Johnson states that he will find solace in reading his favourite books *Paradise Lost* and *Andronicus*. He also states that, "As I am a descendant of Ham, I must bear your reproaches because I beat a white man."

COCKBURN, 1909

During the latest bitter Broken Hill industrial dispute, in which scabs are attacked and a railway line blown up to cut off police supplies, socialist leader Tom Mann is arrested on trumped-up charges of sedition. After he is bailed on the condition that he not hold further meetings in the town his supporters organise the Tom Mann Express to Cockburn. Two to three thousand people board a train adorned with a banner reading "Broken Hill Lockout". The train makes numerous stops in country towns along the way to the South Australian border, allowing its passengers to collect donations and rabble rouse for the cause. Eventually the train arrives in Cockburn, where a picnic is held and speeches heard.

MELBOURNE, 1909

Demonstrators take to walking backwards as a method of circumventing police bans on street marches.

AUSTRALIA, 1911

Although Australian Industrial Workers of the World (IWW) clubs are first set up in 1907 the local wing of the international syndicalist union does not establish an official branch until 1911. Having initially based itself in Adelaide the organisation soon creates further chapters around Australia dedicated to the formation of "One Big Union" to overthrow capitalism.

By 1914 the union's militant stance and repudiation of party politics sees its members regularly harassed by police and employers. This situation only increases with the publication of an incendiary paper called *Direct Action*, whose opening editorial reads, "For the first time in the history of the working-class movement in Australia, a paper appears which stands for straight-out direct-actionist principles, unhampered by the plausible theories of the parliamentarian."

It is the organisation's militant role in opposing conscription during World War One that tips the scales into outright repression, however, as leading members in WA and NSW are soon framed and jailed for sabotage, treason and arson. By the end of 1916 the Federal Parliament passes the Unlawful Associations Act specifically aimed at banning the IWW, with Prime Minister Billy Hughes stating, "This organisation holds a dagger at the heart of our society, and we should be recreant to the social order if we do not accept the challenge it holds out to us. As it seeks to destroy us, we must in self defence destroy it."

Although the union is at first able to work around these legal restrictions, the tightening of the Unlawful Associations Act in 1917 sees any member not willing to repudiate the organisation threatened with six months in prison. This effectively cripples the group and shuts down their paper, but former members continue to campaign for the release of their jailed comrades and various incarnations of the union make a return from the 1920s onwards.

Throughout its history the IWW makes particular use of humour and satire to stir up sympathisers and ridicule its enemies. Other than famously composing parodies of popular songs the group also adorns lamp poles, signs and any and all available surfaces with stickers, otherwise known as "silent agitators", bearing such slogans as "Fast Workers Die Young", "Someone has to be last let it be you", "The hours are long and the pay is small, so take your time and _____ them all", and "A bad day's work for a bad day's pay".

In an interview with historian Eric Fry former *Direct Action* editor and leading IWW member Tom Barker also recalls the graffiti that the group would utilise to spread its name and message:[1]

Of course, all the work wasn't inside the city. All kinds of movements and strikes were going on outside. There were troubles in Broken Hill; there was a great build up of IWW sentiment in North Queensland, from Cairns and Townsville to Cloncurry. The engines and box cars on the railways were carrying our slogans ...

One night at Central Station I saw an engine come in from the shops ready for going out on the road, and the way it had been done reflected light on the side so that you could distinctly see the letters IWW shining on the engine. We used all kinds of methods like that in order to make

the organisation well-known through the country ...

The same thing applied in Sydney Harbour, where we had a big following amongst the ship repairers and painters. When they were painting the side of a ship they would first draw IWW in very big letters on it, and then they would start on the outside and work gradually towards this, so that during the whole of the time anybody coming into the Harbour or passing would see these enormous letters on the side of the ship.

COLLIE, 1911

A number of women in this West Australian coal town assemble at the pit head during a miners' strike to pelt scabs with rotten fruit while others gather on the road leading to the pit to wreck the strikebreakers' bicycles.

BRISBANE, 1912

A citywide General Strike kicks off after 480, out of 550, tramway workers are suspended on January 18 for pinning on union badges at a rally outside the General Post Office. Building on recent successful solidarity strikes 42 unions come out in support of Queenslanders' right to join a union in what is hailed by their Strike Bulletin as the "first Simultaneous Strike" in the world.

Twelve days later, faced with sabotage and the threat of mass action the following day, the manager of the tramways shuts all public transport down. Over the next few days tens of thousands rally and march across the city whilst the government lets loose 3,000 hastily sworn-in "special" constables, many of whom attack strike supporters at random. Undaunted, mass protests continue with breakaway groups raiding elite restaurants and closing shops and businesses who have refused to recognise the call to stop work.

Tensions increase on Thursday February 1 when police charge strikers at various points where they have overturned vehicles carrying scab goods. Batons, mounted police and vehicles ramming crowds of protesters are met with showers of rocks and window breaking. Panicked, the state government in turn calls unsuccessfully for the military deployment of

Commonwealth soldiers, a British warship and sailors from the German *Condor*, which has been stranded offshore.

Despite these ominous signs, 15,000 strikers and their supporters gather the next day in what is intended as a peaceful show of strength. Finding themselves blocked by police parading with rifles and bayonets, the legal demonstration refuses to back away. Led by Police Commissioner Cahill, who reportedly rides about screaming, "Give it to them lads! Into them!" thousands of police tear into the protesters, badly injuring dozens and possibly killing two.

Terrorised and unarmed, the crowd disperses beyond a few rocks, but police continue to hunt down stray protesters for the next hour, beating any they can find. Cornered, a group of female marchers draw their hatpins to use them against charging horses. During this unequal battle, leading feminist socialist Emma Miller topples Cahill from his mount, leaving him with a permanent injury.

Failing to have properly organised a defence effort, faced with the deployment of further specials including Boer War veterans, and unwilling to take advantage of widespread anger concerning what becomes known as "Baton Friday", the Strike Committee backs off from further confrontation. Although the dispute slowly winds down over the following month rank-and-file strikers continue the struggle by picketing businesses, harassing scabs and sabotaging trams and tram tracks through the use of explosives, boulders and fog lights.

AUSTRALIA, 1912

Three years after the introduction of compulsory military training for boys and young men, an Adelaide newspaper reveals that there have been close to 10,000 prosecutions for the non-performance of military drills under the Conscription Act, with another 10,000 individuals failing to register for training in South Australia alone. The Australian Freedom League, which boasts 55,000 members, claims two years later that there has been an average of 131 prosecutions a week between 1911-13, rising to 327 a week in the six months to December

BROKEN HILL LOCK-OUT, 1909

Broken Hill has a long tradition of union militancy, which grew out of the desperate and dangerous conditions miners toiled under in the late Nineteenth and early Twentieth centuries. One of the most bitter and protracted battles between local workers and employers took place in 1909 when the Broken Hill Proprietary Company (BHP) and ten other firms sought to slash wages to 1906 levels in order to maintain profits.

Well aware that a showdown was about to take place the combined unions of Broken Hill hired the esteemed socialist Tom Mann to organise their ranks, which he subsequently and successfully did, raising membership to include 90% of the area's workforce. Despite this show of unity the town's employers, led by BHP's John Darling, announced that from the 1st of January 1909 they would lock out any worker who refused to accept the new less than minimum-wage rate. To bolster their cause they also sent for fifty armed police from Sydney, a move which rather than intimidating the Amalgamated Miners Association (AMA) only served to galvanise it further.

Come New Year's Day 1909 the dispute began in earnest, with unions picketing and closing down three mines and the Port Pirie smelters. Within ten days of the lock-out kicking off, the police moved in to arrest 28 union leaders for sedition and unlawful assembly. These included Tom Mann, who was banned from speaking in New South Wales, an impediment he overcame by arranging to speak before 3,000 supporters in Cockburn, just over the border in South Australia.

Amidst much violence locals stood firm. All played their part, with women enforcing a boycott on hotels and shops serving scabs and police, and families joining in Socialist Sunday Schools and regular parades. Pro-strikers wore badges identifying their position and a coupon system was set up allowing unionists to exchange time spent on picket lines for goods and services. Mock graves and executions (see images) were set up outside the mine gates to name and shame the employers and scabs who sought to drive down wages and destroy the AMA.

Despite an early ruling by the Federal Court of Conciliation and Arbitration prohibiting Broken Hill employers from cutting wages, the lock-out dragged on until the 23rd of May. Even though the unions agreed to return to work, BHP kept their mine closed for another two years, at which time they consented to pay the improved rates which other employers had already agreed to.

The "Thousand" We Would Like to See.

CIVILISATION: "WHAT HAVE I DONE?"

—Adapted from "Arabian Nights" Tales.

THE SPOILS ARE HEAVY.
AUSTRALIAN WAGE-EARNER: "They may say I'm ungrateful; but, somehow, I can't get enthusiastic over the 'Victory' celebration!"

ANTI-WAR CARTOONS, 1915 – 1919

Top left: *FAT (intoxicated with "Patrotism"): LONG LIVE THE WAR! HIP HIP, 'OORAY! FILL EM UP AGAIN!* Syd Nichols cartoon which led to the jailing of Direct Action editor Tom Barker, 1915. **Top right:** "The "Thousand" we would like to see", Taken from *Worker*, 1916. Artist unknown. **Bottom left and right:** *CIVILISATION: "WHAT HAVE I DONE?"*, Claude Marquet, 1917. • *THE SPOILS ARE HEAVY. Australian Wage-Earner: "They say I'm ungrateful; but, somehow, I can't get enthusiastic over the 'Victory' celebration!"*, Claude Marquet, 1919.

with a further 90,000 of those registered failing to actually train. Other than leading anti-conscription campaigners, such as Harry Holland and Alfred Giles, few parents and anti-war activists are prosecuted as the government fears that such action will only increase the existing backlash.

BRISBANE, 1912

In the face of government repression soapbox speakers use a variety of tricky tactics to flout restrictions on free speech. One man has a blacksmith rivet a chain around his body before padlocking himself to a pole and throwing away the key. He then declares himself a "bridge by which comrades can pass over from capitalism to socialism". In the process of removing him one policeman smashes his thumb, much to delight of the assembled crowd. Once in the lock-up the man goes on hunger strike before being jammed into a mental asylum by the exasperated authorities.

In another protest against restrictions on public speaking, two men dressed as Cossacks and bound with red gags come tearing down Queen Street on horseback. Upon their backs reads the message, "Sorry to say can't speak to you today — Commissioner Cahill won't let me."

Angry at the State Government for arresting his mates, Jimmy Quinton engages in a further protest by parading down Queen Street bound and gagged and draped in a Union Jack. When confronted by police he cries to the crowd that he has been, "brutally bound and gagged." Asked who had bound and gagged him he replies, "A rotten constitution." Two months in Boggo Road prison is his reward for taking such a stand.

The following year Socialist Bob Bessant caricatures police censorship before a crowd of 2,000 by riding up and down Queen Street with a placard reading, "Sorry to say I must be quiet, for if I speak I'll cause a riot."

BRISBANE, 1913

Facing court on a variety of charges related to the socialist cause, defendants elect to waste as much of the court's precious time as possible. One man pretends to be deaf and, standing as still as a statue, forces the Judge and police to scream in his ear. Others ask frivolous questions of witnesses such as, "And where was the moon in the heavens that night?"

SYDNEY, 1913

When the IWW first begins selling its paper on the streets of Sydney it encounters resistance from police and censors. This is defeated by a series of actions as recalled by *Direct Action* editor Tom Barker:[2]

We decided that we would make an issue of this trying to prevent us selling the paper in the Sydney Domain. We went to Macquarie Street to see the Minister, Flowers. We got into the office all right. Two cabinet ministers were there and Flowers said to us, "How are you fellows getting on at Newcastle?" We said, "We're not from Newcastle. We are from the IWW." So we were ushered promptly by the attendants down into the street. That didn't satisfy us.

We waited a while, saw the miners go in and come out, and went into the Domain to sit down and think it out. We discovered that there was a ladder up to the Minister's window. Some work had been going on, the men had gone away for lunch, and this ladder was standing right up into the office. We didn't know what the chance was, but Glynn went up first, I went up second and we appeared at the window. You ought to have seen the faces of those two cabinet ministers, standing there with their cigars and the whisky on the table.

Flowers wanted to prevent us coming in, but we told him straight out that we wanted his prohibition on selling papers in the Domain stopped. We wanted our rights established permanently. He was going to ring for the police and do one thing or another until Glynn said, "Look Flowers, I knew you a couple of years ago when you had the seat out of your pants. You were the leader of the unemployed then. Today you're a cabinet minister. Now you come down to earth. I'll tell you what, if you don't put an end to this business of stopping us selling our papers, we'll have ten thousand unemployed down to these offices in a couple of days." That brought Mr Flowers to time and he allowed us in at the window and we had a big wrangle. He wouldn't let us have any whisky, but finally he said he would go into it.

That wasn't the end of it, because a few days later the Political Labour Leagues of New South Wales were holding their annual conference. All the Cabinet Ministers were there, including Holman, the Premier, David Robert Hall, who was Attorney-General and Minister of Justice, and a whole crowd I have forgotten, just the same as the people of New South Wales have forgotten them. It was in the Oddfellows Hall in Elizabeth Street, I think.

Our plan was that some speaker from the body of the Hall should raise this matter and at that moment our fellows should barricade the outside doors and put the light switches out. I was sitting at the back, for a number of us had gone into the public part of the hall. The question was raised, D.R. Hall began to make a statement about it, then, at that moment the light switches were pulled out and the barricade boards put across the doors so that nobody could get out, and the place was in darkness.

Well, there was pandemonium inside the hall. Somebody got up in the dark and suggested they send for the police, so a resolution was carried that the Premier himself, Holman, should go and fetch the police. He was just as helpless as any baby, even if he was Premier of the State. They broke a window and made a big shout and finally the police came and released the whole lot of us.

Out of these various battles we established the right to sell the paper in the Sydney Domain and cleared every other body for the same thing. That was the real gain we made for the freedom of the press in the State of New South Wales.

NSW, 1915

War veteran, Communist and former Prahran Mayor Fred Farrall recalls a series of strikes undertaken by recently recruited members of the First Australian Imperial Force (1st AIF):[3]

On Christmas Eve, we were camped at Yarra, five miles out of Goulburn, which had been decorated for a recruiting rally with flags and seating for the V.I.P.s. Mr Orchard, the Minister for Recruiting, and Major-General Ramashott were to be there. Now, when the march started from Wagga, certain promises had been made. These were that we were to have leave for Christmas Day and Boxing Day to go to our families, and three days leave when we reached Sydney. But, on Christmas Eve, Captain McLeod, who was in charge of the march, announced that the leave had been cancelled, and the recruits were to stay in camp and attend the rally in Goulburn, and march on to Sydney on Boxing Day. This was only one of many promises to be broken, but it was a first for us, and we were very upset.

At this time, the line between Sydney and Albury was being duplicated, and some of the recruiting had been done from the navvies working on it, so that among the soldiers on the march were some members of the AWU. They raised objections to the broken promise and announced, "No leave, no march." We were on strike! And I had only been in the army a few days! A navvy named Green was the leader, and I can remember being amazed at the bravery of the men who stood up to the officer in charge. But it was a good learning experience for me — in modern jargon, a "growth" experience. I learned that one could stand up to those in charge of us and sometimes win.

At five o'clock on Christmas Eve, the recruiting rally was abandoned, as the men had stood firm, and we were given permission to go home, and to be back to join the march at Marulan on 27th December. But no rail passes! The men swarmed on to the trains, just telling the ticket collectors to "send the bill to Billy Hughes". My mate, Gus Stevens, and I travelled free as far as Junee where we had to change for the train to Ganmain, and here, because we wanted to arrive respectable, we jumped the fence, and went around to the ticket box and bought tickets home.

The promise of three days' leave in Sydney was also broken. Most of the men had never seen Sydney, the ocean, or even a tram, and were excitedly looking forward to three days' sightseeing. When we arrived in Sydney, we were marched around and given a dinner at one of Sargent's restaurants, at which we were at first praised up for offering ourselves as recruits to help the "boys over there". And then we were told there would be no leave. We were to march to Central Station and there join a train for Goulburn for training.

Another strike was called, but this time without success. One of the AWU chaps, a big, hefty bloke, stood up and spoke for the men. I was prepared to support him because, in those days, I followed along like a lamb. But we were no longer in blue dungarees, but in khaki army uniforms, and no longer in the bush. On the contrary, we were very close to Victoria Barracks, and we were told that if we did not obey orders there were men there armed with rifles and bayonets who would be called out to make us.

All we achieved this time was to delay the train back to Goulburn for three hours. Just as the army is called out now to enforce the will of those in power, so the army was used then against men who were going out to fight and die for these officers. And all to deprive the men of a paltry three days' leave!

NSW, 1915

A drinker in a bar in Tumbarumba is arrested by police and later fined £100 under the War Precautions Act for saying that World War One is a "capitalists' war and should be fought by capitalists".

MELBOURNE, 1915

The Women's Peace Army, whose slogan is "We war against war", is founded to fight militarism with "the same spirit of self-sacrifice that soldiers showed on the battlefield."

SYDNEY, 1915

Tom Barker recalls IWW attempts to avoid arrest for publishing seditious statements in their paper *Direct Action*:[4]

It wasn't long before the authorities got curious about who was editing the paper, and they couldn't decide whether it was Tom Barker, Tom Glynn, or who it was. We got the idea that we'd make it a little more difficult, so we put on the paper: "Editor: Mr A. Block." For this A. Block we got a block of wood and a dingy old top hat somebody had inherited. We put the hat on this block of wood and kept it behind the editorial room and if anybody came wanting to see the Editor, we took him in [and said], "Allow us to introduce you to the Editor, Mr A. Block." When the detectives came around they got very mixed up. Some were annoyed about it and some thought that it was a bit of a joke. As it happened, it probably made the difference between Tom Glynn getting a long jail sentence and me getting it. He got it, because on one occasion they decided, after they'd had a talk, that I was the fellow they wanted and took me away. I got a short sentence — well,

it wasn't too short, it was a year — but things happened when I was in prison that got Glynn ten years later on.

MELBOURNE, 1916

After anti-conscriptionist and Labor politician Frank Anstey is labelled a "pigeon-livered man" by W. Watt he challenges the ardent pro-conscription politician's convictions by stating that he will sign up for the front if Watt does it first. Anstey names a date and time, but unsurprisingly the "stay at home patriot" Watt leaves others to do his fighting for him.

SYDNEY, 1916

Tom Barker recalls a second domestic troop strike during WWI:[5]

I think it can be said that our influence on the Australian Army was at that time quite considerable, apart from what we did on the industrial front, because it was natural enough that men who had been influenced by the IWW would join and, when accommodation and food and that kind of thing got bad, their minds would revert to "direct action" as a means of rectifying it. In the Liverpool camp there was a famous break-out, when thousands of the soldiers decided they had had enough of the lousy food and the discipline. They went to Liverpool station and stopped the Melbourne Express by standing on the line. They cashed everybody off the train and compelled the engine driver to take the whole gang, in the train and on top of the train, into Central Station. Then they went to town in a big way. They really ruled Sydney for about three days.

I remember being in Bathurst Street, not far from Anthony Hordern's store, when about six of these big diggers were standing around a nice, pleasant businessman. They had him in a corner and one bloke said to him, "Now, look you, aren't we going to fight for you?" The man said, "Yes, yes, yes." "Well," the digger said, "What are you going to do about it? Dip into your pockets, son!" That's a fact. I used to get round the streets and observe what was going on among these fellows that were on the lam, and they were really knocking coppers about; they were breaking places open; they were raiding the pubs. They certainly had possession of Sydney for a good three days, and it took a long while before they caught up with them.

Early this year (1964) I took part in a controversy in the British *Telegraph* about this. When news of the discussion reached Sydney, up rises a mighty man who comes to denounce me for saying such things, spreading scandals about a great army in which he fought himself. "Of course," he said, "there was trouble up at Liverpool Camp. As a matter of fact a number of us did decide that the food was too bad to be stood, so we just went down to Sydney quietly for a decent meal." He didn't mention how long this meal took to get! The claim was also made by one correspondent that nothing very much happened to the leaders. That wasn't true. When I was in Parramatta Jail later I ran into one of these fellows there, he was doing ten years for being mixed up in it.

Under the volunteer system, before conscription was mooted, the Army wouldn't take anyone who said he was a member of the IWW. Maybe a man's boss would tell him he had to join up or get a clearance from the Army. If a fellow wanted to get a discharge before he started, he went up, flashed his IWW card in front of the recruiting Officer and he was out for good. We had to stop taking members for a long time because we knew a lot of them only wanted the card to get out of the Army."

BRISBANE, 1916

IWW member Percival Mandeno is arrested for prejudicing recruiting after he makes a speech pointing out that during the Boer War he was "footsore and lousy". Embarrassed by the imprisonment of a war veteran the government offers to pay his bail, but Mandeno elects to stay put.

SYDNEY, 1916

Tom Barker on internal military resistance to conscription:[6]

Just prior to the first conscription referendum the government, [Prime Minister] Hughes and rest of the gang were cocksure that they were going to get away with conscription. They'd promised it and they were certain they could deliver it so they'd already called a lot of the lads up in advance. They used to dress these lads in blue dungarees and they were called the 'Hugheseliers'.

The day before the conscription vote — I remember this very vividly and plainly — I was in Wentworth Avenue at the bottom of Elizabeth

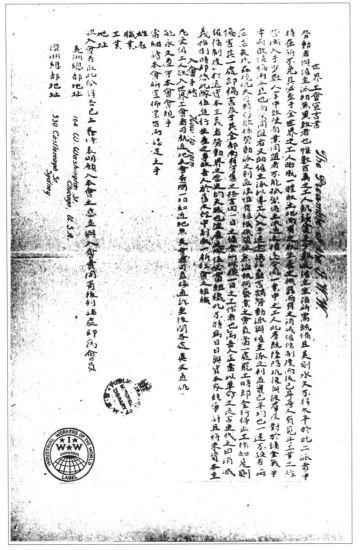

Conscription.

Workers, when the rifle is forced upon you and you are told to shoot, shoot in the right direction.

INDUSTRIAL WORKERS OF THE WORLD

Top: IWW newspaper masthead designed by Syd Nicholls, 1915. **Far Left:** One of the few political organisations of the era to oppose racism, the IWW distributed its Preamble and other propaganda in Chinese during the first decades of the Twentieth century. **Left:** "Silent Agitator" sticker, 1916. **Below:** Syd Nicholls cartoon, 1915.

Street when a battalion of these kids came along. Whatever they were there for, they weren't carrying out orders. They started to shout, "Vote No, No, No." In short, it had just the opposite effect to what Hughes intended because, once they got out on the road there, they became, like Australians are, very vocal and they let everybody know that they were against conscription and that they didn't want to go to fight. This army streaming down Wentworth Avenue, and all these lads bellowing at the top of their voices, "Vote No, No, No," will never fade in my memory.

PERTH, 1917

Western Australia's peak union body, the WA Trades Hall Council, warns that strike action will meet any attempt to sack workers for refusing to enlist.

AUSTRALIA, 1917

Warrant Officer Clarence Wilbur Baker applies to resign his officer status and revert to the ranks, stating that, "The world today is obedient to the war maker (Russia apart) and only a few men remain who dare follow where the facts lead." As a result Baker holds that he too must join "that small, but strong body of men opposing war."

AUSTRALIA, 1917

A strike by 6,000 NSW public transport workers in early August against the introduction of speed-ups and "scientific management" rapidly spreads after coal miners refuse to load trains staffed by scabs. Wharfies in turn walk off the job when they are ordered to load scab coal. Strikes against handling goods unloaded by scab dockworkers then spread the industrial action to ships, factories and other workplaces along the East Coast.

Waitresses at Central Station join the General Strike after they walk off the job in response to being ordered to serve strike-breakers. South Australian police withdraw from protecting scabs in Broken Hill after municipal workers refuse to collect 'night soil' (human waste) from the quarters and hotels where they are staying. In Australia's biggest city thousands jeer and rain blue metal down on scabs housed at the Sydney Cricket Ground. One strike meeting sees militants drown out

moderates by playing ragtime tunes on a handy piano. The lack of coal and other goods also affects the ability of munitions workers to provide materiel to the war front and sees power cuts in Melbourne and Sydney.

Despite the opposition and sabotage ranged against them by conservative union leaders, which ultimately dooms the strike, the anti-scab craze extends to eventually include 100,000 workers who stop work for up to 6 weeks. Daily rallies, including the singing of the recently composed IWW song *Solidarity Forever*, peak with a gathering of up to 150,000 in the Sydney Domain.

MELBOURNE, 1917

Authorities attempt to prohibit demonstrations in the city after women, protesting against rises in food prices which have outstripped wage increases by two to one, disrupt Parliament. The day after the order comes down in mid-August, 3,000 immediately break it by rallying near Parliament. During the demonstration Lizzie Wallace, from the Victorian Socialist Party, and British militant suffragette Adela Pankhurst are arrested for addressing the crowd.

Undaunted a crowd of around 8,000, singing The Red Flag and waving umbrellas covered with red ribbons, rally once more on August 22. Women again lead the demonstration with socialist Jennie Baines, amongst others, arrested for telling the crowd, "If people want food, they should go to the cool stores or to the bakers and the butchers and the other places and take it." Daily protests follow for the next 13 days, after which demonstrators begin heeding Baines' words by smashing businesses windows and looting food.

The campaign peaks on September 19 when a torchlight procession, lights being out due to coal shortages sparked by the NSW general strike, of 10,000 battles with mounted police for hours. After being pushed out of the city centre demonstrators attack businesses involved in strikebreaking. The tumult only ends after shots are fired in South Melbourne over protesters' heads.

AUSTRALIA, 1917

When Billy Hughes invites Lieutenant Albert Jacka, Australia's first recipient of the Victoria Cross, to speak for the pro-conscription cause, the officer, whose father and brother are helping lead the anti-conscription fight, informs him, "Mr Prime Minister, you can go to sweet buggery!"

BROKEN HILL, 1917

Pro-conscriptionists, many of whom had declined to enlist during the Boer War fourteen years earlier, attack anti-conscriptionist rallies across the country. Speakers are tarred and feathered, thrown in rivers, beaten up, and have their platforms set on fire. In reply, Broken Hill activists form a Labour Volunteer Army, and their Melbourne comrades an Anti-Conscription Army, to sort out any war-mad brawlers. Broken Hill's LVA soon boasts 2,500 volunteers whilst the Australian military can draw only 206 men from the area.

BALLARAT, 1917

Victoria's banned anti-conscription paper *The Ballarat Evening Echo* avoids government seizure when railway workers smuggle it into Melbourne in their coal piles. In Melbourne it is snuck into horse stables from which 60,000 copies are distributed daily.

AUSTRALIA, 1917

Following the Russian Revolution and the Australian Labour movement's success against conscription, the conservative Hughes' Government puts a ban on the flying of the red flag. In response radicals across Australia proudly fly the "worker's flag" with a campaign to beat the ban being carried out over a number of years. With the Women's Socialist League spearheading many actions, activist Jennie Baines is arrested on a number of occasions. When finally jailed, she secures her release after a four-day hunger strike. Another flag flyer, Dick Long, pleads "Deliberately Guilty" when his case comes up.

AUSTRALIA, 1918

The Industrial Workers of the World (IWW) parodies military recruiting propaganda with a sticker stating, "Wanted: 1,000 Good Men and Women Not Afraid of Death or Jail—YOU Join the IWW".

FRANCE, 1918

With the end of the war in sight Australian soldiers serving in France engage in a series of mutinies to avoid further lives being wasted. On 14 September the 59th Battalion initially refuses to redeploy to the front and a week later over half of the 1st Battalion go missing. The 119 men involved are charged with desertion rather than mutiny, probably to avoid what would have been massively unpopular executions, and all sentences are later dropped with the end of the war. In the meantime the threat of punishments fails to deter further action as on 23 September a number of Battalions refuse to disband in order to reinforce others.

AUSTRALIA, 1918

The following song is brought back to Australia by disaffected soldiers:

He went up to London and straightaway strode,
To army headquarters on Horseferry Road,
To see all the bludgers who dodge all the straff,
By getting soft jobs on the headquarters staff.
Dinky-di, Dinky-di,
By getting soft jobs on the headquarters staff.

The lousy lance-corporal said 'Pardon me, please
You've mud on your tunic and blood on your sleeve,
You look so disgraceful that people will laugh'
Said that lousy lance-corporal on headquarters staff.

The digger just shot him a murderous glance;
He said "We're just back from the shambles in France,
Where whizzbangs are flying and comforts are few,
And brave men are dying for bastards like you."

DARWIN, 1918

Following seven years of agitation over work conditions and a lack of voting rights up to 1,000 Territorians surround Government House breaking its windows and burning an effigy of Administrator John Gilruth (as well as roughing up the real thing). With Darwin out of their Administrator's dictatorial control the Federal government initially censors news of the rebellion and stations warships offshore before removing Gilruth to Melbourne.

BRISBANE, 1919

Labor Premier Tom Ryan sends champagne and oysters to unionists and socialists, including recently returned servicemen, jailed, under the Federal War Precautions Act, for flying the red flag.

ADELAIDE, 1919

Striking dock workers pelt scabs with potatoes.

NORTHAM, 1919

The West Australian Premier and a large audience of fellow patriots receive a shock during Peace Day celebrations marking the end of treaty negotiations with Germany. Having expected remarks about victory and Empire the crowd sit in silence as Captain Jim Throssell, a Gallipoli veteran, Victoria Cross recipient and son of a former WA Premier, presents an address on "Why The War Made Me A Socialist". During his speech the war veteran describes searching in vain for his brother's body in trenches full of dead and wounded soldiers before going to argue that war is the product of an unequal society and only serves the interests of the powerful.

AUSTRALIA, 1919

IWW member Bill Casey composes *Bump Me Into Parliament*, one of the Wobblies' most famous satirical numbers.

Come listen all kind friends of mine,
I want to move a motion,
To make an El Dorado here,
I've got a bonzer notion.

CHORUS:
Bump me into parliament,
Bump me any way at all,
Bang me into parliament,
On next election day.

Some very wealthy friends I know,
Declare I am most clever,

While some can talk for an hour or so,
I can talk forever.

I've read my bible ten times through,
And Jesus justifies me, but the man,
Who doesn't vote for me,
By Christ he crucifies me.

I am a sitting Liberal,
I sit upon a goldmine while,
Earnest members lose their seats,
I drink all day and keep mine.

Oh yes I am a Labour man,
I believe in revolution
The quickest way to bring it on,
Is by talking constitution.

So bump them into Parliament
Bounce them any way,
Bung them into Parliament
Don't let the Courts decay.

FREMANTLE, 1919

Despite losing one of their number to police fire, strikers expel scabs from the wharfs during what becomes known as Bloody Sunday.

MELBOURNE, 1920

The ALP Member for Kalgoorlie and Irish sympathiser Hugh Mahon is expelled from Federal Parliament after making a speech denouncing the British Commonwealth as a "bloody and accursed Empire".

QUEENSLAND, 1920s

In *Sixty Years Of Struggle: A Journal of Communist and Labour History* former Communist Party of Australia member Doug Olive recalls his early exposure to unionism on the North Queensland cane fields:

The early struggles by the AWU rank-and-file against the [right-wing union] bureaucracy were led mainly by the Industrial Workers of the World (IWW). They were very courageous militant characters. They were flamboyant and excellent agitational speakers. They held union officials in the same contempt as they held politicians. They said that the only man who ever went to parliament with good intentions was Guy Fawkes—and he went to blow the bloody place up!

My first contact with the IWW was at a railway camp between Kyogle and the NSW/Queensland

CIVIL LIBERTIES MARCH, BRISBANE, 1919

Following physical and legal attacks on socialists for exercising free speech and flying the red flag, protests take place across the country demanding an end to repressive measures enacted under the War Precautions Act. Tensions in Brisbane over the issue are particularly high. The authorities jail a number of activists for defying the law whilst thousands of right-wingers engage in three days of attacks on the offices of the Russian Workers Association. Despite this civil liberties campaigners continue to hold demonstrations, including this procession down Edward Street, and the Act is repealed in 1920. Photographer unknown.

border. I was an impressionable lad of 17 or 18 who had just come from the salubrious Sydney suburb of Turramurra which was remote from strikes and militant action. In a railway gang near the border a strike had broken out over the sacking of a powder monkey.

The powder monkey's job was to bore a hole in the rock which was to be blasted out, to set the dynamite in the hole and light the fuse. He used to allow himself 20 seconds to get clear after he lit the fuse. But 30 seconds before, he would call out, "Fire oh!" to give the other men time to get clear. The ganger, aptly known as "Flash Harry", considered this to be time-wasting and told the powder monkey, "You can get out of the place in 20 seconds; why the bloody hell can't they?" But the powder monkey felt that some of the old blokes weren't active enough and needed the extra time, and he wasn't going to be responsible for fellow workers being injured. The ganger then fired him. The men went on strike and sent speakers to other gangs.

This was about 56 years ago and the impact

on my immature but rebel mind was so strong that I still remember how one speaker summed up the ganger and his action. He said, "You've all heard of the philosopher of olden times who went around trying to turn base metal into gold, but here we have a man in more modern times who makes the boast that he can turn human flesh and blood into ready cash—here's your time, go and get your bloody money!" Now this was tremendous stuff for us young blokes to hear.

Later in the Queensland sugar industry, there was an IWW character who used to bob up at pre-seasonal meetings of the canecutters—the AWU meetings held before the start of the cane cutting season—and he would always be elected chairman. In those days most of us were not very well educated; we could hardly put two sentences together, let alone get up and give a speech. But this bloke could speak. For these pre-seasonal meetings the AWU officials would always bring along a stooge to pop in the chair, and just as regularly we'd pop him out.

At the meetings the IWW man who we'd elect as chairman had a novel and unique way of putting the question: he'd say, "Now I'm going to put the question to you boneheads. Men to the left, cockies' fucks and bastards to the right," and then he'd turn to the AWU officials cowering on the side, and add, "and AWU officials to the shithouse." Now this may seem to bypass the norms of democratic procedure and to smack of intimidation, but nevertheless, by Jesus, it was effective. In the parlance of the cane fields at that time, the term 'cockie's fucks' meant that the man was a crawler, and no red-blooded canecutter would willingly nominate himself as a crawler. So they would all move to the left.

They had an equally novel way of persuading cockies — the cane farmers — to grant higher rates and better conditions on the cane fields: this was to let the "red steer" loose, the "red steer" being a fire in the sugar cane. The IWW, at the pre-seasonal meeting, would get the OK on a demand for a higher rate, then they would go to the largest cocky and put this demand to him. The cocky, of course, would refuse. That night, one of the boys would take a candle and go for a walk into the middle of the canefield where there was no wind. He'd put the candle firmly in the soil, bank up trash (rubbishy stuff from the sugarcane) around it, and then light the wick of the candle. By the time the candle burnt down and its flame caught the trash, and ultimately the cane, this lad would be well and truly in his bed.

When a farm was burnt out, the cane had to be harvested within three or four days of its being fired, otherwise it would deteriorate in sugar content. So all the cutters from the neighbouring farms had to be brought in to get it cut in time. But before the boys would start work on this, they would meet and decide to demand that they be paid the higher rate, otherwise they'd go back to their original farms. They had the cocky where the hair is short. The other cockies, fearing the same fate, would then comply with the new rate.

With the higher rate having thus been won, it became an established practice that the AWU officials would then prepare a lengthy legal case for the rate and go to the arbitration court. The new rate would thereupon be written into the award and the Queensland AWU official journal, *The Queensland Worker*, would then claim full credit for the new rate. But the men knew better and they knew that, no matter how brilliant the argument in court, it was the action that had taken place outside the court, in the industry itself, that had counted. The workers get from arbitration only what they are organisationally strong enough, only what they're determined and militant enough, to force arbitration to give them, and this applies in all industries.

MELBOURNE, 1921
The Freemason-controlled Melbourne City Council decides to take on both Irish Republicans and the Left by decreeing that all marches through the city must be headed by the Union Jack. In a shrewd move, Archbishop Mannix agrees to abide with the order on St Patrick's Day by sending a lone, filthy derelict, carrying the British flag, ahead of the main procession. The rest of the march, headed by the Irish Republican flag, follows at some distance. When Mannix addresses the crowd he states, "We paid

an Englishman fifteen shillings to carry the Union Jack for we could not find an Irishman prepared to carry it." Father Phelan chips in saying, "I am proud of the fact that no Irishmen could be got to carry the Union Jack. No Irish-Australian would carry it either."

MELBOURNE, 1923
Special constables are sworn in as people crowd the city and loot stores during a wildcat strike by police.

BRISBANE, 1924
Socialists beat anti-free speech laws by speaking from boats that are tethered just offshore and thus exempt from on-land legislation.

SYDNEY, 1924
Unionists boycott salons on Saturday afternoons in support of reduced working hours for hairdressers.

MELBOURNE, 1925
Hundreds of British sailors are rounded up and arrested for breaking ship's orders in support of an international seamen's strike. Many go to jail happily claiming that they are extending the life of the dispute by saving the strike committee the effort of finding them food and lodgings. On the way to court the men are joined by a massive crowd of supporters marching behind a banner reading, "Prison Before Slavery—Heroes in 1914, Slaves in 1925."

SYDNEY, 1925
ALP officials lock out journalists at the Labor Daily after the scribes refuse to stop using the word "scab".

NORTHERN TERRITORY, 1926
Shortly before helping to wipe out the cattle run at Mount Peak an Indigenous local warns a pastoralist named Matthews that, "This land no more longa white fella, longa black fellow. White fella can't sit down longa black fella. White man shift."

AUSTRALIA, 1928
Throughout a national waterfront dispute waterside workers use a number of tactics

to shame and harass scabs, including hiding on roofs to dump garbage on them and their police escorts. After an acrimonious battle in Melbourne, during which police fire on pickets, killing one and injuring others, wharfies' wives invade Parliament to disrupt proceedings. Port Adelaide sees even more riotous scenes as strikers storm ships and push scabs into harbour waters before soldiers are eventually brought in to patrol the docks.

ADELAIDE, 1929
Police fail in their attempts to prevent unemployed diggers from carrying banners reading, "We had a job in 1914-1918. Why not now!" during the annual ANZAC Day parade.

SYDNEY, 1929
Striking timber workers' wives crash an ALP "Industrial Peace" conference, abusing and attacking the assembly.

ADELAIDE, 1929
A large demonstration of unemployed people occupies the Myer department store in the Rundle Street Mall. When ordered out by police (who quickly move to guard cash registers) the protesters proceed upstairs to occupy the tea room and demand food for their children.

NSW, 1929
Following police action that leads to the death of a picket, Norman Brown, striking coalminers form their own Labour Defence Army at Cessnock.

MELBOURNE, 1930
A furniture removal company that specialises in helping people do midnight flits begins advertising their services with a sign saying, "Why Pay Rent? Keep Moving!"

SYDNEY, 1930s
Chalked Salvation Army graffiti bearing the legend "God Saves" is amended to read "With Eno Salts".

MELBOURNE, 1930s
In *Sixty Years Of Struggle: A Journal of Communist and Labour History* veteran Communist Jim

Munro recalls the anti-eviction actions he took part in as a member of the Unemployed Workers' Union during the Depression:

Around Fitzroy, Carlton and Collingwood I think we stopped every eviction. In some of the outer suburbs they weren't as successful although we were that well organised in the finish that we'd go out by train or tram when we heard of an eviction case. We wouldn't pay fares, we'd jump the trams and trains to the place and we were fairly successful.

There were a few bashings at the time. They caught us at Fitzroy one day on an eviction in a very narrow street. We were packed in front of a house when two furniture vans appeared; one coming up the street and one coming the other way. We took no notice, but when they got close to us they unloaded and there were 30 or 40 cops in each van. They had us hemmed in and they belted the insides out of us; men, women and children.

Just before this we had stopped an eviction at Collingwood. On the Saturday night the police went down illegally with the agent and bluffed the woman out. She had a couple of kiddies and her husband was up the bush looking for work. They had no right to be there, because once we'd stopped the eviction in the first place, they had to take out court orders the second time. So someone went down there on the Sunday night with picks and crowbars and wrecked the place inside and out.

After the Fitzroy bashing there was one much same at Burnley. Ernie Thornton was jailed over it. There were nine estate agents in Richmond and we organised groups of two to smash the windows of every office at fifteen minutes to nine on a late shopping evening. Every estate agent's windows were smashed to pieces. You should have seen *The Herald* on the Saturday night. Sidney Myer issued a statement that it was shocking and disgraceful to think that people who were out of work should be thrown on to the streets. The government had to do something so they introduced a rent allowance of eight shillings a week for rent. The only problem with that was they found houses in far away places for all the well known militants. However, it put an end to the evictions; you could get a reasonable place for 10 shillings. Most agents would give it to you; they'd prefer to get only eight shillings rather than have a place standing open because

nine times out of ten they'd be wrecked.

Incidentally, we got a firewood allowance of a hundredweight of wood a week to each unemployed person. People were wrecking places, pulling down fences and cutting down trees to get firewood. We found that taking militant action influenced public opinion and influenced what the Government did as well.

Another struggle we had was against selling people's furniture to pay for overdue rent. The police would go into your home, mark your furniture, take it to the police station and auction it to help pay your rent. The proceeds of the auction were given to the agent. The first one we knew of was in Napier Street, Fitzroy. They seized a family's furniture, but we got hold of a horse and cart, raided the police station and carted it to Clifton Hill at 12 o'clock at night. Early the next day the police saw that there was no furniture there and went straight to the chap who'd carted it and said, "We know you carted that furniture away last night, it's to be sold at the police station at two o'clock. You have it there or you'll be going in." So, Harry Guinane was his name (he'd been right through the timber workers' strike with me), came up to us at the unemployed rooms and told us about the police threats. We said, "Oh well Harry, there's nothing to do but take it back. Cart it down to the police station and we'll have to find another way out." So we had a talk and decided that the only thing left to do was to buy it back. Bill Donald, who later became an organiser for the Railways' Union, said, "If nobody bids for it, it won't bring much, will it?"

We all went around the Fitzroy shops having a quiet chat to any prospective buyers of the furniture. I went with Bill to a big shop on the corner of Gertrude and Brunswick Streets. We saw a Mr Clements who was a well-known second hand dealer in the district. We asked him if he was going to bid for the sale of furniture at the police station that afternoon. He replied, "I'll bid for it if I think the price is right." We advised him against it, told him that we were from the Unemployed Workers Union and that we weren't going to have our members' furniture sold up like that. He stood his ground, so we asked him whether there would be much profit in it. He said, "What's that got to do with it?" Bill replied, "You've got big windows there Mr Clements and you'll have to make a profit to

have them repaired." On that note we left.

There were two or three auctioneers there that afternoon, but none of them were game to bid. We were more worried about some of the women who were keying up to bid. Our wives and everybody got alongside them and growled, "You bid for this, you bitch, and I'll tear your bloody hair out." "You open your mouth and I'll kick your guts in." We bluffed them out of it, so the furniture was put up in full lots. The first lot went up and Bill Donald said, "I'll bid sixpence." Sergeant Murphy, a vicious dog, nearly fell off the box. He couldn't get another bid, so we bought the four lots for two bob and carted it back to the house.

ADELAIDE, 1931

The aftermath of the national 1928 waterfront strike causes waves in football when a game between West Adelaide and Port Adelaide is boycotted by a number of Port players. The boycott stems from West Adelaide's selection of a policeman named McInerny who is known to have been involved in protecting scabs and breaking picket lines. The game goes ahead as planned, but as the majority of Port Adelaide players and supporters are drawn from the ranks of the local Wharf and Seamen's Unions the heckling and abuse is intense. At one point a ball that is kicked into the crowd comes back sliced in two.

SYDNEY, 1931

In the period of a month a spate of evictions are contested, a house at 81 Booth St Annandale occupied and two evictions in Balmain similarly frustrated. In Bondi a house due for eviction has a banner placed out front and local streets are chalked up with information. A house at 41 Richie St Granville sees the landlord cancel eviction orders after being confronted in his office. On hearing of another eviction in Granville, Unemployed Workers' Movement members attempt to roust the landlord out of bed at night, but are chased off by his shotgun-wielding daughter. Despite receiving a fright they later see off the eviction after 60 picket the property for a fortnight.

BELKA, 1931

Local farmers attending a forced auction in the West Australian wheatbelt remove their hats

INTERNATIONAL WOMEN'S DAY, SYDNEY, 1929

Jean Thompson, of the Militant Women's Group, speaks in support of the wives of striking timber workers during a rally held in Belmore Park, Sydney. Along with another rally in the Domain and a dance this formed part of the city's second annual IWD celebrations. Primarily organised by the CPA and Unemployed Workers Movement meetings, protests and other events took place in a number of other towns and cities around the country with one march in Hobart led by children and women carrying banners reading "Fight or Starve." Photographer unknown

as if at a funeral each time an item goes up for sale. Due to pressure from these protesters there are no bids made and Wheatgrowers Union of WA (WUWA) members buy back equipment for a pittance. They later remove wheels from a wagon and put them in a dam to prevent future repossession.

MELBOURNE, 1931

The Commercial Banking company obtains a court order to evict an unemployed family in Brunswick, but when the bailiff arrives he is confronted by a crowd of 100 who evict him from the property instead. The crowd then grabs the family's furniture and marches to the Brunswick Town Hall where they dump it in the portico. Having done so they return to the house to punish the owner by demolishing the front fence before breaking all the windows,

doors and fireplaces. Finally they smash water pipes and flood the property.

PERTH, 1931

Thousands of unemployed marchers demanding three meals a day and free healthcare fight police after they move in to arrest speakers outside the Treasury Buildings.

BALLARAT, 1932

Unemployed activists protesting against work-for-the-dole schemes and carrying placards reading "Men Fight—Fools Starve" defy the Ballarat Council's decision to refuse them a public meeting permit. Rallying outside the council chambers they are set upon by police, but when two of their number are arrested for addressing an assembled crowd of thousands, agile orators take to shop verandahs and the top of buildings to deliver their speeches.

MELBOURNE, 1932

When the police and bailiffs evict a household from Cuthbert Street in Preston, unemployed activists and locals turn the tables by returning the family's furniture to their home. During the ensuing fracas chairs and bicycles are brandished against baton-wielding police, who fire a shot from a pistol before reinforcements are brought in to overwhelm the 500-strong crowd. Eventually the real estate agent agrees to postpone the eviction for a fortnight, after which the property is burnt to the ground.

TOWNSVILLE, 1932

The Italian consul is attacked and has his regalia torn off by local anti-fascist immigrants.

On the wheelbarrow: CAPITALISM 4683 MAY TREMBLE. THE FUTURE IS OURS

"Confidence is everything". Relief workers on a work-for-the-dole scheme. Maitland, 1930s. Photographer unknown

S.S. SILKWORTH DISPUTE, NEWCASTLE, 1937

Following the Japanese occupation of China's ports in 1937 the Chinese crew of the British vessel, *SS Silkworth*, refuse to sail the ship back to their homeland. Engaging in protests they make public their appalling treatment at the hands of their employers, as well as the atrocities taking place in their birthplace. Supported and housed by local communists, unionists and members of the Chinese-Australian community the strikers are able to force the ship's owners to allow them to disembark when they reach Singapore.

Photographer unknown.

NEWCASTLE, 1932

Faced with 300 picketers a Police Inspector offers to pay the rent for residents he has been sent to evict.

NEWCASTLE, 1933

Doug Gilles recalls that:[7]

In Newcastle [the extreme right New Guard] carried out regular drilling, but hid this as much as possible from the public gaze. Look-outs were stationed during manoeuvres and New Guard members paraded in old uniforms carrying military rifles ... Some of the local unemployed, knowing the location of one of these parades, turned up one day with a bag full of snakes which they let loose. Chaos ensued as the snakes disrupted manoeuvres and the New Guard members chased the unemployed down suburban streets. Three hunted men in desperation hid in a nearby church knowing that if caught they would receive a severe bashing.

MELBOURNE, 1933

After the State Government attempts to force the unemployed to work in relief schemes for under-Award wages, a dole strike is called. When the strike fails, unemployed dock workers forced into shovelling sand run competitions to see who can work the slowest.

MELBOURNE, 1933

Following a crack-down that has seen police break up public meetings the length and breadth of the city and suburbs, Brunswick becomes the focus of a concerted civil liberties campaign from early 1933 onwards. With the local council being one of the few to withstand pressure to ban street rallies, police begin arresting speakers in Phoenix Street under obscure traffic regulations concerning "potential obstruction". After scores of orators are arrested and the Government agrees to amend legislation to properly define "obstruction", Police Commissioner Blamey, a leader of the neo-fascist White Army, defies the Police Minister by ordering his officers to deliberately drive cars up and down the otherwise abandoned street.

Faced with hundreds of mounted and uniformed police bashing crowds gathered to witness the regular Friday night showdowns, local radicals decide to up the ante in May. While a decoy, 'Shorty' Patullo, keeps police busy by delivering a speech from the top of a tram, activists carefully wheel a lorry into Sydney Road. After Patullo is silenced, having been bashed and shot in the leg by members of the Riot Squad, a hessian cover is pulled from the vehicle to reveal local artist Noel Counihan. From behind a steel mesh lift, and with the use of a gramophone horn, the young Communist addresses the crowd for 25 minutes on the importance of free speech as well as any other topic that comes to mind. Laughing at forlorn attempts by the police to crack him out of the cage, the assembled crowd of thousands takes to counting the police out, boxing-style.

Having made his point, and worried that a battering ram wielded by the Riot Squad will gouge out his stomach, Counihan eventually surrenders. Although Patullo serves a month in jail and Counihan is given a heavy fine (which is later overturned on appeal) the protest not only humiliates the police, but forces the Government to finally rein in their excesses.

MACKAY, 1933

Children of Pacific-Islander descent go on strike demanding they be allowed to continue at the school they have gone to for years rather than be forced to attend a new, segregated one.

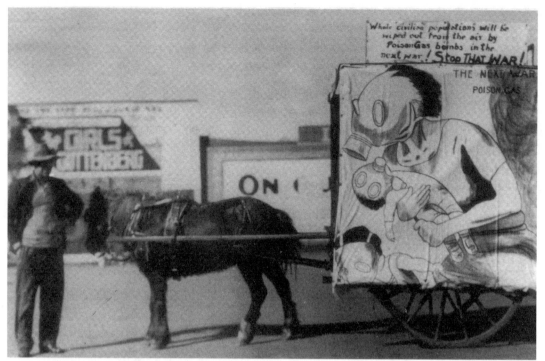

ALF BATTLE
BROKEN HILL, 1935

Anti-fascist and unionist Alf Battle was famous in Broken Hill during the 1930s for reproducing the works of cartoonists such as George Finely and Jack Maughan on striking canvases. Using a horse and cart he would grab the attention of both fellow marchers and passers-by. Broken Hill, 1935.

Photographer unknown.

DAY OF MOURNING
SYDNEY, 1938

While most of NSW was celebrating the 150th anniversary of the invasion of Australia, a group of Indigenous Australians decided to spoil the jingoistic party by reminding the population at large of what the true cost of British colonisation had been. On January 26th 1938 a widely-publicised march and Aboriginal-only public meeting was held to mourn the legacy of invasion and demand equal rights. Henry Fergusson, Jack Patten, Pearl Gibbs, William Cooper and other Indigenous leaders braved the threat of arrest to hold the first-ever national Aboriginal civil rights gathering. It was a harbinger of times to come later in the century. Photographer unknown.

"You have almost exterminated our people, but there are enough of us remaining to expose the humbug of your claim, as white Australians, to be a civilised, kindly and humane nation. By your cruelty and callousness you stand condemned in the eyes of the civilised world."

William Ferguson and John Patten at the Aboriginal Day of Mourning, 1938.

MELBOURNE, 1933

Labor Party Attorney-General Frank Brennan is stoned in his car by protesters angry at the fact that his family are being housed in the luxurious Windsor hotel at taxpayers' expense whilst others have no shelter at all.

MELBOURNE, 1933

Following a government decision to hand out bags of food, rather than relief coupons, unemployed workers in Carlton declare the scheme black. Each week after collecting their food bags they proceed outside to hurl the rations back through the office windows.

MELBOURNE, 1933

Protesting against the hosting of opulent events during a time of widespread poverty, unemployed people in St Kilda steal the council's red carpet just before the opening of a ball by the Governor-General.

MELBOURNE, 1934

During Armistice Day commemorations members of the Victorian Committee Against War And Fascism lay their own wreath pledging "to do our utmost to prevent the imperialist war which now threatens." The wreath is quickly removed by the police who deem it "offensive."

MELBOURNE, 1935

The Shop Assistants' Anti-War Committee calls for a boycott of Myer department stores after the company proposes creating a Men's Infantry platoon made up of its shop staff.

TORRES STRAIT ISLANDS, 1936

30 Islanders working on Native Affairs Department pearl luggers are arrested after they go on strike demanding improved wages and "home rule".

PERTH, 1937

Local commies paint "THE GREAT RED DAWN IS BREAKING" on the Perth Central Railway Station in red letters over a metre high.

BRISBANE, 1937

A Communist Party member chains himself to a chair in the Trades and Labour Council to ensure he gets a say during the evening's meeting. Police are called in by the right-wing leadership to heave him out, chair and all.

PERTH, 1937

Following the Japanese Government's attacks on China and the "Rape of Nanking", the Communist Party of Australia attempts to institute a boycott of products from the military dictatorship. In Perth, activists regularly spend their Saturday mornings wandering through the city's largest stores, Boans, Foys and Bairds, pasting "Boycott Japanese Goods" on various imported items. When shop assistants attempt to remove the stickers they find that they leave the goods in an unsaleable state.

MELBOURNE, 1938

A massive demonstration of 20,000 shuts down the wharves at Port Melbourne after Italian fascists beat an Italian-Australian anti-fascist who was visiting their ship. Following the demonstration and numerous threats, the captain of the *Raimondo Montecuccoli* gathers his crew to flee Australia's shores.

THIRROUL, 1938

During a coal strike, miners slip into a train and proceed to shovel around 60 tons of scab coal onto the surrounding tracks. The next day *The Bulli Times* carries a story claiming that high winds had carried the coal away into the night. Being somewhat wiser to the truth, the mine's owners elect not to remove any more coal from the area until the dispute is settled.

MELBOURNE, 1938

Weeks after the Kristallnacht pogrom devastates Jewish communities across Germany, William Cooper, the 77 year-old co-founder of the Australian Aborigines' League, a man who has no citizens' rights in his own country, leads a protest march from his home in Footscray to the German Consulate. Rallying at Collins Street in the city, the group, members of whom had recently protested during Australia's sesquicentennial celebrations, carry out what is later described by the Yad Vesham Holocaust Museum as "the only private protest against the Germans following Kristallnacht." Despite collecting around 2,000 signatures the delegation fails in its attempt to present a petition to the ambassador. Nevertheless it goes on to decry, "the cruel persecution of the Jewish people by the Nazi Government of Germany" asking, "that the persecution be brought to an end".

WOLLONGONG, 1939

Wharfies at Port Kembla refuse to load pig iron on ships bound for Japan, declaring, "success for the Japanese militarists in China will ... inspire them to further attacks on peaceful people including Australia." Despite it being obvious that the exports will come back to Australia and other Pacific nations in the form of bombs, the pro-Fascist Lyons government attempts to break the boycott, with the result that the wharfies down tools. The strike lasts for two months, during which the Attorney-General and Minister for Industry Robert Menzies (who had made an official visit to Germany the previous year expressing his admiration for the Nazi regime) is thanked by the Japanese Government for his support. In contrast Fred Wong, the president of the Chinese Youth League, makes regular trips from Sydney to deliver fruit and vegetables collected from market farms to help the strikers and their families.

During the tussle Menzies pays a visit to Wollongong, where he is given a reception he will never forget. Thousands strike across the city and all ten South Coast coal mines are shut down. Placards along the Princes Highway greet the politician, who is faced with a massive demonstration upon his arrival. The crowd jostles and abuses him with cries of "Japanese Agent", "Fascist", and "Pig Iron Bob". Children also join in the fun, poking Menzies and his entourage with placards as they enter the Town Hall.

NEWCASTLE, 1939

William Laidlaw is arrested and later does jail time for addressing a crowd with the following comments about the local police force, "They are so low, they could crawl under the belly of a snake with an umbrella up and still have a bit to spare. Norman Brown did not die in vain. He was shot down by parasites—tools of the capitalistic class." Three friends of Laidlaw's also receive jail time for leading a chorus of abuse against the police upon their pal's arrest.

SYDNEY, 1939

Bea Miles, eccentric at large, becomes well known to all taxi drivers, tram conductors and other transport workers due to her ardent belief in the provision of free transport for all. Putting her views into practice sees her banned from a number of taxi companies and leads to numerous court cases. Her favourite methods of gaining a free ride include jumping onto the front of trams and the back of cars as well as leaping into taxis (whether others are already inside or not) and refusing to leave until given a free trip. In the many cases where drivers become abusive she takes revenge by jumping out of the taxi to pull the doors back until the hinges snap.

NSW, 1939

Sick of the hazardous and sub-standard conditions they are forced to live and work in, and incensed at the arrest of activist Jack Patten, up to 200 Indigenous people walk off the Cummeragunja Mission. Breaking the NSW laws governing their lives they cross the Murray River to live in a protest camp in South Australia.

AUSTRALIA, 1939

Union members and others hold massive outdoor meetings across Australia to protest PM Robert Menzies' attempts to set up a national draft register for the coming war. Young men burn their draft cards whilst others fill out forms in the name of Menzies, Franco, Hitler, Stalin, Chamberlain, Blind Freddie and other notable figures.

NEWCASTLE, 1939

After Communist Party public meetings are disrupted by right-wing stone throwers, the organisers move them to the front of department stores with large plate glass windows. The assaults soon cease.

PERTH, 1939

When PM Menzies comes to address a public meeting at a Returned Services League (RSL) hall, local troublemakers arrive early and take seats near the front. As "Pig Iron Bob" makes his grand appearance two of them jump up, pulling out placards and denouncing his right-wing policies. Police drag them outside, but are forced to repeat the spectacle over and over as others leap up at opportune moments.

Following the removal of the last of these male hecklers, Menzies barely draws breath before being interrupted by well-known Perth actress Phil Harnett. When she ignores his patronising request that as a "member of the fairer sex," she quietly sit down, he destroys his reputation for witticism by screaming, "Throw that bitch out!" Since the talk is being broadcast live on radio his difficulties are heard by millions across the nation.

MOORE RIVER, 1940s

Aboriginal people imprisoned at the Moore River Settlement sing the following parody of a hymn in complaint at their treatment:

> There is a happy land, far far away,
> Where we get bread and scrape three times a day,
> Bread and butter we never see, no sugar in our tea,
> While we gradually starve away.

MELBOURNE, 1940s

One former student recalls:

> Six years after I had left school and was married, I went back one day in school uniform, attended some classes where certain teachers were not really aware of their students, and also joined the queue at the staff room door for fun. It was good to see what went on in the classes, etc, with my "adult" eyes and to remember what it was like to be treated as a child.

NEWCASTLE, 1941

Charlie Skene, a union militant and wounded ex-serviceman, is beaten up by racist thugs after intervening in their assault on a Koori man to lecture the abusers on the "dignity of man". When he reports the matter to the local police they fail to take action, instead asking him, "What sort of a man are you, going against your own race?"

TOWNSVILLE, 1943

When Chinese merchant seamen serving with the Allies in the Pacific aboard the SS *Empire Hamble* strike over pay and conditions the US military charges them with mutiny, locking them up in the Townsville jail. In a show of solidarity the Australian Seamen's Union steps in, threatening to take industrial action, with the result that the *Empire Hamble*'s captain, wartime restrictions not withstanding, withdraws the charges, allowing the men to sign on with another ship.

MELBOURNE, 1943

Female munitions workers vote to strike if they are not granted immediate wage parity with men.

PERTH, 1943

Angry at being forced to walk home in the dark and risk the dangers posed by the presence of large numbers of off-duty US and Australian troops, female munitions workers shut down rail services by occupying the train tracks. The action receives much publicity and soon results in safer public transport.

SYDNEY, 1943

Despite pressure from media outlets, their employer, the government, and their union, women at the Daly and Hanford Munitions plant successfully strike for 10 weeks against the employment of non-unionists who had recently scabbed during industrial disputes.

SYDNEY, 1944

Striking newspaper workers produce their own broadsheet selling over 100,000 copies.

AUSTRALIA, 1945

Opposing attempts by the Netherlands to crush the Indonesian independence movement, Australian dockworkers refuse to load Dutch cargo delaying 559 vessels.

Members of the New Housewives Association wear protest aprons during a march on Parliament to circumvent a ban on carrying political placards. Melbourne, 1949. Courtesy of Union of Australian Women.

1946–1959

The immediate post-war years were ones of much contestation, and some victories for the Left. With the population refusing to return to the penury of the 1930s, militant strikes saw major improvements in the workplace as wages increased and the 40 hour week was secured. Similarly, activism at the community and political level impelled the Chifley ALP government to legislate reforms in housing, education and healthcare. Having expanded its powers during wartime, the Federal Parliament also expanded the public service, sponsored manufacturing and increased funding for research and public works.

Less popularly, the government also began to alter Australia's ethnic mix. Desperate to boost population, and unable to source enough people from the UK, immigration was opened to non-British Europeans. Initially giving preference to Germans and Dutch, and fudging the degree to which people would be coming from Greece, Italy and the Baltic states, the ALP presided over an increase in immigration from 32,000 in 1947 to 167,000 in 1949. Newcomers faced discrimination and racism, but their arrival greatly changed Australian society and fed into the nation's slow turn from Britain.

In the meantime the ALP government remained committed to the "Mother Country" and its decision to continue petrol and food rationing in order to support Britain's reconstruction, lost it much support. By 1949 the Chifley government found itself increasingly wedged between the demands of restive sections of the working class and resistance from the wealthy to financial reform. With the Cold War dawning, the ALP smacked down a Communist-led coal strike before a new conservative party, formed in 1944 and named The Liberals in a concession to the progressive tenor of the times, took power.

Led by a resurrected PM Menzies conservative forces launched an anti-communist crusade. In the midst of Australian military involvement in the Korean War, and the signing of the ANZUS defence pact with the US and NZ, this served to drive fear into the populace and divide the labour movement. Backed by the Catholic Church, anti-communist 'Industrial Groups' augmented these attacks by fighting Communists and other leftists for the control of union bureaucracies. Following Menzies' 1951 attempt to outlaw the CPA the ALP split; its right-wing Catholic faction going on to form the Democratic Labor Party (DLP). The ban on the CPA was narrowly defeated in a referendum, but outside of radical elements in the union movement conservatism prevailed.

During its 23-year reign the Liberal government vastly expanded the powers of the Australia Security Intelligence Organisation (ASIO) to spy on and interfere with the activities of leftists, and also used the military and courts against Maritime and other militant unions. It was careful, however, to balance this pressure with concessions to the population as a whole. It retained a number of the reforms won in the 1940s and, enjoying the post-war "long boom", Anglo-Australians experienced higher living standards than ever before, buying up white goods and homes in the expanding suburbs.

Post-war prosperity and Australian citizenship, established in 1949, did not extend to the nation's first peoples. A growing trend in government policy towards "assimilation" did nothing to reduce marginalisation, but continued the practices of child removal and state control whilst intensifying pressures on communities to abandon their languages and culture. In the most callous instance of ongoing subjugation some of the few Central Australian Indigenous people still living a nomadic lifestyle were displaced and injured by Australian-British nuclear and conventional weapons testing.

Indigenous Australians had joined the strike wave of the late 1940s with actions in WA and NT and campaigning, often with the support of progressive religious groups and the CPA, continued during the 1950s. New organisations, such as the Federal Council for Aboriginal Advancement (FCAA), were created. Using film documentaries and reports these highlighted the plight of their people. For the most part activism was restricted to the circulation of petitions and lobbying, although occasional strikes took place and a major revolt on Palm Island erupted in 1957.

Following the war's end women had been forced out of many jobs and back into the domestic sphere. With the rise of suburban lifestyles separate gender roles further solidified during the 1950s. New groups, such as the Union of Australian Women, campaigned for peace and childcare, but, outside of equal pay campaigns, tended to confine their activism to traditionally maternal areas. Gay, Lesbian, Bisexual, Transgender and Intersex (GLBTI) people continued to remain morally and legally suppressed, only able to openly express their desires in the cafes, nightclubs and other spaces they created.

As part of the trend towards rising living standards, consumerism and Americanisation came the rise of the adolescent. The emergence of the rock'n'roll teenage lifestyle challenged the moral and workaday expectations of parents and, in putting pleasure before duty, helped create the conditions for the youth revolts of the 1960s. In the meantime small Bohemian groupings such as Sydney's Anarchist Push continued to explore personal and radical politics beyond the increasingly staid conventionality of the CPA.

"The land was taken away from Aboriginal people by force, by the power of the gun. Now it is being taken away from us by the power of the law... We have had to change in meeting the whites and it is time they changed for us."

Francis Yunkaporta, 1948.

PILBARA, 1946

After four years of meetings involving strike leaders travelling from station to station, around 600 Aboriginal stock workers from 26 different language groups walk off stations in the Far North of Western Australia demanding a living wage. The strike, which comes to be known as the Black Eureka, sees police called in to arrest leading activists Clancy McKenna and Dooley Bin Bin along with Anglo-Australian communist Don McLeod, whom the strikers had appointed their adviser back in 1942. McLeod is soon freed after up to 400 strikers march on the Port Hedland jail armed with hammers and crowbars. McKenna and Bin Bin are later released before the expiration of their sentences as part of a series of concessions, including increased wage offers and improved rations, extracted by the continuing strength of the strike.

With the strikers continuing to hold out, their opponents soon return to playing hardball, with the police cutting off the supply of rations before arresting McLeod and strike supporter Reverend Hugh Hodge for being near an Aboriginal camp without the permission of a Native Protector. The two eventually beat the charges through an appeal to the High Court, and the attempt to starve out the strikers fails, with up to 200 people living in each strike camp by November.

While most strikers survive through gathering bush tucker, they are also able to generate some income by selling buffel seed and pearl shells through networks of unionists, churches and others who come together to support the walk-off economically and politically. At one point McLeod is also able to get some strikers work on the Port Hedland docks. When the police use their powers, under the Aboriginal Act, to order them out of the area, their fellow wharfies decide to stop work until they return. The introduction of white scab labour sees seamen walk off the job as well, until the Australian Workers Union (AWU) leadership ends the strike within a strike by removing the right of Aboriginal people to join the union and thereby work on the wharves.

With the strike continuing on into 1948, animal production in the Pilbara grinds to a complete halt after the last remaining stockmen walk off the job following the arrest of 30 strikers. In 1949, further arrests see the Seamen's Union place bans on wool from the few stations still operating. By this point the station owners begin to capitulate as, in the face of Aboriginal intransigence, the Department of Native Affairs withdraws its opposition to the strike, providing a lawyer for those arrested and assisting in their eventual acquittal. Although many win increased wages, in some cases the first wages they have ever received, others refuse to return to work at all, engaging in mineral exploration and forming the Pindan Cooperative Mining Company before acquiring their own pastoral leases decades later.

DARWIN, 1946

Communist and key organiser for the North Australian Workers Union in the 1940s and early 1950s, Murray Norris recalls the Great Beer Strike of 1946:[8]

> During the war we had been given a ration of two bottles of beer a week (not all the time), and in 1946 [shopkeeper] Cashmans got a load of beer on one of the first boats to bring civilian goods up. He wanted to charge three shillings and sixpence [about $8-10 by modern standards] a bottle, hot, and you took it away to drink. A broad strike committee was set up and a black ban was placed on all beer unless it was sold at the pre-war price of two shillings a bottle. Pickets were set up under their captains and it lasted six weeks before Cashman gave in. Imagine that in a place like the NT where the blokes hadn't had a drink-up for years!
>
> Some of the moves to break the strike deserved to be on films. After about a month of the strike, Cashman or some of his employees tried a sure fire method, so they thought. Hornibrooks' old camp had been taken over by the union to house about a hundred single men, and every day some of these men used to walk up past the union office and through the long grass to the mess in Cavanagh St for their meals. Two of the thirstiest men in Darwin were old Jack Lloyd and Tommy Heath. Their skins were fairly cracking but they were also two of the very staunchest unionists in the NT.
>
> This particular day as old Jack and Tommy were going up for their meal they discovered, strategically placed along the path that they had to follow, bottles of plonk, gin, beer etc. Their eyes

bulged out of their heads. They carefully gathered it together and sat down to decide what to do with it. One said, "We will take it and hide it until the strike is over"; the other said, "We wouldn't you know, we would sneak away and drink it and that would be the start of the end of the strike." They looked at it a bit longer, then old Jack said with great sorrow in his voice "The spirit would be willing but the flesh would be weak," and he started smashing the bottles. Tommy joined in and when they had finished, with their backs a little straighter, they went up and reported to the Strike Committee. From that day onwards the committee knew that they would win, and they did.

NSW, 1946

A campaign against the continuation of wartime wage controls closes 14 mines and shuts ports for 7 days. Whilst continuing to shackle wages the ALP government does little to fight price rises leading to a number of protests, including one in Sydney which blocks traffic in Macquarie Street.

BRISBANE, 1946

Wharfies, who have been stood down from work due to a lock-out by employers, force their way on to the docks to ensure that fresh fruit is unloaded for the people of Brisbane.

MELBOURNE, 1947

Hundreds gathering at Malvern, Kew and Collingwood shopping centres demonstrate against rising food prices. A mock funeral is held with the coffin reading, "How John Brown solved the cost of living," and banners are hoisted stating, "Graziers can't milk me, don't let them milk you," and, "I'll finish up in the soup and so will you if meat prices aren't fixed."

BRISBANE, 1948

During a massive railway dispute the State government orders the arrest of union leader E.J. Rowe for his role in supporting the strike. Despite raids on homes in three states the wily Rowe cannot be found having "disappeared into smoke". Upon the resolution of the strike he makes a dramatic reappearance at the Trades Hall, revealing he had criss-crossed the state and NSW in the previous days assisting in the organisation of the strike before submitting to voluntary arrest.

While imprisoned for his role in supporting the railworkers, Waterside Workers Federation official Ted Engelhart subverts a rule requiring prisoners to salute their warders every morning by always making sure he has his 'piss' tin in his hand when doing so.

SYDNEY, 1948

Posters for the anti-Communist film *The Iron Curtain* are plastered with stickers reading "Approved by the Armament Kings" and "Authorised by Adolf Hitler."

DARWIN, 1948

During a six-week hospital strike, Aboriginal domestic workers show solidarity by refusing to clean the houses of white women volunteering as scab labour.

MELBOURNE, 1948

A student at Scotch College gets his revenge on a teacher who delights in grabbing students by the hair by filling his dark, curly thatch with printers' ink.

SYDNEY, 1948

Central city traffic is held up for two hours by a demonstration of thousands calling for rent control.

CESSNOCK, 1949

During their 7-week national strike 23,000 members of the CPA-led Miners' Federation stop work in support of a 35-hour week, improved safety and long service leave, leading to severe gas and electricity restrictions. In an attempt to look tougher than his anti-communist rival Robert Menzies, ALP leader Ben Chifley backs legislation which makes it illegal to provide financial support (including credit in shops) to the strikers. His government then goes on to raid union and Communist offices and jail union officials before eventually sending soldiers in to work the mines. Although the latter action, which marks the first use of troops in a peacetime industrial dispute, forces the strikers back to work, the ALP loses the 1949 election ushering in 23 years of (more) conservative rule under the Liberal Party.

Battling opposition from union leaders, and

some of their husbands, coalminers' wives across NSW had set up Women's Auxiliaries from 1938 to allow them to take part in industrial struggles and organise campaigns around the issues affecting them and their families. Unsurprisingly during the strike these groups now lead the fight within coal communities, as recalled by Grace Scanlon in the pages of feminist newspaper *Mabel*:

> We picketed the shops, some of them sold goods to the police. I can still feel his hand on my shoulder when the police came to break it up... they were basher gangs of police, sent to control... just thugs in uniform... I was terrified... we dispersed them. I smile today [1970s] when I see the young women demonstrating and standing up to the police. We pioneered that I think... They called us brazen hussies... it was unheard of...
>
> A Liberal woman came to Newcastle once... Mrs Stanley Vaughn, to downgrade the miners' strike and how terrible the miners were holding everything up... We decided to go to a public meeting she was holding in Newcastle and take a stand. We went into the hall and let her go for a while... We began to call and interject, then we got up and walked out... half the meeting came with us. We went to a park nearby and set up our own meeting... nothing organised. Before we knew it, we were surrounded by the police, but the women just kept on getting up and speaking. We had a good meeting and then lined up and marched through the town to Trades Hall. She was a Liberal woman and a good speaker, but we wrecked her meeting."

SYDNEY, 1949

In response to failed attempts to seize Communist Party files and materials, activist Stan Moran publicly declares that, "The police couldn't find an elephant in the snow even if it wore gumboots."

PERTH, 1949

The Perth branch of the Communist Party of Australia defies thugs who have been breaking up their meetings by mooring a boat 50 metres off shore from the Esplanade from which Paddy Troy addresses the gathering crowd. When five right-wingers commandeer a row-boat and come within cooee of the Communists, the militant unionist and two compatriots start up an outboard motor and roar off down the river, thumbing their nose all the way.

Anti-conscRIPtion graffiti on train crossing by a member of the Communist Party of Australia. The CPA, following the German invasion of Eastern Europe, had supported military conscription during World War Two. With the advent of the Cold War it resumed its long held oppositional stance.

Photographer unknown, *Tribune*, 1951.

MELBOURNE, 1949

A delegation of four women from the New Housewives' Association are denied entrance to Parliament House to deliver a protest resolution concerning rising prices. Standing their ground in pouring rain 50 members of the group call out to passers-by that, "women want homes, peace and lower prices – not bombs."

SYDNEY, LATE 1940s

Veteran Communist Hal Alexander recalls his part in assisting his namesake in establishing the closed shop for actors:[9]

Hal Alexander [no relative- Alexander was his stage name] was the Secretary of Actors Equity. The union was having trouble in unionising the industry. Hal made us an offer we could not refuse. The union would get us some freebies to the gallery of the Theatre Royale where Gladys Moncrieff was starring in the musical Maid Of The Mountains.

Our task was to interject at appropriate moments. A hasty "rehearsal" gave us the idea. "Our Glad" would trill something like, "Oh what shall we do?" (say), to which the claque would reply, "Join the union." Or if the junior lead sang, "Who is this who comes?" (say), we'd reply, "The union organiser." And so on. Until they called the coppers.

It must have been a hard night for the performers, but we thought it was a buzz.

The union grew into a strong force in the theatrical world and an important banner for Oz culture. Yes. They did join and Glad became an active Equity member.

NEWCASTLE, LATE 1940s

CPA member Jack Williams Jr, a sign writer by trade, keeps himself busy throughout the decade by painting immaculate slogans on billboards and walls calling for the nationalisation of BHP and revolt against the rich. He is eventually caught in 1949 and bashed by police, who also pour a tin of paint over his head for refusing to name his accomplices.

DARWIN, 1950

Despite not having citizens' rights 200 Indigenous workers strike demanding basic pay rather than rations.

VICTORIA, 1950s

Concerned about the arrival of former Nazis fleeing Europe, left-wing Jewish Council member Sam Goldbloom goes undercover as a plumber's mate at the Bonegilla migrant camp near Wodonga. With the help of unionists and the use of a camera hidden inside a bag he takes photos of men bearing SS tattoos, embarrassing the Federal Government and forcing a crackdown on the migration of fascists.

PERTH, 1951

Workers at Garden Island Naval Base report that people have been wandering in and graffiting warships with hammer and sickles and Communist slogans.

DARWIN, 1951

Indigenous performers refuse to dance for American tourists until two men recently jailed for striking are freed.

VICTORIA, 1951

Indigenous leader Mary Clarke speaks out against the eviction of a woman and her children from the Framlingham Mission for not paying rent telling the *Argus* that, "The white people never thought of paying us rent for the whole country they took from our ancestors. Leave us this tiny corner where our homes are. Why should we pay rent for it all? We regard that little bit of land as ours still."

SYDNEY & MELBOURNE, 1951

The Seamen's Union of Australia avoids a government crackdown on support for striking New Zealand wharfies by smuggling funds across the Tasman in the motor vessel *Wanganella*.

During the same dispute graffitists respond to criticisms levelled at the strikers by A.E. Monk, the head of the Australian Council of Trade Unions (ACTU), by painting "Monk Scabs on NZ Workers" in huge letters on the footpath outside his Essendon home.

VICTORIA, 1952

Around 1,000 Dutch, Italian and German migrants housed at the "barren and boring" Bonegilla Reception Centre for months stage a protest over the substandard conditions and tin sheds they are forced to live in whilst awaiting work. Demonstrating outside the administration block, and threatening to march on Canberra, they demand the camp director provide them with employment or "compensate them for breaches of their Migration agreement." During angry exchanges threats are made to burn buildings and an interpreter is held hostage. 200 soldiers and 5 armoured cars are brought in to parade outside the camp in an effort to quell the protests, which the media misleadingly brand a "riot".

When the Italian Consul and Vice-consul arrive the next day their car is rocked and almost overturned by demonstrators fed up with the consulate's inaction. The residents' anger is only placated after Immigration minister, and future PM, Harold Holt agrees to create temporary jobs with a guaranteed two months employment. Even then, wary of a double-cross, the protesters only agree to demobilise if the Vice-consul remains in the camp until all are working.

MELBOURNE, 1952

Unrepentant drag queen Max du Barrie, who has recently been charged with "having committed unnatural offences with a male ballet dancer", embarrasses authorities by attending the National Theatre's Arts Ball and selling kisses for charity. The dancer in question, Noel Tovey, recalls in his memoirs that, "The Governor of Victoria, not knowing Max was a man, bought a kiss and posed for photographs with him. This led to a witch hunt for Max." du Barrie later appears in court in full drag where, in trying to establish his credentials as a female impersonator, he sings to the jury. Later sentencing him to a year in prison Judge Mitchell states, "I cannot close my eyes to the fact that this is a strongly antisocial form of crime, the viciousness of which cannot be disseminated and communicated to the young." In response du Barrie, who later makes the list of the city's most sensational figures in *Truth's* Follies of 1952, blows a kiss to his mother before being hauled away.

NEWCASTLE, 1954

Women who are paid five pounds less a week for the same work as men at a ball-bearing factory introduce an overtime ban in which they stop work for 15 minutes a shift to ensure their work rate reflects their pay rate.

SYDNEY, 1954

When two members of the Waterside Workers Federation are called before the Petrov Commission into Soviet Espionage, 5,000 of their fellow unionists decide to join them for the day. Pickets are thrown up outside the courts and proceedings are interrupted by human caricatures of PM Menzies, the Petrovs and judges.

MELBOURNE, 1956

Comedian Barry Humphries plays his infamous Ashburton Line prank. Boarding a first class, non-smoking carriage one morning he has an accomplice come on board at the next stop and silently pass him a grapefruit. At the following stop he is given some cornflakes and thereafter bacon and eggs, toast and coffee. Whilst the entire carriage is transfixed no-one has the guts to ask what is going on.

SYDNEY, 1956

Barry Humphries causes chaos at a clothing sale by slipping pieces of ham into the bargain boxes.

HOBART, 1956

The Hursey brothers kick off a major wharf dispute when they attempt, on behalf of right-wing Catholic interests, to break the WWF's closed shop by quitting the union and continuing to work on the wharves. Brought in by police to work, the brothers are prevented from entering the docks by union pickets. When the brothers, dressed in the traditional green, abuse and harangue picketers on St

RESISTANCE TO ANTI-COMMUNIST CAMPAIGNS, 1949-51

The election of the Menzies government in 1949 saw a Cold War crackdown on the CPA and the Left in general. After an attempt to ban the CPA in 1951 was ruled constitutionally invalid by the High Court, the government held a referendum requesting the public grant them the power to overcome such legal obstacles. The campaign which followed brought together a coalition of civil libertarians, unionists and ALP members to oppose the amendment. Although it was narrowly defeated on September 22 1951 repression of radical voices and movements via media demonization, state infiltration and other means continued.

Left to right, top to bottom: Cartoon, Tribune, 1949, Artist unknown • May Day float, Sydney, 1950, Photographer unknown. • Cartoon, Tribune, 1951, Artist unknown. • CPA pamphlet, 1951. • Bank cheque parody, 1951, Artist unknown.

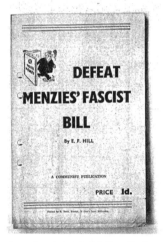

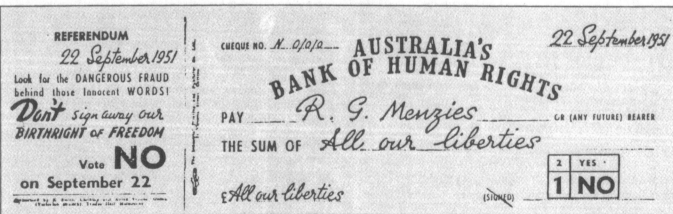

Patrick's Day, incensed Irish wharfies respond by sweeping the brothels and police escorts out of the port and into the water.

QUEENSLAND, 1956

Despite the use of scabs and the declaration of a State of Emergency by ALP Premier Vince Gair striking shearers hold out for ten months against attempts to reduce their wages.

SYDNEY, 1956

Reacting to the Communist Party of Australia's official line that Khrushchev's first speech attacking Stalin is a forgery, CPA member Jim Staples decides to take action. Having noticed that his neighbours, the conservative Clerks Union, have left their duplicator out on a landing, he persuades a friend to type up the speech before running off thousands of copies outside of office hours and without the owners' consent. Completing this task Staples then rushes down to the CPA printers just before that week's *Tribune* is about to be mailed out. Having stuck the speech in as a supplement, thereby reaching 5,000 supporters and members, he ensures that the party ranks learn the truth and is predictably expelled for his efforts.

MELBOURNE, 1956

As part of a strike to maintain wages and conditions Melbourne dockworkers hold up to 50 street and factory meetings a day and distribute over 170,000 leaflets in 14 languages. After the daily newspaper the *Herald* runs a front-page editorial slamming the port strike 1,000 take their message directly to its anti-union editors. Marching to the newspaper's headquarters, the strikers and their families force their way into the machine rooms shouting, "We'll go to the workers first!" After explaining their position to the compositors a number head upstairs to occupy the reporter's workspace. Faced with the possibility that he may not be able to get out the next day's edition editor Jack Williams eventually agrees to run an article giving the wharfies' side of the story.

PALM ISLAND, 1957

After years of suffering under the rule of Superintendent Roy Bartlam, Aboriginal people at Palm Island, originally set up as a penal colony for Indigenous Queenslanders, go on strike for five days. Having tired of rules requiring them to salute all passing whites, to work without pay, to queue for rations and to allow their homes to be inspected at any time, the majority of the island's residents begin organising the first ever strike on a Queensland reserve after Bartlam forces men to build a jail for themselves over the Easter break before going on to demolish a number of Murri homes and boats. When the Superintendent moves to deport Albie Geia for "answering back" to a white supervisor a protest is held and, following scuffles with police and attempts to have a further eight men arrested, the island is shut down by a general strike. One small group of strikers composes a letter, never answered, to the Director of Native Affairs demanding increased wages, decent food and for the Superintendent to be removed, while a group of women up the ante by throwing sand and unsavoury rations of meat at Bartlam's office. Having laid siege to the building the women go on to occupy the main streets, which they are normally banned from using under the island's apartheid laws.

Following these acts of defiance, the Superintendent brings 20 police reinforcements to the Island. Despite the immediate deportation of strike leader Fred Doolan, the island's Indigenous residents remain united, with only 7 out of 1,400 signing a petition disassociating themselves from the strike. When supplies arrive on the third day of the strike, along with more police, a number of strikers reverse the usual order of things by smashing bottles of alcohol and distributing meat to the community while denying it to white staff.

On the fifth day of action, Bartlam and the police move in at 4am, smashing down the doors of a number of homes and placing strikers in handcuffs before deporting them and their families at gunpoint to the mainland (from which, ironically, many of their parents had previously been exiled).

Over the following days protests involving the clanging of pots and pans are held, but with machine guns trained upon the deportation point there is little that residents can do to prevent the removal of 47 of their fellow Islanders. Despite the breaking of the strike and the further deportation of another 50 Palm Islanders, the strike nevertheless forces the Queensland Government to raise wages, build better homes and allow Islanders into previously forbidden areas.

PERTH, 1958

An attempt by six members of the Union of Australian Women (UAW) to get around anti-protest laws by wearing aprons and scarves bearing slogans in opposition to nuclear testing fails when they are arrested for "parading with placards". After an appeal to the Supreme Court the charges are later quashed.

MELBOURNE, 1959

After the *Herald* runs a story falsely claiming that the Victorian Secretary of Seamen's Union, Bill Bird, is standing down from his position due to internal faction fights in the Communist Party, when he is actually quitting due to poor health, 100 maritime workers take action. Appalled at the newspaper's red-baiting the deputation, bearing placards reading "Tomorrow's 'Lies' Today" occupy its offices. Although editor Jack Williams refuses to run a piece admitting his writers had made up the allegations, he does run short statements from the CPA and Seamen's Union a few days later.

SYDNEY, 1950s AND 1960s

During elections members of the Sydney libertarian milieu The Push put up posters encouraging people to vote informal. Many are adorned with the slogan, "Whoever you vote for, a politician always gets in," and, "Give the man a vote, but tie his hands in every way." During a 1961 referendum people are encouraged to lodge their vote as:

YES—we have

NO—bananas today.

1960–1969

OPPOSITE: Demonstrators at Central Station farewell conscripts, Sydney, 1966.

A lthough the early '60s saw a continuation of the suburbanisation and conservatism of the Menzies' era, a series of societal shifts would cause a significantly different Australia to emerge by the beginning of the next decade. Demographic changes, with three million post-war baby boomers reaching adulthood between 1962 and 1971, drove many of these changes. Many of the new generation were far from radical, but, enjoying the highest educational and living standards on record, they were more predisposed to challenge the opinions and morals of their elders and the government. Operating in times of rising expectation and personal freedoms, progressives, young and old, ramped up workplace and community action opening up new fields for activism.

Australian military involvement in Vietnam, and the movement that grew in opposition to it, sparked and fed into much of the new radicalism. In 1962 the Menzies government sent 30 military advisers to South Vietnam, with the first Australian casualty occurring in 1964. Compulsory military service was reintroduced that same year, with conscripts chosen via a lottery based on birth-dates. Lobbying the US to get more heavily in the conflict, and by extension Asia generally, the Liberal government sent troops to Vietnam in 1965.

Conscription and the Vietnam War were opposed by the Calwell-led ALP opposition, and sections of the union movement, from the beginning. Grassroots campaigning began with lobbying, union bans and protests as well as conscientious objection, which saw would-be conscriptees submit to prison rather than serve in the military. Following the Liberals' 1966 election victory, and the intensification of the war, opposition took a more strident tone. Whilst the Federal ALP leadership flip-flopped over the extent to which it would pledge to remove troops, a mass movement seeking complete withdrawal emerged. Using theatrical and militant tactics, radical elements began to outrightly flout the law by disrupting courts, engaging in occupations, and going 'underground' to avoid conscription.

As anti-war feeling became more popular, an overall revival and transformation of left-wing politics took place. The burgeoning youth culture created vibrant arts and musical scenes, giving rise to a counterculture that increasingly fused with oppositional politics. New Trotskyist, Maoist and Anarchist groups, many based in the emerging radical student subculture, also appeared feeding into the broader, more creative, and largely non-party based politics of the New Left. The CPA, which had already lost its pro-Chinese wing in 1964, moved with the times, criticising the Soviet invasion of Czechoslovakia in 1968 and adopting a more independent, less vanguardist line to the point where a pro-Moscow faction left in 1971.

The progressive drift of the population also fed into the gradual dismantling of the White Australia Policy. This began with a new generation of bureaucrats introducing incremental changes in immigration policy. With British trade, diplomatic and military ties fading in favour of the Asia-Pacific, and up to 12,000 students from the region already studying in Australia, vociferous opposition from old guard politicians was overcome. In 1965 the ALP removed the White Australia Policy from its party platform and the following year, with PM Holt taking over from Menzies, the Liberal government removed restrictions on non-European immigration. Since migrants continued to suffer disadvantage, and pressures to 'assimilate' to the dominant Anglo-Australian culture, activism against discrimination also increased.

Whilst far from complete, this shift away from racism also opened opportunities for Indigenous people. New activists emerged and actions, such as the Lake Tyers protests, Yirrkala Bark Petition and the Freedom Rides raised consciousness about dispossession, discrimination and segregation amongst non-Indigenous Australians. Granted the Federal vote in 1962, and gaining it in all other states by 1965, a long campaign culminated in 90.8% of Australians voting in the 1967 referendum to remove two negative references to Indigenous people from the constitution. These changes saw Indigenous people included in the census and allowed the Commonwealth government to legislate laws concerning them. Although this did not automatically confer civil and legal rights the referendum was seen as a mandate for reform. In the context of these changes the struggle for equality, as well as land rights, took off with a wave of protests, court actions and walk offs.

Society also began to change in terms of gender roles. The widening availability of contraception and gradual abortion reform gave women more control over their bodies. Increasingly involved in wage-work they won limited recognition for equal-pay in 1969 and calls for childcare, maternity leave, and provisions forbidding sexual harassment were raised as key demands. Dissatisfaction with male inaction, chauvinism and hetero-sexism within unions, the Left and society as a whole saw a new feminist movement emerge that, along with a push for GLBTI rights, would explode in the early 1970s.

Workplace militancy also climbed over the period. The early 1960s saw the unionisation of non-manual workers in education, banking and the public services with many in these fields undertaking their first strikes and stop-works by the decade's end. The ability of anti-union penal powers to constrain industrial action was broken through mass action in 1969. With anti-union laws neutralised and class confidence on the rise workers unleashed a strike wave that saw twice as many working days lost through industrial disputes than in any year since 1956. Within unions, women and migrants also began to demand more of a say with the rank and file in general, exerting more influence than it had for decades.

"I am ready to go to jail because it is useless saying the same things over and over about a war I believe to be futile and immoral."

Author Patrick White on the war in Vietnam, 1969.

VICTORIA, 1961

Refugees and migrants at the Bonegilla Reception Centre riot for two days demanding they be sent to the jobs they were promised before they immigrated from Germany, Italy and Yugoslavia. On the first day they march within the centre carrying placards reading "Your barbarian system is only worthy of the Stone-Age" and "We want work" before damaging an employment building, jostling the centre's director, and fighting with police. Later in the evening stone throwers break street lights and canteen windows before being dispersed by a baton charge by police.

When police reinforcements are brought in the next day, the residents boo them and stone their cars. Later in the evening, in the context of an enforced curfew, police officers raid residences to prevent further protests from being planned. Following widespread media coverage, the government drops all charges against eleven arrestees before moving the unemployed to city hostels where they stand a better chance of finding work.

SYDNEY, 1961

150 students at the University of NSW protest the administration's leasing of their ballroom to the ABC show *Television Ballroom* by invading the dance floor during a live recording to play jazz and throw paper aeroplanes and pennies.

MELBOURNE, 1963

When the state government attempts to disperse the Indigenous community living at Lake Tyers by closing their settlement, around 40 people defy the reserve's management by travelling hundreds of kilometres to hold a rally in the city. With support from other activists and non-Indigenous people from around the country and overseas, the residents eventually gain control of their land in 1970.

NORTHERN TERRITORY, 1963

The Indigenous people of the Gove Peninsula grab international attention when they present the Federal government with a petition pasted on bark and partially written in their first language. Demanding that a proposed mining operation at Yirrkala be halted and ownership be ceded to the original owners of the land, they launch Australia's first land rights legal case five years later.

MELBOURNE, 1964

The pamphlet *American Atrocities In Vietnam* is seized from bookshops by the Victorian Vice Squad. In response the Peace Quest orders 500 more copies and writes to the Police Commissioner informing him of their plans to sell them at the CML Plaza on the corner of Collins and Elizabeth Streets. Copies sell out within three minutes, with the Vice Squad having little time to do anything other than take names and look flat-footed.

SYDNEY, 1964

Copies of the satirical magazine *Oz* are seized and burnt by authorities after the editors include a copy of Martin Sharp's illustrated board game "Coppers' Snakes & Ladders". The game includes such instructions as, "Beat the suspect unconscious and leave no bruises— LADDER," and, "Pick up another cop in a public lav—SNAKE."

SYDNEY, 1965

Students block Anzac Parade demanding concessions for travel on public transport.

NSW, 1965

Inspired by the US civil rights movement Indigenous activists and their supporters organise a "Freedom Ride" bus-tour of western and coastal NSW to highlight the inequalities and discrimination Aboriginal communities are suffering as well as support those locals struggling against them. Demonstrating outside and desegregating picture theatres, pools and veteran's clubs in Moree, Kempsey and other towns, the group encounters hostility from white locals, including being run off the road at Walgett. Media coverage and footage captured by the riders themselves exposes the rest of Australia to the regions' endemic racism and fuels the wider campaign for Indigenous people to receive full citizens' rights.

May Day rally, Sydney, 1962.
From *The Seamen's Union of Australia, 1872-1972*

SYDNEY, 1965

The Sydney branch of the Waterside Workers Federation holds up 37 ships in Sydney Harbour during a 24-hour strike over the Menzies government's decision to send troops to Vietnam.

SYDNEY, 1965

Four Aboriginal men desegregate the Prince of Wales hotel by refusing to leave until they are served alcohol. Although the publican initially rejects their request their sit-in action and the presence of the media eventually forces him to relent.

AUSTRALIA, 1966

During the 1966 elections three conscripts run for office on an anti-war platform, taking advantage of measures that require the Army to discharge them if they are able to prove that they are "bona-fide" candidates. Since all three fail to receive enough votes to get their $100 deposit back they are soon forced to re-enlist. One, Brian King, refuses to do so and is subsequently court martialled and sentenced to 60 days in jail.

SYDNEY, 1966

Thumbing their nose at the threat of conviction under the Commonwealth Crimes Act, as well as the ACTU's decision not to support anti-war industrial action, members of the Seamen's Union of Australia (SUA) hold a demonstration outside the Vietnam-bound *Boonaroo.* Holding aloft banners reading, "No Kids For Ky [South Vietnam's dictator]," "Y Die For Ky," and "Boonaroo seamen oppose war in Vietnam," the crew prevent the ship from leaving for three hours. In the following year the SUA places a complete ban on carrying ammunition and weapons to Vietnam and offers instead to work without pay to bring Australian troops home.

WOLLONGONG, 1966

A pub is picketed by wharfies after it refuses to extend credit to regulars who are out on strike. After a week of no trade the pub owners change their position.

NORTHERN TERRITORY, 1966

Following the decision by the Arbitration Court to delay the granting of equal wages to Aboriginal workers for a further two years, stockmen and their families at the Newcastle Waters and Wave Hill stations walk off the job to set up a strike camp on the banks of the Victoria River. After Lupgna Giari tours the Eastern seaboard rallying union support, and harassment from pastoralists fails to bring the strike to a close, the NT government backs down, offering an immediate wage increase of 125%. Although this improves conditions across the Territory, the Gurindji people at the heart of the dispute decide to extend their demands by moving their camp to Dagu Ragu (also known as Wattie Creek). With the help of Communist author Frank Hardy and other non-Indigenous supporters they then send a petition to the Governor-General demanding the return of 600-700 square miles of their ancestral land. Despite the Federal Government only offering them land at the desolate Drovers Common, the Gurindji continue their occupation, attracting increasing support from around the country, until the Federal ALP finally begins handing back their lands in 1972.

MELBOURNE, 1966

Walter Hoystead, a member of one of Australia's most famous horse-racing families and a former jockey himself, decides that the whipping of racehorses is an act of unnecessary cruelty. He launches a one-man crusade against the practice by walking onto the course at Flemington with a loaded shotgun. Races are delayed for sixteen minutes while officials attempt to move him on. Eventually the police succeed in doing so, but Hoystead is not to be deterred as he spends the next year driving a van around Melbourne decorated with placards listing the number of times horses were whipped on the previous weekend.

SYDNEY, 1966

Teenager and future playwright Louis Nowra, angry at Australia's increasingly servile relationship to the US, tears bullet holes in the Australian flag, smears it with tomato sauce to simulate blood and hangs it from his school flag pole.

MELBOURNE, 1967

Two brothers, David and Greg Langley, defy 750, 000 Victorians gathered to greet LBJ by splattering the US President's vehicle with green and red paint, the colours of the Vietnamese National Liberation Front.

MELBOURNE, 1967

When Monash University students discover that the administration plans to award conservative Liberal Premier Henry Bolte an honorary degree they decide to take action. Unable to prevent him from receiving the award, the students begin a "No Pedigree for the Pig" campaign culminating in a ceremony in which a piglet receives his own degree.

MELBOURNE, 1967

After he is banned from school for having long hair, Fabian Douglas and his father lobby to get him reinstated. During the campaign they unsuccessfully petition the Supreme Court and the UN, with the father stating that Fabian showed "definite temperamental changes for the worst and developed a stutter" whenever his hair was shorn and that his son "associates long hair with all the good things he knows".

MELBOURNE, 1968

After John Zarb is sentenced to two years for resisting conscription he receives a life-time membership from the Amalgamated Postal Workers Union in support of his stand. Taking a different tack, the State Secretary of the ALP, Bill Hartley, requests permission from the Post Master General to use a special postal franking stamp, stating, "We have attached thousands of yellow stickers to our correspondence, but thought it would be easier if our franking machine was adapted to carry the message 'Free John Zarb'."

MELBOURNE, 1968

Anti-war activists bring a July 4th speech by ALP Opposition Leader Gough Whitlam to the Australian-American Association to a chaotic close by shouting, "What about the slaughter of the Vietnamese people?" A

FREEDOM RIDE,
MOREE, 1965

Indigenous activist Charlie Perkins (on right) talking with local people about issues they faced in their community. Courtesy *Tribune*.
Photographer unknown.

scuffle develops and the next day's newspapers are full of pictures of an activist tangling with Carlton footballer John Gould. Later that night the same activist is arrested as part of a group who cut down the US flag at the American consulate.

MELBOURNE, 1968

A speech by Prime Minister Gorton at Caulfield Town Hall is disrupted by a sit-in by 30 members of the Draft Resisters Union as well as by heckling and 'Sieg Heiling'.

MELBOURNE, 1968

Members of the Draft Resistance Movement and Save Our Sons groups chain themselves across the driveway of the Swan Street Army Barracks in Richmond in an attempt to prevent the intake of new conscripts.

MELBOURNE, 1968

Inveterate student protester Albert Langer is arrested for inciting an attack on American diplomats by wearing and producing badges that read "Light Up An Embassy" and "reading, rioting, rithmetic". In the eventual court case he successfully proves that the "Light Up" badge is simply a parody of an advertisement for a popular cigarette brand of the time.

MELBOURNE, 1968

In response to a La Trobe University referendum over the right of the army to establish a unit on campus, the radical group Enrages encourages a Yes vote so that a Revolutionary Students Militia might be set up. The group states that, "This referendum involves more than a decision as to whether you support a University Regiment or a Guerilla Training Militia — it involves our basic freedom to kill."

MELBOURNE, 1968

When the Vice-Chancellor demands footprints that have been painted walking up a Melbourne University building "come down", graffiti artists add a second lot of footprints doing just that.

MOUNT ISA DISPUTE, 1964-65 QUEENSLAND

In August 1964 an industrial campaign, initially involving work-to-rule and go-slow tactics, by workers at Queensland's remote Mt Isa mine soon mushroomed into an eight month long dispute. During this time all manner of attacks were mounted upon the workers and their community including a lock out by the multinational American Smelting And Refining Company (ASARCO), the sacking of militants, vilification of strikers in the media, and attempts by the Australian Workers Union to overrule the rank and file. A widespread backlash following the Queensland government's declaration of a State of Emergency in January 1965, allowing police to seal off Mount Isa and conduct raids without warrant, saw the order cancelled after 4 days. Although the dispute collapsed in March, most of its demands were eventually granted in the August 1965 Mount Isa Mines Award.

Vindictive to the end the company, Federal government and mainstream media outlets continued to hound New Zealand born strike-leader and IWW member Pat Mackie after the dispute had ended. Although he was unable to work in Mount Isa again, attempts to deport him were defeated when he was able to prove his Australian citizenship. He later went on to win a case against the *Daily Telegraph* for defamation winning $30,000 in compensation.

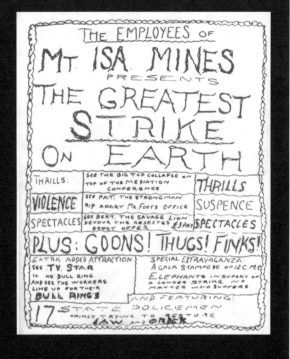

for the growing draft resistance movement.

A rare case brought against eight high-profile unionists two years later sees them found guilty and fined for "inciting young men to refuse to register for National Service." The unionists refuse to pay their fines and release a statement declaring that:

> As trade union officials, representing many thousands of organised workers, we firmly believe the continued conscription of young Australians to be sent to Vietnam to kill or be killed is a criminal act. We therefore, as a matter of conscience with 30 other like-minded trade union officials deliberately handed out leaflets in Flinders Street outside the Department of Labour and National Service ...
>
> [The National Service Act] is both immoral and corrupt. As such it is totally indefensible, acting against the best interests of both Australia and Indochina. The Nuremberg War Crimes Trial established that it was the duty of individuals to oppose and fight to defeat immoral and unjust laws. Therefore such laws must be defeated by the organised, conscious actions of increasing thousands of people, particularly organised workers, even if it means deliberately breaking the law to defeat the law. Accordingly, we declare our intention actively to encourage people to incite others into direct confrontation with the Federal Government in respect of the National Service Act and the dirty war in Vietnam. Further, we declare our complete solidarity with all 20-year-olds who refuse to register, regardless of the consequences. Fines and gaol sentences will not intimidate trade unions into silence.

MELBOURNE, 1968

Students at University High distribute their paper *Ubique Underground*, whose slogan reads, "Power comes out of the barrel of a gestetner." The group also regularly paste up anti-school posters only to see them torn down by prefects. School assemblies are held warning students to keep away from such "scurrilous and evil material" and some students are expelled for their involvement. Despite police being brought in to question students and shut down production, another eight issues are distributed before the year is out.

AUSTRALIA, 1969

Thousands of copies of a leaflet urging "all male persons resident in Australia who are about to turn twenty to refuse to register for National Service when the law requires them to" are handed out around the country. The text also states, "this breaches the Crimes Act," daring the Federal government to take action against the 100 people who have put their name to it. Despite this flagrant challenge to its authority, the Liberal Party generally opts to sit on its hands in fear of generating yet more publicity

MELBOURNE, 1969

After police swoop in during a performance to arrest nine actors at La Mama Theatre for using "obscene language" in a public place the audience, with the backing of a rock band, begin chanting the offending words en masse.

SYDNEY, 1969

A naked student with the words, "The more I make love, the more I make revolution" daubed on his body disrupts the Chancellor's Orientation Week speech at the University of NSW.

GURINDJI STRIKE
WAVE HILL STATION, NORTHERN TERRITORY, 1966-1975

In August 1966 Gurindji stockmen walked off Wave Hill Station demanding equal wages instead of the rations and occasional pittance they were paid for working and living in appalling conditions. Much of the local Indigenous community moved to a nearby sacred site at Daguragu (Wattie Creek) where the focus of their campaign soon shifted from wages to land rights. Despite offers of improved pay and conditions and threats of eviction and a halt to their food supplies, the community held out for close to a decade. With assistance from left-wing trade unions and other activists, support for the struggle grew around the country, and in 1975 the Whitlam Government negotiated a partial handover of traditional land from the British pastoral corporation Vesteys who had exploited the Gurindji for so long.

Above: Detail from Gurindji Solidarity Demo Poster. Sydney, 1970. Photographer unknown.

MAY DAY
1969

Equal Pay Campaigner Nancy Anderson, worked at the Liquor, Hospitality and Miscellaneous Workers' Union.

Photographer: Doug Howitt

AUSTRALIA, 1969

After five years of refusing to pay fines for breaking anti-union laws, known as the Penal Powers, the Victorian Tramways union's secretary Clarrie O'Shea is summonsed to court for contempt. After leading a march of thousands of members from 27 left-wing unions through Melbourne, O'Shea refuses to take the oath or hand over his organisation's accounts telling the court, "I am a paid servant of my members, I am directed to protect their interests at all times, whether it is in regard to their wages, working conditions or their funds, and I am doing what appears to me and our members to be the only logical course I can take to protect their funds." Unimpressed, the judge chooses to imprison him. In response half a million workers across the country down tools, with up to a million joining the following week. Faced with this general strike O'Shea's fines are paid by former Australian Financial Review advertising manager Dudley Mac-Dougall, "on behalf of a public benefactor." Although this lets the government off the hook the Penal Powers are effectively dead as, in the face of union intransigence, no employer now dares use them.

ADELAIDE, 1969

Students at Flinders University set up a Draft Resisters' Sanctuary, hiding out resister Bob Hall in the Religious Centre for 42 hours.

MELBOURNE, 1969

After PM John Gorton expresses Australia's relationship to the US with the words, "We'll go a-waltzing Matilda with you," peace activists respond by singing their own version of the old folk chestnut, "Bombing and burning, burning and bombing, we'll go a-bombing and burning with you."

SYDNEY, 1969

10 anti-war protesters attend the Good Friday Morning Prayer and Litany at St Andrew's Church, taking up places on the pulpit to hold up placards reading, "Christians Crucify Christ In Vietnam," and, "Silence Is A Potent Political Weapon Of Oppression."

MELBOURNE, 1969

Sick and tired of government and union foot-dragging over equal pay for women, Zelda D'Aprano decides to chain herself to the Commonwealth Building in Spring Street, Melbourne. She recalls:[10]

> Diane Ronberg [secretary of the Insurance Staff Federation], and I both agreed that something more than just talking was needed to draw attention to the pay injustice meted out to women and more positive action was required. We began to fantasise women chaining themselves up like the suffragettes did and jokingly asked ourselves where women could chain themselves to make their protest effective.
>
> I began to think seriously of the chaining-up idea, then decided I would be prepared to chain myself to the Commonwealth Building as part of the Victorian Employed Women's Organisation Council (VEWOC) demonstration. Little did I realise the effect this event would have in changing the entire course of my life. I felt that the Commonwealth Government should set the example by giving equal pay to women in government employment and, after assuring Diane that I was serious in my intent, she became excited and undertook to contact Don McSwan, the elderly secretary of the Garment Workers' Union. He had played a main role in establishing VEWOC, but he was shocked by the suggestion. He didn't think the chain-up was necessary or wise, so I decided to do it as an individual, but requested moral support from other women.
>
> The day of the meeting at the city square had arrived—21 October 1969. I had already spent several lunch hours distributing leaflets advertising the meeting and again I went with several other women and distributed leaflets. After the leaflet hand-out, I made my way to the city square and the number of speakers had been reduced to two women. It was almost impossible to hear them because of the traffic noise and, although the press, radio and television had been notified of the meeting, they were not present. However, when they were told to be at the Commonwealth Building at 2pm they all turned up.
>
> I had planned the entire strategy for the event. The door system had to be examined in order to determine how much chain would be required. Then, having done this, I asked the late Jim Donogan, the then secretary of the Painters' and Dockers' Union, if he could get me some chain.

I explained the purpose for which the chain was needed and Jim said he would be glad to oblige, but on the condition that I refrained from revealing the source from which it was obtained. I agreed for I had already priced chain and it was very expensive. I simply purchased the locks.

I felt strongly about the need for women to begin fighting their own battles. The placards were all ready for the event and I refrained from eating or drinking for several hours prior to the chain-up as it would be embarrassing to find that I needed to go to the toilet while still in the chains. Following the meeting at the city square, several of the women accompanied me to the Commonwealth Building where, within seconds, I was chained across the doors. The other women walked up and down with the placards which called upon the Government to grant women equal pay.

I did not know how long I would be there; I was very nervous, but it had to be done and I was prepared for anything. A Justice of the Peace was already lined up in case of arrest. The press, radio and TV arrived and it was on. They asked why I was protesting in this manner and what I hoped to gain from this demonstration. I explained that I was protesting against the injustice done to women over the right to equal pay and, when asked how I felt about being the only woman prepared to do this, I told them that today it was me, tomorrow there would be two, then four women, and it would go on until all women were demanding their rights. They asked ridiculous questions like "Do you now feel like Mrs Pankhurst?" and such, but I made light of these inane questions. I explained why the Commonwealth Building was selected and they then asked where I got the chain from. It was a very heavy chain and with a smile I stated that it was donated by an all-male union, which was not a lie, but refused to name the union.

The entire building became a mass of faces at the windows when they learnt of what was taking place. I had given the keys from the locks to another woman and, after some time had passed, she went off to purchase some sandwiches. It was during her absence that the Commonwealth police arrived and ordered me to unlock myself. I refused to do so. They again told me to unlock myself and again I said I did not have the keys, which in fact was true. The building warden stepped forward and read a meaningless script to me. The police then cut the chain with a pair of bolt cutters. I was amazed how easily the bolt cutters snipped through the thick chain, it was as if they were cutting paper.

I returned to work and ate my sandwiches on the way. I trembled for several hours after my ordeal and gradually regained my calm. The press, radio and TV featured the event; however, the press distorted what was said during the interview. I was convinced that genteel meetings at the city square would never achieve anything. Women would have to fight for what they wanted.

ADELAIDE, 1969

Anti-war activist Peter Hicks threatens to publicly immolate his border-collie, Plato. Following a media outcry, he points out that while some would condemn the burning of a dog in Australia, they continue to ignore the burning of children in Vietnam.

MELBOURNE, 1969

Ten days after her first groundbreaking direct action for women's equal pay, Zelda D'Aprano links up with two other women to chain themselves to the doors of the Arbitration Court. Sadly much of the union movement, supposedly radical or otherwise, refuses to help out, as D'Aprano recalls:[11]

The next day [after the first action], Sharon, a young woman who worked in the office of the Drink Workers' Union, called in at our office and eagerly displayed her support. She was most anxious to participate in any similar action which might be held in the future. I received a phone call from Alva Giekie, a woman congratulating me on my courage and requesting to be brought in on any further chain-ups. She also had a friend who might come along, so we arranged to meet to discuss the issue.

Alva was very enthusiastic to get into action and we decided to chain ourselves across the doors of the Arbitration Court, the institution which refused to grant women equal pay for work of equal value. Alva's friend, Thelma Solomon, was a willing participant, but they were both schoolteachers and it was difficult for them to take time off from school for a demonstration. There was a dispute pending within the teaching service, and a stop-work of teachers was possible. We decided to wait for the outcome. Meanwhile, I went and examined the door system at the Arbitration Court to determine how much chain was required, and where the chain would have

to go. I made various enquiries in my search for chain and was able to obtain some from the Builders Labourers' Union. I purchased more locks and all was set to go if the teachers went on strike.

Alva was so keen that she suggested we carry out the chain-up strike or no strike, but I realised there would be media publicity and both Alva and Thelma would be in strife. Alva, having had no previous experience of the media, thought if we asked them to refrain from photographing her and Thelma, then all would be well. I explained that this wasn't possible and they could not risk such action. The teachers' strike was planned for the Friday, but it would not be known until the Thursday evening's negotiations if the strike was on or off, so we had to wait for the late news Thursday night before we could act. I listened to the news and negotiations had broken down so the strike was on.

We had discussed the need for several women to come along with placards and give us moral support, and I undertook the responsibility of getting this support. The next morning I went to work earlier than necessary, for I did not consider that I could do as I liked while working for the Union. I was "Mary Ann" in the children's page of the union journal, and did almost all of this page at home where I could apply myself without interruption. I never asked for payment from the union, so a little time in return still put the union in my debt.

My early arrival at the Trades Hall gave me the opportunity of calling in to Jerry, the secretary of the Drink Workers' Union and my comrade [fellow member of the Communist Party], and I told him about young Sharon and her eagerness to lend support. I asked if she would be able to take one hour off in order to give us some badly needed moral support. Jerry stood there stuttering and stammering, "Oh," he said, "She couldn't possibly go along; after all my Union is a right-wing union you know. If the members saw her there they would want to know what she was doing there." He continued to stutter and stammer. "Forget it," I said and walked away.

I then rang the Steelworkers' Union, another left-wing union, and spoke to one of the organisers about getting some support from a woman. He advised me to ring back and ask Lennie McMichael, the secretary of the union. Lennie was also a comrade and when I rang and explained the situation, he said he would not let a woman go for this purpose. When I asked for his

reasons for refusing, he stated they did not work this way. I tried to explain about the teachers' strike and why it had to be a last minute decision, but he said, "The answer is still no." There was no one else I could ask for only two of the women comrades had made an approach of support for my stand, but didn't indicate any interest in activities of this nature.

Alva, Thelma and I chained ourselves across the doors of the Arbitration Court on 31 October 1969 without any support from other women. The media was present and again there were photos and interviews. I suggested that we must not be provoked for it was important to preserve our sense of humour in such situations. There was just sufficient chain to allow the door to open slightly and people had to bend down and crawl in sideways to enter the building. This was so undignified for the "important'" people and one commissioner told a union official in the building that he was lucky I didn't know who he was or I may have wrapped the chain around his neck.

Again there were questions from the media concerning the demonstration and, eventually, we were paid a visit by several Commonwealth policemen, one being the policeman who had cut my chains on the previous occasion. The three of us were asked to undo the locks and leave the building, but we refused to do so. We were again asked and again we refused, until the building warden arrived and we were cut loose. We were lined up like naughty children to stand before the warden as he read his text for the day from his book of legal jargon. His voice trembled as he read.

The experienced chain-cutting cop approached me and said that this was the second occasion on which I had acted in this manner, and he warned me that serious action would be taken against me if I behaved in this manner again. I asked if this only applied to Commonwealth buildings, knowing his jurisdiction full well, and he replied yes. "Oh well, there are plenty of State Government buildings" was my reply. We then caught a taxi and I returned to work.

AUSTRALIA, 1969

Reverend Billy Graham's revival tour hits a few snags when students dressed in white bedsheets and sandals attempt to take his microphone from him in Sydney. Billboards advertising the event are regularly defaced with Hitler moustaches added to his likeness, along with slogans condemning his support for President Nixon and the war in Vietnam. Hammering home the point, at the Melbourne Cricket Ground (MCG) two men run across the turf carrying a banner reading "Thou Shalt Not Kill ... Vietnam."

MELBOURNE, 1969

Pro-choice activists disrupt anti-abortion Right To Life meetings by standing up to declare, "I've had an abortion. Arrest me!"

SYDNEY, 1969

During an address to 800 students at Sydney University, Professor Charles Birch, Professor Charles Martin, and Doctor Terry Smith openly call for resistance to conscription. The Federal government had thus far avoided bringing charges against prominent figures inciting non-compliance with National Service, but in this case PM McMahon calls for immediate action against the three. Within days over 500 academics from around the country sign a similar statement calling for draft resistance and requests to place an advertisement bearing their names are refused by *The Australian* and *The Sydney Morning Herald*. Two months later the Attorney-General Nigel Bowen informs Parliament that he has dropped the idea of prosecution as legal advice holds that it would fail, but as the list of signatories to the Statement Of Defiance has grown to 8,000 it is more likely he simply wants the matter brought to a close.

MELBOURNE, 1969

A meeting of 200 union shop stewards issues a statement reading, "We encourage those young men already conscripted to refuse to accept orders against their consciences and those in Vietnam to lay down their arms in mutiny against the hideous barbarism perpetuated in our name upon the innocent, aged, men, women and children." Following the launch of an investigation into the statement by the Attorney-General another union meeting, this time by the NSW Teachers Federation, sees 180 delegates sign a petition calling on Australian servicemen "to lay down their arms in mutiny." Despite strong condemnation by the media and the

government, the strength of anti-war feeling ensures that charges of incitement to mutiny, which carry penalties of up to life in prison, are never brought against the unionists.

AUSTRALIA, 1969

In the build-up to the July registration period, National Service Minister Billy Snedden is briefly trapped in his Treasury office by a sit-in, while occupations also occur at his Sydney office and the Victorian Liberal Party HQ. During a raid on the National Service Department in Adelaide furniture is trashed, telephone lines cut and pig's blood poured over files.

MELBOURNE, 1969

Anti-development activists hang out their dirty underwear in North Melbourne's Abbotsford Street during a protest against the Victorian Housing Commission's decision to demolish the only laundromat in the area.

AUSTRALIA, 1969

During the year's Fill In A Falsie campaign, activist Harry Van Moorst estimates that up to 6,000 fake conscription forms are sent in. Topaz, a race horse, receives the call-up, as do several Liberal Party politicians. Others prank their buddies as in the case of the middle-aged Ted McCormick, a unionist and waterside worker, who receives a call-up notice stating he is a night-soil collector. During a number of public Fill In A Falsie events police prove reluctant to make arrests despite a Department of National Service spokesperson stating that, "The possibility of receiving 10,000 false registration forms wouldn't be very attractive. The Department would waste a lot of time checking them."

WOLLONGONG, 1969

A draft resister successfully halts a train carrying conscripts by sitting on the railway line.

MELBOURNE, 1969

All manner of shenanigans kick off when Laurie Carmichael Jr, the son of a prominent communist and union leader, appears at Williamstown Magistrates Court to face charges relating to his refusal to appear for a National Service medical examination. Having disrupted the opening of Federal Parliament the day before, and having

read a short statement outside the court, Carmichael is whisked off by his supporters. Embarrassed police react angrily, attacking those present and punching the defendant's mother in the head before arresting her, his father and numerous others. Further arrests and clashes then ensue as word of the violence spreads, leading local dock workers to walk off the job and join in the fray. When Carmichael's case is called the pandemonium spreads to the court itself as various young men leap up Spartacus-style to claim, "I'm Laurie Carmichael!", "No, I'm Laurie Carmichael," etc.

A few days later the real Laurie Carmichael Jr addresses the Melbourne Unitarian Church, explaining that he wishes to stay out of the clutches of the law in order to raise the profile of draft resistance. When those arrested at the protest front court, 1,000 demonstrate outside with workers at the Naval Dockyard downing tools in solidarity. Despite the protest being non-violent the *Herald Sun* runs a headline claiming, "Angry Mob Storms Court." When the paper's editor refuses to meet about the matter union leader Ken Carr calls the *Herald Sun's* industrial reporter to warn him that the Seamen's Union will black-ban the newspaper's newsprint if a retraction fails to appear. Suitably chastened the editor runs just such a statement within 24 hours.

HOBART, 1969

Professor Roebuck of the University of Tasmania becomes one of many academics to defy the Federal Government's attempts to stifle anti-war dissent, calling upon Australian soldiers to refuse orders in Vietnam and asking them, "How often have you said that the German people were responsible for Nazi war crimes? They must have known. Well, now you know too. You too are responsible."

MELBOURNE, 1969

Anti-war activists create the John Michael Sullivan Award, named after a Commonwealth Police Chief notorious for targeting protesters, to be given to the person who can fill in and post the highest number of false draft registration forms to the Department of Labour and National Service.

Gary Foley at the Springbok (South African Rugby Team) tour demonstrations, Sydney, 1971. Photograph courtesy of Gary Foley.

1970–1979

The progressive trend unleashed during the 1960s peaked in the early years of the new decade. A series of anti-Vietnam war moratoriums, the largest demonstrations in Australian history, saw hundreds of thousands protest across the country. In the face of mass opposition and non-compliance with conscription, and in line with US policy, the ailing Liberal government began to draw down Australia's troop involvement.

Alternative medicine, organic food, experimental arts and music, appropriate technology, Eastern spirituality and communal living practices all served to create a countercultural niche in society whilst also changing mainstream values. The increasing consumption of illicit drugs amongst countercultural scenes, and beyond, was met with repression by new government agencies who persecuted grassroots users and drove up prices leading to increased involvement by organised crime.

Women's Liberation established itself as a major movement from 1970 onwards. Hundreds of consciousness-raising and activist groups were set up across the country and grassroots services dealing with health, abortion, domestic violence and other issues founded. As the movement spread it also diversified with factions devoted to electoral politics, migrant issues, lesbianism, separatism and Marxism emerging.

Australia's first Gay and Lesbian rights organisation, Campaign Against Moral Persecution (CAMP), was founded in 1970. Operating an advice line and engaging in lobbying it raised the acceptance and visibility of same-sex communities. In the midst of more militant groups, such as Gay Liberation and Radicalesbians, engaging in consciousness raising and in-your-face direct actions, the variety of GLBTI friendly venues and meeting places slowly widened. Legislative reform, excepting SA, was slow, and homophobic attacks, official or otherwise, continued, most notably highlighted by police assaults on a series of Sydney Gay and Lesbian marches in the late 1970s.

Indigenous demands for justice mushroomed during this period. Community empowerment and action peaked with the setting up of the Aboriginal Tent Embassy outside Federal Parliament in 1972. This brought together activists from across the country and raised the issue of Indigenous dispossession internationally challenging the rest of Australia, the Left included, to take real action towards equality and land rights.

Ecology emerged as an important issue in the early 1970s. Whilst some campaigns focused on the protection of forests and rural areas, the movement also demanded cleaner air and safer workplaces. As part of a push for healthier and more equitable urban environments, heritage and community activists joined with squatters and building unions to defend metropolitan bushland and inner city areas from destruction. Opposition to uranium mining and nuclear power would extend from submissions and lobbying to massive demonstrations by the end of the decade.

A new ALP Commonwealth government, led by PM Whitlam, was empowered and driven by Australia's progressive turn to undertake a series of wide ranging reforms from its election in 1972. Introducing free university education, universal healthcare and abolishing the last vestiges of the White Australia Policy, the new government also legislated land rights for parts of the NT, advocated a multicultural Australia for Indigenous people, and formally ended Australian involvement in Vietnam. Amidst a flurry of reforms, money flowed into the arts and many of the grassroots initiatives established by activists in recent years – including women's shelters, free legal services and advice lines – received funding, gradually losing their political edge in the process.

The conditions activists operated under, and many of the issues they faced, had always differed on a state-by-state basis, but variations were particularly stark during the 1970s. Whilst the South Australian ALP government enacted many reforms from 1973 – including decriminalising homosexuality, relaxing censorship and drinking laws, and introducing consumer protections – the governments of Queensland and WA were deeply reactionary. Both states introduced anti-association laws, resisted progressive Federal reforms, and continued to heavily repress and dispossess Indigenous people. In response free speech protests were held in Perth and strikes and protests by Aboriginal people undertaken at Noonkanbah and other locations, whilst Queensland saw illegal street marches and Indigenous resistance against state policies occur across the state.

Both reform and radicalism would be blunted in the mid-1970s as the 'long-boom' came to an end, and capital strikes and the global oil crisis created unemployment and inflation. The previous conservative government had suffered electorally from increasing economic uncertainty, but media attacks and widening public disaffection over a series of government scandals and blunders saw the ALP wear most of the blame. Following a narrow election victory in 1974, manoeuvring on the part of the conservative opposition saw the Commonwealth budget blocked in 1975. A constitutional coup followed with Governor-General Kerr sacking the government and placing the Liberal-Country Party coalition in control. Mass opposition to this move was channelled by the ALP and union bureaucracies into electoral channels and, following further media opposition, PM Fraser consolidated his hold on power in a landslide victory.

Although liberal in some of his attitudes, particularly in relation to South African apartheid and in pushing the acceptance of tens of thousands of Vietnamese refugees, Fraser's key message was that the good times were over as, misquoting George Bernard Shaw, he stated, "Life wasn't meant to be easy." In the face of a series of government and employer attacks, many Australians disputed this. Although industrial disputes dropped off gradually, strike levels were still at record highs and major campaigns limited the degree to which the gains of recent years could be unravelled. Action in the community similarly challenged funding cuts, whilst changes in the expectations of women and migrants could not be undone. Multiculturalism continued as government policy and law reform finally allowed people to divorce freely, but Aboriginal land rights were curtailed. Despite some successes the collapse, and rightward turn, of the ALP, and the exhaustion involved in holding the line, saw grassroots movements and the Left operating in a much tougher environment by the decade's end.

"Male chauvinists start shakin',
Today's pigs are tomorrow's bacon."

Graffiti, 1978.

AUSTRALIA, 1970s

With the advent of free-posting (for magazine subscriptions, utility bills, etc) pranksters find a new way of distributing propaganda, art, stories, paintings and other oddities. Not only do the stuffed pre-paid envelopes provide a new avenue through which to distribute a variety of creations, they also hopefully brighten up the day for those employed to open them in large clearing houses.

MELBOURNE, 1970s

For decades after it is first applied, the painted slogan "MONEY DOES NOT TALK, IT SCREAMS" remains on a bridge over the Glen Waverley railway line, proving that location is indeed everything.

ADELAIDE, 1970

The annual Miss Fresher beauty contest at Adelaide University is shut down when 60 feminists and their male supporters occupy the catwalk.

MELBOURNE, 1970

In a case heard at the City Court, three ministers of religion claim that a mock crucifixion held on the previous Christmas Eve was not offensive, and indeed may have prompted parishioners "to ponder the true meaning of Christmas". Regardless of this interpretation, the Court fines two men $50 for offensive behaviour in displaying placards reading, "Born at Christmas, Killed in Vietnam."

CANBERRA, 1970

While most Liberal politicians remain silent on the subject of their own children and conscription, leading cabinet member Billy Snedden informs the media that, "I have two sons, the eldest will be 19 in May, and both tell me that they are looking forward to doing National Service." Snedden's words came back to haunt him a year later when the *Nation Review* reveals that his son Drew has registered to seek permission to leave Australia before his marble rolls in order to "further his career as a Qantas clerk". The newspaper also points out that, "Anybody who shares Drew's enthusiasm for conscription can fill out an 'Application for permission to leave Australia.' Indeed 3,000 such applications are made in Victoria each year alone."

BRISBANE, 1970

During a protest against the Queensland Government, Pastor Don Brady sets alight and throws into the gutter a copy of the repressive Aboriginal and Torres Strait Islander Act.

MELBOURNE, 1970

300 students at Mordiallac High School strike over the right of males to have long hair.

SYDNEY, 1970

Scuffles with police break out during a rally to commemorate the massacre of anti-apartheid protesters at Sharpeville after a South African flag, stolen from the apartheid regime's Canberra Embassy, is burnt.

MELBOURNE, 1970

Paul Francis Perry recalls one university occupation as follows:[12]

> As the meeting closed and students drifted off to lectures, a Labor Club rally was formed and invaded the Monash Uni Careers and Appointments Office (due to their involvement with the military). This occupation differed from those in the administration building in a very important way. The C&A occupation involved the actual USE of the offices and equipment, with a great deal of leaflets being produced on gestetner and photocopy machines.
>
> The first step taken by the Uni administration was to cut off the power by removing the relevant fuses. The occupiers were stunned, but a freelance anarchist replaced the fuse. The fuse again disappeared and the box was locked. The anarchist then pulled out part of the ceiling and, wrapping his hands in plastic bags, cut insulation from leads to an air pump motor. A power lead was attached and run back to the wall socket, restoring power, to the consternation of those listening outside. The same person was to restore telephone communication to the outside world.

BATHURST, 1970

During the first of a number of riots that are to plague the Maximum Security Bathurst prison, one wag demands that Johnny Cash be appointed mediator.

SYDNEY, 1970

Fifth and sixth form students at Cleveland Boy's High School cancel a planned one-day strike after the Education Department accedes to their demands that construction work around the school be cleaned up and blocked toilets fixed.

MELBOURNE, 1970

The recently formed Women's Action Committee holds a protest at the Miss Teenage Quest where they drop leaflets into the crowd and hoist a banner denouncing the "exploitation of women's bodies for charitable purposes". Later in the year they go on to hold demonstrations in which women board trams and only pay 75% of the full fare "as a protest against women receiving lower salaries, but paying full price for commodities and services".

SYDNEY, 1970

Nine people are arrested during an anti-conscription demonstration held outside the home of Federal Attorney-General Tom Hughes. At one point Hughes attempts to attack protesters with a cricket bat, prompting 50 others to stage a cricket match outside his home the following weekend.

BRISBANE, 1970

Poet Oodgeroo Noonuccal (Kath Walker) writes to the Queen threatening to return her recently awarded MBE if the Australian Government does not hasten the pace of awarding Indigenous Australians human rights.

SYDNEY, 1970

Battles between school authorities and radical teens accelerate, following an inaccurate report in *The Australian* asserting that permission has been given for NSW high-school Principals to allow the "passive wearing of Moratorium badges" in support of upcoming anti-Vietnam rallies. Despite a retraction from the newspaper students refuse to remove said badges and are expelled or suspended from several schools, including Manly, Ibrox Park, Fort Street, Sydney Girls and Dover Heights. Some schools, such as Seven Hills, threaten to also suspend teachers for wearing anti-war badges, while a few progressive institutions, such as Hunters Hill and Pittwater, allow their students to wear whatever they like.

MELBOURNE, 1970

Having issued a challenge to police to arrest him at Monash University, draft resister Adrian Bissett and 200 supporters draw further attention to his defiance of military orders by blocking Dandenong Road.

SYDNEY, 1970

Aboriginal protesters throw wreaths into Botany Bay as tens of thousands, including the Royal Family, attend a re-enactment of Captain Cook's landing.

MELBOURNE, 1970

During the first massive Melbourne anti-war Moratorium gathering anarchists reject support for both the Southern and Northern Vietnamese regimes and parody popular pro-NVA slogans by chanting, "Ho Ho Ho Chi Minh, drop him in the garbage bin."

SYDNEY, 1970

The Campaign for Action Against Censorship (CAAC) protests in Sydney against cuts to the film *Medium Cool*. Brandishing placards reading, "Obscenity Is Cool," "Don't Buy Damaged Goods," "This Film Has Been Cut," and "Sex Starved Censors Scissor Films," the 35 protesters are eventually pushed away from the entrance of the Greater Union cinema by police.

MELBOURNE, 1970

Julie Ingleby is separated from her children and jailed for contempt after protesting in the City Court against the sentencing of her husband for holding a placard reading, "Fuck the Draft—Not the Vietnamese." Sentenced to three days of "mending socks" at Fairlea Prison, Ms Ingleby learns that in addition to her prison stay, she has also been sacked by the Education Department. Warning others that, "Anyone who is working for a State Department is at the same risk," she links up with the Technical Teacher's Association to fight for the "so-called democratic right to speak freely and act according to one's conscience."

SYDNEY, 1970

UNSW student paper *Tharunka* decides to challenge NSW's censorship laws by publishing the bawdy poem *Eskimo Nell*. Drawing a storm of condemnation from the mainstream media, politicians and other student papers, *Tharunka's* editors are charged with obscenity over the sexual content of the paper, while their decision to also print instructions for the creation of thermite bombs, napalm and chlorine gas goes strangely unnoticed. Upon her appearance at Sydney Central Court, *Tharunka* editor Wendy Bacon racks up yet more charges for wearing a nun's habit emblazoned with the words (from her banned poem *Cunt Is A Christian Word*), "I've been fucked by God's steel prick."

ADELAIDE, 1970

During the second Vietnam Moratorium march, anti-war protesters decide to occupy the city intersection at North Terrace and King William Road. Having announced their intentions in advance the protesters receive the support of the State Premier Don Dunstan, who asks the police to divert traffic to allow the sit-down protest to take place. The Police Commissioner John McKinna has other ideas, however, and when the 5,000 protesters halt at the given point he sends in his men to brutally break up the demonstration and arrest 130 people. During 40 minutes of scuffles demonstrators chant "Old McKinna had a farm" and "Oink Oink" before moving on to occupy the steps of Parliament. In response to the police violence two ships at Point Stanvac Oil Refinery go out on strike for 24 hours.

MELBOURNE, 1970

Following the traditional May Day march those of a more radical persuasion decide to continue on from the Yarra Banks towards the American Consulate. En route two red flags are placed on the "secret" ASIO headquarters.

NSW, 1971

In 1971 locals at Kelly's Bush request the help of the NSW Builders Labourers Federation (BLF) to save remnant bushland in their area. After an investigation the union agrees to place work bans and the Green Bans movement kicks off. By 1974 the BLF has imposed 42 green bans holding up over $3 billion worth of development, asserting in the process the right of workers to determine that what they create be of a socially useful nature. Over 100 National Trust buildings are saved from the wrecker's ball while the BLF also prevents The Rocks area from being developed, the Botanical Gardens from being turned into a car park and Centennial Park from being levelled. Although unable to wholly save Victoria St in Darlinghurst, the union's support for residents and squatters helps them prevent it from being completely demolished, despite the opposition of police and organised crime figures who evict, kidnap and even kill protesters.

Just as importantly the union puts the rank and file in charge, holding regular workplace meetings, encouraging initiatives from below and introducing limited tenure for elected leaders, who are paid wages at the award rate, to avoid the creation of an ossified, timid bureaucracy. In other moves the NSW BLF also imposes industrial bans over prisoners' rights, discrimination against a gay student at Macquarie University and in support of a Women's Studies course at the University of Sydney. Threatened by the union's independence, the Federal arm of the BLF, led by Maoist Norm Gallagher, joins together with developers and the conservative NSW State Government to deregister the union and decimate its membership in March 1975.

AUSTRALIA, 1971

Within hours of US President Nixon announcing an escalation of bombing over North Vietnam, wharfies and seamen stop work to join demonstrations outside US consulates around the country. During the protests demonstrators in Queensland pour blood over the trading floor and brokers at the Stock Exchange, while their compatriots in Perth disrupt the sitting of State Parliament.

MELBOURNE, 1971

Wanted draft-resister Michael Hamel-Green makes a surprise appearance at the Year 12 end-of-year exams held at the Melbourne Exhibition centre. He advises students to resist conscription, before disappearing ahead of the arrival of police.

SYDNEY, 1971

After the Harco Steel factory announces the dismissal of five boilermakers and one ironworker, the company's workers decide to buck their employer's right to hire and fire by declaring their boss "surplus to requirements" and taking control of their workplace. Attempts by the police to remove the workers fail. The occupation lasts for four weeks, during which the occupiers implement the 35-hour week and refuse demands by their union, the Federated Ironworkers Association, to strike and therefore end the occupation before they are ready.

MELBOURNE, 1971

Pirate station Radio 3DR (Draft Resistance) is born when 150 people barricade themselves into the Melbourne University Student Union and begin transmitting from the 3rd floor. A number of draft resisters wanted by police choose to hole up in the George Paton room while amplifiers and a transmitter are set up to broadcast the station throughout the University and across most of the adjoining suburbs.

The station broadcasts with only a few minor interruptions from Air Cadets and the like until, on the third morning, the police decide to move in at 5am. Having assembled a large contingent of supporters, 3DR is given ample warning of the impending raid with flares and sirens going off across the university. On arrival the police smash their way through windows before being forced to scale three levels of barricades composed of chairs, chains and tables. During this time the wily draft resisters are spirited from the building to safety while their supporters link arms, singing, "Power To The People". Although it only takes the police 20 minutes to enter and clear the building they remain on campus for an extra four hours smashing Union property in a petty attempt to discredit the draft dodgers.

SYDNEY, 1971

Eight female cleaners stage a sit-in strike on a Pan American jumbo jet after one of their co-workers is given the sack. After a 1-hour stand-off union representatives are called in and the woman is given her job back.

MELBOURNE, 1971

Students at Preston East Technical College strike for a half day after a number of their peers are threatened with expulsion over the length of their hair.

SYDNEY, 1971

Appearing in court dressed as a "soldier of peace", draft resister Geoff Mullens receives 12 months in prison for refusing to be conscripted. During his trial he delivers a submission to the court reading:

I DEMAND THE REPEAL OF THE *NATIONAL SERVICE ACT* AND I WILL REFUSE MY CO-OPERATION WITH THE GOVERNMENT UNTIL THAT AIM IS ATTAINED.

I pity you all, I pity you war-criminal politicians who must feed like carrion on other people's lives to sustain your own. I pity you beaten soldiers who kill and are killed for lies. I pity you revolutionaries whose fear condemns you to sterile games. I pity you Australians whose lives are a mere progression from school to home to work to bed to death, and yet must all the while be accomplices to slaughter. None of you are free. None of you are human before all else.

Look around you. Imagine that the man nearest to you has been burned by napalm. His face has melted, his features run into each other, his skin is charred, flaky, perhaps the bones in his arms are exposed where the skin has evaporated. See the woman near you. Her baby is dead, body pockmarked with holes from anti-personnel bullets. But you don't need that imagination in Vietnam.

This is a country, like others, governed by a compulsion to manipulate. In the factory or office you have no more significance than any other working machine. For the government you are liable to be used for whatsoever they choose.

I AM NOT A MACHINE. I AM NOT TO BE USED AS OTHERS WILL! I CAN, AS BERTRAND RUSSELL ASKED, "REMEMBER MY HUMANITY". IF YOU CANNOT, I PITY YOU.

MELBOURNE, 1971
Gay Liberationists make their presence known by noisily testing out beds at the Myer Department Store.

ADELAIDE, 1971
Feminists set up a birth control information booth outside the St Francis Xavier Catholic Cathedral.

SYDNEY, 1971
During a parliamentary debate destined to defeat proposed pro-choice abortion legislation women invade Parliament carrying banners attacking NSW's Premier reading, "Askin Babies—A Liberal Disgrace" and "When are we going to legalise abortion?" Scuffles break out when the women are eventually removed.

In the same year, as part of international abortion law reform rallies, 250 march in Sydney led by a float featuring a pregnant Liberal Premier Askin and a pregnant member of the clergy.

MELBOURNE, 1971
Despite being wanted for draft resistance Paul Fox is interviewed by TV reporters and marches straight by police during an anti-conscription rally in the city.

DARWIN, 1971
By way of a letter signed by nine people, Aboriginal activists threaten to cut the Darwin to Adelaide telegraph line, and with it the city's contact with the rest of the world, unless the government agrees to their demands for land rights.

MELBOURNE, 1971
Fully prepared for the traditional July 4th anti-American protests, police surround the US embassy. To their surprise, the protesters march straight past and proceed to get stuck into the South African one instead.

SYDNEY, 1971
Members of the gay and lesbian rights organisation Campaign Against Moral Persecution (CAMP) hold a demonstration outside the Liberal Party's headquarters urging them to support former Attorney-General Tom Hughes in the seat of Berowra over his challenger Jim Cameron. Although no fans of the Liberals, the assembled protesters remind passers-by and the media of Cameron's recent tirades against gay law reform with helium balloons and banners reading, "Advance Australian Fairies," "Even Hughes Is Better Than Cameron," "Don't Let The Wowser Spoil The Party," and, "Cameron Hates Homos, But He'll Sure Bugger The Liberal Party."

MELBOURNE, 1971
With anti-conscription sentiment and draft resistance reaching an all-time high, 7,775 men are balloted in for failing to register. At the same time the Federal Government's will to deal with resistance begins to falter, with only 1,089 being prosecuted in any way, of whom a mere 10 are jailed. In an attempt to further push the envelope, a group of draft dodgers chain themselves to the Pentridge Prison gates daring the Government to come and get them. When this fails to get a response they board a tram (still manacled) and repeat the performance outside the Labour and National Service building. Only one is arrested, and later released on a $200 bond. The Government however is seriously embarrassed and the effectiveness of forced conscription is further undermined.

ARMIDALE, 1971
During the Springbok tour a number of classes at the University of New England are cancelled for two days so that teach-ins can be held for students and lecturers to discuss apartheid, racism and civil rights together.

MELBOURNE, 1971
Dissident students at Upwey High School form a Red Mole Party and distribute a manifesto advising students that, "If you want to be happy/Hang your teachers and prefects/Cut your parents' throats/And destroy the Coles 'Back To School' counter."

CANBERRA, 1971
Having been clued in to the fact that Austra-

Above: Anti-war Moratorium poster and badges, early 1970s. Unknown

lian National University Student Association President Michael Wright will be judging the Miss ANU competition on the basis of the "biggest boobs", the Labour Club enters Miss Daisy Bovine, a calf with four teats "who [makes] up in number what she lacks in size".

MELBOURNE, 1971
Paul Francis Perry, in his self-published book *The Rise And Fall Of Practically Everybody: An Account Of Student pPolitical Activity At Monash University, 1965-72*, published in Balaclava in 1973 recalls that:

The secret ASIO headquarters in St Kilda Road were rather a joke at this time. Peter Bailey, who was easily amused, used to spend hours wandering around the reception area asking people what building it was. Of course no one was permitted to tell him, and no one could therefore tell him to go away. It was alleged that one agent got to know Bailey so well as to satirise him by asking for a cigarette whilst casually displaying a full packet.

SYDNEY, 1971-1972

Michael Matteson, a draft resister, continually eludes police in their attempts to send him to jail. On one occasion he narrowly escapes arrest, after publicly debating and humiliating the enraged Attorney-General on ABC TV, by climbing out the studio's back window. On ANZAC Day 1972 he is caught after making a speech and police arrest and handcuff him. However, before they are able to bundle him away his driver alerts supporters from the nearby University of NSW who produce bolt cutters to free the captured activist. Having been delivered to safety, Matteson promptly gives another press conference condemning conscription.

CANBERRA, 1972

Veteran Aboriginal activist Gary Foley recalls how the Aboriginal Tent Embassy came to be:[13]

A series of demonstrations emerged ... in the aftermath of the Springbok tour, that we called the Black Moratoriums. The Aboriginal land rights demos started getting huge numbers of people, which hadn't happened before. For the first time, land rights demos in Sydney and Brisbane and Melbourne started to have an impact, to be noticed in the media. Towards the end of 1971 they started to make the then Prime Minister pretty nervous. We were bunging on a demo in Brisbane, then a week later we'd bung on another in Sydney, then a week later in Melbourne—we had a little hit squad of Aboriginal organisers just cruising up and down the east coast and around to Adelaide, and we created the impression that there was this massive community uprising.

By Australia Day 1972, [then Prime Minister] McMahon felt compelled to make a major pronouncement on Aboriginal land rights in response to all this agitation. And in doing so he really stuffed it right up and triggered the Aboriginal Embassy—which helped bring down an Australian government. Actually, Billy McMahon shot himself in the foot and brought

himself down, but it was us who seemed to have made him so nervous as to do a series of stupid things that just completely wrecked the credibility of his government. So by the time I was 21 I knew what people could achieve if they were prepared to stand up and be united and go for it.

When Billy McMahon made his pronouncement in 1972, we had a meeting in Redfern that night and the consensus was very clear. After the Prime Minister made it clear he wasn't going to do anything, we needed to up the ante, turn the blow-torch up a bit. So we dispatched the guys to Canberra that night. Their instructions were to go and set up a demo on the lawns of Parliament House and try to hold the fort until we could organise for more people to come in over the next few days.

We fully expected them to get arrested that night and that would have been it. But when they got there and put their beach umbrella up on the lawns of Parliament House, it was the police who informed them that there was at that point no law against camping on the lawns of Parliament House, and that as long as they only had eleven tents there was nothing the coppers could do. If they had twelve tents they'd be deemed a camping area and the coppers could have them removed, but eleven tents was okay. So next morning the Prime Minister came to work, saw this demo of Aboriginal people across the road and tried to get the police to do something about it. Only to be told, "Well, sorry, there's nothing we can do. It's not against the law."

So we were there legally. And the big catch-cry among conservative people in the '70s when it came to Aboriginal people agitating and demonstrating was, "We don't mind you demonstrating, just as long as you stay within the law." That was their favourite line. And here we were, demonstrating, but keeping within the law.

Because we were so pleased with what we'd accidentally managed to do, the whole tone of the Aboriginal Embassy was humorous rather than aggressive or threatening. We went to a great deal of trouble to play on the humour of it all and to capture the Australian people's imagination. Australians like larrikins, and this was very much a larrikin achievement. And I think we succeeded in doing that, to the point where by July 1972 the Aboriginal Embassy enjoyed tremendous popularity. Tourists would turn up in droves, we became one of the new tourist attractions of

Canberra. And more important politically, the television cameras of the world started to turn up. For the first time ever, the Indigenous political struggle in Australia was put on the international map. People all over the world began to find out what was going on in Australia. This was one of the great achievements of the Aboriginal Embassy: it put the Australian Aboriginal people's struggle on the world stage.

This freaked out the Prime Minister and eventually he did his really silly act, which was in the middle of one night in July. He came up with a law that made it illegal to camp on the lawns of Parliament House, and at nine o'clock the next morning he moved the coppers on us. And it was inevitable that if he did that there was going to be violent confrontation. We'd always said, "If they try to pull that, we'll regard that as trying to change the rules mid-stream and we'll react in an appropriate way." And we did.

It resulted in three weekends of some of the most violent demonstrations Canberra's ever seen—but they were only violent because we were attacked. We defended ourselves. If you look at the film footage it's quite obvious that we're standing there linking arms to protect ourselves, and it's the police who move in and attack us. You see how many police they put against us. In the third demonstration, they had every ACT policeman on duty in front of Parliament House— it would have been a good day to rob a bank somewhere else in Canberra—plus two NSW riot squads on standby at the back of Parliament House, and they even had troops from Duntroon on standby. It was overkill like you wouldn't believe. And when Aboriginal people in those political circumstances in that era were attacked by police it was inevitable that we would defend ourselves. We weren't Martin Luther King non-violent types, we were the real thing.

Me and Bobbi Sykes got arrested that first weekend, and I ended up in hospital. I got knocked out in the melee and was fairly concussed when they took me back to the cells. I don't remember, but I think I must have vomited or something and the police freaked out and carted me off to Canberra hospital— where I found the casualty ward was full of coppers getting their injuries treated. When Whitlam came in as Prime Minister a lot of the sting was taken out of things; too many people on the fringes of our political group sat back and said, "It's all okay now, Whitlam

International Women's Day
march, Sydney, 1972

will save us." By the time Malcolm Fraser got in, significant changes had taken place—but people were disillusioned by Whitlam, too, very early in the piece.

MELBOURNE, 1972

A Day of Action against the Vietnam War begins with two separate marches, one from Melbourne University and the other from the Shrine of Remembrance in St Kilda Road. The first includes a 90-second appearance by draft resister Michael Matteson, while the second sees police prevent protesters from laying a wreath reading "To the unwilling, led by the unqualified, to do the unnecessary … In memory of all those who have served in Vietnam."

ADELAIDE, 1972

300 people march with bags of discarded bottles and cans in tow to Coca-Cola's headquarters to award the multinational Friends of the Earth's first King of Krap award.

MELBOURNE, 1972

A network of people calling themselves the Dairy Liberation Front liberate crates of fresh milk from dairy processors for redistribution in the more hard-up areas of the city. Around the time of a Sydney Anarchist conference in a squatted church four years later people repeat the action, forming the Milk Liberation Front to redistribute dairy products from wealthy areas.

ARMIDALE, 1972

After a radical student is arrested during an anti-conscription demonstration for carrying a banner reading "Fuck the N.S.A" [National Service Act] hundreds of others stage a spontaneous sit-down in the street chanting, "Fuck, Fuck, Fuck." Following further arrests the crowd moves on to the police station, which they surround before running a red flag up its flagpole.

MELBOURNE, 1972

Paul Francis Perry[14] recalls the setting up of a Draft Resisters Sanctuary at Monash University:

> Copying an idea used successfully a year earlier at Melbourne Uni, the Draft Resisters Union set up a symbolic fortress in the Monash Union

building and challenged the Commonwealth police to capture the draft resisters there. A pirate radio (3DR) was set up and transmitted successfully to the amazement of [the adjoining suburb] Clayton. Unfortunately the only record available was one of Melanie and everyone was thoroughly sick of it.

A VHF radio network was established to warn of approaching police. The New Left Communist Party of Australia (revisionist) group who were running the radio were mystified by an extra party on the frequency who kept saying, "mumble, mumble, BULLFROG, mumble, BULLFROG." It was discovered that the Maoists, who had been excluded for security reasons, had set up their own network and managed to get on the same frequency, much to the chagrin of the revisionists. The Commonwealth police for their part just cruised around the block freaking out the DRU sentries by telling them their VHF sets should be licensed. A proposal that the police should be given café coffee was defeated on the grounds that one wouldn't give café coffee to one's worst enemies.

SYDNEY, 1972

Gay Liberationists set up a kissing booth at Sydney Uni and sell confectionary to passing students under the slogan of "Get your floss from a fairy!"

MELBOURNE, 1972

During the Easter break slogans such as "Christ Chunders At Congress" and "Insurrection Not Resurrection" appear on the walls of inner city churches.

PERTH, 1972

Indigenous activists set up an Aboriginal Consulate outside the West Australian Parliament demanding the government build 1,500 houses to meet what they regard as their people's minimum housing needs. Supported by trade unionists and university and high-school students the group also stages Perth's first Black Moratorium march.

MELBOURNE, 1972

Police drag away Sebastian Jorgenson after he disrupts an Apex event attended by Prime Minister McMahon at Montsalvat in Eltham. Furious that the artists' colony which his father

had helped to found, and which he believed "had always stood for humanitarian ideals", would host those supporting the Vietnam War, Jorgenson had snuck into the dining hall before tipping over drum cymbals, slamming piano keys and giving the PM a serve.

CANBERRA, 1972

Four Indigenous women chain themselves to the railing outside Parliament House to protest against the continuing repression of the Aboriginal Tent Embassy.

MELBOURNE, 1972

Demonstrators celebrate July 4th (American Independence Day) with a series of actions at the U.S. Embassy. Crowds of 2,000 engulf the area carrying banners reading such things as "Sabotage is Super" and "Independence Day for Whom?"

MELBOURNE, 1972

During the July National Mobilisation Against Conscription protesters incur the wrath of the RSL by laying a wreath at the Shrine of Remembrance reading, "To the unwilling, led by the unqualified, to do the unnecessary. In memory of all those sacrificed in Vietnam."

MELBOURNE, 1972

Bob Easton, a draft resister on the run from the police, makes a five-minute appearance at a Young Labour conference at Trades Hall before being spirited away by supporters. Having been underground for over a month he tells those assembled that, "People are refusing to comply with [National Service] in greater numbers, but today only about 8% of them are being prosecuted. This shows that the Government is not serious in enforcing the Act. The Government can be made to look ridiculous by mass non-compliance."

AUSTRALIA, 1972

Liberal PM Billy McMahon is haunted by hecklers wherever he goes during the 1972 Federal Election. Signs are erected saying "Hello Wingnut" and he is also greeted with calls of "Hello Big Ears". On other occasions he and his wife are set upon by angry anti-war demonstrators, although action by the police generally prevents things from getting too out of hand. Under such pressure McMahon's usual gaffe-ridden speeches become even more absurd with him promising "increasing opportunities for unemployment in the New Year" and to "honour all our promises on the problems we have made." The coup de grâce comes when he asks voters "to study our record and vote Labor".

SYDNEY, 1972

Gay candidate David Widdup runs against Prime Minister Billy McMahon on a platform of gay reform. Capitalising on rumours about McMahon's sexuality he campaigns as the "only openly gay candidate" in the area under the slogan, "I've got my eye on Billy's seat."

MELBOURNE, 1972

"All Space To The Spaced" and 'We Demand Everything" are painted on the walls of suburban schools.

AUSTRALIA, 1972

Despite waning street protests, due to the election of the ALP and the ending of conscription, anti-war trade unions rapidly respond to the escalation of US bombing against North Vietnam. The Victorian Branch of the Seamen's Union refuses to service any US vessel hoping to dock in Melbourne and is soon joined by the State branches of the Waterside Workers Federation, Shipwrights and Ship Construction Union and the Ship Painters and Dockers Union. The Miscellaneous Workers Union also chips in by refusing to guard American ships, while other unions call on the ACTU to place bans on postal and financial dealings with the US. The ACTU has no such plans, however, with its President "Fireman" Bob Hawke, famed for his ability to "hose down" disputes, negotiating an end to the bans after the US right-wing AFL-CIO labour federation bans all Australian ships from the Atlantic Coast.

MELBOURNE, 1972

1,000 anti-war demonstrators take part in New Year festivities by burning a ten-foot effigy of US President Nixon before going on to block traffic and throw crackers and rocks at the Pan Am building.

BRISBANE, 1972

Bowen Hills residents defy the state government's compulsory purchase of their homes for the construction of a freeway by engaging in occupations and eviction resistance. Despite police brutality and the use of scab labour to demolish homes the campaign was eventually successful and the freeway scrapped.

ARMIDALE, 1973

Following a spate of attempted suicides, students at the University of New England hold a march demanding an end to the practice of basing student marks entirely on examinations. Dubbing their protest the Peasants Revolt, 300 radical students, led by bagpipers and carrying pitchforks and banners reading, "We've Had Enough," "Examine The Examiners," and more ludicrously, "Smash Kill Destroy," march through the University picking up supporters before heading to the administration offices.

Upon their arrival they find the building locked up, but four students scramble inside through hastily smashed windows only to be thumped by campus security. Witnessing the agro, those outside burst through the front door to evict the security guards and occupy the building. When the police are brought in to throw them out, the occupiers tape all of the Administration's art treasures against the windows and doors, forcing the authorities to allow them to stay until the following night. During the occupation 700 blank, pre-signed university degrees are also liberated.

In the days following the occupation the anti-examination campaign continues, with one attempt to put the exam hall out of action failing after glued-up locks are removed by tradespeople. A second attempt proves more successful when students toss butyric acid, a harmless but extremely smelly compound, around the hall.

150 Classical Marxism students take a different tack by pulling their chairs into a circle to collaborate on their papers. When a supervisor attempts to intervene he is told he is disrupting the exam and ordered to leave the hall. The police are then called in, but after the students refuse to budge the Dean of Arts and the Vice-Chancellor accede to their demands, agreeing to let them sit their examination at home in their own time. This in turn inspires those in other courses to demand similar reforms.

With their right to dictate to the student body increasingly challenged, the administration strikes back by taking out injunctions under the Summary Offences Act to ban five students from entering the University grounds. This strategy backfires however, as the injunctions must be served in person. After Sue Gray is served with her injunction she tips off the other four, who go underground, leading the police on a merry chase around the district. Despite raids on various homes the four hide out with friends and sympathetic lecturers while making surprise appearances around the University grounds. In the face of a general student revolt as well as work bans imposed by the Builders Labourers Federation (BLF) and questions from Civil Liberties groups and the Federal Attorney-General, the administration admits defeat after only two days, with the five returning to campus for a victory celebration complete with local rock bands.

WOLLONGONG, 1973

Local women, angry at the fact that a subsidiary of BHP is refusing to hire females while complaining of difficulties in finding staff, chain themselves to the fence of Australian Iron and Steel's office. Following the company's refusal of a site tour the women get together a few weeks later with the Federated Ironworkers' Association to disguise themselves as male union officials. Wearing overalls and blackening their chins with greasepaint, the women make an unofficial tour of factory sites, scattering feminist literature in their wake.

SYDNEY, 1973

During a strike seeking the 35-hour week, power workers in the grassroots Electricity Commission Combined Union Delegates Organisation (ECCUDO) elect two members to ensure that enough power is generated to avoid mass lay-offs in other industries. When the Liberal government tries to isolate the strikers by cutting power to factories, ECCUDO places advertisements in daily newspapers instructing workers in how to turn the electricity back on. With their own deeds exposed as the root of the problem, the Liberals hurriedly lift power restrictions in response.

MELBOURNE, 1973

"The forest precedes man, the desert follows," is sprayed on inner-city walls.

SYDNEY, 1973

A Telecom maintenance worker notices that one cable too many is running into the Communist Party of Australia's offices. Deciding to take full advantage of the situation, a CPA official invites ABC TV's *Four Corners* and other members of the media to attend a ceremonial cutting of the wire. This is followed by a trip to the other end of the wire, an ASIO listening post hastily vacated some hours before.

NORTH WEST CAPE, 1973

A Maoist "Long March" to Western Australia's remote US military base also features a "Quick March" for lazy and/or busy lefties.

SYDNEY, 1973

Members of Gay Liberation hold a series of "zap" actions throughout the city handing out "Are You A Poofta?" leaflets and engaging in defiant displays of same-sex affection. They then go on to set up a stall selling "homosexual" brains (originally belonging to sheep) outside the practice of the notorious Harry Bailey, a psychiatrist who specialises in electro-shock operations designed to "straighten out" gays and lesbians. Bailey, whose use of deep sleep and other therapies at the Chelmsford Private Clinic sees 26 patients die under his care, later receives a serving of brains mashed into his shagpile carpet.

MELBOURNE, 1973

Having already defeated school regulations governing hair length and uniforms via a campaign of concerted noncompliance, 400 out of 900 students at Upwey High School go on strike in support of teacher stoppages over staffing cuts. When the teachers finish their industrial action around 150 students elect to stay out, marching down to the Ferntree Gully National Park to hold a day-long festival. The next day most students return to school, but a number decide to drop out altogether by forming a commune in Auburn.

ARMIDALE, 1973

Lacking any formal grievance procedures for dealing with sexual harassment and rape, female students at the University of New England take matters into their own hands by locking one offending staff member in a cupboard at the Mary White College before expelling him from the university.

SYDNEY, 1973

The traditional, male-dominated May Day march goes off in a big way when women's liberationists and their supporters crash the boys' parade. Angry at the "May Queen" beauty contest, feminists leaflet the crowd and demand to be allowed to speak from the all-male platform. Scuffles break out on stage as women wrestle with union hacks for use of the microphone. The police stand by mystified, unable to decide whether they should be bashing reds or women's libbers. Faced with a large crowd, the official organisers relinquish control of the stage only to attempt to drown out proceedings through the use of loudspeakers attached to a nearby truck. Eventually, however, they are forced to acknowledge that the new generation has the numbers and instead stoop to heckling rank-and-file female and Aboriginal unionists with cries of, "You've never done a day's work in your life, bitches!"

MELBOURNE, 1973

After they put up posters near the home of a Melbourne spy, three members of the Committee for the Abolition of Political Police (CAPP) are arrested for publicising the names and addresses of ASIO staff. Two of them are fined $200 each for "harassment", yet the named agent remains free to continue his creepy stalking of activists.

SYDNEY, 1973

Graffiti seen around Sydney include slogans such as, "Keep The War Going — It's The Only One We've Got!," "If You Keep Shitting On The World, The World Is Going To Reply—Forcefully," "I Hate Crowds — Use the Pill," and "God Loves You — He Just Doesn't Want to Get Involved."

ADELAIDE, 1973

200 secondary students strike and march down Rundle Mall to the Education Department where school ties are burnt in a protest against mandatory uniforms.

MELBOURNE, 1973

In an attempt to clog up the courts and expose the hypocrisy of Victoria's "Don't Ask, Don't Tell" abortion laws, women between the ages of 18 and 72 arrive at Russell Street Police Station to turn themselves in for having undergone the procedure. While the police follow a few cases up, the law's bluff is called and no one suffers prosecution.

ADELAIDE, 1973

Inspired by the success of the Draft Resisters Union in defying military conscription, a bunch of South Australian druggies form the Dope Smokers Union (DSU). Offering to help arrested smokers go "underground" in order to avoid prison, the group also distributes legal information, growing guides and joints to anyone who wishes to try out marijuana for the first time. Of particular consternation to the Adelaide Drug Squad, the Union also specialises in tracking down and publishing the details of undercover police and their vehicles. In 1974 the organisation ups the ante even further by starting their own marijuana mail order service in an attempt to slow the dominance of organised crime and protect smokers' consumer rights. After both the union and its customers are busted the DSU forms the Apolitical Party to contest state elections.

MELBOURNE, 1973

Police shut down a march through the city by environmentalists, taking into custody a 275 metre long "crocodile" made out of non-refundable drink cans.

PERTH, 1973

At the Perth Parliament buildings a mixture of Condy's Crystals and soap powder turn the fountains into a pink foam machine. Strong winds soon have the suds spilling onto the freeway. The Pink Panther Action Force later claim responsibility on behalf of the plebeians of Perth, who have to endure politicians windbagging on about nowt of interest to anyone but themselves.

MELBOURNE, 1973

The Victorian branch of the CPA lays a trap for ASIO break-and-enter men by coating doorknobs at their headquarters with a special chemical and leaving an envelope marked "Confidential" on a desk in full view. A sophisticated voice-operated microphone is also set up. The next day a break-in is revealed when a second chemical activates the first indicating that someone had gone through the party's filing cabinets and desks. The tape further reveals that a safe-cracking operation has taken place and that sensitive files have been tampered with. This information is released to the public, but is largely ignored by the mainstream media.

SYDNEY, 1973

450 pro-choice protesters are prevented by police from laying wreaths, in remembrance of all those who have died through backyard abortions, at the Cenotaph on Mother's Day.

MELBOURNE, 1973

In response to a suspected speedup at the AMI car plant, migrant workers impose their own work rate, and upon completing 50 cars, knock off for the day. When the foremen attempt to force them back to work they are met with a unified, "No speak English." Spanish workers also begin instructing their colleagues in the art of sabotage by teaching them how to weld pieces upside down so that the job is slowed during product checking.

SYDNEY, 1973

The owners of the Clifton Hotel in Redfern agree to begin serving Aboriginal patrons after unions threaten to cut off their supplies.

MELBOURNE, 1973

Hundreds of pro-choice protesters force anti-abortionists to call off a planned rally in the City Square by arriving there first and refusing to leave.

ADELAIDE, 1973

The Happy Birthday Party contests the State Election by running a Mr Susie Creamcheese for the seat of Unley. The candidate outlines his party's goal as being, "To fundamentally assert the existence of a reality different to that propagated by both political parties in South Australia whose entire activities are based on their allegiance to the WASP-progress-work ethic ... we assert the possibility of a people-centred society based on a sense of life celebration, playful eroticism and levity."

MELBOURNE, 1973

"Justice Is Just Arse" is painted on the walls of the Carlton Court House.

ARMIDALE, 1973

Student environmentalists cut down every billboard on the highway between Armidale and Glen Innes in a protest against consumerism and visual pollution.

SYDNEY, 1974

Following their beating of a Glebe rapist, the Feminist Action Front release a statement promising to "terrorise men as men have terrorised women for centuries". They also spray "Rape Will Be Revenged" on walls around the inner city.

MELBOURNE, 1974

During an inner-city drug raid one Detective Sergeant "Ding Dong" Bell leaves behind his notebook. Within days pages appear in the radical paper *The Digger* exposing Bell's systematic harassment of an activist who had earlier revealed the policeman's practice of carrying around blank warrants to justify snap raids on hippy households. How was the activist able to prove this? Because "Ding Dong" had left a pile of said warrants behind during a previous raid. Unsurprisingly Bell's stay on the Drug Squad is not an extended one.

WYONG, 1974

Hearing that rain is forecast, the employer at a shopping centre under construction cancels weekend work ahead of schedule rather than pay his employees for missing a day's work. Turning the tables on him, members of the BLF call the Bureau of Meteorology themselves and walk off site the following Monday, claiming "wet money" for that day instead. When the boss refuses to pay up and sacks an injured employee to boot, the workers decide to occupy the site, shutting down all work in progress. Before long 167 employees have been sacked and the police move in to roughly evict the occupiers.

Unfortunately for the owner, seven wily workers are able to evade the long arm of the law by scrambling up a crane and hanging on for grim death. Despite the police refusing to allow supplies in, some of the occupiers' mates are able to stage a diversion while the rest toss bags of food up to the crane. Two days later another attempt to break the siege occurs with meat pies and a roast chicken making it through. Finally after four days of occupation both the police and owner back down, ceding the site once more to the workers and their local supporters.

MELBOURNE, 1974

A Miss Teenage beauty contest attended by the Victorian Governor Sir Rohan Delacombe is disrupted by feminist demonstrators chanting, "This degrades women." Despite being quickly removed by police the women's cries temporarily drown out the official TV coverage of the ceremony.

ADELAIDE, 1974

Inspired by tales of post-war squatting and the founding of a similar project in Sydney named Elsie, members of South Australia's women's liberation movement set up one of Adelaide's first women's shelters in a squatted house in Brompton that had been earmarked for road building.

SYDNEY, 1974

During a Right to Work demonstration a group demanding the Right Not to Work intrude, complete with banner, chanting anti-work slogans and distributing a leaflet attacking the worship of wage-slavery as the solution to survival on the dole.

MELBOURNE, 1974

Students at Monash University occupy their administration building for over a week demanding an end to the existing examination procedures and calling for student control over course content.

SYDNEY, 1974

NSW BLF members and anti-development activists quietly infiltrate a swanky dinner party held by Frank Theeman. Theeman, who is widely believed to be involved in the kidnapping, bashing and killing of those opposed to his Victoria Street development, ejects the gatecrashers after they quietly distribute small cards reading, "Under concrete and glass, Sydney's disappearing fast" and, "The person next to you may be a demonstrator."

MELBOURNE, 1974

Angry students, parents and teachers across Melbourne take action against Education Department plans to further increase class numbers by removing portable rooms. At Watsonia High locals blockade entrances to the school by parking cars across them. When contractors cut holes in fences and try to get the portables out people prevent them by lying down in front of trucks. At Eltham High students barricade the front gate to the school, weld up bolts to hold gates together, entangle fences in barbed wire and flood the surrounding area to bog trucks down. In Kew students stage a sit-in and refuse to exit portables until the department agrees to leave them in place.

GEELONG, 1974

300 students protest over the destruction of local habitat to make way for a staff carpark by replacing a number of the trees already removed.

MELBOURNE, 1974

The entire population of Brunswick Girls' High School marches out off campus, down Sydney Road and into the city to demand an end to chronic overcrowding.

SYDNEY, 1974

When the Masters Builders' Association and the Federal Secretary of the Builders' Labourers Federation (BLF) Norm Gallagher move in to destroy the radical NSW branch of the union a number of members resist, as recalled by Russ Hermann:[15]

Gallagher's main tactic was to set up a Federal Branch and with the help of the Master Builders Association [he] started issuing Federal tickets. The first job to sack workers who refused to join the Federal Union was the E.A. Watts job at the NSW Institute of Technology (now UTS) building site on Broadway. The State Industrial Commission had ruled that they be reinstated, but when the men again refused, they were dismissed. This happened on October 18.

Naturally the officials and the rank and file were a little upset. A meeting was called, in fact there were meetings every afternoon in the office and it was decided that we would occupy the crane the next evening.

We arrived at the next afternoon's meeting, expecting that volunteers would be chosen and that it would all happen. Instead, the officials and a couple of [Communist] party members all argued against it. There was a lot of discussion in the pub that night and four people, including one party member said that they were still going to occupy the cranes. I was asked to go as well, but said that I was reluctant because I was in a new relationship and didn't feel like sitting up in a crane for a few days, but if they were desperate, I would. At 2am there was a knock on my door. One of the four had disappeared. So off we went.

We had no trouble finding a staircase, but it only went up two flights. We then searched for a while and after crawling through scaffolding found it. Then up about 20 flights of stairs. We arrived on the roof and assessed the situation. One crane, the one nearest Broadway, was on the concrete slab and only needed a short ladder to climb aboard. The other one was on a steel tower. Brian and I climbed the tower. A small problem. There was a padlock on the trapdoor on the floor of the crane. Brian suggested we climb out under the bottom of the crane, up the sides and then onto the crane platform. I looked down, it was about a 200-foot

drop, and said no way.

I went onto the roof and found a hammer and chisel and proceeded to attack the padlock. By this time it was daylight and we could hear the scabs arriving on the job. I was frantically hitting the lock, sometimes my hand, and finally broke the lock as they were arriving on the concrete slab. Then we were the lucky ones. A 30-gallon drum on top of the trapdoor and there was no way they could get in.

The other two were only about 10 feet above the concrete, but they were courageous. They stood with crowbars over their shoulders and didn't say a word, they just looked. After a while, the workers gave up and went back down the stairs. We had done it. But it wasn't a great victory. We didn't have any crane drivers to get supplies or change shifts. But we did have a flagon.

Joe Owens [BLF state secretary] was furious. He came up onto the concrete slab and talked to us. We didn't think we'd quite made our point. We told him that we'd come down when we'd finished the flagon. So about lunchtime we came down and Joe led us away without any recriminations from the workers on the job or the police.

Brian and I went back to our job on the Monday. The foreman was furious because we hadn't told him. But he and the owners respected Brian and didn't want any action from the union ...

A couple of weeks later at the daily afternoon meeting the President, Bob Pringle, said that they wanted me to go up the crane again. I said I'd already been up once. Bob answered that they needed someone who knew the way up. Reluctantly I said OK. So on the very early morning of the 6th November, we went up again. This time we had crane drivers, dogmen, labourers and a pair of bolt-cutters. There were four on the Broadway crane and three on the tower crane.

We were much better prepared. We had sleeping bags, a gas stove and a means of getting supplies. The press loved it. TV interviews, the front page of the *Herald*, and heaps of union members showing support. And the view was fantastic.

We had a lot of fun playing games with the cops. To get supplies the dogman would go down in the box and hover just above their outstretched hands. I would be standing on the platform next to where the crane driver was sitting, giving him directions. He would slowly swing the box around with the cops chasing it. Then at a signal from below, he would swiftly swing the box to where the people with our supplies were. They would quickly load the box and it was up and away before the cops could get to it. This was always the highlight of the day as we would then check to see what goodies they had given us.

We now had a sheet of masonite to sleep on and we were getting very comfy, even to the point of getting upset if our supporters woke us up too early. On the second day we were surprised to see Deano, one of our city organisers, suddenly arrive in the Broadway crane box. Although the union executive were a little annoyed, as was the other city organiser, we were very pleased to have him up there. He would come over to visit us and we'd have lots of argument, discussions, etc. He certainly brightened things up.

So things went on in a fairly regular way. By now we also had walkie talkies. This was useful in giving directions to our suppliers. They also caused me to make a fool of myself, for which I'm still reminded.

We'd just had the usual fun with the cops and my unit was still switched on, when I heard someone say that the helicopters were coming. I nearly shat myself. Was this training for the SAS? I sang out to the other crane. We decided that we would make it difficult. The crane drivers raised the jibs and we started to go round and round. This would make it hard to land. Then we saw them. We waited.

They flew straight overhead and on to Garden Island. What a relief. What an idiot.

After 4 days, it was my turn to come down. Maybe it was because of the helicopters. I wasn't game to ask. Anyway I'd had a great time and it was time to return to the mastic and my relationship.

The sit-in lasted 19 days. As well there were sit-ins at the Prouds job next to the Hilton Hotel and a Kell & Rigby job at Rose Bay.

Except for a couple of days off the crane having a much needed shower, the organiser stayed up there 'til the end. One of the cranes broke down and Hal Alexander went up to have a look.

Then on the 17th day, while the occupiers were asleep, one of the cranes caught fire. No one knows how it happened. Some of the people on that crane then moved to the other one. Two days later the cops came up onto the concrete slab. "You'd better come down," the cops said. "There's a milk crate full of Molotov cocktails on the deck and we can't guarantee your safety."

So they came down. It had been a marvellous effort. We held out for another four months, but with the weight of the Master Builders behind Gallagher, we were in a no-win situation. Every new job started up with his Federal Tickets and that was it.

The final crane occupiers including the crane driver Bobby Chandler were all charged with trespass. The magistrate dropped charges on the organiser, because he could have fought it on the right of entry.

Veteran agitator Hal Alexander also recalls his part in fighting the destruction of the NSW Builders Labourers Federation.[16]

I make it to university. Sort of.

The Poet Lorikeet calls them the Green Ban Fusiliers. The Builders Labourers Federation.

A healthy rambunctious turmoil pervaded the industry. Like the Miners, Ironworkers, Maritime and other unions in earlier periods, the BLF had become the fighting vanguard of the working class. It had won improved conditions and pay rates through militant actions.

The Master Builders were savage ... Other bosses and many union officials were snarly because their own troops were talking darkly that the BLs' way was the way to go. Like they used to about the Wharfies and other aforementioned.

In the meeting halls of power, where these things were discussed, some even spoke with certitude that we could blaze the way, show the world that here in Oz the unions were potential organs of revolutionary power and the vehicles of future proletarian emancipation. Such proclamations led to the usual fulminary esoterics and many trees were sacrificed.

However, justice where it's due. The NSW Builders Labourers Federation won many a victory, many hearts and minds, had songs and poems written in its honor and put new political concepts on the agenda. Above all, it fought for its members and their rights.

[Federal BLF leader] Stormin' Normie Gallagher had his own pan of fish to fry and moved in from the Federal Melbourne office to take over the NSW branch. The fur flew and splits appeared. In the [Communist] Party and the Union leadership arguments were heated and unresolved. The rank and file (or some of them)

opted for job site occupation.

The University of Technology was a skeletal frame of steel and concrete of 30 stories. The big crane on the Broadway southern side was occupied by a group of union members. The site was enclosed by a five-metre high wooden fence. The back Haymarket stretch had a three-metre cyclone wire counterpart.

Hindsight does not allow a telling of the names of the aerial campers or who supplied them, relieved them or otherwise helped. Likewise of the two union officials who came to Glassop Street to proposition me, but this is the story.

Somehow (someone?) the starter wiring on the back crane was tied in with the building and as it rose it had suffered a circulation seizure. Would I go up next day and try and fix it? They made it sound like the world revolution could depend on it. This bunny said yes but with the odd presentiment that it might be like poking one's prick into a cage of hungry ferrets.

5am. on Broadway, at about opposite to where the main entrance is now, about a dozen BLs and some others like Pat [Fiske] taking piccies had gathered. A whistle up and they've barricaded the road a hundred yards either side. Cars queue as a rope snakes down over the hoarding and the blokes heave on it to swing the box over the high wooden fence onto the road. When it thumps down I climb aboard with the doggie. We lift, another heave, the box clears the woodwork and shoots straight up to the top of the structure where I'm deposited.

Great view. Stretching to all horizons.

Sydney. Home of all my homes.

I look down. I shouldn't have.

Vertiginous (ver. tij' a. nas) - adj - giddy, dizzy, causing giddiness, whirling, revolving.–Websters.

Yes. All of that. When the fundamental orifice and other organs had resumed their more or less normal functions, I looked over to my comrades in their crane cabin a long way away. They toasted me with a couple of tinnies. Very helpful.

Hoisting the toolbox ahead I wound the cable over my shoulder and edged across the narrow girder to the crane motor. Sussed out there was no way to reach the burnout without crawling under the motor sump. Nice. There was a tray of sticky oil, black and congealed, under it. I dice the tee shirt and thongs.

They reckon that Cleopatra bathed in oil. She didn't have to rewire a huge metal diesel object at the same time. I did and did it.

Back under and out, looking like ready to sing Mammie, I hoy the lads across the way. They wave back, someone presses a starter control and the beast roars into life. Cheers all round. They shut it down and give me the old clenched fist.

Then I yell, "How do I get down?"

The big bearded one leant out of his cabin and replied, "Walk." The erstwhile dogman joined him at the window. "Yer an angel, brother, maybe you can fly." So can pigs.

The bastards never told me about this.

So down the raw concrete narrow stairway or by ladder where it stopped. The bastards never told me about this. Thirty floors.

Down on the paddock. Sudden realisation that there is no way out to Broadway. The solid timber wall stared back.

And I looked and felt like a furry Exxon oil spill victim.

Or a cormorant in the Gulf War. Bloody undignified.

The bastards.

So I head for the cyclone fence backing onto Thomas Street and stop. Outside the only gate are a bunch of blokes. Two seemed to have some sort of security insignia on their shirts. No seeming about the holsters at their hip or the contents. Two others were, to my scrambled senses, Big Norm's boys from Melbourne. They were likely enough looking customers that way. And where were my back up buddies? Where indeed?

What was that about getting a steady job and sticking to it?

I head for the part of the cyclone fence furthest from the hoons, running. As I hoist the toolbox over the top, there's a yell. Something like, "Who are you and where the fuck did you come from?"

Stealing a fraction of time I yell back, "Been fixing that sump," then hit the top strand on the fly, land in a sprawl on the other side. This was no time for pleasant exchanges of political opinion or any other kind for that matter and I headed for the markets and Chinatown.

From where would you go in Chinatown in just a pair of footie shorts, carrying a tin toolbox, with no money, having the hard boys on your hammer and everyone staring, partly because you have a wild staring look yourself and partly because you're covered in black shit and the wildness is because the bastards never told you about this?

Deadset right. The Trades Hall to find my procurers of the night before.

Into the Labourers' office first looking for sympathy and that ratbag place can't stop laughing. I enquire as to where my two benefactors might be found. Just a little job they said.

I'm ushered around the corner and along the corridor. (A giveaway if you know anything of the weird geography of the warren that was this history soaked, grey edifice. And of a sheltered-world-within-itself to an often grog-soaked troupe of numbers men of left and right who haunt its corridors and crannies. Even the best meaning had to learn to count and, for a few, drink. You could write a hundred books about a thousand characters of a colour and life who schemed, wheedled, raged, fought and laughed within its walls. And of the staff, mostly women, who ran the union offices and without whose efforts and devotion most organisations could not have survived.)

Anyway. Escorted by one of these unsung still smiling ladies, we arrive to confront the perpetrators of stares and laughter. After they had stopped staring and laughing they said they'd run me home. So down and out into Sussex Street.

From there into the Union Secretary's new Kingswood. "Fuck him," they said, not so carefully lining the seat with the *Sydney Morning Herald*. Back to Balmain, a full body detergent and hose down. Oh, Cleopatra!

You'd think enough was enough! St Jude you have deserted me. Working next day at the Royal Prince Alfred hospital there's a phone call.

"Jim Staples here. Can you come down to my office right away?"

Jim Staples? Hadn't seen Jim Staples since we expelled him [from the Communist Party of Australia], late '50s or so for being rude and out of order. What could he want?

What's that? Some problem about yesterday? Serious?

So I told the boss I was clocking off sick — again. "Like yesterday," he said. "Yair, only worse", I told him.

Cut short, the thing was (as related by my "two best mates" and Jim) the contractors' inspectors had examined the crane and there was either sugar or water or piss or something in the hydraulics that ensured its continued immobility, that that little number would cost a horrible big

bundle of big ones to repair and that noises about industrial sabotage were made and possible proceedings under the Crimes Act mooted.

Not all that much really except that we could all be in deep shit. Especially me.

They were all sweetness and light. Jim didn't appear to be wearing any grudges and said they would fix it up somehow.

The important thing was to keep me out of it. They just thought I ought to know.

Ought to know?

That was the trouble.
THE BASTARDS NEVER TOLD ME!

CANBERRA, 1975

A ten-metre blow-up whale floated on Lake Burley Griffin by FoE during a meeting of the International Whaling Commission is ironically lifted by the wind to land smack in the middle of a freeway that the green organisation is also campaigning to stop. When the "whale" makes a comeback the following day, appearing outside the pro-whaling Japanese delegation's hotel rooms, it is hacked to pieces by hotel staff before being given a funeral procession through the city's Civic Centre.

SYDNEY, 1975

Angry at a lack of facilities for children, Redfern locals take matters into their own hands. Designating February 22nd "Takeover Day", residents begin gathering together materials donated by local merchants or appropriated from the Public Transport Commission. On the day, homes adjacent to Douglas Street are leafleted and, thanks to a huge turnout, a vacant lot left unused by the Rachel Forster Hospital for 40 years is quickly transformed into a "People's Park" replete with swings and other play equipment. Faced with such community solidarity the Hospital backs down within a few weeks, allowing the playground to remain.

ADELAIDE, 1975

Peter Arend is jailed for contempt of court when he refuses to accept the sack from the Chrysler motor company. Despite being re-trenched, alongside 150 other car workers, he continues to report to the Tonsley Park Plant for 20 days. An attempt by Chrysler

Top left: Leaflet, Sydney, 1976. Artist unknown. **Bottom left:** Queer Badges, 1970s-80s. Courtesy Australian Gay and Lesbian Archives **Right:** Stop sign street sculpture found in Thornbury, Melbourne 1977. Photographer unknown.

IN THE INTEREST OF ......

PUBLIC
SAFETY

WE RECOMMEND THAT
THE FIREARM
DISPLAYED ON
THIS LEAFLET
BE ADOPTED AS THE
OFFICIAL SIDEARM OF.

ALL ....

c o p s

(police, military, judiciary, trade and student leaders, politicians,
social workers, editors, managers, executives, shop detectives, professors, teachers,
ologists, & ismists, e.g. psychologists, psychiatrists, pop stars, TV stars, movie
stars, leftists, rightists, anarchists, nihilists, moderates, liberals, priests,
nuns (non-exhaustive ...

WE BELIEVE

that
this uniquely designed weapon will act as a deterrent to a police state....if adopted by the above.

that
this weapon will solve the problem of the above who force their own frustrations with the misery of their lives on others in the forms of brute force, authoritarism and greed.

that
this weapon, if adopted by the above, will bring an end to the reign of terror currently being engineered against those of us who don't want to be cops.

F19 ANTI-FREEWAY BLOCKADE
MELBOURNE, 1977-78

In 1977 the Victorian State Government announced its plan to demolish a number of residential homes in Melbourne's inner north in order to make way for the construction of the F19 freeway. A coalition of older residents, political activists and hippies from the Carlton area came together with the local council to resist the resulting wave of compulsory evictions. Over a period of months, the anti-Freeway campaign saw Alexandra Parade transformed into parkland before brick walls and barricades built out of cars and scrap material were erected to slow the pace of construction. Although the blockade was eventually broken and the freeway completed, the protests achieved victories further afield with proposed road projects cancelled and planning processes reviewed.

Photographs courtesy of Friends of the Earth, Melbourne, and *Barricade!: The Resident Fight Against the F19 Freeway.*

to send him home via a court injunction merely spreads the dispute as unionists still working at the plant vote to back his stand. Despite moves by the leadership of the Vehicle Builders Union to simmer things down, 200 press-shop workers defy their orders and strike the day after Arend is locked up by police.

MELBOURNE, 1975

Members of Women's Liberation, demanding investment in public housing, squat two Housing Commission flats in Fitzroy which have been left empty for more than two years.

CANBERRA, 1975

Incensed with the sexist portrayal of a women's conference, 300 attendees march on the offices of *The Canberra Times*. Forcing their way in they occupy most of the building while the offending editorialist hides in a cupboard. Another employee promises the women the right to reply, but later reneges on his promise with the lame excuse that, "I can't publish material that is critical of the media." Incensed the women reoccupy the newspaper's offices, but are prevented by police from disrupting the distribution of the next morning's edition.

ARMIDALE, 1975

Responding to a violent attack on a celebration held at the University of New England by students and members of the local Vietnamese community to mark the ending of the Vietnam War, members of the Socialist Action Movement (SAM) set up their own karate squad. When right-wing students next show up to attack a demonstration held in the wake of the sacking of the ALP Government, they turn tail and run after being confronted by both the karate kids and 1,200 anti-Liberal protesters.

AUSTRALIA, 1975

Following the constitutional coup of November 11, in which Governor-General John Kerr removes the Whitlam Government to hand power to the conservative Liberal Opposition, protest action is swift. Within hours of the news being broadcast, 3,000 people march in Sydney with 10,000 also coming out in Melbourne and 2,000 in Canberra and Adelaide. The following day 400,000 join a half-day strike in Melbourne while 15,000 march in Brisbane and 10,000 rally in Adelaide. In the week that follows, huge rallies are held in all of the capital cities and many regional centres, but fearing the consequences of such mass action the Australian Labor Party (ALP) and the Australian Council of Trade Unions (ACTU) move quickly to cancel any further action in the streets in favour of focusing on the ballot box. Having well and truly lost the initiative and given the Liberal Party and the enemies of the ALP's progressive policies plenty of time to continue their attacks in the media it is unsurprising that Whitlam leads his party to catastrophic defeat in the subsequent election.

Protests and actions continue for a few more years, however, as Whitlam calls for opponents to the Liberal coup to "maintain their rage"; a number maintain it far longer than he intended (i.e. till the next election), making the politicisation of the Governor-General a continuing problem for both Kerr and the new PM Malcolm Fraser. In a typical protest held during the year following the Dismissal, police attempt to keep anti-Kerr protesters away from the G-G during a visit to the Canberra School of Music by erecting steel barricades. One protester unlucky enough to get on the wrong side of the fence is thrown head-first into the crowd, but despite the heavy police presence Kerr's Rolls-Royce is still egged. Having made it into the concert relatively unscathed, the G-G is given an unwelcome reception with half the crowd booing him and refusing to stand upon his entrance.

MELBOURNE, 1975

Over 300 cyclists pedal from Melbourne to Sydney to protest against the Federal Government's pro-uranium policies. During the build-up to the marathon former Olympic champion Nino Borsari lends a hand with coaching.

MELBOURNE, 1975

Friends of the Earth (FoE) members stage a sit-in in the Melbourne Airport's toilets to draw attention to the Fraser Government's decision to allow supersonic flights to Australia ahead of the finalising of an Environmental Impact Statement.

SYDNEY, 1976

At a large Movement Against Uranium Mining rally, 1,000 free tickets to a Bob Dylan concert are distributed. After realising that many people have gotten in for free the concert managers offer a cash reward for information leading to the capture of those responsible. Nobody is dobbed in, but the culprits later appear on Sydney radio station 2JJ to explain why and how they'd pulled off the action.

MELBOURNE, 1976

When the *USS Truxtun* arrives in Australia, the warship is "greeted" by thousands of maritime workers who walk off the job in Port Melbourne to support a strike and bans on all US military visits. The ship is forced to berth under its own power as union-staffed tugboats refuse to assist, and the Americans are further hampered by a mini-flotilla of protest boats. Having finally docked, the crew is met by a demonstration of over 1,000 peace protesters, with the result that the ship is eventually placed under the guard of 100 Victorian police.

CANBERRA, 1976

Over 1,000 protest at the official opening of Federal Parliament with the Governor-General John Kerr being greeted with boos and jeers of "Dictator," and "Why don't you resign?"

SYDNEY, 1976

ABC TV in Sydney is blacked out for half an hour in response to a decision by the new Chairman of the ABC, Sir Henry Bland, to cancel the production of the comedy show *Alvin Purple* following complaints from moral crusaders the Festival Of Light. Bland had already incurred the wrath of his staff for previously censoring a *Today Tonight* segment dealing with atrocities in Vietnam and for banning Radio 2JJ from announcing forthcoming demonstrations.

WOLLONGONG, 1976

Wharfies at Port Kembla place a seven-day

black ban on cargo heading for Indonesia, demanding that union-sponsored relief ships be allowed to land in occupied East Timor.

SYDNEY, 1976

During a visit to the Royal Motor Yacht Club, Governor-General Kerr is met by a demonstration of 300, including a group of 80 early birds who had arrived before the starting point to secure themselves a prime heckling spot.

MELBOURNE, 1976

A visit by Governor-General Kerr sees streets leading into Richmond blocked off as police attempt to remove protesters carrying photos of Norman Gunston (their preferred candidate for Governor-General) and banners reading "Sack Kerr" and "P.O.Q. G.G." Closer to the destination, cars entering the event are attacked and their windows smashed. Upon Kerr's arrival things get really heavy when protesters throw a smoke bomb in front of his Rolls-Royce. While his driver is caught up in trying to make his way through the smoke, other protesters run in, pelting the car with rocks, eggs and ink bombs. Attempts to drag Sir John from the car are defeated by police who are in turn 'Sieg Heiled' by the crowd.

SYDNEY, 1976

Musicians performing the opera *Lakmé*, starring Joan Sutherland, read out a statement and hold up the start of their performance for over 40 minutes as part of a protest against the retrenchment of orchestra members in Melbourne and Sydney.

BRISBANE, 1976

Having had his unemployment benefits cut while he was in Adelaide seeking work, unemployed bio-chemist Lew Blazenvich begins a hunger strike in the City Square, calling for an inquiry into the administration of the Department of Social Security.

SYDNEY, 1976

Anarchists bearing a banner reading "An Island Of Hope In A Sea Of Despair" conduct a march on May 1st to commemorate May Day rather than waiting, like the rest of the Left, for the closest convenient weekend. Marchers

wearing bizarre garb (bearded men in dresses, etc) address passing crowds while halting traffic in the city's main streets.

AUSTRALIA, 1976

Rail workers hold a 24-hour stoppage demanding the reinstatement of a shunting supervisor in Townsville after he is suspended for refusing to handle supplies destined for the Mary Kathleen Uranium Mine. Although the ACTU's national bans are under attack, and later defeated, by conservatives from the Australian Workers' Union (AWU), the supervisor's actions are in line with Australian Railways Union policy of calling on its members to refuse to "handle goods which contribute to the mining or processing of uranium."

WESTERN AUSTRALIA, 1976

During a visit to WA, Governor-General Kerr is heckled at the Perth airport by 100 protesters before being spontaneously hassled by passers-by in the streets. An official dinner at the Parmelia Hotel is disrupted when 350 gather outside chanting, "Sack Kerr," forcing the G-G to sneak in through the rear entrance. Labor Senator Peter Walsh has his name and address taken by the police after he addresses the demonstration, and the crowd begins marching through the city to protest a police attempt to arrest other speakers.

Despite the presence of 200 police the Curse Kerr Committee confronts their target with cries of "Kerrupt" when he appears at the Catering Institute of Australia the following day. The G-G's woes continue when a visit to the Leslie Salt Company in Port Hedland sees maintenance workers close down the plant in disgust at his presence.

CANBERRA, 1976

A decision to introduce bus fares for school students sees 150 of them march on Parliament House, where a flustered Minister for the Capital Territory, Tony Staley, jokes that the impost will be good for the students' health as it will encourage them to walk more. A 13-year-old's retort that the same

could be said for the removal of Commonwealth cars for politicians and bureaucrats draws no reply.

SYDNEY, 1976

When Prime Minister Fraser attempts to open an exhibition at the Art Gallery of NSW he is heckled by members of Artists For Labor who hold up a banner reading, "Fraser-Kerr Vendetta."

MELBOURNE, 1976

Despite timing his visit to coincide with the term break, PM Malcolm Fraser is met by 2,000 people protesting budget cuts during a visit to Monash University. Upon his arrival he is forced to enter the Alexander Theatre through a side door and an attempt to deliver a speech is disrupted by noise. Eventually the protesters invade the stage, trapping the PM in an office until police reinforcements arrive to clear the area and whisk him away in an unmarked car.

BRISBANE, 1977

Activists get busy after Premier Joh Bjelke-Petersen announces, "The day of the political street march is over. Don't bother applying for a permit—you won't get one. That's government policy now." Despite the state already being the least democratic in Australia, thanks to a gerrymandered electoral system that allows the ruling National Party to govern with less than 30% of the vote, and activists being regularly under surveillance, raided and harassed, the protest ban nevertheless marks a new era in the criminalisation of dissent.

The revised rules are put to the test within days when 5,000 rally in support of Storeman and Packers' Union organiser Ted Zaphir, who has been charged with "threatening to cause a detriment" after refusing to supply a Toowoomba fuel agent during an industrial dispute. Over 800 police, including 180 reinforcements from the country, are drafted in to harass the protest, with Acting Police Commissioner MacDonald ordering them to "follow demonstrators anywhere to make arrests." When 400 students attempt to march from Queensland University to the city they are blocked by over 200 police and forced to make their way there individually. A similar march of 200 waterside workers, however, forces the police to back off allowing them to march through the city, albeit on the pavement.

SYDNEY, 1977

1,000 demonstrators occupy a wharf at Glebe Island in June, delaying the export of uranium ore for 90 minutes. A similar attempt a few months later to maintain an anti-uranium vigil at the Whale Bay container terminal sees 21 arrested and news crews attacked by police.

MELBOURNE, 1977

15,000 gather as part of 50,000 strong nationwide Hiroshima Day protests, holding a die-in and rallying under a banner reading, "Take A Stand Australia, Stop Uranium Mushrooming".

SYDNEY, 1977

Female students at Auburn High School stage a sit-down strike in the school playground over their Principal's refusal to allow them to wear pants in the winter.

BRISBANE, 1977

Queensland "Right To March" protesters catch the police flat-footed by jogging along footpaths in the city. By the time the members of Special Branch who are spying on them get a message through to police headquarters the protesters have already dispersed.

MELBOURNE, 1977

Acting before the State Government has the opportunity to remove their jurisdiction over the area the Fitzroy and Collingwood councils begin laying down three kilometres of kerbing alongside Alexandra Parade, filling in all but one of its lanes with soil to create gardens and parkland. This attempt to cut inner-city pollution by rendering the proposed Eastern Freeway ineffective leaves Transport Minister Joseph Rafferty stunned. However, despite a carnival in which thousands celebrate the opening of the new park, he quickly moves to reassert control and demolish it in favour of laying down more tarmac.

SYDNEY, 1977

A speech by visiting US academic Hans Eysenck, who claims to have proven that American whites are more intelligent than African-Americans, is disrupted by protesters blowing whistles and chanting, "Go Home Racist." Eysenck is hit in the face with a water balloon but splutters on before a smoke bomb brings proceedings to a close.

BRISBANE, 1978

Jessica Harrison recalls the pieing of right-wing Christian campaigner Mary Whitehouse:[17]

Whitehouse was the 1970s forerunner for much of the Christian fundamentalism that was to follow. She was based in Britain where she was the core of a right-wing 'family values' push. She and her followers would campaign for increased censorship of television, in the media, and generally against what was known then as the 'permissive society.' Behind her demure little old lady image, she was very much against abortion and any kind of rights for women.

She came to Brisbane as part of a national speaking tour. Given that the State of Queensland was incredibly conservative in the 1970s, she probably thought that she would be very popular there.

People forget now, but back in the late 1970s, there was a general ban on street marches and public protests in Queensland. Supposedly you could apply for a permit to protest, but the authorities would never give you one. Whenever people just went ahead and held a demonstration anyway, the police would come in and beat everyone up. They were extremely keen on stifling any form of public dissent. In fact, it was so repressive that one time when some friends and I were just zooming around having fun in the back of a flatbed truck, we were threatened with arrest for laughing too much!

We were always looking for ways around these laws. At one point, we formed a religious sect devoted to the Holy God of the Bankbook, which gave out weird and political tracts in shopping malls. On another occasion, we rode around on bikes with protest placards on our backs.

In this case, we were inspired by what we had read about [American Yippie activist] Aron Kay's spectacular pieing actions. It was meant to be a menstrual blood pie, though no one was willing

to donate at that time! So we had to use cochineal in an attempt to make it bright red, but the dye made it purple. Flavour-wise it was pretty soapy as we used what we regarded as the traditional recipe – shaving cream.

Once prepared, we all dressed up in our finest and entered as members of the public. One woman was actually a mother, but since she was quite small, she dressed up in a school uniform. Another of our members, a tall young guy, dressed in a suit to do the deed. I remember feeling very uncomfortable wearing a dress, but I was also excited. In some ways, we were pretty scared since there weren't many of us—luckily Whitehouse's supporters didn't get violent.

When Whitehouse made her appearance, our friend let fly with the pie. Sadly, it didn't hit her right in the face, but it went all over her chest. A number of male voices immediately rang out in incredulous outrage that we could do such a disrespectful thing. She was totally flabbergasted, yet managed to make the comment that at least the pie matched the colour of her dress. We all rushed to the front to support the pie thrower, but were hustled out quickly. A few people were arrested, but they were let off as often tends to happen in these situations. Basically, no one wanted to have to fly Whitehouse back from Britain to appear as a star witness.

It got into all the newspapers. I remember seeing a photo of Whitehouse with pie running down her dress just after it happened. We weren't really doing it for media coverage, however, we just wanted to make her feel unwelcome. I guess we succeeded.

TWEED HEADS, 1978

200 people from NSW attend a rally and begin a march to see how far a demonstration can make it into Queensland. At the state border the marchers are held up by 300 police warning that they will arrest anyone who crosses over under the state's anti-protest laws.

MELBOURNE, 1978

400 rally outside Festival Hall against the visit of "morals" campaigner Mary Whitehouse, with one group carrying a 60-foot banner reading, "Festival Of Light — Keep Your Filthy Morals Off Our Bodies."

ANTI-URANIUM BIKE RIDE,
CANBERRA, 1977

From 1975 to 1977 hundreds of cyclists rode across Australia to Canberra to protest against uranium mining. The journey in 1977 saw riders once more spread the anti-nuclear message along the way before engaging in an occupation of the Department of Natural Resources offices and setting up an Alternative Energy Festival campsite outside Federal Parliament. On their way into the city, the massed group were attacked by police after they held up traffic on the Commonwealth Avenue bridge in response to a car knocking over a rider.

Photographs courtesy of Friends of the Earth, Melbourne.

'70s POSTERS

CLOCKWISE from top left: Homosexuals Fight Back! c. 1978. Courtesy of Gay and Lesbian Archives Collection. • Stop Uranium Mining, Without Authority Poster Collective, 1978. • International Women's Day, Marie McMahon, Jan Fieldsen, Bridgit Bogart, 1979. Earthworks Poster Collective, The Tin Sheds Art Workshop, University of Sydney. Screenprint. Poster Courtesy of JURA Collection • Dole Bludger Picnic, Smudge Posters, Sydney. Poster Courtesy of JURA Collection • No God, No Master, Michael Callaghan, 1977. Earthworks Poster Collective, Sydney. Screenprint. • Land Rights Teach-in, Gary Robinson, 1979. Earthworks Poster Collective. Poster Courtesy of JURA Collection.

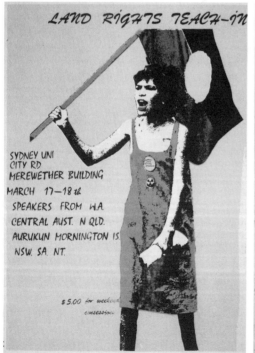

QUEENSLAND, 1978

When coal workers shut down every mine in Central Queensland as part of action against the Federal Government's plans to tax subsidised housing they also announce they will be holding street marches regardless of whether the State Government will grant them permits or not. With the protests set to involve virtually the whole population of remote towns such as Blackwater and Moranbah, the Bjelke-Petersen Government realises it will be unable to prevent the rallies and relents, handing over the necessary paperwork.

PERTH, 1978

A group of decorators paint the slogan "Soon To Be Picturesque Ruins" on Parliament House. Unknown to the ignorant artists, who were too lazy to read the newspapers, the work is carried out the night before the ceremonial opening of Parliament with the result that the police run to the newspapers with stories about "a serious bomb scare."

WOLLONGONG, 1978

Students lie down in front of bulldozers at Wollongong University to protest against the construction of a $30,000 duck pond at a time when the administration is threatening to close the Philosophy Department due to a lack of funds.

BRISBANE, 1978

Anti-uranium activists disrupt the shipping of uranium for export via the Brisbane docks by occupying a railway supply line. They follow this up by locking police out of the dock area whilst cutting through a fence to form a picket line that wharfies have agreed not to cross.

MELBOURNE, 1978

Hare Krishnas locked up in Pentridge prison for refusing to pay fines arising from begging go on hunger strike, demanding they be provided vegetarian food not cooked alongside meat and fish.

ADELAIDE, 1978

Protesters marching on Hiroshima Day present mining company CRA with a number of "body bags" as a reward for its contribution to the nuclear industry.

BRISBANE, 1978

During a feminist demonstration in King George Street, the police move in to arrest a woman for saying "fuck" during street theatre and a man for chanting the same word in response. Further arrests ensue when the remaining protesters give the F-word the full work out with a rendition of the feminist ode, "Tired Of The Fuckers Fucking Me Over."

MELBOURNE, 1978

After being on display for a number of years, the skull of Australia's premier outlaw Ned Kelly is stolen from its display at the Old Melbourne Gaol. In a statement issued years later the thief claims he took it because he "simply wanted to keep the skull away from the sick people who had custody of it and abused the privilege."

At some point the skull is offered to left-wing author Frank Hardy, who before his death informs friends that he knows of its whereabouts. A formal offer to return the skull to authorities is made in the 1980s and then withdrawn after police raid the homes of those they believe are connected to the theft.

Nothing more is heard of the relic until March 1998 when the thief contacts the former chaplain of the Old Melbourne Gaol. Father Norden reports that the caller wishes to return the skull providing it is buried in dignity with the rest of Ned's body. Kelly historian Ian Jones is also contacted by the man who he describes as "a very down-to-earth fellow who just said that Ned Kelly's skull should never have been on display and that's why he took it. He didn't feel it was proper."

Following criticism of the thief as "disrespectful" he and his supporters release a ten-point statement pointing out that:

1. We did not hang Mr Kelly by the neck so that his knees contracted twice to his chest before passing on.
2. We did not mutilate his body.
3. We did not hack off his head.
4. We did not remove his brain, put it in a preserving jar and give it to an unnamed medico.
5. We did not remove the flesh from Mr Kelly's skull.
6. We did not brand the initials E.K. into Mr Kelly's skull.
7. We did not declare the skull an official police trophy.
8. We did not pass the skull around Victorian townships as part of a grisly exhibition.
9. We did not mount the skull in a glass case and put it on display as a trophy.
10. We did not behave in a ghoulish, barbaric and uncivilised manner that is more in keeping with the head hunters of old than with supposedly sophisticated twentieth century and soon to be twenty-first century human beings.

Shortly after the release of this statement the Ned Kelly Memorial Society come forth to offer a $10,000 reward for the skull. Negotiations begin, with Northern NSW activists Fast Bucks and JJ McRoach representing the thief. The pair, both of whom had run for the Australian Marijuana Party in the 1980s, claim to have met the thief shortly after he obtained the skull. Fast Bucks also claims to have paid the man $8,000 in 1978 to prevent him from selling it to a number of overseas collectors. Amongst these collectors was Mick Jagger, who had appeared in a film of Ned Kelly's life. Fast Bucks was apparently shown the skull, which was hung from a coathanger in a cupboard. In connection with this he states that, "There is no doubt that (the thief) took it. It's a bit disgusting, it's a creepy thing to do, but why should the cops have it as a souvenir? So they can humiliate Ned Kelly even further?"

After negotiations stall the thief, later revealed to be West Australian Tom Baxter, contacts a journalist at the Melbourne *Age* to demand that Kelly be given a posthumous pardon and that his body be moved from Pentridge and buried with his skull in the Kelly homeland around Greta. During the conversation Baxter identifies Kelly as an early Australian republican and an Australian icon. He further states that Kelly's rebellion could be traced "back to the government stuff, them trying to split up families. They pretty much had a down on the Kellys. I'm not trying to say he is blameless ... but in the circumstances of Stringybark Creek, he was obviously fired upon first by people who weren't in uniform ... He's not the common criminal people make him out to be ... of course the police take a dim view because he killed some."

In 2004 Baxter appears on ABC TV's *Rewind* program once more stating that his aim in "liberating" the skull had only been to help Kelly escape "eternal incarceration". Leading journalists through the Kimberley scrubland he retrieves the skull from one of its many hiding places using the occasion to reiterate that, "The law did the wrong thing by Ned. He was wrongly executed. His trial was ... even for the standards of the day, it was not a good trial and it was designed to please the government of the day and was designed to execute Ned Kelly."

Kelly's tale, however, takes yet another twist when the ABC employs a forensic anthropologist to do a facial reconstruction based on a cast made from the skull in Baxter's possession. Following a comparison to Kelly's death mask it is discovered that the stolen item, bearing the chiselled-in letters E.K., was never Kelly's cranium, but in fact came from Ernest Knox, who was executed in 1894 for murder.

BRISBANE, 1978

Police attack 80 members of the group Concerned Christians after they meet in the Roma Street Mall and attempt to illegally march in pairs down the footpath to Queen's Park. Ordered by Special Branch to stop singing hymns they begin humming and whistling before 11 of their number, including a clergyman, are arrested for loitering. The following day the Queensland Trades and Labour Council holds two protests in support of those arrested with 1,000 rallying in Roma Street and another 250 in suburban Rocklea.

AUSTRALIA, 1978

The management of the ABC brings a world of trouble upon its head when it sacks Switch Room Operator Lionel Barr for refusing to broadcast Federal Parliament as part of a union work ban over funding cuts. In response to the sacking, NSW members of the ABC Staff Association begin a seven-day series of strikes while Queensland ABC staff strike for 24 hours. With

industrial action spreading to include members of the Sydney Symphony Orchestra and the Australian Journalists Association, Barr soon finds himself back at his job and management back at the negotiating table.

BRISBANE 1978

Transcendental Meditation advertisements on buses that read, "Don't Just Sit There — Meditate," are changed to "Don't Just Sit There — Masturbate."

WODONGA, 1978

120 Sanyo workers strike and occupy their workplace after they are informed that another 14 workers will be made redundant on top of 145 who have already lost their jobs in the previous year. The strikers hold a "sleep-in" at the company canteen over two nights before marching on the administration building to inform their manager that they are sacking him. The company responds with its own letters of dismissal, which are burnt, and attempts to end the occupation by turning off the power to the factory and sealing its gates. However the strikers get in first, managing to keep one gate under their control and setting up a roster to continue the occupation for a number of days.

BRISBANE, 1978

250 environmentalists meet in King George Square for a FoE bike rally that thumbs its nose at the state's anti-protest march laws by riding through the city chanting anti-uranium slogans.

SYDNEY, 1978

Lance Gowland[18] recalls the events that led up to and dominated the first Mardi Gras, "Australia's Stonewall":

> The idea for the first march [which was in solidarity with a Gay Pride event in San Francisco] came about when we were talking to a friend who was on the CAMP (Campaign Against Moral Persecution) executive, Ron Austin, about demonstrations and what we could do instead of just marching with our banners. He said, "Why don't we do what the Americans do and have a party, a street party. We could have a Mardi Gras," and he suggested that we go to a Stonewall

committee meeting to see what they'd say.

> They were a bit reluctant and said that if we wanted to do it we could as long as we were prepared to put the work in as they had enough to do already. So we did it. We formed a separate committee to organise it with a march planned in the morning and a Mardi Gras in the evening. We did a lot of posters and had a lot of advertising for the whole of Stonewall week. We wanted it to be political, but fun too, with a party atmosphere, so we encouraged people to dress up. On the day, June 24th 1978, we hired a P.A. truck, put a few banners around it and at 10 o'clock on Saturday night we parked it in Taylor Square with music playing really loudly.

> And people came from everywhere — we were surprised to see that there was a crowd of about 1,000 people when we left Taylor Square and by the time we got to the bottom of Oxford Street we had about 2,000 ... they'd all come out of the bars and joined us. I have to say the police were hostile to the idea of the parade from the start — they'd warned me that if we stopped along the route our permit would be revoked.

> They harassed us along Oxford Street and then when we got to Hyde Park, where we'd planned to finish up with some music and speeches, we were denied entry. I was told to drive down Liverpool Street, but when I drove into College Street instead they tried to arrest me. Confusion reigned and so when someone yelled out, "To the Cross," we continued on up there. I still clearly remember the mood of the march that night ... there was a magic, a feeling of excitement and solidarity. And I'll never forget this kid who came flying past me at one stage yelling out, "I'll never hide again!" That was just great! When we got up to King's Cross the crowd became incredible, but by then the police moved in and it became a nightmare. They blocked both ends of Darlinghurst Road so we were caught in the main part of the Cross and couldn't get out. They parked vans across the road and were arresting people indiscriminately, dragging them by the hair and punching them in the face. It was a radical confrontation. (Even bystanders were arrested —I was working on the waterfront at the time and some of the wharfies got arrested who were up there.)

> There was a feeling of support towards us,

though, from the crowd in Kings Cross (who didn't like the police much anyway). And there was a great feeling of solidarity amongst us, especially from the lesbians in the march who played a major role in fighting off the police. In fact, the way the crowd fought back during the arrests was the first time I'd ever seen a situation where people didn't get arrested peacefully in Australia. When one of us was being arrested someone would come up and try to pull them away. For example, when they tried to arrest me, the police were pulling me by the legs while the crowd grabbed me by the arms and there was a tug-of-war. I had two cops on my legs and half a dozen demonstrators pulling me by the arms and they won, the crowd rescued me. That happened quite a lot that night and it was mostly the women who fought back.

So the police tried to arrest me and confiscate the truck. They couldn't arrest me but they did take the truck and drove it away with a lot of the people still on the back. They parked it up near Darlinghurst police station and I went up and got it later. Over 50 people were arrested that first night and all of them were taken to Darlinghurst police station. So the crowd all went to Darlinghurst police station and we were there all night until daylight chanting out, "Let them go, let them go!" and raising money. We raised thousands of dollars for bail and then of course we had public meetings to organise a fight-back, and demonstrations to get the charges dropped. Then, two days after those arrests, there were more violent confrontations when police lined the court entrance and tried to prevent us from going inside.

Neville Wran, the Labor Premier at the time, went on an overseas trip around that time and we let our friends in the international gay movement know what had happened ... Everywhere that Neville Wran went he was met by gay and lesbian demonstrators and when he came back from that trip we were waiting for him at Sydney airport, 30 or 40 of us with banners and things. He apparently said that he was sick and tired of all these gay demonstrators everywhere he went. We also stationed a caravan outside his house so there was no escape there either! So the drop-the-charges thing was really international and went on for 12 months, with more people arrested in the follow-up demonstrations. It

took a long time and a lot of struggle before the charges were dropped for almost everyone.

TOWNSVILLE, 1978

Queenslanders hold a "lightning" march at a suburban shopping centre and disperse before the police can arrive to arrest them for rallying without a permit.

MELBOURNE, 1978

Over 700 students stage a walk out at Newlands High School over the lack of a library, gym, assembly hall, cafeteria and other basic facilities. The students march around the school blocking traffic and holding banners reading, "Make Newlands A School, Not A Slum."

QUEENSLAND, 1978

A statewide day of action for civil liberties sees most of the 570 people who live in Collinsville take part in an illegal march down the main street as the two local cops watch balefully from their car. Waterside workers and coalminers strike for 24 hours and 30 collieries are closed with demonstrations also held in Townsville, Mackay and Bundaberg. In Gladstone, the local Trades and Labour Council somehow gets a permit to march, which 300 take advantage of, whilst in Rockhampton 400 attend a rally where 35 are arrested. 4,000 people gather in Brisbane's King George Square, but when 1,500 attempt to march they are met by 1,300 police brought in from all over the state. 346 people are arrested with the remainder being brutally dispersed. Sympathy from the protesters' southern cousins comes in the form of a solidarity rally involving over 700 people in Sydney.

CHRISTMAS ISLAND, 1979

A general strike shuts down the Australian territory after drivers of Chinese, Malaysian and Singaporean descent walk off the job at the British Phosphate Commission alleging abusive behaviour by their Caucasian supervisors. Before the dispute ends the WA Trades and Labor Council calls for an embargo on supplies to the island.

BRISBANE, 1979

Rumours circulate that glam band Jimmy and the Boys are planning to burn an effigy of the Baby Jesus at a Christmas Eve concert. In response ultra right-wing Country Party Premier Joh Bjelke-Petersen promises that police will be on hand to prevent any such action. On the night, uniformed officers stand aside as undercover police provoke a riot by wading into the audience to beat people at random.

MELBOURNE, 1979

Following the sacking of ten painters and dockers for taking action over nightshift safety standards, 1,600 workers at the Williamstown Naval Dockyard vote to sack their bosses and run the facility themselves. In dismissing their employers the workers decide to remain on the job, but only take orders from leading hands elected by their own delegates' committee. The General Manager of the shipyard, Commodore Dalrymple, is handed a resolution to the effect that his services are no longer required and a sign is posted outside the dockyard advertising vacancies for his job and that of the works' manager.

Commenting on the situation, Brian Baxter, an organiser for the Amalgamated Metal Workers and Shipwrights' Union, states that, "We are putting the Commodore on the dole queue. He is sacked and we won't be talking to him. We are challenging the right of employers to act like gods and treat workers like slaves." Another occupier, Carl Tulloch, the President of the Combined Unions' Shop Committee, puts it even more simply, "We've had a lifetime experience of these blokes. They're bastards and they're cunning."

During the work-in the occupiers carry out much-needed safety audits and invite the public in for tours, with the result that one socialist is arrested by the police for trespassing on a "defence establishment" after he takes some photos of the occupation. Having made their point, and with their access to tools and supplies cut off and their timecards removed, the workers reinstate their management after eight days at a demonstration outside the Department of Defence.

Above: Feminist rally, Sydney, 1970s.
Photographer unknown.

BRISBANE, 1979

Constable Michael Egan becomes the first Queensland cop to officially resign over the State's anti-protest laws after he is arrested for going to the aid of a friend who is nabbed marching down the footpath following an International Women's Day rally. He later suffers further arrests for traffic offenses, and decides to leave the state after being followed home from a civil rights meeting by Special Branch operatives.

NORSEMAN, 1979

After he condemns ongoing strike action at the local mines everyone in the Western Australian mining town's main bar, except for his Liberal advisors, refuses to allow PM Malcolm Fraser to buy them a beer.

SYDNEY, 1979

Aboriginal activists Bill Craigie and Cecil Patten remove six paintings by Gunwinggu artist Yirawala from Hogarth Galleries in Paddington to draw attention to the ongoing theft of Aboriginal art. Despite arguing that the pieces have sacred significance and that Aboriginal people have never renounced their claim to the paintings, the pair are arrested by police. Facing court 18 months later the activists pay tribute to the jury, telling them, "After 200 years you have given black people in this country hope," after they find them not guilty despite directions from the judge to ignore cultural arguments in favour of strict interpretations of NSW law.

ADELAIDE, 1979

During a charity appearance Prime Minister Fraser is pelted with fruit and howled down with cries of "Let him eat yellowcake!", an allusion to his Government's aggressive support for uranium exports.

QUEENSLAND, 1979

After two seamen are jailed for refusing to pay fines levied upon them for taking part in illegal street marches, the Seamen's Union responds with a strike, tying up at least 30 ships across the state.

SYDNEY, 1979

Disability activists disrupt the official opening of the inaccessible Eastern Suburbs Railway. After footage of the protesters being abused and jostled by attendees is aired on the media, the government is embarrassed into agreeing to introduce transport subsidies and accessible taxis.

MELBOURNE, 1979

Following a complaint arising from the band's performance of their song *Why Doncha All Get °ucked)* at a gig in Eltham, the Vice Squad raids Festival Records, seizing copies of Skyhooks' fourth album *Guilty Until Proven Insane*. When the matter reaches court the magistrate quickly dismisses the case on the basis that the song "may be indecent, but it's not obscene". He also laments that a single complaint could lead to such a waste of police resources.

The matter does not end there, however, as *The Age*, in reporting on the case, makes use of the word "fuck", leading three members of the Vice Squad to visit its editor Michael Davie. Davie remains unbowed in the face of possible prosecution warning them that, "If the case goes to court, every newspaper in Victoria will want to report it. In doing so, to make any sense of the case, they will have to use the word, since otherwise the reason for the editor of *The Age* being on trial will be unintelligible. Suppose the word is found to be indecent and I am found guilty. Then all the other papers that have used the word will have to be prosecuted. Then *The Age* would have to report on their prosecution and in doing so would be bound to repeat its original offence. Then there will have to be another prosecution of *The Age* and myself. Then the other papers, to report that case, will have to repeat their original offences." Leery of creating any further publicity and swayed by this logic, the guardians of public morality decide not to press charges.

PERTH, 1979

The first ceremony of Prince Charles' tour of Western Australia for the state's 150th anniversary is disrupted by Aboriginal protesters carrying placards reading, "What About Aboriginal people's 30,000th anniversary?" "150 Years Of Deprivation Of Land Rights, Poverty And Oppression," and "Celebrate What?"

SYDNEY, 1979

Having just become an Australian citizen, Rolo Mestman Tapier infuriates the Returned Services League, and other ardent monarchists, by publicly renouncing his pledge of allegiance to the Queen on the basis that he will only recognise a democratically elected Head of State. Two years later, Tapier is arrested for appearing at an Australia Day parade wearing a sandwich board reading, "Abolish the Monarchy," and, "Royalists are kow-towing colonialists suffering from an inferiority complex." Having defeated charges of "behaviour likely to cause serious alarm and affront," the prankster claims to have been converted to the Royal cause and proves it by changing his name to Lord Bloody Wog Rolo. He also sets up the British Ultra Loyalist League Serving Historical Interests Today (B.U.L.L.S.H.I.T.) organisation under whose moniker he runs for Senate in 1986.

In the course of various campaigns against racism, organised religion, and corporate greed, Rolo is repeatedly arrested for offences relating to the decoration of his car with slogans. Following much police harassment, including a forgery charge placed by an officer who could not believe that a real license could read "Lord Bloody Wog Rolo", the prankster adds slogans such as "Support honest police, they both need you" to his repertoire.

When BUGA-UP first comes together, Rolo successfully disrupts a supermarket trial of shopping bags bearing tobacco advertising. Having filled up their shopping trolleys and proceeded to the checkout he and an accomplice refuse to pay for the goods or remove them due to dubious receptacles on offer. After much disruption ensues the supermarket's manager eventually relents in calling off the promotion.

Having revised many a billboard, including one located atop a five-story-building in North Sydney, Rolo meets his wife, soon to be Lady Bloody Wog Rolo, when the two go to deface the same billboard. The pair soon go on to become BUGA-UP ambassadors attending many an action and events such as Campbelltown's Fisher's Ghost parade. During the course of such ambassadorial activities, Rolo spends three days in Long Bay Jail after he and fellow activist Ric Bolzan are successfully convicted for "maliciously injuring" a racing car which they had chained themselves to and dumped cigarette butts on during an anti-tobacco sponsorship action.

QUEENSLAND, 1979

More than 3,000 coalminers strike after two union officials are jailed for refusing to pay fines arising from their involvement in illegal street marches in Brisbane.

MELBOURNE, 1979

Rather than accept forced transfers, three Humanities teachers at the Footscray Technical School decide to stage a work-in by continuing to teach according to their old timetable. Following their sacking and threats by the Education Department to send in the police to remove them, a ten-day strike is undertaken at the school and vigils held at Parliament House, with the eventual result that all three are reinstated.

QUEENSLAND, 1979

Ten schools in Northern Queensland stop work for 24 hours after a teacher at the Lutheran run Hope Vale Mission School is forcibly transferred for supporting local Aboriginal people in their fight for independence from his employers.

SYDNEY, 1979

The Unemployed Workers' Union throws a huge party just outside the gates of the Liberal Party's own Yuletide celebrations. Despite the presence of 500 police the 400 unemployed revellers get close enough to abuse conservative partygoers and greet them with banners reading, "Merry Xmas People Bashers." One UWU member slips through police lines disguised as a waitress and enters the party as a latecomer. When Prime Minister Fraser makes his entrance he is greeted by the sight of the unemployed activist hurling food trolleys and trays across the room at him. Food flies into the Tory crowd as she is dragged from the room by bouncers, but before she is finally arrested she gives police the slip by hiding behind a cupboard.

ANTI-CLOCKWISE FROM TOP LEFT: Protest against public transport cuts, Melbourne, c. 1989. Courtesy of www.greenleft.org.au • Squatter's protest, Melbourne, 1980s. Unemployed Workers Union Newsletter • Strike at Philip Morris, the makers of Marlboro cigarettes, 1980. Courtesy of www.greenleft.org.au • NSW Nurses rally against funding cuts under the Wran ALP Government, 1981. Courtesy of www.greenleft.org.au

1980 –1989

The early years of the decade saw the Federal Fraser government hit stasis point. 1981 saw workers from cinema ushers and public servants through to teachers and truck drivers undertake successful industrial action with some gaining reductions in working hours, including a 35 hour working week for some metal workers. The resources boom collapsed during the following year and unemployment reached 10% whilst inflation and interest rates continued to soar. As employer displeasure at the government's inability to rein in wages fused with public anger at declining living standards, the Fraser era came to an end with a resounding electoral defeat in 1983.

Where the Liberal government had bickered over the introduction of monetarist policies and failed to restore corporate profits, the newly elected ALP succeeded, ushering in a new era of neo-liberalism. Breaking with the bi-partisan policies of the past eight decades the Labor party introduced financial deregulation, floated the Australian dollar, began privatising state assets and wound back protectionist tariffs. It also relaxed media laws, leading to some of the highest concentration of ownership in the world. These policies led to a short boom, fuelled by cheap credit and asset stripping, and with it the rise of a new coterie of flashy multi-millionaires. Over the longer term they saw the national goal of profit creation trump all others and returned Australia to an almost wholly primary export-driven economy, with Asia now the focus rather than Europe. They also presided over a massive increase in public and private debt, left the country wide open to currency and commodity speculators, and, despite the introduction

of some subsidies to industry, accelerated the shutdown of Australian manufacturing. Meanwhile most Australians experienced decreased job security, rising workloads and a drop in real wages as the wealthy increased their share of profit.

Unlike in the US and UK these changes did not result in major social ruptures. Moving on from the confrontational approach of the Fraser years the ALP, led by former ACTU leader Bob Hawke, preached consensus. Bringing employers, government and union bureaucrats together under the auspices of the Prices and Incomes Accord it convinced the latter to agree to 'economic rationalist' policies, the introduction of job-destroying technology, and wage control in return for health reform, an increased safety net, jobs growth and low inflation. Despite these dividends never being fully realised, union leaderships became progressively enmeshed in high-level negotiations and spent more time preventing industrial disputes than supporting them. The tendency to police the membership had always been strong and Australian unions had, with a few exceptions, always fought within the constraints of the capitalist system rather than for its abolition. However, the 1980s saw power centralised in the bureaucracy to a degree not previously experienced. In the midst of industrial peace and the sidelining of rank-and-file participation, earnings and membership declined. The few unions that resisted the trend towards collaboration with government and employers were broken, or absorbed into more compliant organisations via a wave of amalgamations.

Similar deals were struck with the leaderships of various social movements. Whilst some gains were won in terms of expanded anti-discrimination laws and funding for various projects, the incorporation of sections of feminist, Indigenous and other movements led to a demobilisation of their base and the creation of new bureaucracies designed to manage the economy and society rather than revolutionise them. This in turn further bound key activists and factions to the government as the loss of extra-parliamentary influence made them more reliant on government favours as well as fearful of the return of a Liberal-National coalition going ever further to the Right.

Plenty of radical action was still happening, however. The environment and peace movements particularly grew during the 1980s. The former had employed direct action against development projects and the clear-felling of native forests from the late 1970s onwards and continued to pioneer blockading techniques that would come to be adopted globally. A massive blockade challenged the damming of Tasmania's Franklin River in 1983, and whilst the government deal that sealed this victory saw many leading activists focus on wheeling and dealing with the ALP, others retained a focus on grassroots protest and the development of truly sustainable alternatives. Some also began to form Green parties and electoral tickets with the first such MP elected in Tasmania in 1983.

Indigenous communities fought on for land rights, but – outside of the South Australian government confirming an earlier Federal hand back of Pitjantjatjara land (minus the right to veto mining) and limited reforms in NSW – significant change was scuttled nationally via mining company pressure and ALP manoeuvring. The massive overrepresentation of Indigenous people in prisons and their deaths at the hands, and under the charge, of police saw widespread demonstrations lead to the 1987 Royal Commission into Aboriginal Deaths in Custody, the majority of whose 339 recommendations were sadly ignored. A large demonstration at the 1983 Commonwealth games and a series of protests during the 1988 bicentenary of British invasion, including 40,000 marching in Sydney on Invasion/Australia Day, brought together Indigenous people and their supporters nationally to demand a treaty, autonomy and compensation. This helped trigger a new upsurge and interest in Aboriginal and Torres Strait Islander culture, with increasing numbers of people coming to identify with their Indigenous ancestry in the decades to come.

The Federal Labor government remained in lock-step with US foreign policy and embarked on an expansion of military spending and aid from the mid-1980s, further enhancing Australian dominance and power in the Pacific. The nation's involvement in the US military machine was challenged by a massive movement that saw hundreds of thousands demonstrate against nuclear weapons and close to one million people vote for anti-nuclear parties, electing one senator in 1984. US naval visits and uranium mines and exports, which had been targeted by peace and environment activists since the beginning of the decade, continued to attract blockades and pickets whilst remotely located American bases, mainly involved in spying and weapons targeting, also became the focus of national protests. As part of the reaction to the threat of global destruction and the "New Australian Militarism" women targeted ANZAC Day commemorations to raise the issue of rape and civilian deaths in war.

In 1987 the economic boom turned to bust. Over the next few years inflation and unemployment soared and the stock market and a series of financial institutions crashed. In response the Federal government cut social spending whilst the Federal Treasurer, and future PM, Paul Keating excused the downward spiral as "the recession we had to have." Despite the failure of the Accord to control anything other than wages, union leaderships stuck with it out of loyalty to the ALP and fear of emboldened New Right employers out to destroy them. Some maritime and construction unions continued to undertake solidarity actions, but most abandoned anything but a token commitment to non-industrial matters.

With Australian migration patterns having changed from being almost entirely European to include large numbers of people from Asia and the Middle East, xenophobes at all levels of society became active. At the same time as tiny neo-Nazi groups physically attacked immigrants and leftists, and plastered cities like Perth with racist posters, Liberal Party leader John Howard attempted to whip up anti-Asian sentiment. Efforts to completely turn the clock back failed as the era of full blown support for the White Australia Policy was over, but such agitation fed into the everyday social and economic prejudice immigrants continued to experience.

The late 1980s also saw the collapse of National Party led government in Queensland under the weight of corruption and decades of election rigging. Radicals across the country welcomed the end of a repressive administration that had hounded activists for decades. Predictably the ALP government that succeeded it joined other state governments of a similar stripe in accelerating neo-liberal reform whilst conceding minor improvements, primarily around social issues.

By the end of the decade much of the socialist Left had withered. The CPA was soon to dissolve due to a loss of direction and the desertion of sections to the ALP, whose own Left factions were on the decline. In contrast, with previously cosy relationships with government delivering little or no reward, significant sections of Australia's broader Left and social movements, particularly amongst the burgeoning environment movement, progressively spurned the ALP to re-engage with extra-parliamentary action. Coupled with the ALP's decision to reintroduce fees for tertiary study these developments sparked a new wave of occupations, protests and blockades that would continue into the early 1990s.

"A whiff of how important class is in Australian society is how fearfully Australian politicians run away from it."

Craig McGregor, 1987

CANBERRA, 1980

Anti-nuclear protesters squat Parliament lawns, setting up an Atom-Free Embassy in the process. After 94 days the police move in using the same anti-camping laws that had been applied to the Aboriginal Tent Embassy years earlier. Following the eviction the protesters return with a piece of cardboard and a flag to try to create the Atom-Free Embassy Mark II, but are forced by the cops to remain on foot to avoid arrest. Weeks later the protest goes fully mobile, engaging in an illegal banner drop at the Commonwealth Heads of Government Meeting in Melbourne before taking over St Martins Square in Sydney for a week.

QUEENSLAND, 1980

Responding to moves by the Federal Government to expand the uranium industry, workers at Evans Deakin Industries and the Sergeants-ANI engineering firm refuse to supply steel for the Ranger uranium mine. The Electrical Trades Union (ETU) also withdraws its services from members working at the Mary Kathleen mine.

ADELAIDE, 1980

A student strike at Marion High School forces headmaster Brian Hannaford to stop punishing students by hitting them with a cane.

SYDNEY, 1980

In anticipation of the Critical Mass rides that will take place 15 years later, a large group of cyclists take over Sydney streets to protest car culture.

PERTH, 1980

A man carrying a shovel is arrested in the garden adjoining Premier Sir Charles Court's Dalkeith mansion. When asked what he is doing he informs police that he is the chairman of a mining venture and that he wishes to gain insights into the local tribe's sacred sites — their rose bushes — before beginning mining.

SYDNEY, 1980

Myer Department Store launches a contest entitled "The Cheekiest Jeans in Town", in which women parade behind a screen with their denim-clad bums popping out. Some members of the crowd, however, prove too cheeky for Myer's security and are arrested after booing and disrupting the sexist contest.

TASMANIA, 1980

ALP Senator Michael Tate swears not to drink another drop of alcohol until marijuana is legalised. Is he still waiting?

PERTH, 1980

During a Christmas rally against the State's Section 54B anti-demonstration laws, Santa is arrested for protesting without a permit.

MELBOURNE, 1981

Maintenance workers at the Union Carbide plant in Altona occupy their workplace after more than 30 workers are sacked by the company for taking part in an industrial campaign seeking the 35-hour working week. With up to 150 people on the picket line at any time the "52 behind the wire" hold volleyball matches across the fences and conduct tours of the plant, while receiving "wages" in the form of cash donations from neighbouring workplaces. Further support comes in the form of circus performances, jazz music, film screenings and other entertainment laid on by supporters whilst the occupiers also begin practising their Christmas carols should they still be inside in the months to come.

One activist interviewed by *Direct Action* explains that the workers had opted for an occupation after they'd "struck on a number of occasions in the past and the managerial staff scabbed on us. It's no use us being outside the gate whilst they're inside producing. We're making our point in a way the company can't ignore."

When the occupation enters its third week Union Carbide sends out threatening letters to the wives and families of the occupiers, who are also targeted by obscene and threatening phone calls. A fortnight later the company moves to force the Workers' Union to deregister them with the result that the ACTU and local ALP members finally get behind the occupation. After 51 days the workers march out having forced their employers to reinstate all of those previously sacked.

NSW, 1981

The Building Workers' Industrial Union (BWIU) black bans the construction of nuclear shelters, condemning those recently advertised in national newspapers as a "blatant confidence trick which specifically seeks to exploit for profit the current arms race".

MELBOURNE, 1981

Incensed at overcrowding, parents remove their children from Footscray Technical School. Having defied threats from the Education Department to take them to court, the families end the boycott with a funeral procession from the school to the Education Department's headquarters in the city.

ADELAIDE, 1981

Members of Actors' Equity continually interrupt and delay the beginning of performances of the musical *Evita* until the Adelaide Festival Centre Trust agrees to pay all the actors involved union rates.

CANBERRA, 1981

The winning entry in a competition to name a new police launch is submitted by an academic who suggests PLATYPUS on the grounds that it is uniquely Australian, amphibious and gentle, but still able to defend itself when under attack. Only after he has won the competition is it revealed that his true reasoning was that platypus is derived from the Greek word for FLATFOOT.

BRISBANE, 1981

Sick of sanitised protests featuring one droning politician after another, anarchists at a major city rally hoist a banner reading, "We're Bored! How About Open Platforms?" behind the speaker's rostrum.

MELBOURNE, 1981

As part of a host of activities carried out during the International Year of the Disabled Person a group of feminist protesters crash the patronising Spastic Society's Miss Australia Quest. Demanding autonomy for people with disabilities, and an end to the sexist spectacles supposedly held in their name, the demonstrators take to the stage disrupting proceedings and garnering widespread media coverage.

HOBART, 1981

When PM Malcolm Fraser arrives to open a new Commonwealth building he is met by a demonstration of 400 unemployed people complete with a soup kitchen. A sympathetic police request that people not throw soup at the PM only gives them an idea that hadn't occurred to them previously. Sure enough when Big Mal arrives he is showered with soup and tomatoes. Media reports that the soup had been urinated in are believed to be just that- only rumours.

ADELAIDE, 1981

Workers at the bankrupt company Cook Engineering save their jobs by blockading their factory for six days and nights to prevent a liquidator from removing materials before a receiver can be appointed.

QUEENSLAND, 1981

During an industrial campaign to gain wage parity with their NSW peers, plumbers, electricians and mechanics employed by the State Government place bans on the servicing and repair of air conditioners, lights and cars used by key politicians in the Queensland Cabinet.

SYDNEY, 1982

After a tour by ultra-conservative Christian evangelist Jerry Falwell is announced, gay and lesbian activists around the country register the business name "Moral Majority" in an effort to forestall the formation of right-wing groups under the same name. The NSW group produces official stickers bearing slogans such as "Moral Majority Says Keep Abortion Safe And Legal," "MM Says Lesbians And Gays Should Be Blatant," "MM Says Sodom Today, Gomorrah The World," and "MM Says Matthew, Mark, Luke And John, They're All Queens Where I Come From."

CANBERRA, 1982

Demonstrators from organisations such as the Barefoot and Pregnant Ball and Chain League, Australians for Divine Illumination by Nuclear Blasts and the National Association for the Advancement of Rich, White and Straight Men stage a rally outside the National Press Club where an address by US Evangelist Jerry Falwell is being held.

BRISBANE, 1982

Ciaron O'Reilly recalls how libertarians responded to the state's draconian anti-free speech laws:[19]

> The Commonwealth Games Act (1982), with its threats of severe punishment and its purpose to silence Aboriginal dissent during the period of the Games, was a catalyst for libertarians to take up the issue of free expression. The view of those participating was that the only cheap accessible means of communication available to ordinary people was being denied in Queensland by the police permit system under the Traffic Act, the municipal permit system under the City Council Mall Ordinances, and the occasional State of Emergency legislation like the Commonwealth Games Act. The 'Committee of 50' was formed to carry out a day of action on September 15th (1982) when it would declare a 'Free Speech Mall' and 'Freedom of the City' and would openly break the permit systems as a way of encouraging community non-cooperation.
>
> The nature of the 'Committee of 50' day of action was one of 'propaganda of the deed' – with a theatrical opening of the 'Free Speech Mall' complete with ribbon cutting and a top-hatted robed Mayor who introduced the civil disobedience in verse. The leafletters, buskers, speakers, actors and picketers were all introduced with a systematic tearing up of application forms for permits. The message was clear – end the permit system, exercise free expression. The City Council ordinances were not enforced, although $25 on-the-spot fines had been threatened earlier that week by then Acting Lord Mayor Len Ardill. These fines were also threatened later in the campaign but never enforced [and so] a sub-goal had been realised on the first day of action.
>
> Another ribbon was cut and 'Freedom of the City' was declared. The Committee took civil disobedience outside the Mall in defiance of those authoritarian regulations existing under the Traffic Act. Humour was an important ingredient of the campaign from the outset, both for the value of communicating ideas to the public and enriching the morale of the activists involved. Posters proclaiming 'Bill Posters is

Innocent' appeared around the city next to the official injunction proclaiming 'Bill Posters will be Prosecuted', some 'Committee of 50' activists dressed as clowns, while the banner leading the final march proclaimed 'PERMIT SCHMERMIT.' To the tune of 'Ten Green Bottles' the marchers sang 'Ten smiling marchers marching down the street, ten smiling marchers marching down the street. If a Queensland cop one should accidentally meet, there'd be nine smiling marchers marching down the street' etc.

As the marchers were being arrested and placed in police vans a recently arrived busker spontaneously joined in by playing 'The Last Post' on his trumpet. He too was arrested after complying with a police direction to put his trumpet away, but insisting on his right to remain with other onlookers on the sidewalk. Twenty-two people were arrested.

SYDNEY, 1982
A blockade of the NSW Transport Ministry by striking truckies is serenaded with *Tiptoe Through The Tulips* by Tiny Tim after the eccentric singer stumbles upon the protest. The strikers reply with a rendition of *Waltzing Matilda*.

CANBERRA, 1982
After an ALP Senator claims that the food served at Parliament House "would kill a brown dog", catering staff walk off the job leaving the politicians to fend for themselves.

MELBOURNE, 1982
300 pro-choice demonstrators disrupt an anti-abortion protest by seizing the front spot, and prime banner position, during a march through the city by 1,500 Right To Lifers.

SYDNEY, 1982
Members of Billboard Utilising Graffitists Against Unhealthy Promotions (BUGA-UP), furious at the NSW Art Gallery's decision to display a racing car plastered with cigarette advertisements, decide to take action. One artist chains himself to the car and presents an open letter to the gallery trustees informing them that he will not leave until the advertising material is removed. Supporters in the crowd shower the car with

Marlboro packets and butts collected from surrounding streets and also cover it with anti-smoking stickers. While the artist is eventually separated from the vehicle by the police, and BUGA-UP activists arrested on charges of Malicious Damage to a Racing Car, the gallery cries Uncle, removing the vehicle the following day only to see it paint-bombed during its journey back to Alfa Romeo.

BRISBANE, 1982
When the Prime Minister attempts to leave the Young Liberals' National Conference at the University of Queensland he finds his official convoy blocked by a 100-strong crowd chanting, "One more cut, Fraser's throat!" Well used to being targeted, the PM leaps out of his car to rush past the assembled crowd who, in taking up the pursuit, allow his chauffeur to speed through and collect him.

MELBOURNE, 1982
Aboriginal activists opposed to the building of an aluminium smelter at Portland disrupt a 200-metre race being held as part of an international athletics meet sponsored by Alcoa. Dashing onto the Olympic Park track, and knocking over contestants in the process, the Land Rights activists unfurl a red, black and gold banner reading "Alcoa = Unemployment" before escaping down Punt Road.

SOUTH AUSTRALIA, 1982
During three days of protest at the Honeymoon uranium mine, anti-nuclear demonstrators defy police attempts to prevent them from setting fire to a massive three-tier cardboard "yellow cake."

DARWIN, 1982
An unemployed labourer is arrested and later fined $175 for shouting "objectionable words" at the Queen during an informal walk through the Smith St Mall.

MELBOURNE, 1982
Members of the Women With Disabilities feminist collective disrupt the Miss Victoria fundraising pageant by invading the stage to hoist a banner reading "Equality Not Charity".

ALICE SPIRINGS, 1982
A plucky crew of anarchists break into the US military spy base at Pine Gap spraypainting the message "No To This Madness" and a "circle-A" on the base of a radar dome.

MELBOURNE, 1982
The elite Melbourne Club, home to Prime Ministers and captains of industry, plays host to unwanted guests on two occasions during the year. The first, in October, sees luncheon delayed after unemployed activists, armed with sandwiches in plain paper bags, occupy the dining room demanding the premises be remodelled to provide free meals, childcare and accommodation for the jobless.

A month later a much rowdier crew of protesters storm the entrances of the club at the conclusion of a 3,000 strong anti-unemployment rally. Having already burnt Australian flags flying outside the Stock Exchange, and hoisted Eureka and red flags in their place, hundreds force their way into the club's lobby. Faced with a police scrum, most are rapidly evicted, although 15 manage to make their way into the inner sanctum. Wealthy patrons are hurried away from the fracas and staff remove valuable paintings, while three of the occupiers make it out to the windows, where they are cheered by the thousands locked outside. After an hour-long standoff the police agree to free all but three of the occupiers, who are taken to the Carlton police station. The remaining demonstrators move on to block traffic outside the Russell Street watch-house where they erroneously believe their comrades are being held.

SOUTH AUSTRALIA, 1982
Stony Point steel workers facing redundancy jeer and heckle PM Fraser before blocking his car with a crane.

MELBOURNE, 1982
150 protesters roll up to Victorian Premier Lindsay Thompson's Glen Iris home after his government pledges $70 million in aid to home buyers, but bugger all for tenants. In order to rectify this omission, "Housing Minister" Mr Jeff Kennett, suitably bedecked

in an old Scotch College blazer and cricket cap, unveils a "Nature Strip Housing Scheme" aimed at offering "a no-frills, no-cost approach to housing" for the poor.

WOLLONGONG, 1982

During the 16-day occupation of the Kemira Mine, striking miners' wives occupy the company canteen to keep the food flowing to the occupiers. When retrenchment notices offering bonuses are posted to their homes the women respond by returning them as a group to BHP's offices.

VICTORIA, 1982

18 are arrested during a wild anti-nuclear protest at the Omega Military Navigation Base near Yarram in South-West Gippsland. One group of demonstrators use a grappling hook and ropes to try and bring down the 2.5-metre electric fence surrounding the base, while others merely attempt to scale it. After police baton charge the crowd, cars are parked across the base's entrance to prevent the removal of arrestees.

BRISBANE, 1982

Brisbane anarchists convert a West End cigarette billboard into a community notice-board. The billboard originally carried a Drum advert until persistent vandalism forced the advertisers to give up on the idea. Noticing that the space is now empty the anarchists convert it to a socially useful function by adding a suitable title and gluing up a few posters to get the ball rolling.

MELBOURNE, 1982

After a flotilla of kayaks, led by a burning *HMAS Anzac* made out of papier-mâché, fail to halt the US warship *Goldsborough* from docking at Station Pier, protesters react in a myriad of ways. One group, responding to a call from ALP Premier Cain for all Victorians to extend their "traditional courtesy and hospitality" to US servicemen, invites the crew to join them for a BBQ with "yellowcake and submarine sandwiches" at an anti-nuclear embassy set up on nearby Port Melbourne beach. Another less friendly bunch scuffle with police after a man

dressed in black robes and a death's head mask leaps in front of a consulate vehicle carrying the ship's captain. Feminists, meanwhile, enrage serviceman by chanting, "Take your syphilis elsewhere" and an Anglican priest from the group Clergy For Peace conducts a service aimed at purifying the area of "demonic spirits".

SYDNEY, 1983

The following statement is found etched into the body of an expensive continental car: "This represents the transfer of wealth from the property owning class to the panel beating class."

PERTH, 1983

During a 1983 visit by the US Navy members of the Peace Fleet attempt to blockade the aircraft carrier *USS Carl Vinson* with a flotilla of protest ships, before Project Iceberg (PI) goes on board the *USS Worden* to hang banners reading "Not Here, Not Anywhere" and "The Human Race Or The Arms Race?" PI continues to disrupt public tours of visiting warships over the next two years with many of its members and supporters being arrested as a result. When the authorities attempt to prevent the protests by searching bags in 1985 their efforts are easily circumvented by protesters who smuggle stickers and banners on board in their toddlers' and babies' clothes and bags. One action, taken just before the campaign successfully finishes the tours off, sees two women and their children hang a banner, with each letter printed on a nappy, reading, "Bombs Kill Babies."

BRISBANE, 1983

Ciaron O'Reilly[20] recalls how People for Free Expression stymied moves by the Queensland Government to ban street speakers from appearing in the Queen Street Mall:

> A street theatre was developed that embodied the contending forces [with a] soapbox, [cardboard cut-out] television, a street-speaker, the mall manager, a policeman and a politician. [It] contained a scriptural malleability that changed with new events and developments. The theatre became a three-dimensional mirror as the real-life mall manager, street-speakers

and police hovered around it. Its thrust had the mall manager, a politician and policeman rejecting the humble soapbox, calling press conferences and extinguishing street-speakers from the mall. The theatre never failed to attract a large crowd who would be leafleted and then addressed by street-speakers.

> On May 6th amidst an unusually high police presence we premiered the street theatre in the mall. At the end of the theatre a libertarian stood up on the soapbox to address the crowd. After a few words the police moved in and informed him if he continued he would be arrested. He dismounted, and a process of "take-your-turn" began – as other activists took the box, said a few words and were ordered off.

> Activists moved around the large crowd that was gathering, inviting people to "Take the box for free speech" and say a few words. Some of the public responded to the call. One Vietnam veteran got up and made a speech about how he had fought against the communists for the right of free speech and how it was now being taken away.

> One anarchist turned to the crowd and called for a vote. The hundreds of people who had gathered voted overwhelmingly that we should be able to speak – the police responded by arresting him. Resolve set in, and activists began to address the crowd for a second time demanding the release of the man who had been arrested and the right of free expression. Eight libertarians were arrested and taken to the watch-house and charged, others moved to the outside of the watch-house to picket. Five refused to pay cash bail and were not released until the following morning.

> The arrests had occurred less than 50 yards from the Hoyts Theatre where the award-winning film *Gandhi* extolled the virtues of civil disobedience and the struggle for human freedom. The irony was not missed by libertarians, who issued a pamphlet picturing Gandhi threatening, "I won't eat another thing until they let them speak in the Mall!". The leaflet took up these ironies as well as the demands and was distributed at intermission of the film for several weeks ...

> One Friday night the street-theatre was under way when the Special Branch police moved in to give people directions to stop speaking. Actors responded by tying a gag around their mouth. All the libertarians in the crowd tied on gags and handed them out to enthusiastic onlookers.

CAMPAIGN FOR FREE EXPRESSION
BRISBANE, 1982

In response to Queensland's draconian anti-free speech laws, under which people could apply for, but never be granted a permit to protest, activists carried out a number of actions during 1982 and 1983. Regular civil disobedience and street theatre in the Queen Street Mall eventually saw the space opened up to public speakers. The Campaign For Free Expression then celebrated the creation of this "Free Speech Mall" by entering a runner in the Townsville to Brisbane "Mall To Mall" race. Taking advantage of Queenslander's love of all things "Big" the group created a giant soapbox and mounted it on their race support vehicle.

Photographs courtesy of Ciaron O'Reilly.

From the state that gave you the Big Pineapple comes "The Big Soapbox".

Above: Anti-electoral postcard, Melbourne, 1987. Libertarian Workers for a Self-Managed Society.

The gags were decorated with colourful "Queensland Made" stickers expropriated from the Department of Primary Industries earlier in the week. The stalemate was deafening – a silent movie of political repression – until a tug of war developed over the soapbox. A policeman picked up the box, our lawyer placed his hand on it and began a legal argument over property rights; an activist misread this as a sign "to defend the soapbox" and was arrested quite violently. Another activist who attempted to calm the police down was arrested. He went limp in protest, and was dragged some 50 metres down the Mall making speeches all the while ...

[The following] Friday night saw the Special Branch and Public Safety Response Team gathered around where we usually spoke. The street theatre group began a decoy action up at the Albert St. end of the Mall, attracting a crowd and drawing the police away from our usual gathering place. As the police moved away from the usual gathering place two libertarians chained a third to a nearby tree. As the street theatre was winding down under police threats the anarchist chained to the tree began his speech. Activists, the police and the crowd that had gathered moved down to the tree. Gags and leaflets were handed out as Drew spoke. One libertarian was arrested for leafleting, another for "miming without a permit" when he stopped leafleting and put on a gag, and also a civil liberties lawyer on his way to a dinner engagement for attempting to engage police officers in a dialogue over their interpretation of the law.

The speech went for 25 minutes with the crowd peaking at 2000. Business-as-usual was derailed as people stopped consuming and spontaneously participated in an unlawful assembly. As Drew's chains were finally snipped and he was led away by Special Branch he yelled "We must break these laws to remain committed to democracy. It is right to do so. We have nothing to lose but our chains!"

Leafleting of the *Gandhi* film and unannounced lunchtime speaking and street theatre continued. On Thursday lunchtime Special Branch officers appeared in the Mall, but failed to act on the illegal street speaking and theatre. When Special Branch members were referred to by name one of the officers approached a People for Free Expression (PFE) activist and said "If you don't mention us we won't bother you!." A strange offer that hinted a shift in police policy was occurring.

When PFE activists arrived in the Mall [that Friday] the Democratic Rights Organisation had been speaking for a couple of hours with no trouble from the police. The Special Branch hint was correct, a shift in policy had been realised. There were no arrests. We celebrated with some anxiety-free theatre and speaking. The strategy of creative acts of civil disobedience on a weekly basis had been effective ... [A month later the police admitted to the press that] they would not be enforcing the laws silencing political speeches in the Mall.

WOLLONGONG, 1983

A NSW magistrate rules that it is not criminally offensive to refer to the police as swine after hearing a case in which a man was arrested for parading out the front of a temporary police office with a sign saying, "This building is now inhabited by pigs." The NSW Attorney-General agrees with the decision by stating that police should not be oversensitive in such matters.

ALICE SPRINGS, 1983

The Women For Survival protest camp holds its own CIA Olympic Games outside the US Pine Gap spy base, including the "CIA Open (Top) Secret Sprint" in which contestants charge at a car containing the Northern Territory's Chief Minister.

SYDNEY, 1983

Three members of Women For Survival manage to paint "No" on the *Invincible*, but are chased off by police before they can add "War" to the side of the UK aircraft carrier.

MELBOURNE, 1983

An auction aimed at privatising a Telecom-owned mansion descends into chaos after Housing Worker Joan Doyle grabs the microphone to shout, "Shame, Shame, Bona Vista for public housing!"

QUEENSLAND, 1983

Having won the right to speak in the Queen Street Mall, anarchists encourage the public to exercise their civil liberties via a week-long series of actions, as recalled by Ciaron O'Reilly[20]:

> The opportunity to publicise the Mall as a free speech area was provided by a promotional stunt organised by the city council, State Government and City Heart Business Association. The Mall to Mall Race — from Townsville Mall to Brisbane Mall – was an invention: to promote the Mall as a prime business area and as a monument to the administrations of Lord Mayor Harvey and Premier Petersen. The race would provide us with the means to celebrate (and entrench) our victory in the Mall, take the struggle for free expression outside the Mall and into the streets of the Queensland countryside and escalate our counter-cultural attack on conservative Queensland ...
>
> We were for a culture of participation, they for a society of the spectacle; alienation not only at the point of production (boring jobs, meaningless university courses) but also at the point of consumption (in the disco, supermarket

Anti-clockwise from top right: Wharfies picket the loading of uranium, Darwin, 1981. • National Aboriginal Conference chairman Steve Mam at a Brisbane land rights march. c. 1982. • Rallying against Fraser's budget cuts, 1981. • Rally and march against uranium mining at the Honeymoon lease on Kalkaroo Station, 75km north-west of Broken Hill, 1982. • All images courtesy of www.greenleft.org.au

and the Mall). The Mall to Mall Race was to be another orchestrated spectacle for the masses following the 1982 Commonwealth Games and preceding the Student Games 87 and Expo 88. The organisers' hope was to fill the Townsville to Brisbane Race (over 1,600km) with participants that embodied the nature of their Queensland ethos: trendy entrepreneurs, military machines, khaki warriors, captains of consciousness and company-sponsored volunteers. Our hope was to stain their social fabric with a symbol of resistance to their domination and a sign of hope, freedom and counter-culture.

A giant soapbox was constructed and mounted on the back of a 1964 utility, "Soap from the Soapbox" was produced to raise funds and on August 21st the People for Free Expression entrant headed north. On their way there Jim and Ciaron made contact with local activists organising support gatherings for their race back, where they would speak and leaflet in defiance of the Traffic Act restrictions on free expression.

On the day of their departure the *Sunday Sun* ran a human interest story on "A Cop's Beat in the Mall," featuring a photograph of "The Neutron Bomb Minstrel Players" with the explanatory note, "Peaceful demonstrators in Queen St. Mall get on with the act without fear of being arrested." The article confirmed a change in police behaviour and the Mall as safe territory for political activity.

Ciaron spoke in Townsville Mall on the two days preceding the race and on race day to those gathering at the starting line. Thousands of Townsville people lined the streets for the "event" and as the giant soapbox rolled up the main street, Jim, behind the wheel, leafleted the crowd and Ciaron, standing on top of the box, addressed the captive audience. The speaking went on for about half a mile with a good response from the crowds before police moved in and "gave a lawful direction".

Over the following five days [the pair] spoke in Mackay, Rockhampton, Bundaberg, Maryborough, Gympie and Nambour.

On [the final day], fifteen minutes after the official ending of the race, the giant soapbox limped into Queen St. It had suffered total destruction that morning 30km north of Nambour and had been rebuilt. Anarchists had organised a "civic reception" for the soapbox with a gigantic (cardboard cut-out) cup in the Freedom Stakes being presented to Jim and Ciaron by a tuxedoed anarchist mayor. Street theatre included a lap of honour of the Mall pursued by a policeman. A celebration of free expression— five hours of soapbox speaking—then followed. This celebration was occurring approximately one year after the Committee of 50 opening of the Mall as a free-speech zone. The variety of libertarians taking turns in speaking reflected how many activists had been empowered in the instrument of street speaking.

ALICE SPRINGS, 1980s

The entire front gate of the Pine Gap spy base has to be removed after peace activists jam it up with bike locks.

BRISBANE, 1983

During the trial of a number of free speech activists, Special Branch operatives unwittingly reveal that they have been compiling lists of those who sign petitions. To highlight this revelation activists picket the court proceedings, chanting "Lop the Branch" while mysterious figures dressed in overcoats, hats and sunglasses with badges claiming to be from ASIO, KGB, CIA and KAOS mill about in the crowd. One man appears in a red dressing gown claiming to be Cardinal Bernie Maloney from the Vatican Secret Police. As with any gathering in Queensland at this time arrests inevitably ensue.

SYDNEY, 1984

A mobile BUGA-UP embassy is set up outside the offices of Leo Burnett, an advertising firm responsible for marketing Marlboro cigarettes through billboards which turn the "Land of the Dreamtime" into "Marlboro country". BUGA-UP erect a large billboard on site with a picture of a typical WASP ad exec bearing the slogan, "Greed breeds mean deeds." The Embassy also displays 15,000 cigarette butts collected from Aboriginal sacred sites around Australia.

On Thursday May 10th an envoy is sent into the offices of Leo Burnett in a vain bid to establish diplomatic links with the Marlboro country. As a token of esteem a trophy comprising a map of Australia, constructed from recycled billboard components, with cigarette butts marking the Aboriginal sacred sites from which they had been collected, is to be presented to the Philip Morris account executive, but he manages to hide behind a locked door.

Shortly after this mission, the advertising company abandons its tactic of ignoring the embassy and strikes back. The first sign of trouble comes in the form of a visit by officials from the Education Ministry who claim the embassy will have to move as it is on their property. However, following consultations with the BUGA-UP Ambassador, the bureaucrats decide that the embassy is fulfilling an educational purpose and can stay.

Next come the local police who claim shopkeepers have complained that the embassy is harassing the public. The hapless constables inform the Ambassador that they have traced the registered owner of the embassy van to a Phillipa Morris and want to speak to her. It is only after much prompting and the explanation that she is away caring for her mother who is dying of lung cancer that the penny drops and the police abandon their efforts.

After three weeks the embassy is raided. Despite claiming diplomatic immunity its Ambassador is arrested and later that night the embassy removed. The next morning contractors from the Education Ministry construct a fence around the site to prevent further disruptions.

AUSTRALIA WIDE, 1984

In a nationally coordinated action, groups of troublemakers hostile to the gentrification caused by Fremantle's hosting of the impending America's Cup yachting competition spraypaint "Fuck the Cup" in numerous cities. After much media coverage, in which the offending word is censored, cheeky blighters change the slogan to "F... the Cup."

MELBOURNE, 1984

Over a month-long period, members of the Unemployed Workers' Union (UWU) occupy five different Commonwealth Employment Service (the government-run predecessor to the Job Network) offices. Since the unemployed are often forced to spend hours waiting around for mandatory appointments, the UWU demands seating, toilets, childcare and other facilities.

STREET THEATRE
WA, 1980s

Top: War Resisters die-in outside Australian Military Recruitment Centre. Perth, 1980s.

Bottom: Dressed as Smurfs Campaign Against Nuclear Energy activists protest outside BP's offices over the company's connection to the Roxby Downs uranium mine. At the time smurf dolls were only available from BP service stations. Perth, 1981.

Both photographs courtesy of People for Nuclear Disarmament (WA), *Stepping Out for Peace*, 2004.

During the actions activists are tackled by staff and police when they attempt to install coffee urns and a portaloo as well as remove cards advertising jobs which are temporary and/or pay less than Award rates.

DARWIN, 1984

Two stowaways and a protest flotilla made up of canoes, small boats and surfboards delay the uranium carrier *Clydebank* from leaving port.

BRISBANE, 1984

After years of raids, frame-ups and stop and searches, the anarchist community finally gets their chance to retaliate when the police hold a public relations exercise called "Police Week". In an attempt to show the other side of the story, activists organise a Know Your Rights stall alongside the various police exhibits. Two leaflets are distributed, one outlining people's rights when dealing with police and the other detailing the long history of police abuses in Brisbane. Radio ZZZ also comes along to interview police and chronicle the various confrontations that occur. The activists score at least one victory when the police are forced to remove a faked poster of demonstrators laying into cops (suspiciously, the "demonstrators" had short hair and appeared to be police cadets).

ADELAIDE, 1984

An anti-uranium demonstrator splatters Prime Minister Hawke with yellow paint as he enters the National ALP Women's Conference.

AUSTRALIA, 1984

Women hold actions across Australia on ANZAC Day to commemorate the women and children killed and raped in war and to bring to light the fact that Australian veterans have participated in such atrocities. In Sydney women force their way through hostile crowds to lay their own wreath at the ANZAC Memorial, while Hobart sees women dressed in black and wearing white face masks also lay a wreath. The next day the cenotaph is graffitied with slogans such as "Even Heroes Rape In War" and "Lest We Forget The Women Raped In Wars". Police make arrests, but are hard pushed to identify the women since they were all masked during the protest.

In Melbourne a large group of women march with a banner reading "We Recall All Women Raped And Killed, Now And In War — Lest We Forgive". After being battered by police and the crowd the group finally succeed in making their way to lay their own wreath. During the rally they also demand the abolition of ANZAC Day as a nationalist festival.

In Perth 70 women choose a less confrontational path by holding their own memorial rally and vigil before the official one. However, controversy still occurs as it is discovered that other women had sprayed the monument with anti-war slogans the previous evening.

Adelaide also sees women lay a wreath while a separate and independently organised action is held during the ANZAC march with 50 women gathering at Parliament. As the march goes by they turn around to hold high a banner stating "Women Turn Their Backs On War".

In Brisbane 30 women dressed in black, singing, "Its Not Only Men In Uniform Who Pay The Price Of War," disrupt the dawn memorial by waiting until the traditional one minute's silence to really crank up the tune.

CANBERRA, 1984

Eight Greenpeace activists wearing white disposable suits and gas masks walk into Parliament House carrying low-level nuclear waste found in suburban Sydney.

SYDNEY, 1984

Demonstrators disrupt an anti-immigration speech given by historian Geoffrey Blainey by chanting, "Blainey out, Asians in!"

ROXBY DOWNS, 1984

During actions against the construction of the Olympic Dam uranium mine two protesters superglue their hands to a gate to prevent the entry of vehicles. While the police manage to remove them with the use of an oxy-cutter, the pair appear in court the following day with sections of piping and a lock still attached to their bodies.

VICTORIA, 1984

Anti-war activists sell apolitical New Age Confest attendees "Holy Tibetan Water" drawn from the nearby Murray in order to raise money for protest activities.

ALICE SPRINGS, 1980s

In the run-up to the Henley-on-Todd dry-river boat race, members of the "Alice Springs Peace Squadron" accuse US competitors of cheating by using nuclear powered vessels. On the day of the event a lone protester tackles servicemen from the nearby Pine Gap spy base by boarding the US vessel with half a surfboard strapped to his waist.

CANBERRA, 1985

With the help of the Canberra Trades and Labour Council, anti-apartheid protesters build a brick "Laager" (traditional Afrikaner hut) to house an ongoing protest outside the South African Embassy.

SYDNEY, 1985

A failed attempt by a hang glider pilot to land two yellow paint bombs on the deck of the US guided missile destroyer the *Buchanan* ends in a high speed car chase after a policeman dives off a launch, swims to shore and commandeers a vehicle to pursue the bomber and his accomplice through the streets of Watson's Bay. Despite some headlong and dexterous manoeuvres the pair are eventually captured in nearby South Head.

MELBOURNE, 1985

On the same weekend as the commercial Home Show expo, squatters and the homeless hold their own No Home Show in St Kilda's Catani Gardens, setting up a tent city for over 200 people.

DARWIN, 1985

Six anti-nuclear protesters hold up the loading of yellow-cake uranium onto the *Clydebank* by chaining themselves to its mast.

ALICE SPRINGS, 1985

With the Pine Gap spy-base undergoing a major overhaul, peace activists attempt to prevent the US military from bringing in supplies. Veteran Communist and all-round troublemaker Hal Alexander[22] recalls the planning and eventual execution of a daring plan by four plucky cyclists to occupy the Alice Springs runway and thereby prevent massive

Galaxy C-5 transport planes from landing:

There was quite a large group at Priest St. After general discussion the "bikies collective" met outside on the front lawn. There was a lot of discussion about "morality." What if we made the plane crash? What if the crew were killed? And I thought to myself —the crew? What about US! What were the actual dangers? Did we really know what we were in for and so on. Someone reported on landing patterns, on how long it took for the plane to circle and land from a certain spot once it was seen, the role of the control tower, how it had been arranged to check the Richmond Air Force Base departure and when it might arrive ...

Rumble (I think it was) suggested a contingency plan — race out when it landed and paint a symbolic sign on it. Things got more confused. Then Gabriel, a Chilean anarchist, said, "Enough of this shit. We either do it or we don't. I will be in it, but to hell with contingency plans. Once it's landed that's it for me."

That did it. A clear challenge. Gabriel mumbled something like "Pajaro". Wanker in Spanish.

So it was on. Boiled down, four riders, Laurie's truck with Rumble as driver. With Gabriel we had Bob, Brian, and faced with put up or shut up, me. I must have been pissed. An Anarchist, two Comms and a Social Democrat. Not a bad cross-section.

Early on I'd been introduced to a big bloke with a beard who looked a bit Nedkellyish. Brother Dennis Doherty, Marist teacher at Yarara Aboriginal College in the Alice. He offered to come and photograph the action from the front line as it were, carry the water bottle, whatever. We agreed. Having a Catholic priest (of a sort) gave me a feeling of broadness. Maybe he could administer the last rites ...

Up at sparrow fart next morning we met in town, picked up the bikes, stowed them in the back of the truck under the canvas and headed for the airport 5km out. Rumble drove the twin-cab and we circled the terminal parking lot, checked out the various entrances, then headed south towards Santa Teresa mission, 100km plus south. We drove past the end of the tarmac fence line and kept going.

Suddenly, Rumble, looking in the rear vision said, "Shit, there's a wagon tailing us."

"Put your foot down and keep going."

"I have got me bloody foot down. Fucking near through the floor. Bloody Laurie ought to get this old bastard tuned."

The cloud of red dust behind us got closer. Around a bend and we hared off into the desert scrub and into a lonely scraggle of trees. To our amazement the Budget hire kept going. A hurried and somewhat argumentative discussion and we wheeled back towards town. About a mile from the tarmac we off-roaded again and unloaded the bikes, told Rumble to keep going while we went for cover.

Ten minutes later, back came the CIA mob and followed Laurie's beat-out towards town. Rather, its cloud of billowing dust. We couldn't believe it. We'd lost them. J.R. led them back to town, lost them and returned to the airport.

So here we are. Phase one over. More animated disputation. Then, "Let's go, we're in this far, we might as well keep going."

Carrying our conveyances we crept through the stunted coolibahs and spinifex until we reached the road once more. Over the barbed wire and towards the tarmac baking and shimmering in the heat haze of a Centralian summer. The terminal seemed miles away ...

We reached a small stand of bush shrubs, about 500 metres from the end corner of the runway, and dived into the skimpy shade. Bob and me close together, Brian off to the right with his own bush and Gabriel to the left, still clutching the binoculars he'd carried all the way. The Brother was 50 metres to the rear. We waited. The sun belted down. We were hot, we were thirsty. Brian produced a can of drink from his bag and toasted us. Well-chosen epithets convinced him to share. Suddenly a low flying plane skirted the edge of the runway and made several passes.

"We must have them worried," said Bob. Got them worried? This is crazy. More time passed. Gabriel kept bobbing up to scan the surrounds through his binoculars.

"Keep your bloody head down," I remonstrated. "And cover up those bikes with grass and dirt." The chrome was glinting in the sun. Another baking half hour passed. Then a car appeared along the runway. The airport security wagon deposited two guards at the far corner and the driver pulled over to our side. The driver got out. And still we waited.

Brian produced a bamboo stick from his pack and Bob and me watched bemusedly as he attached it to the back of his bike. "What's that," asked Bob. Brian said, "Lukey made me a little banner last night. It's got peace symbols and other stuff written on it." He attached the calico to his little mast. No sooner fixed than it bent at the base and flopped over. "Just like the peace movement," says Bob, "you can never get it up when it's needed."

All frivolities stopped dead. "Holy bloody Mary," says Brian, "there it is!" Out of the south east, a great rumble. Then this huge grey-green monster appeared, wings swept back, heading towards the terminal like a thing from the past.

AWESOME!

We had four and a bit minutes, according to our researchers, before it hit the tarmac after a wide circle over the MacDonnell Ranges (Yipirinya) and back towards us.

"LET'S GO." And we went. Across the rutted flintstone and sandy gullies. Dodging the desert bushes. Sweat streamed into my eyes. Arse over turkey at the halfway mark. Up again, cursing our stupidity. The guard at the station wagon saw us coming, waved his arms and yelled something incomprehensible, ran towards us and then made his blue. He ran back to his motor and roared off to pick up his mates. Maybe he thought the odds too great with four crazy, yelling, stumbling lunatics getting closer.

We hit the runway almost together.

I looked up and tried to see through the blinding sweat and haze. There was the monstrosity. It had turned and was coming back to land. Huge, its roar getting louder.

On the bikes we headed towards it. It towards us. Start praying for us, Brother Dennis.

Closer came the Galaxy. Time? What's time? An abstract, they say. Nothing abstract about the enemy as it dipped over and down below the Ranges. We spread out four abreast a few arms length from each other.

We yelled. We cheered. We'd done it. We'd killed them! Punching the air with our fists in exultation! Almost, it seemed, the plane was upon us. It probably wasn't, but nothing seemed to matter with our neurons scrambled and adrenalin pouring out of our ears.

What mattered was that it stopped descending, began to lift. Its engines on full throttle it screamed overhead, turned westward then north and disappeared back over the Ranges. Landing aborted! Bikes had defeated their technology!

Looking back, the security mob were on our hammer. I was dimly aware Gabriel had disappeared. They'd got him half way down the runway. Ahead the tarmac swarmed with vehicles—the coppers, the security, the CIA. Bob did a wheelie as the security wagon pulled alongside. They stopped and came at me. I dodged and whipped around the back of their car. Bob took off and I followed. A copper jumped out of his car to grab Bob. Again we took off and he had to race back to his vehicle. This kept being repeated, one way or another. No wonder they had the shits with us back at the lock-up.

And where was Brian? Not that I dwelt on it, me and Bob still had our own problems. Ducking and weaving we almost came abreast of the terminal. A mob of about fifty peaceniks were cheering (and laughing) their heads off. A bloody audience. We're not dead. And we stuffed the CIA. Would have been a great time to die.

Mind you, the local lawmen weren't thinking about the CIA. They were after us and would have gladly fulfilled the death wish.

Behind, his hands aloft and off the bike, Brian was being grabbed by the N.T. constabulary. A wave to our troops as I swept past. Bob must have been a goner, nowhere in sight. "The time has come, the walrus said." Two paddy wagons and a car encircled the lone survivor.

A copper jumped out, shouldered me to the ground and my foot caught between the front wheel and the handle bars. The big Sarge started pulling on my shoulders and the rookie on the bike.

"Get up," said the Sarge.

"I can't get up. Your bloody mate won't let go of the bike." Finally we sorted it all out and into the paddy wagon I went. "Greetings, Comrade," one of the ensconced trio said. The four were a unit again. Christ knows, and if he doesn't, who does, where Brother Dennis was.

Driven away from our laughing, cheering supporters we sweated out a seeming two hours in the wagon, so dry and exhausted we gave up, yelling, "Close Pine Gap" and rocking our prison. Forty degrees in the shade and us in a tin three by two out in the sun. For the fourteenth time we were discussing how a cold green snake (or a white death or even a few XXXXs would go) when our guardians climbed aboard and we went to town.

Meanwhile back at the desert, the Bruv had wended his weary way through the desert to the terminal. By this time the plane had finally landed and was unloading its cargo ...

At the airport Rumble's rumble went into action. Suddenly, Jane and Linda went over the fence. Pigs came from everywhere. Within seconds the two women were hoisted high off the ground by the coppers and hustled away. There was a break in the police lines. Over went Rumble. They say he was poetry in motion, like the great Magic Dragon himself as he side-stepped two wallopers, slipped behind their defensive line (he played for Cronulla once) and reefed a plastic bag of orange paint from his kick, smearing it all alongside the Galaxy and a sizeable portion over himself as well.

TOUCHÉ, Madam Defarge said as another aristocratic head lobbed in the basket. Touché's right. They hit Rumble like the wall of a brick outhouse. Another doll over!

While all this nonsense was going on the four muscatels were singing themselves silly, demanding lawyers (stopping short of "guns and money," after all we didn't want to give the wrong impression). We had the watch-house to ourselves. No blackfellas even. Cops all out at the airport and no time to do the rounds of the Todd River to get their quota for the day.

Exhausted from bellowing every song we knew and abusing our captors, we'd just about collapsed what with all the excitement and all when in comes Rumble between two coppers. Orange paint all over him. We were ecstatic as they slotted him into another cell. We exchanged the usual pleasantries that one does under such circumstances and then they carted him off to hospital to have the paint washed out of his eyes.

SYDNEY, 1985

Green guerrillas begin planting fruit and other food-producing trees across Sydney, breaking up much concrete in the process.

MELBOURNE, 1985

Radical Christians scale several barbed wire fences at the Watsonia Army Base to paint "Messenger of Death" on a satellite dish before daubing it with ashes and human blood.

PERTH, 1985

Ten people are arrested by police for painting "human shadows" on the footpath as part of an international action to mark the fortieth anniversary of the bombing of Hiroshima.

MELBOURNE, 1986

A group calling itself the Australian Cultural Terrorists pulls off possibly Australia's most famous art heist. A recently-purchased Picasso painting, The Weeping Woman, worth around $2 million, is stolen from the National Gallery of Victoria over the weekend of 2nd–3rd August. The theft is not discovered until Monday 4th, when a ransom note is sent to the Minister of Arts, the media, and the gallery, reading: "We have stolen the Picasso from the National Gallery as a protest against the niggardly funding of the fine arts in this hick state and against the clumsy, unimaginative stupidity of the administration and distribution of arts funding. Two conditions must be publicly agreed upon if the painting is to be returned:

1. The Minister must announce a commitment to increasing the funding of the arts by 10% in real terms over the next three years and must appoint an independent committee to enquire into the mechanics of the funding of the arts with a view to releasing money from administration and making it available to artists.

2. The Minister must announce a new annual prize for painting open to artists under 30 years of age. Five prizes of $5,000 are to be awarded. The prize is to be called The Picasso Ransom. Because the Minister of Arts is also the Minister of Plod we are giving him a sporting seven days in which to try and have us arrested while he deliberates. There will be no negotiation. At the end of seven days if our demands are not met the painting will be destroyed and our campaign will continue."

The thieves also leave a note in the form of a typed gallery card on the space once occupied by the painting reading, "Removed for renovation". There are no clues to their identity and police are left dumbfounded. The Minister for Arts and Police, Race Mathews, quickly states that Arts funding will not be decided by blackmail, while the gallery's administrator is left with egg on his face after earlier that year stating, "This face will haunt Melbourne for 100 years. Everyone will come to know it very well indeed, I hope."

WARSHIP ACTIONS,
FREMANTLE 1982-1985

As the main Australian port for US military rest and recreation Fremantle has also been the primary site of resistance to warship visits. During the mid-1980s regular protests were held at the docks, out to sea and on US warships. Photographs courtesy of People for Nuclear Disarmament (WA).

During the search for the painting police and gallery staff search art students' studios at the Victorian College of the Arts. While they fail to turn up the original they do discover a suspicious number of copies and interpretations left by students annoyed at the intrusion.

After failing to secure their demands the kidnappers eventually return the painting some weeks later, leaving it carefully wrapped in a locker at the Spencer Street [now Southern Cross] train station.

PERTH, 1986

As a promotional exercise the US Navy and WA State Government set up a Dial-a-Sailor phone line so that people can meet and host visiting US servicemen. Some peace activists enthusiastically respond by inviting sailors home to try and persuade them to join the fight against the war machine, while others leave politicians home addresses, resulting in uncomfortable and unwanted visits.

MELBOURNE, 1986

Peace groups picket the Myer Department Store's "Fête de France", calling for a boycott of the nuclear nation.

FREMANTLE, 1986

During a rally against a visit by nuclear-powered US warships, protesters sing, "Lock up your children, lock up your wives, the sailors are in town endangering our lives."

CANBERRA, 1986

Members of the Shopping Trolleys Against Apartheid group take action against the Coles supermarket chain, a major distributor of South African goods in Australia. Causing a scene in the Monaro Mall they take noticeably full trolleys to each supermarket checkout only to "discover" that the last few items have been made in South Africa. Upon making this "discovery" the shoppers inform the checkout operators that they cannot possibly buy from a store that sells apartheid goods and hand over leaflets explaining why.

YALLAMBIE, 1986

Peace protesters invade the Victorian Army base at Yallambie en masse, blocking roads and creating havoc during an Armed Forces promotional Open Day.

PERTH, 1986

After timber retailer Bunnings decides to sponsor the Festival of Perth their detractors take action by redesigning the official flyer (showing the shadow of a saxophonist with the words "Bunnings thinks you should take to the streets") to depict the shadow of a logger with a chainsaw. The flipside carries a "special message" from Mr Bunnings outlining a variety of environmental abuses his company is responsible for and stating that he hopes people enjoy the festivities regardless.

Thousands of the leaflets are distributed at an official Festival of Perth street party where a band make space for an onstage guerrilla theatre performance about the "evils and degeneracy" of the Bunnings company. When ordered back onstage by an infuriated stage manager the band merely punctuate the jokes with drum rolls and light backing. Having been thoroughly discredited the Bunnings family withdraw future support for the festival, but claim in the media that they're more upset at the signing of the leaflet as "Bunmings" (an apparent mistake) than anything else.

MELBOURNE, 1986

Nuclear-capable warships visiting Melbourne are targeted by a peace fleet. With union bans having already limited the number of ships able to enter the port the fleet are only left with one warship to deal with. On the ship's entry into Princes Pier a scuba diver manages to graffiti the side of the ship with anarchist and peace symbols as well as the slogan "U.S. FUCK OFF". During the ship's Open Day pig's blood is thrown across the deck and people walk on board unveiling T-shirts that spell out the word "DEATH". Arrests naturally ensue, but the police van carrying prisoners away is blockaded for over an hour by a Telecom car and a 44 gallon drum dragged in the way by protesters.

CANBERRA, 1986

An 800-strong women's peace camp set up outside Parliament House expels Liberal Party politicians Amanda Vanstone, Susan Knowles and Jocelyn Newman after they attempt to enter the camp with a male member of staff in tow. Nationals leader Ian Sinclair has a cup of tea poured over his head when he tries to push his way into the camp, but anti-feminist sentiment takes a darker turn when an unknown assailant attempts to firebomb the protest.

FREMANTLE, 1986

During a protest against the arrival of five US warships, a peace protester disarms a US marine by throwing his gun into the harbour.

MELBOURNE, 1987

An imaginative shoplifter recalls:

> Me and this other girl used to go nude shoplifting. She wouldn't actually go nude, but would watch out for me. I'd wear an overcoat with loads of pockets and load it up as usual, but wear nothing underneath. I'd walk out of the shop looking really obvious, but it was only after a few occasions that I was stopped by the security guard. He wanted to search me and at first I refused and acted all indignant and eventually I consented and flashed him. Then whilst he was standing shocked and dumbfounded I just walked out of the shop. I managed to get away with this three or four times.

SOUTH AUSTRALIA, 1987

When charged by police, women arrested during a trespass action at the US spy base at Pine Gap all give the name of the murdered US anti-nuclear whistleblower Karen Silkwood.

MELBOURNE, 1987

150 secondary school students, angry at schools cuts, march on the office of Mr Cathie, the ALP minister for Education, chanting, "1,2,3 and a bit, Mr Cathie's full of shit!" After he refuses to meet their representatives the students blockade the building whilst others ride up and down the elevators. When two representatives are finally allowed in they discover the Minister has run away, prompting the chant, "When the going gets tough, Cathie goes on holiday!"

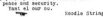

The Empress, which is located at 253 Wellington St, Collingwood, is one up from the corner of Johnston and Wellington. A sizeable building by any standards, the Empress offers huge potential as a place to hold gigs for bands, exhibitions for artists or even space for meditation oriented groups. The people from the Pier Cafe and Squatters' Union have expressed interest in holding cafe nights there once a week, with the place opening for its first night on February 4. Everybody's welcome to come along and help make the night a grand occasion.

Since moving in, permanent members of the establishment have tried to maintain collectiveness as much as possible, by having Mouse Heatings to discuss agreements on long term residents and maintenance of morale on issues that affect the group as a whole. About 8 live here, more or less on a full-time basis, sharing food and domestic chores.

Anyway, until the next we meet on paper, may all the homeless find peace and security.

Yant el our ou.

Noodle String

The Wellington St Empress, or more commonly known as the Factory or Warehouse, first started as a skwot in early December of '87, just prior to the eviction of people from the Princes Pier Cafe, by 3 people, very new to the Melborne street scene.

In its first week of occupation, I met the owner of the premises, who, after seeing the effort we had made in cleaning the place, granted us permission to stay for 5 months, rent free. The owner also gave me his telephone number for assistance in any hassles we might come across, police etc. Since then, many more have decided to stay, some permanently, some temporarily.

AUSTRALIAN SQUATTING SCENE, 1980s

Although people had been taking over disused buildings for housing and social purposes for as long as owners had been leaving properties empty, the 1980s saw a new wave of activity and organisation. Echoing campaigns of the 1930s and 1940s, and in some cases growing out of those of the 1970s, squatters around the country supported one another in finding homes and resisting evictions as well as raising issues related to homelessness, speculation and waste.

Clockwise from top left: Flyer by Jo Waite and story about Empress Cafe squat from Squatters Union of Victoria magazine *Squat It!*, 1988. • Flyer for Port Melbourne's Princes Pier, *Squat It!*, 1987. Artist unknown. • Squat Poster by Heinz/David Pope, *Canberra Crimes*, 1980s. • Melbourne squatters radio show flyer, Squat It!, 1987. Artist unknown. • Wal Larkin cartoon, *Squat It!*, 1988. • Cartoon about the International Year of Shelter For The Homeless, *Squat It!*, 1987. Artist unknown.

ALICE SPRINGS, 1987

Writing in 1998 veteran troublemaker Hal Alexander recalls mass trespass actions at the US Pine Gap spy-base in 1987 as well as the connections between Australian independence and Indigenous struggles and those of French-controlled Kanaky:[23]

Alice Springs activists had worked hard all the year and before. The Alice is the geographical centre of Oz and the focus of a contradiction. Local Arrernte people are engaged in struggle for restoration of land from which they were driven two generations before. The US spy station is at Pine Gap, 20km from town.

The lines of the contradiction, internal and external, cross right here.

The Australian Anti-Bases Campaign Coalition (ABCC) was formed in 1986 after years of activity. It made 1987 a year to challenge the existing ten-year agreement giving amerikan rights to the base.

The Alice Springs Peace Group researched the project. An office, workers' wages for a year, computer, photocopier and whatever. It was a lot of money unless you said it quickly. As always when the need is great committed friends come good. The money was found.

You'd have to know the Alice to realise the enormity of getting 500 plus bodies to the place in October for ten days. How they would eat, sleep and shit, and where? Once again the nameless and unknown started acting as though they'd done it all their lives. It all came together.

The week [included] seminars, cross cultural gatherings with Arrernte people, workshops, Non-Violent Direct Action (this NVDA gets me), media collectives, garbage collections, shit disposal units, kid disposal (sorry) child care centres, print facilities, transport coordination, women's committees, bolt cutters (no connection? No?), and so on. I'm still not clear on NVDA policy when a copper's got you down and his balls are in easy reach.

It was all great and the unsung heroes did it all. What everyone learned in the two days of action that followed was matched by the direct eye-ball stuff with the real "owners" of the patch of desert on which sits the abominable amerikan and his pile of high technology jeopardy.

And so we come to the crotch of the problem. That should be crux, but the NVDA question intervened. The problem is—what to do about the Yank at the front line. And so it came to the last two days. People made their own internal resolutions as to whether to be arrested or not. Mine was, seeing that I owed them still for the bike ride [in which Hal and three other cyclists had blocked a US supply plane from landing], to keep out of it. You never know anyway. These things have their own dynamic.

A lot of stuff is on video. Jumping fences, shinning up the gate surveillance camera tower and superglueing themselves to the metal, cutting fence wire, running from police, climbing trees. Dozens got themselves knocked off. In the heat of summer and the events I went over the fence, done the thongs and got a feet full of Centralian thorns and lumbered by one of the most inept pigs you'd never want to meet.

The yanks kept out of direct contact. Cunning. Protection of the external base area was handled by Federal Police. Complete hoons, more used to patrolling the corridors of power in Canberra where they are pretty useless anyway, they were innocents at large in the desert.

One fat slob was after [ABCC organiser] Doherty. Now Dennis is not one of your Speedy Gonzales over either a short or long course, but he left this prawn for dead. The copper fell turse over arkey on a rock. Ever the solicitous Christian, Den went back, picked him up and asked if he was alright. The ungrateful bastard grabbed our mate and told him he was under arrest. My Arrernte brother Blue Tongue, when I told the story said, "Brother Dennis shoulda kicked shit out of him while he was down."

The Septic Tanks had built three adjoining holding pens (great foresight or rather a spawning of the despicable CIA/ASIO coupling) a few hundred metres inside the base. Women in one, blokes in the others. Sexist pigs. Our captors even gave us oranges and water, again showing they weren't real police. Then, as Steve said later, "You'd whinge either way." After a while, out of the hills comes Polly and her Melbourne mob. They had been camped there all night. Dumb? Not the Vics, the Feds.

We were finally photographed and processed ... Our protectors (Christ help us) finally loaded us in a bus for Alice Springs lock-up. More crazy demonstrators were at the main gate so we were taken on one of the back roads out. Get to a gate and the dills haven't got the right key. Radio base for instructions. More delay. Boring ... And so to the familiar surrounds of the watch-house.

That night the Grandparents drew up a petition for next day.

Next morning the camp meeting decided to have another go. At the base main gate, after all the song and dance routines and speeches, the Oldies, led by Blackfellers Mum Shirl, Bobby Anderson, Newcastle Glad and others tried to hand their statement on behalf of their children and grandchildren in at the gate. When they got nowhere the perimeter wires were cut again and they led the new invasion through the perimeter wire. Many more were arrested ...

And so to the story of Alphonse Dianiou and his uncle Djoubelly Wea. David Bradbury had turned up to record this new attempt to batter down one of the side gates of history. We drove down to the base and he started swinging his anti-yank cam. I was introduced to Alphonse. Bradbury disappeared.

From Kanaky (French New Caledonia) Alphonse was one we helped to get to the Alice. Along with indigenous mob from New Zealand, Belau, Solomons, Philippines and other South Pacific dwellers. He had met Rosie and her mob.

After the dust from the plodding coppers' feet had died down and another big number of souls were safely in the can, Alphonse and I drove back to town.

At Miguel and Christina's where empanadas reigned supreme, we had lunch and talked about here and there and there and here. After we had thrown the frogs out of Kanaky and won Yamba station and property back from our own invaders, Alphonse said he would like to visit the family. Rosie had invited him to see how our people lived.

That afternoon we drove up to the Walpiri camp where most were staying. Some missing were likely to be in Alice Springs jail. Introductions. Old man Willie, old woman Hilda. Their offspring Rosie, Janie, Blue Tongue, Mongrel Dog, Carpita, maybe others. And some of their kids, Matthew, Alison, Priscilla, Annie and several others. That old man and woman had a big mob. The deadly Rice gang.

And JB, about three years and less than two stone, wringing wet. We all settled on the verandah. Alphonse starts to talk, Rosie starts to interpret in Arrernte for the kid. He gestures angrily and she shuts up. Alphonse starts again. This is his story.

"My country is over there. Over that desert and ocean a long way. My people are in a big fight to get their land back. Same but different to you.

"I had to make a big journey through the country and the islands. Everywhere people were fighting for themselves and their families. Trouble everywhere. At each of these places I found a nice stone which I kept.

"When we went to the big city where most of the French live, I was arrested and put in jail. There was nothing to do for a long time. So I would look at my little stones and remember the people there. And make up stories about them, with happy endings.

"So I brought these stones to your place. I would like JB to have them so one day he will come and stay with us for a while. He will learn about my people and teach us about your struggle."

JB took the stones, looked at Alphonse then put them in his tattered shorts pocket. He got up and walked to a small desert tree, sat down and dug a hole. The kid put the stones in the hole, took them out again, put them back in his pocket. He repeated this routine. He was still doing it as we left.

Alphonse Dianiou cannot challenge this. He is dead.

You see, he led that group of young Kanaks who captured that mob of French SAS murderers [in 1988] and hid them in a cave on the Island of Ouvea, which is his place. And after the French rounded up all the women and children, herded them into the communal longhouse and threatened ten deaths for every Frenchman and after all the negotiations were over and they released the criminals unharmed, Alphonse and his comrades walked out with their hands in the air.

These cultured descendants of those who stormed the Bastille cold bloodedly shot them down.

One day JB — John Patrick Rice/Furber — will go to Ouvea. He'll meet the children of Alphonse Dianiou.

Maybe he'll take some desert stones from the Red Centre.

And Djoubelly Wea? Alphonse's Uncle/Father. They rang me from Manila. From Peace Brigade headquarters. Could I meet him and mind him for a couple of days? His flight home to Noumea and Ouvea had been rerouted through Sydney. No problem.

His picture's on the mantlepiece alongside the photo of Rosie and the Old Man. I can't describe people very well. You'd have to see for yourself. He looks like the preacher that he was. Dignified.

That's about best.

He stayed and we talked a lot. Saw videos at Tranby [Aboriginal College]. Djoubelly was most interested in the action stuff. Anti-colonial struggles, like the one Alphonse was in. Got Chris at the Metallies [Australian Metal Workers Union] to rush some copies he wanted his people to see. He took them.

I know something about Kanaky. Alphonse and his Uncle Wea told me. In Australia there are too many advisers about what should be done about the problems of others. Often they are people who know least about here on their own dunghill.

On the occasion of the first commemoration of the murder [in 1989] of Alphonse Dianiou and his comrades, Djoubelly Wea and Le Front de Libération Nationale Kanak et Socialiste (FLNKS) resistance leaders, Jean-Marie Tjibaou and Yeiwene Yeiwene, were killed in a gun battle in which French troops were involved.

At this time of writing I do not know the finer details of how or why this occurred. What I do know is that they were all further victims of colonialism.

At least four of Alphonse's audience on that day in October 87 at the Walpiri camp, all young like him, are now also the dead victims of colonial/capitalist genocide.

ADELAIDE, 1988

Students protesting the ending of free education under the Federal ALP use hit and run tactics to avoid arrest while occupying city intersections, the Stock Exchange and offices belonging to "tax-minimising" companies such as AMP and Elders IXL.

MELBOURNE, 1988

Pedestrians paint in their own zebra crossing along the Princess Highway. Cars observe the crossing and it soon proves popular with locals.

SYDNEY, 1988

The Australian Skeptic's magazine *Skeptic: A Journal of Fact and Opinion* reports that:

During February, Sydney was visited by a fraudulent channeler, but far from being like all the other fraudulent channelers who visit Sydney he was different — he was a fraudulent, fraudulent channeler, an elaborate hoax organised by Richard Carleton of Channel 9's *60 Minutes* and U.S. arch-sceptic James Randi. Preceded by a sophisticated promotional campaign including

a press kit with totally spurious newspaper clippings, reviews and tapes of radio interviews, and a stunningly inane little volume called *The Thought of Carlos*, "channeler" Jose Alvarez was interviewed on several Sydney TV shows. There were also references to him on the radio. *The Today Show* appearance achieved notoriety (and a front page in the afternoon *Daily Mirror*) because Alvarez's manager, upset at sceptical questioning by host George Negus, threw a glass of water at him before storming off the set with his charge in tow.

The culmination of the visit was an appearance at the Drama Theatre of the Sydney Opera House on Sunday, February 21st — a free seminar at which Alvarez channeled a 170-times-reincarnated ex-Atlantean spirit named Carlos to share his wisdom. This proved to be the usual facile predictions for the future, New Age "be nice" pronouncements and the sale of crystals. The seminar was further covered on Channel 9 news that night and *The Today Show* the next morning.

The whole point of the exercise was revealed on *60 Minutes* the following Sunday when Richard Carleton exposed the hoax, which he said was designed to show that the Australian media were inadequate in their background research. The programs could have exposed Carlos/Alvarez by simply phoning the U.S. to check his credentials, all of which were fakes created by Randi. They failed to do this and thus allowed Alvarez a free run with the full benefits of potentially expensive promotion in Sydney's media.

CANBERRA, 1988

The Bicentennial Authority, alleging copyright violation, objects to the use of the slogan "Bugger the Bicentenary" by an Aboriginal group.

MELBOURNE, 1988

A merrymaker recalls:

One time we went to the all-night corner shop in the nude. The guy who worked there was Indian and was always really mopey so we thought we'd cheer him up a bit. So me and this other girl stripped down and went up to the shop and asked for a packet of cigarettes. He gave us the cigarettes and the money and then kind of spun out when he realised what was happening. Then we walked out and went home, but some old woman from the Bowls Club who lived two

'80s POSTERS

Top to bottom, left to right: Condoman, Michael Callaghan, 1988. Redback Graphix, Canberra, for NCAAIDS (National Campaign Against AIDS), Commonwealth Department of Health, Canberra. • No Nukes In The Pacific, Pam Debenham, 1984. The Tin Sheds, Sydney. Screenprint. • Boycott the Bicentennial, Artist unknown, 1988. Courtesy of Jura Archives. • Save The Franklin, Damn The Government, Bob Clutterbuck, 1982. Red Letter Press Collection, Melbourne. Courtesy of the State Library of Victoria. Screenprint. • Grow Your Own Grassroots Defiance, Frances Budden, 1984. Matilda Graphics, Gordon Darling Fund. Screenprint.

doors up dobbed us in to the cops. They turned up to the party and tried to bust people for being naked, but couldn't do anything because we were all clothed. They were asking if we'd seen any naked ladies and we were saying, "No, none of them around here." The funny thing was that we were sacrificing cardboard cut-out effigies of policemen and politicians in a bonfire at the very given moment the cops came in.

BRISBANE, 1988

A huge factory broadcast speaker is hung out of a building on a quiet street in Fortitude Valley near a stop sign. Hooked up to tape it is looped to play, "Two beans plus two beans is four beans," amongst other strange songs and cut-ups. The speaker cannot be seen and the weird messages reverberate throughout the area with seemingly no origin.

MELBOURNE, 1988

A pamphlet entitled "How To Make It Your Bicentenary", which curiously resembles a similar Federal Government effort, calls on people to defoliate Australian Flag flower gardens, squat disused heritage buildings, burn flags, erect billboards marking massacre sites, redo historical graffiti and perform other acts of disgust at the Bicentennial whitewash.

PERTH, 1988

When the University of Western Australia attempts to force students to pay to use outer car parks they are met with swift but anonymous resistance. For almost two months running newly installed ticket machines are smashed each weekend, allowing students continued free parking.

MELBOURNE, 1988

In an attempt to further AIDS awareness, members of the Prostitutes Collective send condoms raining down on the heads of British sailors as they disembark from the HMS *Ark Royal*.

ADELAIDE, 1988

50 students hold a "study-in" occupying the offices of Federal Senator Rosemary Crowley in protest at the ALP's plans to end free education.

MELBOURNE, 1988

An anarchist activist recalls one of Melbourne's more impressive graffiti actions, targeting ALP Transport Minister Jim Kennan's decision to remove conductors:

Stars were sprayed across the sky like kitsch jewellery, flashing colours from deep darkness. The police helicopter zagged across the sky defying criminality by its presence. A police car cruised slowly past us, but we were 80 foot above them and could have spat on them and they would never have known. We were invisible, which is an easy status to acquire if you exist above or below the periphery of a person's vision. The average person has a 30 degree visual site of connection so it's easy to put yourself outside of that.

The view from the Fitzroy silos is great. Behind us the black chasm of suburbia slumbered into dawn. Brunswick Street with its crafted bohemia and coffee shop radicalism postured and partied in front whilst to the left Northcote hill swept down with a cavalcade of lights. With dreadlocks and ragged clothes, addictions and afflictions, life styles and wrong styles we finish our cigarettes, test out knots and harnesses and start to walk backward down the gently sloping top of the silo, feeding the rope out between our legs as we go.

I check my spray-can which is sitting in the pocket of my overalls and make sure I know which way the nozzle is facing. The first time I embarked on this I went to start spraying only to spray paint into my left eye as I was hanging 50 feet from the ground. Martyrdom whilst doing a graffiti run was never the political death I imagined, it lacks the historical precedence that being squashed by a truck at a logging demo has.

I look to my left at Del, she's confidently striding backwards. She comes to the edge of the silo where it drops 90 degrees straight to the ground and starts down the side as if on a Sunday walk. She's spent close to a year living on tree platforms — height has become her perspective. I get to the edge and slowly climb over it, fighting the urge to look at the drunks below. Instead I look for Del. We're doing a joint effort: for the first time in collective Graffiti history we're going to spray paint the silos, having been inspired by the tram dispute. My hand is shaking and my letters are uneven and sloppy like a child's while Del's are straight and adult like. We can't see what we're writing as a whole perspective because we're too close, but as soon as we're finished and

abseiling down to the ground I walk backwards and look up at the silos and there it is in huge letters in red and black. "SACK KENNAN NOT CONNIES." "OBEDIENCE IS SUICIDE." It looks good and we are happy so we pick up the ropes, throw them into the back of a taxi I sometimes use to mask night-time activities and head off into the night.

Within the week *The Melbourne Times* has the silos plastered on their front page with the writer asking for information on how we managed to graffiti them. And so our prank was born. The idea behind it was that an organisation is only as big as its profile and a profile is only as big as you can make it without getting caught. A few of us got together and made a basic plan and then rang *TMT* to ask for the writer who, like a placid groper, took the bait and proceeded to let us reel him in.

We told him to meet us at a café in Brunswick Street the next day at one o'clock. As we knew his name we'd locate him there. Twelve o'clock the next day and five of us are sitting on the 13th floor of the commission flats in Richmond wearing overalls with ski masks in our pockets. At 1pm I'm in a phone box calling the café, the journalist is put on line and I tell him I'll be there in a few minutes. Next I call a taxi company and request that they pick him up at the cafe and bring him to where we are and tell him to go to the 13th floor. Being so high up we have a good view and before long see his taxi coming down our street. Once he enters the block we give him a minute and then pull our ski masks on. The lift doors open and he stands around looking confused until one of us jumps out from the laundry to usher him in.

He stands nervously staring at the five people in ski masks watching him. We tell him that due to the nature and illegality of our organisation we have to keep our identities secret and make sure he isn't being followed. We explain that the police have been after us for a long time and we can't take chances. Then we tell him how we did the graffiti on the silos so that he can establish we are telling the truth — if the graffiti claims sound true then all the other things will also seem true. He believes that we are the people responsible for the graffiti so we start telling him about our organisation. He's looking very excited, but uncomfortable at our location and asks if we can go somewhere else, perhaps his flat in North Melbourne. There is silence and we tell him to wait outside whilst we discuss this. A few

Protest against
public transport cuts,
Melbourne, c. 1989.
Courtesy of www.
greenleft.org.au

NO TRAINS
= MORE CARS
= CHAOS

minutes later we grab his address and tell him to wait outside his flat till we get there, where one person will go up and check if it's safe. He agrees to all this and leaves, after which we proceed to his flat where all checks out.

Soon we're sitting comfortably in his lounge room drinking his tea and eating his cake and biscuits. He's taking notes as we talk about our Australia-wide Anarchist organisation with international links. We tell him we have cells all over the country, that they are small, that we communicate regularly, and meet once a year. We tell him we are involved in anti-militarism, environmental campaigns and general grassroots stuff. We tell him we have trashed equipment owned by mining and logging companies, that we have money to bail our members out of jail and to buy equipment, that bands raise money for us, that we move around a lot to avoid getting caught. We tell him we are well versed in bush and urban tactics, that we despise large political organisations and are affiliated to no one.

He is frantically writing all this down as we feed him the bait of this shadowy militant Anarchist organisation. In truth we didn't tell huge lies, a lot of what we talked about does go on, but the lie lay in the supposed coherence and organisation we talked about which creates the impression of a level of power and commitment that isn't real. We made things sound bigger than they were and he believed it all. After two hours we were finished and left warning him that if we were exposed in any way he'd be in deep shit as we knew where he worked and lived.

The next week a double page spread appeared in the *TMT* talking about this fictitious "Anarchist organisation that has its tentacles throughout Australia." We had managed to get the profile of anarchism noticed in some small way and had used the media effortlessly to achieve it. Sure we never changed the world, but anarchism is only ever mentioned in the media in relation to chaos and we managed to subvert that.

FREMANTLE, 1989
Slabs of concrete in the main mall are torn out and replaced with indigenous trees. A few days later shoppers are confronted with the spectacle of council workers tearing out the trees to replace them with drab concrete once more.

SYDNEY, 1989
As soon as they enter Oxford Street to protest against the Gay and Lesbian Mardi Gras, 1,500 far-right Christian Festival Of Light supporters are confronted by a crowd of over 8,000 people. With same-sex couples making out in front of the homophobes, one brave fellow kisses the notorious Reverend Fred Nile whilst another grabs a FOL microphone to shout, "Gay love is best. Go to hell Fred!"

CANBERRA, 1989
Anti-McDonald's activists consume large quantities of food colouring before entering one of the nation's capital's busiest food outlets. Proceeding to the counter to order a large meal they kick off a Vomit-In puking green, pink and multi-coloured liquid all over the store.

NSW, 1989
Dave Burgess recalls an uncomfortable landing during anti-logging protests in NSW's Southeast forests:[24]

> It was September 1989 during the Southeast blockades, at a stage where the blockades had moved to Coolangubra State Forest which was a 50,000 hectare wilderness area. Forestry were attempting to build Wog Way Road dissecting the wilderness in two. We'd managed to stop them seven kilometres in with tree platforms, and there were also platforms at the other end of the road with a patch in the middle that they hadn't completed, so we decided to put up a tripod there.
>
> I believe it was the first ever tripod used in blockades. We were at the northern end of Wog Way Road. It was the early hours of the morning on the 18th of September and I was pretty new to blockading. I had been down in the Southeast for probably two months and was still pretty keen to be a guinea pig so I volunteered to go up the tripod.
>
> The tripod was made of steel poles made of scaffolding equipment with proper joins. It was a completely new device so we built it very strong. It took a four wheel drive with a rope at the apex to pull it up. The hollow steel pipes were fitted over stakes in the ground to secure it solid on the ground. It was put up over the gate to the forest. The tripod was about ten metres high and I was sitting in a dentist's chair which was suspended under the apex. It was pretty high tech compared

to the tripods now, but it had never been done before.

> At about 6am the first timber workers arrived, saw what was going on and pulled out, and waited down the road. At about eight o'clock the police arrived and brought the timberworkers back to the blockade site. The police proceeded to arrest everyone and asked the timberworkers to assist them to pull down the tripod. At that point most people were arrested or in the bush. There were no people around the base of the tripod.
>
> The police and loggers lifted all the legs off the stakes. I yelled out to them "You're gonna kill me mate." They said, "Yeah, we know that but you should have thought about that before you went up there," and proceeded to push the tripod over. They would have known as soon as they lifted one of the legs how precarious it was.
>
> I fell approximately eight or nine metres from the pod. I didn't land on the road. I landed in the few square metres that would have been a soft landing. The rest of the area would have been really hard. I missed a barbed wire fence by a couple of feet. I missed the graded road and landed on a slope which also helped.
>
> Then the scaffolding crashed down around me, which weighed a fair bit. After I hit the ground the police came up straight away and tried to drag me off. I resisted, telling them I couldn't walk. I had no feeling from the waist down. I had pinched a nerve in my back, but I didn't know that at that stage.
>
> Following that, the rest of the protesters who'd run away in the bush now ran out, angered sufficiently to overcome notions of arrest and confront the police and tell them what they thought of them. The situation was getting quite close to out of control. I was eventually put into an ambulance about an hour or two later. I was pretty hysterical as far as I can remember, going through periods of intense laughter and then deep depression, shaking fits, basically showing all the classic symptoms of shock, and definitely concussion. I was put in the ambulance and taken to Bombala hospital, but there was no x-ray machine at Bombala hospital and I still had no feeling in my legs.
>
> I was taken to Cooma hospital in traction and it was on the way to Cooma hospital that I felt my knees touching together and then I knew I'd probably be all right as far as having full functions was going. For an hour or two I had feared that I may have become paraplegic.

I got to Cooma hospital and the first thing that the doctor said was, "I'm on their side." He tried to have me discharged from hospital even though I was still dizzy. I was finding it hard to stand up and outside the hospital there was a police car waiting and they were ringing up constantly wanting to know when I was going to be released so they could arrest me. Luckily a nurse saw my condition and said, "Stay out of his way until the next doctor comes on duty and we'll sign you in." All through the night I was there and through the next day the police were ringing up, often three or four times within an hour, trying to find out when I'd be released. The next day when it did come to my being released, I had support there by then from other conservationists.

We rang Channel Nine because the tripod had been filmed going down and the footage had made national news. We rang [them] to say I was about to be released and arrested. As I left the hospital the police car was seen driving away as the Channel Nine news car was driving up. I said, "Well, that's all right anyway cos I'm about to go to the police station anyway to put in a complaint."

I went to Cooma police station. At the desk they initially said that they couldn't accept the complaint because it wasn't their business, but I had been advised by lawyers that they could, so I gritted my teeth and stood there saying, "Yes, you can." Then they all went into the back room for a huddle and finally they announced that the Chief Inspector of the region would see me. I went to his office and got treated like a celebrity with a cup of coffee and he outlined very politely what my options were. That done, I went and stayed in a safe house in Cooma for a couple of days and recovered, though I was still very concussed and vomiting a lot.

Following up my complaint I had one interview at police headquarters in Sydney, and the police then proceeded to have their internal inquiry which found that I'd brought on all the circumstances myself, that I'd been violently yelling at and abusing the loggers and police, and that they'd in fact taken half an hour from the moment they'd arrived to getting me down and that they'd in fact tried to coax me down. They also found that the loggers were in a state of near riot and that I had to be pulled down at whatever cost to prevent a riot.

Luckily the independent cameraman who'd filmed it had timed it on his camera and put in a statutory declaration to the police inquiry saying that the whole incident could have taken no longer than a couple of minutes since the arrival of the police which discredited the police, and loggers' statements. That was considered sufficient evidence for the case to be put back to the Ombudsman, that the police were guilty of negligently endangering my safety. He recommended that they be cautioned by their commanding officers and also that no charges be laid against the police involved.

In July 1992, I was at a protest action at the woodchip mill in Eden. Who should turn up again, but one of the police who had tipped me from the tripod. He came straight up to me and said, "I didn't think you'd be at one of these things after what we did to you last time." That was my last contact with him.

PERTH, 1989

In an attempt to liven up the usual boring Palm Sunday Peace March, activists chant, "Merchant banks, not tanks," "Don't drop on my dope crop," and other silliness, while punks are arrested for taunting the police with "He's not political. He's just doing his job."

CANBERRA, 1989

More than 100 demonstrators protest outside the Australian National Gallery during an elite preview of Van Gogh's *Irises*, a painting recently acquired by the magnate Alan Bond. Bond and wife Eileen are forced to enter by the tradesperson's door and their speeches are disrupted by 20 protesters, who make it into the gallery via a side door, carrying a banner reading, "Alan Bond's investments in Chile = torture and oppression."

MELBOURNE, 1989

Squatters paint "Squat This One" with a big arrow pointing up ALP Planning and Environment Minister Tom Roper's driveway after his department continues to evict the homeless from empty public housing properties.

PERTH, 1989

Stencilled graffiti bearing the slogan "Lest We Regret" and the War Resisters International symbol of a broken gun appear across the city on the eve of ANZAC Day.

CANBERRA, 1989

During the opening of the new Parliament House, Greenpeace activists steal the limelight by scaling the building to drop a banner over the entrance reading, "No More Uranium Mines In Kakadu World Park."

PORT KEMBLA, 1989

Activists stop BHP from pumping toxic waste into the ocean by blocking an outflow pipe.

BRISBANE, 1989

One atheistic phone prankster with a grudge against bureaucracy recalls:

> One of my favourite people to call was this Christian outreach counselling line which would pose as a general help line for depressed people and then hit them with all this religious bullshit. I'd ring them and just go, "I'm fucked, boo hoo, etc," and they'd want to have a prayer with me and I'd start mumbling weird stuff like, "Alfredo Legs," and, "You've got the spam," or whatever. It would tie up their lines, but eventually you'd have to give up because they'd keep you on forever with this crap.
>
> I'd also ring up the Tax Office and play tape loops of explosions and screaming and they'd be going, "Hello, hello?" with all this carnage going on. They'd hang up and we'd ring them again over and over. One time I rang up Social Security and I had this cat Megizor who was pregnant. I was telling them, "I have a housemate called Megizor and she's pregnant and she needs benefits, but she can't speak any English," and crapped on for ages. I was saying, "She can't read or write, she doesn't have any education, she just lays around the house, her language is so strange, it's like, meiouw, meiouw." Every time they got annoyed I'd come back to the point, but eventually I told them she had four legs and was small and they hung up.

MELBOURNE, 1989

Anti-apartheid activists protesting against the presence of South African tennis players at the Australian Open march onto an outer court where one of the sanction-busters is about to play. With the support of a theatre workers' union, and with police and the Lawn Tennis Association agreeing not to intervene, the demonstrators burn an effigy of South African President Botha.

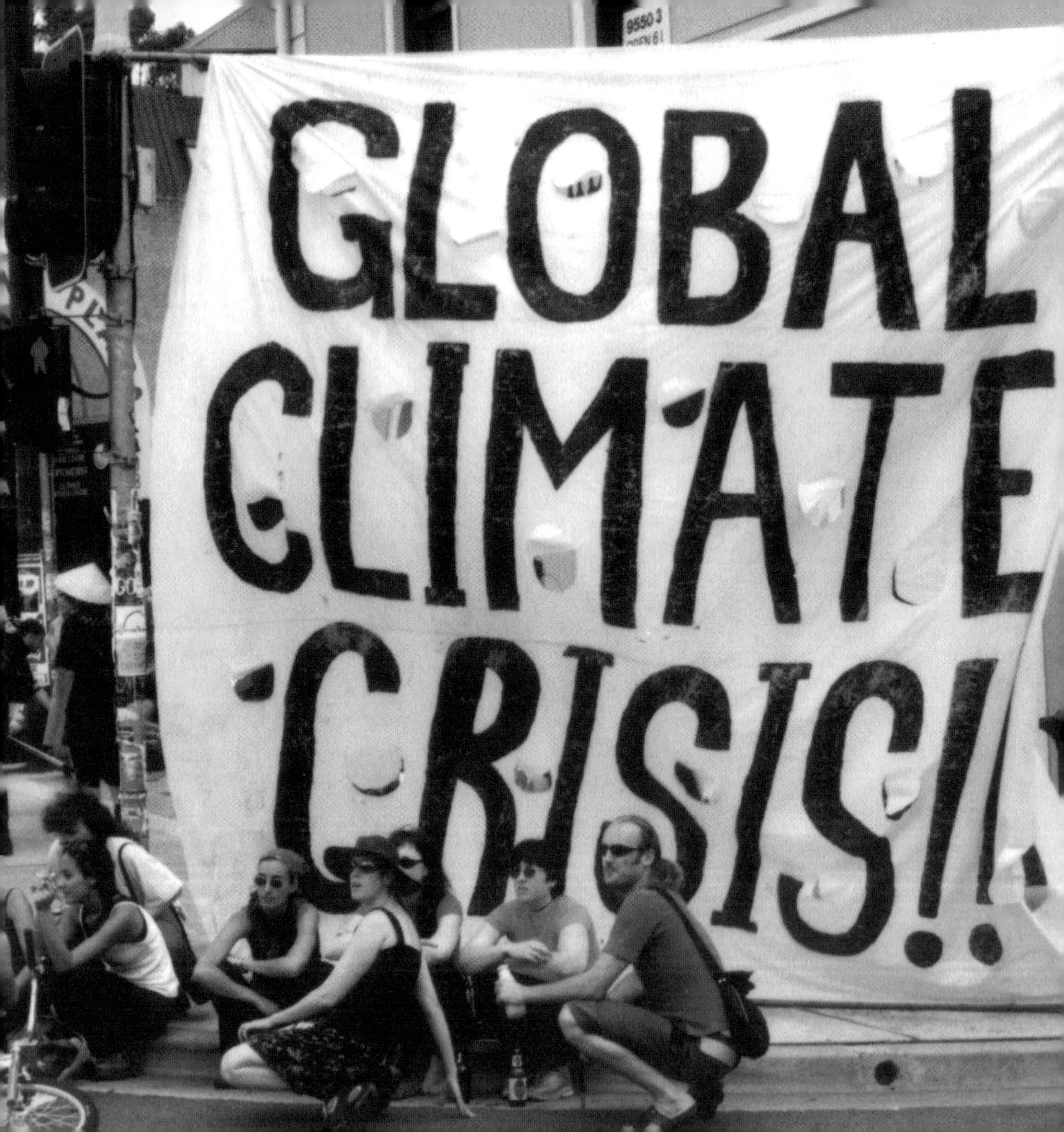
GLOBAL
CLIMATE
CRISIS!!

OPPOSITE: Reclaim the Streets. Sydney, 1997.

Photographer: Ian Sweeney

1990 –1999

The neo-liberal reforms and rightward turn in Australian society that had begun during the previous decade gathered pace during the 1990s. New Right think-tanks, backed by corporate largesse, continued to advocate for the destruction of organised labour and the welfare safety net. Battles between the soft-right (known as "wets") and the hard-right ("dries") within the Liberal Party saw the latter prevail with new governments in Victoria in 1992 and WA in 1993 legislating anti-union laws and imposing major cuts to social services. Although some major employers had also taken up this fight by engaging in stoushes with unions, most were content to stick with the Accord for the first part of the decade.

And who would blame them? In the context of its continuing embrace of market based solutions, and the abandonment of the idea that government should interfere in the economy to protect the living standards of working class Australians, the ALP at Federal and state levels provided investors with major windfalls. Not only did they speed up the privatisation of publicly owned assets in banking, transport and utilities, and the tendering out of government services, but they also convinced unions to agree to further labour market deregulation. Under the concept of "enterprise bargaining" the ability of the state to control wages and conditions via the arbitration system was watered down and unions agreed to make agreements at a workplace rather than industry level. In the context of a stronger economy and union movement this could have been favourable, and was for a few unions, but with unemployment hitting 10% in 1992 and memberships demobilised it further broke down solidarity and influence. Little surprise therefore that between the acquiescence of the bureaucracy and the further destruction of heavily unionised industries in manufacturing – hitting older, migrant and regional workers hardest – union membership slipped to 31% by 1996.

1991 saw the architect of many of the ALP's neo-liberal reforms, Treasurer Paul Keating, take over as PM. Before losing power his predecessor Bob Hawke presided over Australia's first military foray since Vietnam by sending a small force to the Gulf in support of the US invasion of Iraq. Major demonstrations protested this development, spurring on the turn to militancy that a minority in the student, peace and environment movements had already taken. An increase in the level of direct action against logging, the dumping of chemical waste and the importation of rainforest timber was echoed in the membership of all environmental organisations, which topped 700,000 in 1991.

The 1992 culmination of a 10-year court case brought by Torres Strait Islander Eddie Mabo finally saw the High Court recognise that *terra nullius* had been a myth. This could have provided the context for a treaty and land rights, but entrenched interests rapidly whipped up a scare campaign that at its most apoplectic claimed ordinary non-Indigenous Australians stood to lose their homes and property. With the Liberal and National Parties on the rampage, and the High Court providing a restricted definition of Native Title, the Keating government passed off legislation instituting a complex negotiation system and little or no rights and compensation as an equitable outcome. By 2013 only a fraction of Native Title claims would be settled, with Indigenous people remaining the poorest in the nation with a life expectancy 10 to 11.5 years lower than the national average.

John Howard resumed leadership of the Liberal-National Coalition in 1995 and led the parties to victory the following year. A social conservative, the new PM advocated a return to the supposedly "relaxed and comfortable" Australia of the 1950s, where the Left was nullified and nary a non-white face seen. Targeting and scapegoating the unwaged and immigrants, as well as LGBTI and Indigenous Australians, the Coalition further cut social spending, pushed a Christian-Right agenda regarding families and moral conduct, introduced a regressive flat-tax on goods and services and invoked the concept of "mutual obligation" to punish welfare recipients mired in poverty due to neo-liberal reform. In terms of foreign relations the new government refused to sign the Kyoto convention on global warming, repudiated international treaties regarding human rights, simultaneously lorded over and ignored Pacific states, and continued to advocate for trade liberalisation at the expense of poorer countries. Howard personally campaigned against the movement initiated by Paul Keating to make Australia a Republic, and manoeuvring by conservative forces and the inability of Republicans to come up with an attractive alternative saw the majority of Australians vote to retain a Constitutional Monarchy in 1999.

Rejecting the findings of the 1997 *Bringing Them Home* report into the removal of Indigenous children (the 'Stolen Generation') by government authorities, Howard refused to issue an apology, or institute compensation. Spurred on by right-wing commentators (mostly employed by the Murdoch press) his government denied the nation's history of genocide and attacked those who dared criticise his vision of Australia as selfish 'elites'. These efforts were aided by the rise of the ultra-conservative One Nation party, which drew on a racist sector of the Australian population that had suffered under neo-liberalism to recruit 25,000 members and win 23% of the vote in Queensland's 1998 election before collapsing over inner party squabbles and corruption.

Incensed that the previous Liberal-led government had failed to do more against its traditional opponents, PM Howard took advantage of ALP reforms and union demobilisation to push on with further privatisation and workplace deregulation. The 1996 Workplace Relations Act banned solidarity strikes, pushed individual contracts, prohibited compulsory unionism, disallowed the payment of wages to striking workers, and gave the Industrial Relations Commission new powers to end strikes. Hampered to some degree by the ability of the Senate to block it from going even further, the Coalition joined with the right-wing National Farmer's Federation and stevedore company Patricks in 1998 to lock out waterside workers. This attempt to destroy the powerful Maritime Union of Australia and drive fear into the workers of Australia backfired as picket lines of tens of thousands around the country shut down ports and defeated the conspiracy, albeit at the cost of a reduced workforce and poorer conditions.

The Coalition government also sought to expand the nuclear industry. In response ultimately successful national campaigns were undertaken by Western Australians against the creation of a nuclear waste dump in their state and by the Mirrar people against the establishment of a uranium mine at Jabiluka.

Australian governments had long been complicit in the Indonesian occupation of East Timor from 1975 onwards with the ALP going so far as to seize a chunk of the nation's oil wealth via the 1989 Timor Gap Treaty. Australian activists had long supported the independence struggle and a series of mass demonstrations and wildcat industrial action targeted Indonesia after it unleashed militia violence in response to the successful vote for secession in 1999. Responding to popular sentiment, whilst also seeking to continue corporate exploitation, the Australian government provided the bulk of military forces that took part in the subsequent 'stabilisation' of East Timor. This occupation would continue for some years and led Indonesia to discard a previous agreement to block asylum seekers from travelling to Australia by sea. For now, with the Indonesian government in disarray due to popular revolts, the Howard government was content to ignore the complaints of its near neighbour. Indeed emboldened by its perceived success, the Howard government embarked on further military interventions in the Pacific and beyond in the years to come, whilst marketing the military at home as a 'humanitarian' force.

Critical Mass Poster, Newcastle c. 1996. Artist unknown. Photograph by Ian Sweeney

"The power of direct action should not be underestimated. Direct action provokes rebellion, creates cohesion and often changes the values and philosophy of the participants."

Nicole Rogers, 1994

MELBOURNE, 1990

Tram conductors incensed by ALP plans to axe their jobs defy their union's softly, softly approach by staying on the job while refusing to collect fares. Outraged at the idea of free travel, the government responds by switching off power to the trams, locking the workers out of their jobs. Conductors and drivers then proceed to push a number of trams into the city blocking major intersections and disrupting traffic. They also occupy a number of depots, hosing management out of one office in the process. Supporter groups are set up in Brunswick, Preston and South Melbourne to collect food and donations from locals. Although a typical sell-out by union management ends the dispute, the conductors hold the wolves at bay to keep their jobs for an additional eight years.

PERTH, 1990

A missing Christian fundamentalist banner at the University of WA is returned bearing the revised slogan, "Students for Christ AND Satan".

MELBOURNE, 1990

Members of the Melbourne Rainforest Action Group highlight the hypocrisy of Westpac, a major investor in the disastrous Ok Tedi mine in Papua New Guinea, sponsoring National Clean Up Australia Day by delivering a ton of garbage to the bank's city office.

SYDNEY, 1990

Greenpeace divers block a pipeline carrying toxic waste from a Caltex Refinery after tests show that the oil giant is dumping waste into the ocean containing six times the allowed amount of toxic phenol compounds.

PERTH, 1990

In the build-up to the first Gulf War, a cannon at the Fremantle War Monument is repainted from army grey to pink and purple polka dots and adorned with slogans demanding its erection go flaccid.

MELBOURNE, 1991

An artist recalls:

There was this guy and me and we used to go around redecorating the insides of condemned buildings. We'd do it every weekend. We'd go in there and paste it up with photocopied political stuff, usually against the media and technology, and stick up bits of rubbish and muck and whatever else we found. We'd get discarded stuff and put it to new use and then just leave it. We weren't interested in making any particular statement we just wanted to put this space and stuff to use. We mainly did this around Richmond and at the old St Kilda station, but we also did alleyways and other spots.

MELBOURNE, 1991

27 swimmers from the Gulf War Peace Support Team form a peace sign in the water before moving to the bow of the *Westralia* in an attempt to prevent the ship from carrying supplies to the impending war in the Gulf. In the following weeks the group also places a protest wreath at the Shrine of Remembrance, holds a week-long Peace Camp in the city and blockades the Defence Centre building.

CANBERRA, 1991

One anti-war activist recalls:

There we were protesting against the AIDEX arms fair and things were getting really intense. We'd prevented the cops and arms dealers from getting their displays in and having tried to use mass arrest tactics to no avail the cops were resorting to pure violence, busting peoples arms and stuff. Anyway at one point we were all on the road occupying it when the cops start getting ready to crack heads. You could tell when they were going [to] start because they'd put on their latex gloves real slowly, meaning they were going to spill blood. Everyone was bracing themselves for the onslaught when one joker on our side started singing Monty Python's *Always Look On The Bright Side Of Life*. Pretty soon we all started laughing and singing. Even the cops couldn't take the situation seriously and left, so we'd managed to recapture the road and avoid getting beaten up for it, all via the use of humour.

A coarser example of witticism at the same protest emerges after one cop is asked for his badge number at the AIDEX anti-arms fair protest. When he responds with "4946, fuckwit," demonstrators direct a new chant his way "4946 ... Officer FUCKWIT!"

AIDEX, 1991

In November 1991 more than 1,000 protesters blockaded the National Exhibition Centre in Canberra with the goal of shutting down the Australia International Defence Exhibition. Over 12 days AIDEX '91 saw the most police violence and the highest number of arrests in the Australian Capital Territory since the Vietnam era. Amidst round-the-clock picketing of roads and entrances to the National Exhibition Centre activists responded to media negativity and police provocation with determination and humour. Although the exhibition was eventually able to go ahead the blockade caused enough disruption to ensure that AIDEX was never held again.

THIS PAGE **Top left:** That old protest staple, the Grim Reaper, makes an appearance. Canberra, 1991. **Middle left:** Sleeping on the job. Canberra, 1991. **Bottom left:** Picket line. Canberra, 1991. **Top right:** "Crime scene", Canberra, 1991. **Bottom right:** Renegade Activist Action Force's giant prop which was later used to ram the National Exhibition Centre's gates. Canberra, 1991. Photographer: Leo Bild **OPPOSITE PAGE Top left:** Marriage protest. Jules McLellan **Top middle:** Cheers as the OSG leave. Canberra, 1991. Photographer: Leo Bild **Top right:** Photographer: Leo Bild **Centre left:** Tripod sitters. Photographer: Susan Luckman **Middle centre:** One of around 180 arrestees. Canberra, 1991. Photographer: Leo Bild **Top right:** Street theatre by a member of the Sydney Peace Squadron. Canberra, 1991. Photographer: Leo Bild **Bottom left:** A car body donated by a local wrecker for barricading. Canberra, 1991. Photographer: Jules McLellan **Bottom right:** Mass sit-down picket. Canberra, 1991

MELBOURNE, 1991

Police hoax the public by informing the media that they have found evidence at the Coode Island chemical explosion site showing the disaster to have been the work of eco-terrorists. Having harassed environmentalists and diverted attention from the real causes of the explosion, chronic mismanagement, the police quietly reveal months later that this "proof" never existed.

SYDNEY, 1991

Members of Citizens for Accessible Public Transport (CAPT) block traffic in the central city with their wheelchairs as part of a protest over the high cost of taxis and the lack of options for people with disabilities in NSW.

MELBOURNE, 1991

A vegetarian prankster recalls:

> I used to go into the supermarket with these "Warning 100% Clown Fat" stickers. I'd take a hatpin along with me. I'd feel all the weird meat packets and when I was sufficiently grossed out I'd stab holes in the packaging and stick the stickers on them. Then I'd wander around the store acting like a shopper and listen to people's comments. I'd also stick the Clown Fat and other weird stickers at busy tram stops and inside newspapers.

PERTH, 1991

Following disgust at a lack of democracy within their Student Guild, students at the University of WA launch a "Don't Vote, Shoot!" campaign. Posters bearing snipers targets on the faces of all student representatives are pasted up and much graffiti on the theme ensues. In reaction to the campaign more peaceable-minded (although obviously not vegetarian) students launch a "Don't Vote, Fish" campaign.

MELBOURNE, 1991

The creator of Loser Corp. outlines the thinking behind a range of stickers he produced:

> I'm really into stickers, number plates, signs that people put on their desk at work and stuff like that. It's the "people's art" — the means of self-expression for losers outside the culture production monopoly who can't do music or zines to express their angst, but get stickers with opinions to put on the bumper-bar of their car, like, "I'd Rather

Be Surfing." I like job-theme stickers — there's a tradesman's car I see near uni with "Same Shit, Different Day" on it. That's really sad when you think about it.

> I like to extend the range of opinions, or make them more realistic, and so have produced "I'd Rather Be Winning", or "I'd Rather Be Dead", or for Australian bands, "I'd Rather Be Nick Cave". For the "Divers Do It Deeper", "Engineers Do It With Precision" line of stickers I did "Losers Do It Less Often" and "Organisms Do It Competitively". The latter covers all the other stickers on that topic, and pretty much summarises evolutionary biology, or life in general.

> From a sign for putting on your desk saying "You Don't Have To Be Crazy To Work Here, But It Helps" I did "You Don't Have To Be A Loser To Work Here, But It Helps". From the popular TAC slogan "If You Drink, Then Drive, You're A Bloody Idiot" I did "If You Drink, Then Talk, You're A Bloody Idiot", and "If You Think, Then Live, You're A Bloody Idiot".

> Recently I saw two misleading stickers on a car in Fitzroy — "The Goddess Is Dancing" and "Magic Happens" from which I'm making "The Goddess Is Non-Existent" and "Competition Happens".

PERTH, 1992

Perth's dope smokers decide to strike back after Western Australian police advertise their annual Operation Noah "dob in a druggie" day with a poster literally depicting drug users as space monsters threatening children. While some pissed off tokers ride around the city tying up the Noah switchboards by calling the toll-free line from phone boxes and leaving the phone off the hook, others call in to finger politicians, cops and Neighbourhood Watch coordinators as the real criminals.

MELBOURNE, 1991

A former art student recalls:

> At college I used to really hate the segregated art shows, so no matter whose show it was I'd sneak a piece of art up on the walls, steal the price list and re-photocopy it with my piece on there. The funny thing was that the times I did it, the only piece that sold was the one I'd put up. When the Painting Department dobbed me in to the head

of the Arts Department he wound up shaking my hand and saying the college needed more of this sort of dissent.

> I really hated all the "I'm a special girl, I'm a special boy" stuff and I'd go to these people's favourite pub with a tomato sauce bottle and squirt it in their faces and in their hair and laugh and giggle. When they confronted me I'd just go, "I'm mad," and then they'd leave me alone.

> Later on we had to do an exhibition at a professional gallery, which was to consist of serious paintings regarding the meaning of art. What I did was store up all these Vic Bitter labels and plaster them down. I showed the gallery the piece I was supposed to be doing, but on the day instead hung up this grotesque piece with all these Vic Bitter labels in the shape of a bottle with a Vic Bitter border. With that I skipped off never to return.

AUSTRALIA, 1992

With the introduction of the plastic five-dollar bill bearing the Queen's likeness a number of modifications begin to appear on notes. Many thousands either have her head scrubbed out or an incision made through the neck, both symbolically beheading her and reducing the life span of the ugly currency. Other notes have words strategically rubbed out so that "This Australian Note is Legal Tender Throughout Australia and its Territories" comes to read "This Australia Not Legal".

MELBOURNE, 1992

On Invasion (aka Australia) Day Koori activists and their non-Indigenous supporters re-enact the First Fleet's landing with a twist. Instead of engaging in the wholesale annexation of Australia, the sailors, soldiers and convicts arriving at St Kilda beach agree to recognise Aboriginal sovereignty and compensate Indigenous people for the use of their land. When Captain Phillip attempts to scuttle the treaty he is bound on board with convict chains and deported.

TASMANIA, 1992

Earth Firsters and other radical environmentalists blockade and "hijack" a logging train. Dressing as bushrangers, wearing masks, and bearing a banner that reads, "Bushrangers for Bush," the modern day Kelly Gang hold up the train by placing themselves in front of it. Leaflets are passed to train drivers before a tripod is set up and bodies locked onto various parts of it. The train, which is loaded up with dead trees and Chlordane (a carcinogenic insecticide), is held up for over four hours, highlighting the complicity of Tas-Rail in destroying forests — there are no passenger trains in Tasmania — as well as costing them money in wages and profits. Surprisingly, or perhaps not, the raid receives its strongest condemnation not from the logging industry but from the Wilderness Society, which condemns it as an act of eco-terrorism.

MELBOURNE, 1992
An anti-corporate activist recalls:

> My involvement with anti-McDonald's activities stemmed from my background in the anarchist scene and a prank two of my friends pulled off years ago. My two friends were both on the margin of the radical left and were notorious speed freaks. They worked for a certain Student Union which was about to be taken over by a larger and inherently corrupt Union by the end of the year. Faced with the prospect of losing their jobs and, even worse, being unable to satiate their drug appetites they decided to appropriate all the resources they could access for radical causes.
>
> Armed with hundreds of reams of coloured paper, a Pagemaker program and a printing press they churned out tens of thousands of leaflets which would have cost McDonald's heavily. The offending leaflets were exact replicas of the promotional material McDonald's give out to attract customers. Seeing it was coming up to Grand Final day in Melbourne my friends designed a leaflet which gave away a meal worth around $8 to celebrate the Grand Final and McDonald's involvement in the promotion of sport and healthy living.
>
> With the aid of a few pals and untold grams of amphetamines they distributed around 50,000 leaflets by stuffing them under car windscreen wipers and handing them out to the legions of fans leaving the match. Needless to say McDonald's was inundated with orders for the free "Grand Final meal" that Saturday night and for the following week. As a publicity exercise McDonald's didn't refuse the forged vouchers as it was some extra advertising, but it must have been an expensive exercise.

Having admired my friends' exploits and learnt more about the indefensible business practices of McDonald's, as well as having mutated into a vegetarian, I decided I had to act. A good friend of mine who also hated McDonald's with a vengeance had an idea for a voucher and asked me to design it. The voucher entitled the bearer to a free meal if they had collected 10 pieces of McDonald's rubbish. The voucher was supposedly for a new environmental campaign by McDonald's to show their "caring, green" side. I even put a recycling logo with the words, "McDonald's caring for our environment" on it. I made the voucher last till the end of the year to sustain maximum costs for McDonald's. Having no access to a printer I made about 1,000 copies on yellow paper with red ink on a decrepit Xerox copier. The vouchers however were accepted by McDonald's even though kids were constantly raiding their bins to get their 10 bits of rubbish. I also included McDonald's head office phone number with instructions to ring "reverse charges and find out more about our environmental practices."

DARWIN, 1991
One Territorian recalls an attempt to smear the NT's top politician as follows:

> Just a few months after the massacre of East Timorese in Dili, the Northern Territory Chief Minister, Marshall Peron, aka Partial Moron, decided to rip over to Jakarta to see his mate President Suharto. Community feeling was such that a street survey conducted by Murdoch's *Sunday Territorian* found that 8 or 9 people out of every 10 thought he shouldn't go there so soon after the atrocity.
>
> There was a small demonstration at Darwin Airport to see him off. I planned to splatter Partial with red paint as he got out of his limo and then state, "That's for East Timor." I had some watered-down paint in a jam jar, which I poured into a 600ml iced coffee container in the Men's toilets. I then pretended I wasn't part of the demo. Instead I sat on a bench outside by myself near where the car was going to pull up, and placed the container on the ground between my legs. The police outnumbered the demonstrators and were sitting around with nothing to do. One eagle-eyed cop noticed through the window a slight red stain on the spout of my "iced coffee" which I'd been unable to clean off in the toilets. Next thing I knew

there were two cops in front of me demanding to look at my iced coffee. I realised I'd blown my chance.

They demanded the "iced coffee" and wanted my personal details, but I feigned disinterest and finally they left me alone. That was the end of it as I hadn't committed any offence. Partial didn't miss his plane and got through the airport unscathed. Peron realised he'd had a lucky escape and later remarked on *The 7.30 Report* that, "Some people think it's a good idea to pour paint over people."

MELBOURNE, 1992
During a visit by US President George Bush Senior, demonstrators throw mud at police outside the World Trade Centre before marching around the city to occupy government and corporate offices. Whilst all of this is going on outside two activists manage to sneak into the building and head up to the floor where Bush and his fellow dignitaries are chowing down. Security staff are initially gobsmacked when the pair hop out of the elevator, but after they direct a few choice words in the direction of Bush they are hurriedly whisked out of the building.

SYDNEY, 1992
After a busy year of fighting old-growth logging via blockades at Mount Killiekrankie, the Mummel Forest, and the Carrai plateau, as well as helping defeat "resource security" style legislation via lobbying and a tent embassy, the North East Forest Alliance heads to Sydney. As recalled by Tim Somerville:[25]

> The final chapter to 1992 was our storming of the headquarters of the NSW Forestry Commission. It had been the hardest fought, most frantic and probably most important year of the NSW old-growth struggle. NEFA had brought the hill tribes to Sydney and we were as angry as hell after a year in the forests and wanted Sydney to feel the battle that was going on out there. We decided that we would take over the Forest Commission headquarters in Pennant Hills. This was no 1960s style "sit-in" that we had planned, rather it was a cross between a siege and a bloodless coup.
>
> We conducted reconnaissance on the building on the days leading up to the planned action. One guy who worked with the Department

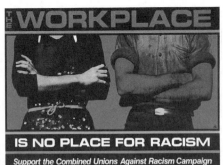

'90s POSTERS: Toppling Sexual Harassment ... Carol Porter, 1994. Red Planet, Melbourne. Screenprint. Courtesy of Trades Hall · The Workplace is No Place for Racism, Gregor Cullen, c. 1995. Redback Graphics. Combined Unions Against Racism Campaign · Kissing Doesn't Kill ACTUP Melbourne. 1990 (AIDS Coalition to Unleash Power). Courtesy of Gay and Lesbian

of Health at the time took in one of our most reliable feral warriors, Rodney. Rodney cut all of his dreadlocks off for the operation. They wore white coats, Heath Department tags, the whole bit, and inspected as much of the building as they could. From these operations we had the floor plan and internal systems well worked out. We also watched from the outside and worked out that at a certain time —7.17am to be precise — you didn't need the electric card to enter, as the security grill in the car park went up, and a security guard was in place with the boom gate down. We decided that that time had to be the optimum time to hit the building.

All we had to do then was get 30 or more ferals, greenies, anarchists or whatever to all appear in Pennant Hills at 5.00 in the morning and somehow not attract attention, and enter this building at 7.22am.

Quite magically we all got to the right place at the right time, took up our respective positions, loaded up the cars and it all happened. It was 7.20, and this morning the boom gate in the car park wasn't even closed, so we just drove two over-full cars, a van and appropriately enough a Landover troop carrier, straight down the ramp and into the underground car park. The plans were perfect. It went like clockwork. People went straight for the lifts, took them to the sixth floor

(the executive suite) and the rooftop as arranged, then blocked them open with pot plants so no one could follow. Someone had brought along ingenious homemade wrought-iron devices which could hold the fire-escape doors secured from the inside. This then locked the whole building.

I was on the sixth floor. Others had reached the roof and abseiled down the side of the building hanging a massive banner reading "Under New Management".

We had succeeded not only in occupying the building, but effectively locking out the whole of the Forest Commission and the police and so began our media offensive, assisted by state-of-the-art fax machines in the Forestry Commission's private suite."

Andrew Culvert picks up the story,[26]

The whole concept was that of a coup, where the old corrupt Forestry Commission was ousted by a popular uprising, and we were the interim administration, the People's Commission for the Forests. We had pre-prepared press releases detailing the coup and had prepared a new Forestry Charter which was immediately faxed out on the Commissioner's group-dial fax to all district and regional offices (with the Commissioner's official

fax header), detailing their responsibilities under the new regime.

Within half an hour, Sydney media had gone into an absolute feeding frenzy, there were helicopters overhead, and people's wives were ringing to seek reassurance that their husbands were safe or asking whether what they had heard on the radio was really true. I had one woman ring and I reassured her that her husband was perfectly safe. There'd just been a bloodless coup, I explained, but it's all sorted out now and working under a new administration. She seemed quite happy, saying, "Oh, all right then, thank you."

We were in the building for five hours all up before the police could chop their way in. The view from the Commissioner Hans Dreilsma's office was excellent. There were fire engines, hosts of police and media and scuffles between police and forestry officials as angry forestry staff harassed protesters outside. At times we feared a full violent Tactical Response Group raid.

The Parliament was in uproar that day, with National Party members calling us terrorists and the Minister banning the Forestry Commission from having any further contact with us. We were eventually arrested and let out on bail to face the media chorus.

MELBOURNE, 1992

Racist "Asians Out" graffiti is revised to read, "Take Asians Out To Dinner—No Borders," and "Asians Shout Death To Racists."

MELBOURNE, 1992

An unemployed activist recalls:

> In 1992 we decided to hold a 'Celebration of Life Under Capitalism.' Basically it was a response to Trades Hall's piteous March for Jobs, which was happening on the same day. We were sick of all these groups calling for full employment when we didn't all want to work and there weren't enough jobs to go around anyway—it was reformist bullshit and a threat to welfare rights.
>
> What we did was plaster posters everywhere that just read, "Celebration of Life Under Capitalism," in big letters with the time, date and place, and no further explanation. On the day we made sure we got there before the other march did and had various banners taking the piss out of it and demanding the sort of things the government would have to do to create full employment anyway—stuff like bringing back conscription, invading Asia, etc. Some of us were also there wearing T-shirts reading things like, "I am in Heaven."
>
> When the cops arrived it was really weird, they thought we were some kind of right-wing loony group and started telling us that they agreed with our views (which to anyone else would be outrageous) and that they'd defend us from these leftie thugs. Of course we got into loads of arguments with the Trades Hall mob, some of whom realised we were a joke, some of whom didn't. By the end of it even the cops finally realised we'd been having them on and I think they arrested someone later in revenge.

PORT AUGUSTA, 1992

Parents freak out and call the police after an overgrown Easter Bunny visits various homes, leaving bizarre gifts and a trail of footprints in white talcum powder.

BRISBANE, 1992

A long-time Queensland activist recalls his part in attempting to expose the farce of electoral politics:

> One of the most successful anarchist posters in the lands of the old British Empire has been the Guy Fawkes [a man captured beneath Parliament House in 1605 attempting to blow it up] poster. All versions of the poster carry a portrait of Guy Fawkes and the simple legend, "The only person to enter Parliament with honest intentions." The huge popularity of the poster reflects more than fond remembrance of Guy Fawkes Night, it represents the cynicism and distrust of Parliamentary politics in the general community. When a version of this poster was produced in Brisbane in 1969 it sold somewhere around 15,000 copies. Interestingly, the celebration of Guy Fawkes Night in Brisbane ended shortly after the appearance of the poster.
>
> My own love affair with Guy Fawkes began in 1986 when I dressed up as him to deliver a protest bomb to the Queensland Parliament. The bomb was a soccer ball painted black with a sparkler for a fuse and I had written a protest poem on it. Needless to say I failed in my attempt to deliver the bomb, though I had a lot of laughs trying.
>
> In 1990 I retired Guy Fawkes, packed his costume away and gave the ball to some kids. But then in 1992 the return of Guy Fawkes occurred due to an event called the Radical Reunion which was to mark the 25th anniversary of the 1967 Civil Liberties march, the first big act of civil disobedience in Brisbane in the '60s. The strangest thing about it was the venue, Parliament House, certainly a controversial choice and one waving a red and black flag at the anarchists. The organisers claimed the choice was ironic, but it showed their now cosy relationship with the Goss Labor Government and I decided to show them irony by announcing I would appear as Guy Fawkes!
>
> To commemorate the occasion I promised to design a special T-shirt. The fact an election was coming further spurred me on since Guy Fawkes is the traditional Brisbane pisstake of any who, like the Greens, try to take the Parliamentary road.
>
> That the irony of it would prove too much for the organisers was predictable. On the Thursday night before the reunion they called me to say they were worried about my plans to appear as Guy Fawkes and would it be okay if Parliamentary security searched me? Now the funniest moment in the original Guy Fawkes protest had been when the Bjelke-Petersen police force insisted on getting their bomb disposal unit to examine my bomb (which was patently a soccer ball with a poem on it). If the committee for the Radical Reunion wanted to look as stupid as the Bjelke-Petersen

> cops then that was fine by me.
>
> It was their second request that made my blood boil as they asked me if I would remove the bomb from the T-Shirt design. I was livid. I mean, you cannot take the bomb from Guy Fawkes. Guy Fawkes is the bomb, the bomb is Guy Fawkes. One expects some hardening of the radical arteries over 25 years, but this was positively sclerotic. I can't say what enraged me the most – their denial of our shared history, their hopeless reformism or their political naivety. On the night I turned up as Guy Fawkes, read my poem, and the committee found themselves as powerless as the previous police force had been to stop me.
>
> Having been reborn, Guy Fawkes decided he would have another shot at Parliament. On the Saturday before the election he appeared at the West End shopping centre to begin a new campaign. He had a stall like the other pollies with a big Vote For Guy Fawkes sign. He handed out leaflets explaining why it was foolish to vote and addressed the crowd through a megaphone. On the Tuesday before the ballot Guy Fawkes appeared on Radio 4ZZZ explaining he would run in every electorate and in every election and that to vote for him was simple. You simply took your pencil and crossed out all the names on the ballot paper, writing, "None of the Above," before drawing a square, putting a one in it and writing "Guy Fawkes" next to it.

MELBOURNE, 1992

A Melbourne Trades Hall May Day banner is revised from "Workers of the World Unite" to "Workers of the World Quit!"

NSW, 1992

Tim Somerville recalls some of the tactics used to temporarily halt the logging of old-growth forest on the Carrai Plateau:[27]

> This was the way 1992 was, it was the middle of the Government's term, they were getting desperate to break the back of the forests issue, with elections safely off in the distance, and we were running hard, ready for any fight, any number of arrests. There were no elections coming up, few avenues for delay left through the courts, so it just had to be direct action all the way.
>
> I went down as part of the forward crew to Carrai. We were determined, we knew this was the last of the old growth on the Carrai plateau, and it was being trashed before our eyes, so we

just decide to stick it out. We needed a strategy to take the forest back from the police. We staged a demonstration in Kempsey at the Forestry office, and meanwhile a number of people, myself included, infiltrated the closed area and began preparing materials for a blockade. It's an enclosed area so we had to move through the bush, cut poles and the whole deal without getting heard or found.

The rest of the crew returned from town and we all knew it was just grim determination, it was now or never. So that night by darkness we got to setting up a full-scale blockade. We had an unregistered vehicle which we ran the police line with, and took it into the closed area as the first line of defence. The point of the car being unregistered was that it was disposable, it was a blockade. We took off the wheels as soon as it was in position. We set up tripods and bipods down the road from the car obstacle. It was on, rucca rucca rucca, from 4am onwards.

There were a couple of cops on the gate at all times, so one person had to take a "fall" and keep those cops busy. One cop was out of action having just arrested our "fall" and the other cop had no more than a radio and the promise of the larger day shift arriving later. There we were just crapping on to the remaining cop, trying to keep him from walking round the corner to where the set up was going on. A role reversal took place at this point where the cops were utterly powerless and we'd taken control of the scene. The cops started protesting that we were on enclosed lands, and to get the car back out and were basically feebly trying to remain in control. At this point in a hilarious bit of cheek, one of our members dressed the cop down and said, "Look mate, you're not in control here, we are, so just stay where you are and wait for your buddies. There's a gaggle of tripods around the corner. The forest is closed all right, it's closed by us."

Come daybreak we'd got a pretty good set up, and we'd prepared to hold them out a second time, and we'd sent a reconnaissance crew into the forest to assess the damage and we held them out for the whole day.

The police were left red-faced. We'd regained the lead. The media came up that day and there were logging trucks lined up the narrow road. The next day the police came in with not only a large, but a particularly nasty, contingent of police. They had done their best to get every nasty cop from Coffs Harbour to Port Macquarie and

they came in with cherry pickers, chainsaws, the rescue squad, the whole bit and the atmosphere was very manic.

The cops blockaded the media out a few kilometres down the road and they were determined to get through. More than any small one-day scene I'd seen, it went off in terms of heated exasperated emotion on both sides. Mainly a sense of defeat from us knowing we were right out on a limb. We'd pushed it as hard as we could and done well, but we couldn't hold it indefinitely. When the log trucks rolled in that afternoon with a cop riding shotgun on each door, there was the scene on our video of the satisfied sergeant pushing his fist into the camera, fuck you greenies. That was it for Carrai, we lost it, it was fucked and the old growth was well and truly destroyed.

MELBOURNE, 1992

Following massive education cutbacks that shut down dozens of schools in working class areas, a series of school occupations occur. Whilst in most cases the seizing of the schools by parents and students is short-lived two occupations see things go much further. Richmond Senior High School is taken over and run by a collective of parents, unemployed teachers and activists for almost a year before being evicted. Pickets and actions follow, but trade union and ALP sabotage undermine their effectiveness, leading the occupiers to accept a relatively poor deal from the government. Northland Senior High School, which had been running a unique program involving Aboriginal community participation, is also occupied and run by a collective of parents, students and others for over a year. They too are evicted, but choose to continue running a "mobile" school squatting the lawns at posh private schools and universities as well as the stairs of State Parliament. Eventually a combination of these actions with a successful court case sees Northland reopen with its original programs intact.

DARWIN, 1992

A Territorian recalls an East Timor solidarity action as follows:

An unknown person hit four targets in one night with red paint bombs for East Timor. These were

delivered to Darwin's Indonesian Consulate and three Northern Territory Government ministers' electoral offices. The funny thing was that the "get away driver" involved didn't know about the attacks until he read about them in the paper. He wouldn't have approved and to this day doesn't know he was involved! He'd simply offered the person a lift home, well insisted really. The person asked him to wait a minute whilst she went to "visit a friend". On her return the driver asked, "Was he there?" to which she replied, "No, but I left a message."

CAIRNS, 1992

The Press Association reveals that plans to form twin cities on the part of West Glamorgan in Wales and Cairns in Queensland are a hoax designed to show how desperate local politicians are for a free holiday. Earlier in the year West Glamorgan councillors had received a letter from the "Cairns Welsh Descendants Association" inviting a delegation to attend a "Sheep Shearing Thanksgiving Festival". The letter claimed Cairns was linked to West Glamorgan through a number of Welsh criminals sent to Australia. Amongst Cairns' founders it was claimed there were a deported horse rustler, a child beater and a mule thief. The Welsh councillors fall for the hoax informing local papers and making travel plans. The truth only comes out when someone in the town admits to setting up the council with the aid of friends in Australia.

MELBOURNE, 1992

The creator of Loser Corp. recalls:

In 1991 and 92 I became obsessed with Darwinian evolutionary theory and its bleak implications for the possibility of a good human society. It made me very depressed for a couple of years, and still does. I wanted to do something dramatic to highlight the issue, like a hunger strike or something. But I thought I'd just get the shit beat out of me if I had to sleep somewhere public at night, so I decided to do a one-day thing, a protest rally against evolution called 'Losers Against Evolution'. I got permission from the council to do it in the City Square on a Saturday. I think they thought it was a religious group protesting the teaching of evolution in schools, whereas actually I totally believe the theory, and wanted to make everyone as depressed about it as I was. There was kind of a joke in the title 'Losers Against Evolution', being that in a sense every protest falls under this heading. I made banners and leaflets, and sat there for the day. Most of the shoppers ignored it. I don't think anyone knew what it was about.

MELBOURNE, 1993

During a Campaign Against Police Violence demonstration protesters receive support from an unexpected quarter when primary school children on an excursion flash them the V for victory sign and shout "Pigs" at the police.

MELBOURNE, 1993

In response to Optus' crass use of surrealist images in their advertising the phone company begins receiving carefully packaged, but very rotten, fish in the post.

AUSTRALIA, 1993

A billboard advertising a Shell petrol company credit card displays a graphic of an eight-lane highway with a gold Shellcard in front of it. All appears normal except for the fact that the card bears the company name of the Vogon Construction Company. Those who have read or watched Douglas Adams' *The Hitchhiker's Guide To The Galaxy* will recall that the Vogons are aliens who destroy the earth in order to build an intergalactic freeway. Insider irony?

MELBOURNE, 1993

Members of the Direct Action Group Survivors (DAGS) picket the Liberal Party's headquarters to protest against cuts to education and services. Small children burst open piñatas bearing Premier Jeff Kennett's likeness to grab lollies with suggestions on fighting the right written on them.

MELBOURNE, 1993

On Hiroshima Day members of guerrilla theatre collective Operation Rhubarb, dressed in bloody rags and made up as war victims, confront shoppers in the Bourke St Mall with howling air raid sirens and numerous die-ins. Later in the day members of the group, along with others, confront Foreign Affairs Minister Gareth Evans during an appearance at Melbourne University.

After a few of the "war victims" howl at him in pain, grab his legs and dribble fake blood onto his suit, Evans cancels the speech and races off from the angry crowd.

MELBOURNE, 1993

When State Treasurer Alan Stockdale arrives at court to defend his public transport cuts against accusations of discrimination he is greeted by, and forced to walk through, two rows of black-clad disability activists maintaining complete silence.

SYDNEY, 1994

False advertisements appear in local Sydney papers taking advantage of the fact that McDonald's sometimes offers free or reduced meals to seniors. The ads state that it is Senior Citizen Week and offer a free meal and drinks to the elderly at a number of stores. After crowds of older folks take advantage of this offer, one store is stripped of supplies and forced to close down for a day.

MELBOURNE, 1994

During an anti-fascist demonstration in Brunswick, National Action's leader Michael Brander receives a direct hit to the mouth with an egg. Later that night the winning lob is replayed in slow motion on Channel 9 news as the Goal Of The Day and a Hole In One.

SYDNEY, 1994

Families and activists from all over NSW set up a tent city in Hyde Park to highlight the lack of alternative accommodation available for intellectually disabled people.

CANBERRA, 1995

Nude statues of Prince Phillip and Queen Elizabeth reclining comfortably on a park bench undergo a series of attacks from forces both hostile and sympathetic to the monarchy. On the night of the piece's unveiling anti-monarchists strike smashing the Queen's head off. Further hi-jinks ensue the following day when off-duty police officer and Vietnam veteran Carey McQuillan travels all the way from Sydney with garments and glue to clothe the couple. While in the process of doing so

he is interrupted by a cyclist who attempts to restore the artwork to its original state.

After chasing the cyclist off McQuillan is confronted by the coordinator of the Canberra National Sculpture Forum, who enters the fray with a hammer and sign stating, "This sculpture has been ceremonially vandalised by someone with a small sense of tolerance and freedom and an even smaller sense of humour." McQuillan responds to this by spraying glue over the interloper. The sculptor at the centre of the uproar welcomes the fuss stating, "I don't care what people think about it as long as they think." A few days later the repaired statue loses its head again, with what's left of the bodies eventually ending up in the courtyard of Community Radio 3CR in Melbourne.

MELBOURNE, 1995

The La Trobe University student newspaper *Rabelais* finds itself the target of government censors after updating and republishing an article entitled The "Art Of Shoplifting" from the NSW anarchist zine *Destroyer 251*. Holding that shoplifting is an art rather than a crime, the article's authors introduce their guide by stating that, "Shoplifting is a topic that is practically relevant to many and it should therefore not become an exclusive craft confined to a small shoplifting elite. On the contrary, shoplifting is an art that deserves the widest possible dissemination ... Sadly, however, many people living precariously on low incomes tend to either: (1) avoid shoplifting for anachronistic moral and/or ethical reasons; or (2) remain ignorant of the better methods and techniques of shoplifting, thus failing to maximise their lifting potential."

Other than exhorting others to take up the practice the authors also attempt to outline their ethics by advising would-be artists that "from the onset, the golden rule of theft should be enunciated: NEVER STEAL FROM SOMEBODY WHO COULD CONCEIVABLY BE A COMRADE. Hence kicking into a house on Bell Street with a beaten up old Mazda in the yard is irresponsible and counter-revolutionary! Be careful, too, about taking stuff from small 'corner store'-type shops—you could be ripping off someone in a situation not dissimilar to your own. On the whole, it is best to play it safe and go straight for the big corporate fuckers."

Ignoring the humorous and political content of the article, the Film and Literature Classification Board decide that one person's art is another person's crime, banning the piece on the grounds that it "promotes, incites or instructs in matters of crime or violence". The students appeal to both the Federal and High Courts, quibbling over the nature of "instruction" and arguing that the relevant authorities are applying political censorship. In the end, despite both courts ruling against the editors, the Victorian Director of Public Prosecutions tires of the affair, opting to drop the charges.

MELBOURNE, 1995

Protesters at Melbourne University shut down an appearance of Premier Kennett whilst chanting "Kennett is a Wanker." The slogan is later described in *The Age* as "unrepeatable".

SYDNEY, 1995

Incensed at state government plans to build a third airport runway, with attendant increased noise and air pollution, residents from a number of suburbs blockade Sydney airport, as recalled by Anthony Kelly in *Non-Violence Today*:

The blockade on December 17 was endorsed by 10,000 people at a protest meeting at Leichhardt Oval in early December and largely planned by a committee from eleven noise-affected local councils, with Mayors and Councillors taking most of the decision-making roles ... In the weeks leading up to the blockade, organising spokespeople including Marrickville Mayor Barry Cotter, continually called for "a peaceful and passive rally" that "mums and dads and kids could come along to" and downplayed any suggestions of arrests or the possibility of going onto the runway.

Secretly, however, a group of approximately 200 people, who had put their names down at the large Leichhardt Oval meeting to take part in an arrestable action had met and been briefed in arrest procedures, legal information, and some non-violence guidelines. These people were not told exactly what their part in the blockade was going to be until the morning of the blockade when they gathered apart from the main crowd and received a short briefing. A separate

marshalling group made up of Greenpeace activists was responsible for this group.

Also planned secretly was the armada of fifty fishing and private boats that gathered at the end of the third runway in Botany Bay. With no fences this was the most likely place for activists to actually get onto the runway to halt takeoffs or landings. Due to the presence of eight water police craft none of the boats tried to enter the 50-metre exclusion zone and risk arrest. Police were also patrolling the runway near the water.

The main body of protesters met at the nearby Tempe oval at 10am on the day of the blockade and from the beginning, the focus was on ten local council representatives including several in full mayoral ceremonial regalia who led the thousands-strong march to the airport. The bulk of the marchers went to the main airport terminals where, through sheer weight of numbers, most of the doors were blocked for some time. Passengers were directed by airport staff to enter various special doors and only people with tickets were allowed into the terminal ...

On the way to the airport terminals the two hundred or so "arrestables", who had remained at the end of the march, broke away and continued walking to the main car park entrance gates. As planned and before the police had even noticed, everybody simply sat down at the car park gates and formed an effective human blockade.

Meanwhile, a kilometre-long convoy of over 100 council vehicles, including dozens of thundering garbage trucks, entered the airport, encircled the domestic terminal access ramps and, to the cheers of the blockading masses, stopped at the most appropriate point to gridlock the road access to the entire airport terminal.

So with the airport surrounded and with the airport car park and traffic blockaded people seemed to settle in to the atmosphere of a festival. While the bulk of the blockaders were entertained by speakers and musicians at the terminals, the car park blockaders shaded themselves from the intense sun and waited for the expected police response. Water trucks, ice-cream and refreshment vans were all surrounded by thirsty and hungry people.

Much fun was had when two people decided to walk back and forth over a zebra crossing and were soon joined by about fifty other people who would nonchalantly walk back and forth in front of the halted cars. The zebra crossers would even stop periodically to allowed the hot

car occupants to drive on.

The 400 police that were present seemed to be mostly occupied with re-directing the chaotic traffic. Many were stationed near and inside the terminals doors, helping the airport security, and there was no concerted police effort to clear or move people over the three hours the blockade eventually lasted for. There were also no arrests ...

Clearly, many other passengers and their friends/relatives felt angry and virtually everybody who caught a plane that day was inconvenienced in some way. However, there seemed to be a balance of passengers who supported the blockade, but wished it was on another day! The blockade disrupted the airport's operations severely, causing 20 of the 118 flights that day to be rescheduled and at least two to be cancelled. The blockade ended at 2pm with a united march out of the airport to chants of "We'll be back".

MELBOURNE, 1995

Red Rooster takeaway stores are hit by a spate of robberies in which thieves remove the S from their rooftop signs. "It drives us nuts," one manager tells *The Age*. "I don't know how they get on the roof, I'm surprised whoever it is hasn't broken their neck by now."

MELBOURNE, 1995

An anarchist who hangs a poster from his lodgings reading "Kennett Must Die" is dobbed in to the police by his landlord. After being charged and fined for minor offences he successfully appeals on the grounds that, whatever the Liberal Premier might think, he is not immortal.

MELBOURNE, 1995

Protesters from Disability Action on Rights and Equity (DARE) blockade trams in the central city for several hours to highlight the demand for accessible public transport.

SYDNEY, 1996

Greenpeace activists campaigning against the use of toxic materials dig up and replace PVC pipes at the Homebush Stadium site before returning the offending items to Olympic authorities.

MELBOURNE, 1996

A 2,000-strong march against education cuts occupies mining company BHP's offices to

GOOLENGOOK
FOREST BLOCKADE,
EAST GIPPSLAND, 1997

A 25-metre quadpod is used to prevent bulldozers and a log-loader
from entering logging coupes in the Goolengook block. Actions such as
these slowed the destruction of old-growth forest for a number of years,
grabbing the attention of the nation in the process.

Photographer: Tony Quoll

highlight how the Coalition's recent budget has benefited big business at the expense of the public.

DARWIN, 1996

A Territorian recalls one East Timor solidarity rally as follows:

> On 13 November 1996 a group of people demonstrated for East Timor's independence at Parliament House. The week before the Malaysian authorities had violently and illegally shut down a private conference on East Timor in East Kuala Lumpur. Participants were beaten, arrested, jailed and deported.
>
> We had heard that the Malaysian High Commissioner was coming up from Canberra for a two-day visit to Darwin. When two official NT Government cars pulled into a side road near Parliament, activists blocked the road and forced them to stop. I rushed over and tried the door on the first car. To my amazement it wasn't locked. I looked in and saw a Malaysian looking dude and asked hesitantly, "Are you the Malaysian Ambassador?" Then I jumped inside the back seat next to him for about one second before being tackled and put in a headlock by a violent plain-clothes cop. People shouted at him to let me go since I hadn't done anything, but he arrested me for trespass on enclosed premises. It was filmed and shown on TV around the nation and Murdoch's *NT News* went on and on about it and had an editorial condemning me. I went to court for it in September 1997 and copped a fine of $1,020, which I'm paying back at $1 a week."

MELBOURNE, 1996

Radio pirates hijack Hitz FM's signal and broadcast their own show, including talk breaks and music. Police fail to track down the culprits or the source of the signal.

BLUE MOUNTAINS, 1996

The Mountains Against McDonald's (MAM) group stage a successful rally and concert outside Council Chambers in protest against a proposed McDonald's fast food outlet. Going against the usual format of rallies, in which a handful of speakers drone on for hours, this protest features around 100 people stating their case against the development in a minute or less. After the development is struck down the following week locals propose hooking up with other groups to form a series of "Mac-Free" zones around Australia.

MELBOURNE, 1996

Ten years after Picasso's *Weeping Woman* is stolen and held to ransom by the Australian Cultural Terrorists a letter is sent to *The Age* from a group called the Australian Cultural Pacifists. The author claims to have been an associate of the original thief and sheds light on various details surrounding the case, claiming Hereward Hogshead (a pseudonym) appropriated the picture as he "Wasn't a celebrity and this was his beef. He really should have been. But his 'de-installation' of a Picasso was celebrated and that was art ... it was a 'crime' of creative genius." The letter goes on to claim that the thief carried the painting out in broad daylight, even getting a guard to open the door for him. He had spent time studying the doorman and ascertained that he only checked items going in, not out, and would assume anyone exiting with a big wooden box would be someone in "authority". Apparently getting the box in had been the difficult part, as the thief had had to smuggle it in piece by piece. Once this was accomplished he had hidden in the gallery after closing time. He then had to remove the frame from the painting, as he had been given the wrong dimensions. This done, he waited until opening time the next day and simply strolled out.

The letter also sheds light on the motives behind the theft by claiming the idea was to get at Race Mathews, who at the time was Minister for both Police and the Arts. Initially the cops threw themselves off the trail since they believed the thief had called them on a silent number only given out to police reporters. In fact it was listed in the telephone directory.

Profiles put together by police at the time were apparently also miles off target, since no arts insiders were involved and the thief relied on his powers of observation. The letter writer points out that many people knew what was going on at the time, but had kept quiet since "contrary to police and media mythology most people do keep things under their hats, even when rewards are on offer. Criminals on the other hand despite their much touted 'Code of Silence' race to see who can rat out who first." The writer concludes by saying that although the thief acted sloppily he still got away with the deed thanks to the fact "that his friends weren't criminals or artists either, so no-one talked."

SYDNEY, 1996

During the Gay and Lesbian Mardi Gras festivities, class-conscious queers graffiti yuppie shops in Oxford Street with "McMardi Gras" and "Pay to be Gay".

MELBOURNE, 1996

The La Trobe University student newspaper *Rabelais* is threatened by police with legal action after it publishes a photograph of Premier Jeff Kennett's face framed in the crosshairs of a gun-sight with the caption, "Is death good enough for this man?" When pushed by journalists for an explanation the paper's editors claim that the picture is a piss-take of the Liberal Party's own use of a rolling gun sight in anti-ALP adverts and state that, "We feel like we have been a target and we [have] turned the tables."

SYDNEY, 1997

Greenpeace activists occupy the roof of the Prime Minister's residence, Kirribilli House, installing solar panels and calling on him to take action against climate change.

MELBOURNE, 1997

A Melbourne troublemaker recalls bringing his love of Australian Rules Football and his hatred of war together:

> I was reading the sports pages during 1997 when I noticed that as part of an upcoming speaking tour former US General "Stormin" Norman Schwarzkopf would be geeing up Collingwood's players before tossing the coin at a match against traditional rivals Carlton. Given that Schwarzkopf had served as the public face of the US military during the Gulf War, I was appalled at this cheap publicity stunt and decided to do something about it.
>
> Forming the group Footy Fans Against Mass Murder (FFAMM), which at that point had a membership of one, I shot off a press release to various media outlets deriding the involvement in

JABILUKA BLOCKADE,
NORTHERN TERRITORY, 1998.

Following decades of opposition to uranium mining the Mirrar people called on supporters from around Australia to take part in blockading construction of the Jabiluka mine on their lands in 1998. Over a period of eight months around 600 people were arrested for disrupting work whilst protests and actions took place around the rest of country, including bank boycotts, high-school walk-outs, graffiti runs and the shutting down of miner North Ltd's Melbourne headquarters for days. Continued resistance by the Mirrar and their supporters, as well as falling commodity prices, saw the project cancelled in 2003.

Above: STOP JABILUKA uranium mine stencil. Alice Springs, 2000. Photographer: Ian Sweeney
Right: Embroidered patch of the Stop Uranium Mining symbol was designed by the Mirrar People with artist Kathleen McCann in 1998 and used in the successful campaign against the Jabiluka Uranium Mine in Kakadu, Northern Territory, Australia.

ReAdvertising stickers by MARCSTA, 1990s and 2000s. www.prdctvsm.com

Top: "One Perfect Day" graffiti, Newcastle 1998. Photographer: Ian Sweeney **Bottom right:** Billboard revision. Newcastle, 1998. Photographer: Ian Sweeney **Bottom left:** Billboard revision. Newcastle, 1998. Photograph courtesy of Sean Healy and Damien Frost.

the Australian game of a man who had presided over the needless slaughter of tens of thousands Iraqi conscripts as they retreated from Kuwait. I pointed out that hundreds of thousands of Australians, many of them footy fans, had taken part in demonstrations against the Gulf War. Given that UN sanctions and continuing air raids were still killing Iraqis in their thousands, FFAMM demanded that an Iraqi bomb victim be given the honour of tossing the coin ahead of a war criminal like the good General. In a twist on the usual right-wing logic around such issues, the press release also decried the decision of the Collingwood Football Club to bring politics into sport by engaging such a controversial figure. It also stated that FFAMM had been convened in response to this outrageous provocation and would be protesting outside the game.

Living in Melbourne I knew that anything connected with Aussie Rules would get a run and sure enough the *Herald Sun* got straight back to me. Over the next few days they printed a series of stories which surprisingly included most of my arguments. Indeed the only derisive comment I received from their journalist was when I told him I was a Dockers [Fremantle Football Club] supporter. The planned protest was also mentioned on 3AW, the ABC and other radio stations, with the result that Schwarzkopf's coin toss was called off for fear that pacifistic footy fans might stage a ground invasion — something I hadn't even thought of!

On the day of the game, myself and a friend who I'd persuaded to help out managed to recruit about 20 or 30 assorted anarchists and malcontents, most of whom hated sport, to join us outside the MCG. We hoisted a hastily spray-painted banner reading "Give Stormin' Norman The Boot!" and handed out flyers to the thronging masses. Surprisingly the ground's security left us alone and we received very little shit from anyone. Most people ignored us and the handful who did stop to argue or hurl abuse were easily matched by those who gave us the thumbs up.

FFAMM made a brief comeback the following year during the MUA dispute when I produced stickers reading "Dockers Fans Say Smash Patricks". Patricks, for those too young to remember, were the company who, with the

connivance of the Howard Government, drove unionists off the docks with dogs and thugs in balaclavas in an attempt to smash the Maritime Union of Australia. The Fremantle Football Club had grown out of two Western Australian teams with a traditional base in the wharves and the team's emblem was an anchor. They really should have been called the "Wharfies" rather than the Americanised "Dockers", but that's a whole other argument. Being a W.A.-based club the stickers didn't get much of a response here in Melbourne, but I sent some over to friends in Perth to put up around the place. I hope that some made it to the picket lines.

I also sent some emails to the Fremantle Football Club's official website pointing out that if Patricks weren't stopped our club's nickname would go from reflecting a proud body of union men to a bunch of parasitic scabs. I didn't receive a reply and none of the online supporter forums ran my emails either. Various people in W.A. did show up to Dockers games with placards in support of the MUA, however, so I obviously wasn't the only fan to give a shit.

FFAMM then lay dormant until 2000 when it was resurrected for the S11 anti-globalisation protests in Melbourne. I set up a website detailing the history of strikes and political action by Aussie Rules footballers and supporters and called on footy fans to show their colours by joining us at the pickets outside Crown Casino. I roped in the same friend who'd helped me years before and we spray-painted another banner and joined virtually every other leftie in Melbourne in shutting down the World Economic Forum.

Only one other bloke turned up to the picket line in his footy gear, but we had a few people stop by with their tales of combining sport and politics. One told us about the time a friend of theirs snuck onto the stage during a post-Grand Final celebration, it was Carlton in the '80s I think, to deliver a speech about the impending dangers of nuclear war. Rather than being booed he was cheered, although probably anything would have been cheered that day.

Another fella told us how a rank-and-file team running for control of the Transport Workers Union in the 1980s would get behind the goals at VFL games. Every time a goal was scored they'd

hoist a banner urging truckies to vote out the incumbent right-wingers, picking up plenty of TV coverage in the process. I'm not sure you'd get away with that anymore as in the AFL era it's only corporate sponsors who get to use such viral marketing methods.

MELBOURNE, 1997

As part of their campaign against the company's destruction of Tasmanian forests, members of the Forest Network dump a tender of woodchips on the driveway of North Ltd's Chief Executive.

HOBART, 1997

Angry at the previous month's Critical Mass debut, in which police cars floundered amongst the 500 non-petrol-guzzling attendees, the blue meanies arrive mob-handed to shut down the ride. Whilst they initially succeed in their goal of controlling and sidelining the massed cyclists they ultimately fail when the riders leave them flatfooted by dispersing into five groups.

MELBOURNE, 1997

The Senior Vice-President of the Real Estate Institute of Victoria is left red-faced after driving around Melbourne's most affluent suburbs unaware that the number plate of his new Porsche had been tampered with. Ian Carmichael, of Carmichael and Weber, had been lunching when he made the mistake of parking his convertible out the front of a rival real estate agency. During his meal someone amended his plate from the pretentious ICOO11 to "WANKER."

NORTHERN TERRITORY, 1998

93 protesters wearing John Howard masks are arrested for trespassing on the Jabiluka mine lease. When asked for their details all reply, "John Howard, Government House, Canberra."

SYDNEY, 1998

The *Sydney Morning Herald* receives and reports on a letter from a group calling itself Concerned Students For A Better World. The

Top: After training wild camels with Coober Pedy local Phil Gee, the cameleers met with Kungkas at the Warina Siding for the trek's launch.
Left: Talking to school kids along the way. Humps Not Dumps travelled from Warina Siding, along the Oodnadatta Track to Olympic Dam uranium mine at Roxby Downs. From there they journeyed through Woomera and then to Maree, Copley and Leigh Creek.
Right: Mel Stron, Wren Redback and Izzy Brown. Photographer unknown.

HUMPS NOT DUMPS,
SOUTH AUSTRALIAN DESERT, 1999

In June-August eight women trekked 1,000 km across Billa Kalina in a bid to draw attention to nuclear activities in South Australia. In support of the Kungka Tjuta's fight, Luna, Wren, Julia, Janine, Mel, Izzy, Sophia and Catherine braved harsh desert conditions for three months on their anti-nuclear camel trek. The Kungka Tjuta is a council of senior Indigenous women from Yankunytjatjara, Antikarinya and Kokatha country who were protesting against government plans to dump radioactive waste in their land, and for the protection of their land and culture. After a sustained community campaign and court action, the government abandoned its plans for the nuclear waste dump in August 2004.

Leaflet, Goulburn, 1999. Courtesy of 7U?

B.M.L.O.

Big Merino Liberation Organisation.

Join us today to help end the exploitation of
the Big Merino.
We believe this the big merino should be
freed from its current state of captivity and
be returned to its natural environment.
Send or fax your letter of complaint to:
Goulburn City Council
locked bag 22
Goulburn N.S.W
2580
fax:02 48234456
Or contact the B.M.L.O to pledge your
support:
po box R420 royal exchange 1225 n.s.w.
sevenuy@hotmail.com

"better just leave that sheep
where it is, or they'll be trouble."

" now listen here, fella.
you leave our Big Merino alone.
goulburnians love that sheep:
its the heart and pride of our
community. thats why we stuck it
next to another one of our
favourite icons, the Servo."

group claims that students working at Sydney Water had triggered the city's water crisis by tampering with samples to make them appear contaminated. After the story hits the headlines Sydney Water conducts tests that prove that the "hoax" is itself a hoax with Sydney's water supplies remaining polluted.

MELBOURNE, 1998

Students disrupt an exhibition celebrating "25 years of excellence" at the Victorian College of the Arts by removing 20 works and replacing them with signs attacking plans to introduce up-front fees.

CANBERRA, 1998

Two ALP staffers are sacked after they give detailed instructions in a party newsletter on how to alter the Liberal Party's website. 32 different people log on and modify the site, linking it to Asian porn sites and changing the Prime Minister's name to "Führer Johnny Hanson Howard."

MEANDER, 1998

Protests against logging on the steep slopes of Tasmania's Mother Cummings Mountain see hundreds of locals arrested for trespass and obstruction. One protester, suitably clad in green and code-named Hector the Forest Protector, spends 12 days sitting on a platform 25 feet up a tree.

MELBOURNE, 1998

Monash students change a slogan on a billboard advertising the university from "Open Your Mind" to "Open Your Wallet".

GEELONG, 1998

After publishing a satirical bumpersticker, locals attempting to stop the destruction of forests surrounding Barwon's water catchments find themselves on the wrong end of Australia's defamation laws. Having already produced a previous effort reading "I Hate The Water Board" they are sued by Board chairman Frank De Stefano for releasing another stating "Barwon Water, Frankly Foul". In his writ De Stefano claims

the Bannockburn Yellowgum Action group imputed that he "was a foul person, was a person smeared with the sewerage of that authority of which he was chairman; was a person who smelt like sewerage and was a person who was unfit to hold the position of the chairman of Barwon Water." Despite the legal move being ludicrously over the top the activists eventually find themselves $10,000 out of pocket.

PERTH, 1998

Anti-nuclear activists disrupt the flow of business by opening and immediately closing bank accounts in protest at Westpac's involvement in uranium mining.

CANBERRA, 1998

Protesters occupy Prime Minister Howard's office, making international phone calls, ordering pizza and defacing a portrait of Johnny's beloved Queen.

MELBOURNE, 1998

Someone at the Melbourne City Council sneaks into the parking division and reprograms a number of infringement ticket machines. Offenders get an extra surprise when they receive parking tickets reading, "Council–Melbourne, Area–Asshole." Embarrassed, the council apologises and drops the fines for all concerned.

TORQUAY, 1999

The Surfriders For Sacred Sites group protests against uranium mining during the Bells Beach international surf competition by unfurling banners reading "No Jabiluka, Not Anywhere."

ADELAIDE, 1999

Following the death of a patient, who lay waiting for treatment for four days in a corridor, 25 nurses occupy a ward at Adelaide's Flinders Medical Centre, which is slated to close due to state government cutbacks. For ten days the nurses continue to roster themselves on for duty until hospital management and board members force their way through a picket line to remove equipment and patients.

AUSTRALIA, 1999

Demonstrators angry at the government's slow response to the destruction wreaked upon East Timor following its independence referendum occupy the roof of Parliament House, dropping banners and spray painting "Shame Australia Shame" on its marble façade. The rest of the country sees large protests in support of the East Timorese, including one in Darwin where rocks are thrown at the Indonesian consulate before its flag is torn down and burnt. Despite threats from Qantas and other firms, workers take official and wildcat action to pressure Jakarta by shutting down flights to and from Indonesia and placing bans on shipping, telecommunications and postal services.

MELBOURNE, 1999

The Victorian Transport Minister Robin Cooper reveals that a major downturn in public transport revenues has occurred since the mass sackings of tram conductors and their replacement with fare machines. Losses are in part a result of increased fare-dodging and in part due to a high level of vandalism directed against the hated Metcard machines. Cooper reveals that 137 out of 485 railway-station machines have been put out of order in the previous three months. Some machines have had coins and chewing gum jammed in their slots while others have had unofficial "Out of Order" stickers placed over their computer screens. In one case a young man is caught pouring battery acid into the coin slots of a number of machines. Apparently a design fault in the equipment has led to a spate of such attacks as when corrosive material is poured into them they malfunction, issuing a cash jackpot for the lucky vandal.

SOUTH AUSTRALIA, 1999

Chuck Foldenauer, head of the Beverley uranium mine, declines to press charges after receiving two servings of public humiliation in the form of "slimings" of green goo from anti-nuclear group Humps Not Dumps.

2000–2012

With even the mildest of Keynesian theories now treated as utopian by mainstream political parties and the media, the new century saw the Howard government pick up the pace of its assault on the legacies of left-wing struggle. In response new movements emerged to reject the individualism, racism and selfishness that had arisen amongst the Australian polity and population during the previous two decades of neo-liberal reform. During 2000, hundreds of thousands rallied around the country for "reconciliation" and justice for Australia's Indigenous peoples and more than 10,000 alter-globalisation protesters blockaded the three-day World Economic Forum in Melbourne. Australian activists had long employed satire, parody and pranks, but utilising new technology, and inspired by local and overseas pioneers, the 2000s saw street art, culture jamming and hacking taken to a new level.

Between 1999 and 2001, 8,000 refugees arrived in Australia by sea. Although these people made up a tiny proportion of the world's displaced the government whipped up a storm over "border protection". In doing so it exploited a number of traditional white fears, including invasion from the North and that Australia's settlers would suffer dispossession to the degree they had imposed on Indigenous locals.

Refusing to let a group of asylum seekers rescued from drowning by the captain of the Norwegian freighter *Tampa* land on Australian territory, and sending SAS commandoes to secure the ship, the Howard government rushed the "Pacific Solution" through Parliament in 2001. Dividing the ALP (which had originally introduced mandatory detention for refugees in 1992) this new legislation tightened eligibility for asylum and benefits, excised Christmas Island and other territories from Australia's migration zone, and exiled refugees to cash-starved Nauru and PNG for processing (from which almost all would eventually be granted refugee status in Australia).

With the September 11 attacks occurring in the US the government further ramped up its xenophobic rhetoric by portraying refugees as potential terrorists, falsely claiming that one group had deliberately thrown their children overboard when approached by the navy. This hyperbolic scare campaign secured the Coalition an election victory, but also brought together a broad social movement. Over the next decade and beyond activists would engage in everything from supporting escapes from detention centres through to running court cases and providing social services to refugees damaged by long term incarceration.

Having previously portrayed Australia as the US government's "deputy-sheriff" in the Asia-Pacific region it was unsurprising that the Coalition rushed to join the invasion of Afghanistan in 2002. Ramping up its bellicose posturing it also threatened to take pre-emptive action against Islamic militants in neighbouring countries after 88 Australians died in a terrorist bombing in Bali. Over 800,000 Australians protested against Australian involvement in the 2003 invasion of Iraq, but the government ploughed on and lacking direction the movement soon faded. Despite sentiments towards peace still clearly surviving amongst large sections of the population, the government's careful cultivation of nationalism and militarism paid it dividends as patriotic symbols and holidays regained a popularity not seen since the Vietnam War.

Amidst setbacks and attacks on their contentious representative body, the Aboriginal and Torres Strait Islander Commission (which was eventually abolished), Indigenous people continued to fight for equality and oppose the destruction of their lands. Campaigns to gain compensation for wages stolen by employers and governments during previous decades gathered pace whilst plans to build a nuclear waste dump near Coober Pedy were scuttled in 2004 by a campaign led by the Kupa Piti Kungka Tjuta Council of female Aboriginal elders.

With the government on their side and unions in retreat employers continued to use lock-outs and other forms of intimidation to force employees to accept individual contracts, insecure working arrangements, and lower wages and conditions. This trend would become an all-out offensive after the Coalition routed a disoriented ALP, led by the erratic Mark Latham, in the 2004 election. Capturing both houses of Parliament for the first time during its reign, the Coalition, in a classic example of double-speak, rammed through "Work Choices" legislation in 2005. This Act expanded the use of individual contracts, undercut minimum wages and conditions, gutted unfair dismissal protections, reduced union access to worksites, and made strikes illegal outside of limited "bargaining" periods, and those within them more difficult to call. A special taskforce, the Australian Building and Construction Commission (ABCC), was given draconian powers, including the ability to jail those who would not answer its questions, in an attempt to remove unions from one of their last strongholds.

In the midst of a resources boom triggered by the expansion of the Chinese economy real wages soon hit a 39-year low and casualisation an all-time high, particularly in the burgeoning service sector. With Australia's top 10% enjoying its largest share of wealth since 1949, and top executives enjoying salaries 97 times that of the average worker, a backlash was not far away.

Despite Victorian nurses successfully defying anti-strike clauses the union bureaucracy chose not to make Work Choices unworkable via industrial action. Instead it channelled mass anger into an electoral campaign which returned the ALP to power in 2007. Hundreds of thousands took part in rallies, but with little pressure from below the ALP, under new leader Kevin Rudd, only softened elements of Work Choices, failing to fully re-establish unfair dismissal protections, abolish the ABCC or restore the right to strike. Rather than attempt to rebuild their still declining membership via industrial struggle, union leaderships accepted this outcome and continued to expend huge amounts of energy, and their members' money, in getting themselves and their factional mates elected to Parliament. By the decade's end there would be small signs of a willingness to defy the law, but for the most part workplace action remained at ebb.

Before being turfed out of power, and becoming only the second PM ever to lose his own electoral seat, Howard launched one final audacious attack in the form of the Intervention. Successfully playing the race card once more, this set of measures saw the government massively extend its control over Indigenous people in the Northern Territory. Using the language of social welfare, playing on a mix of white guilt and racism, and claiming to act in the interests of children, new powers saw the government initially send in the military to oversee porn and alcohol bans in Aboriginal communities, mandate welfare spending regardless of past behaviour, and strip communities of control over their land and assets. In its goal of forcing Aboriginal people out of remote areas and into the mainstream labour force the Intervention also cruelly abolished one of the few government funded areas of paid employment, the Community Development Employment Program (CDEP), thereby removing many essential services from communities.

Upon its election, the new ALP government provided a formal apology to the Stolen Generations, but failed to offer any compensation for their suffering. Most tragically it entrenched the Intervention's punitive measures whilst extending them to other disadvantaged communities. Refusing to build new housing unless Indigenous people signed away control of their land, the bipartisan policy of stripping what little Aboriginal self-determination had been gained in previous decades unsurprisingly entrenched paternalism, dysfunction and powerlessness whilst failing to address the parlous living standards of Australia's first peoples. Despite widespread criticism and a continuing lack of meaningful consultation the ALP chose to extend the program in 2012 by another ten years.

On other fronts, the ALP acceded to the growing movement against global warming by signing the Kyoto protocol and proposing to create a carbon market. Although these moves promised to do little to effectively bring CO_2 emissions down they were vociferously opposed by mining billionaires. Fostering the claims of climate deniers via the media, these interests would eventually defeat the government's legislation in 2009, removing Liberal moderate Malcolm Turnbull from leadership of the Coalition and installing the hard-right Tony Abbott as his successor in the process.

China's ongoing demand for Australian resources largely spared the country from the worst of the Global Financial Crisis. The Rudd government resorted to economic stimulus spending in 2008 and 2009, failing to ease the speculative housing bubble that had lifted rents and put home ownership out of the reach of many Australians, or to reign in the banks that had fuelled it. Having failed to properly regulate schemes subsidising the installation of insulation and solar panels, leading to fires and deaths, the government's credibility nosedived. After it proposed a relatively mild set of new taxes designed to channel money from the overheated mineral sector to ailing sectors of the economy the mining oligarchs revolted once more, initiating a campaign that eventually saw Rudd removed and replaced by Australia's first female PM, Julia Gillard, in 2010.

Corruption, scandals and the obfuscation of politicians at State and Federal level had seen cynicism about Parliamentary politics soar from the late 1980s, reaching an all-time high with the 2010 election. Although this did not translate into an increase in community level direct action or engagement with truly democratic alternatives it did see a spike in informal voting, the spoiling of ballots and support for minor parties and independents. With neither of the major parties able to secure enough seats to rule in their own right the ALP was forced to strike deals with independent MPs and the Greens in order to form a minority government.

Following on 2011's passing of a reduced tax on mining "super profits", the following year saw the ALP, under pressure from its Green allies, finally legislate a tax on carbon, as part of a transition to a market based trading scheme. The government had never intended either package to institute major change and, following pressure from an ascendant Coalition and corporate sector, their final forms were little more than symbolic. Aiming to blunt Coalition attacks on its credibility in the face of a series of refugees drowning, 2012 also saw the government repudiate humanitarian alternatives by once more outsourcing the incarceration and processing of asylum seekers to Nauru and PNG. Despite the at times difficult conditions they were operating in, activists continued to fight on in creative ways, with a series of widespread Occupy-related actions taking place in late 2011, and a national campaign for same-sex marriage equality reaching critical mass in the following two years.

"John Howard, Amanda Vanstone and everyone in Parliament have got to realise that we are the first people of this country ... what right have they got to lock up other people? They got off a bloody boat, or their ancestors did – they can go into a refugee camp, or should I say concentration camp.

It doesn't matter what culture, what religion you are, just try to stand together and stand strong ..."

Linda Dare, Bungala Traditional Owner, speaking at Baxter protest, Port Augusta, 2005.

ALBURY, 2000

In response to Wilson Tuckey's conduct as the Minister for Forestry, an Earth Firster decides to pay the politician a visit while he is attending the AUSTimber 2000 conference. As morning tea is being served the activist comes out of the crowd belting Tuckey with a homemade vegan custard and pear pie. He is immediately arrested and taken away, but not before Tuckey, having regained his composure and with pie dripping down his face, calls on police to release him so that they can settle the matter with their fists. The activist becomes the first Australian pie wielder to face court for his actions, but before long he is joined by another who winds up doing time for pieing Victorian Premier Steve Bracks.

SOUTH AUSTRALIA, 2000

Asylum seekers locked up in the hastily constructed Woomera Detention Centre stage a series of mass breakouts in which hundreds march out of the camp to protest in the main streets of Woomera.

MELBOURNE, 2000

The Department of Human Services rapidly moves to carry out long-delayed repairs on flats in a Port Melbourne housing estate rated "priority zero" after residents embarrass the State ALP Government by moving into a tent city.

SYDNEY, 2000

When the Olympic torch finally reaches the inner city suburb of Newtown it receives quite a different greeting to the rest of the country, as torch bearer and gold medal winning athlete Jane Flemming is resolutely booed by a crowd of 200 locals. The anti-gentrification protesters, bearing banners reading, "Share The Spirit Of Corruption," and, "Bullshit Olympics," also abuse the assembled police and throw fruit at the bus carrying other torch bearers.

NIMBIN, 2000

In a protest against the continuing prohibition of marijuana, locals hold a Hemp Olympix during the town's annual Mardi Grass festival. A Hemp Olympix flame is toted around the local region, beginning its run from the Lismore Court House, the site of many a drug-related conviction. Events held during the Olympix include "Speed" and "Artistic" joint rolling, bong throwing, and the "Irongrower-person" event, which involves having to carry fertiliser and water up steep terrain while covering one's tracks to avoid detection by police helicopters. With the event proving highly popular, the organisers drag the whole thing up to Sydney for a run prior to the official Games.

NSW, 2000

During the annual "Let It Grow" Mardi Grass celebrations in Nimbin members of the Australian Cannabis Law Reform Movement (ACLRM) decide to organise a Freedom Ride tour of all the prisons in NSW as a protest against the jailing of thousands of drug offenders. Described by ACLRM spokesperson Graeme Dunstan as "part cannabis law reform road show and part media circus," the Freedom Ride, aided by prison activists Justice Action, aims to "visit all major rural centres listening to stories of injustice and suffering, talking up civil rights, medicinal cannabis, and industrial hemp."

Despite the NSW Ministry for Corrective Services denying them access to prisons on the grounds "that they would be disruptive to other visitors," the group begins their journey on June 30th with the intention of holding a series of "picnics" outside the institutions. A convoy consisting of Peacebus.com, a heavily decorated bus armed with computers for live web link-ups, and a series of cars bearing flags reading, "End the Drug War/Release the Prisoners," is led out of Nimbin by a Hemp Olympix 2000 torch bearer.

After a weekend in Byron Bay, where police authorities avoid the group despite its policy of openly smoking marijuana, the Peacebus crew crash the annual Grafton Cup race day on Saturday July 7th. After they set up outside the track, stewards request they move their banners for fear of "spooking the horses". Despite the presence of uniformed warders and the Prison Governor, no attempts are made to interfere with protests that later circle the town's prison with a "Big Joint".

The tour's next stop is at Glenn Innes

where, following a public meeting, the group make a stop at the local correctional centre. Supported by local residents, some of whom recently rejected an out-of-court offer of $500,000 in compensation for illegal drug raids, they are initially denied speaking rights by the local police. After lengthy negotiations and a reading of the Summary Offences Act the authorities relent, allowing the group five minutes use of their P.A.

Stiffer opposition is found upon the convoy's arrival in Tamworth as the town's Acting Mayor, Councillor Warren Woodley, is a proponent of the Australian Cities Against Drugs organisation who oppose "harm minimisation policies on the grounds that they encourage drug use". While Mr Woodley's threat on ABC Radio "to move (the convoy) on with axe handles if they go near schools" is not carried out the tour nevertheless loses the use of two of their vehicles after inspections by police.

July 19th sees further difficulties as police and council authorities attempt to prevent a protest from being held outside the Tamworth Town Hall. Undeterred, the activists briefly occupy the Council Chambers, but attempts to torch an effigy of the Grafton Jail fail when a council officer douses it with water. The next day sees the group unceremoniously moved on from their campsite after police once again attempt to prevent them from addressing prisoners.

After taking refuge at NSW's only licensed experimental hemp farm the group raise enough money to repair their vehicles and go on to visit other jails at Bathurst, Junee, Lithgow and Silverwater. Their journey culminates with the burning of a jail effigy outside the US Embassy prior to the holding of the Sydney 2000 Hemp Olympix.

SYDNEY, 2000

100 protesters opposed to the imposition of Goods and Services Tax (GST) on sanitary products and led by a group of red-caped women calling themselves the Menstrual Avengers, march to the city offices of the media magnate Mr Kerry Packer. Having chanted, "Get your bleeding tax off our Tampax," and, "Make Kerry pay, not the poor", the crowd moves on to the Liberal Party HQ,

where women hurl tampons and paste dirty underwear to the front of the building.

MELBOURNE, 2000

In a bid to get him to stop turning a deaf ear to their plight, 50 sacked textile workers hold a barbecue on the nature strip outside the home of Federal Treasurer Peter Costello.

SYDNEY, 2000

Newtown locals throw a street party with vegan food to celebrate the closing of the local McDonald's store.

PERTH, 2000

Riot police smash through a crowd of journalists in order to disperse an anti-GST protest after dyed-red tampons rain down on PM Howard.

MELBOURNE, 2000

Members of the Catch A Tram group blockade trams in the city for two hours demanding accessible public transport for people with disabilities.

AUSTRALIA, 2000

Hackers hijack multinational sportswear manufacturer Nike's website, redirecting visitors to www.s11.org, an activist page promoting anti-globalisation protests against the World Economic Forum in Melbourne. The number of hits on the S11 site rapidly rises from around 50 to 50,000 an hour. Despite an investigation by the FBI and the best efforts of Nike, the hackers evade the long arm of the law.

MELBOURNE, 2000

MOR pop singer Johnny Farnham's record label BMG threatens to sue one of the groups organising the S11 protest after it places a photo of the artist and a link to his song *You're The Voice* on its website. When quizzed by an *Age* reporter as to why anti-globalisation demonstrators have adopted the bland icon's biggest hit, an S11.org spokesperson explains that the number has topped a recent poll of potential protest theme songs. The activist goes on to claim that Farnham's working-class sympathies could be traced back to his 1960s single *Sadie The Cleaning Lady*, that his song *What You Don't Know* quoted

Noam Chomsky, and that his album *Chain Reaction* included lines such as, "Hey all you captains of industry/You line your pockets, but poison me." Despite the legal threats, the track, which includes the lyrics, "You're the voice try and understand it Make a noise and make it clear, We're not going to live in silence We're not going to live in fear", is periodically blasted out from a sound system during the successful disruption of the World Economic Forum (WEF) gathering.

SOUTH AUSTRALIA, 2001

Seven asylum seekers detained in the remote Woomera Detention Centre escape by tunnelling under fences. They remain free for nine days before being recaptured.

MELBOURNE, 2001

Members of the Snuff Puppets performance group grab Australian flags from people during a Federation parade to tear out the Union Jacks before handing them back.

SYDNEY, 2001

During the annual Mardi Gras parade, Gays & Lesbians Against Multinationals (GLAM) take a stand against the pink dollar with a float led by the Revolutionary Cheerleaders, who holler chants against the state, Barbie and capitalism.

MELBOURNE, 2001

In order to highlight the ALP's role in repressing refugees, the electoral office of the Labour Shadow Minister for Immigration (and future Prime Minister), Julia Gillard, is encircled with fencing by activists posing as Australasian Correctional Management (ACM) guards. A spokesperson for the group, which performs the action on the first anniversary of the Tampa incident, states that Ms Gillard is suspected of harbouring escaped asylum seekers and that none of the people inside, including Ms Gillard, have proven that they did not enter the country illegally.

SYDNEY, 2001

During an anti-aeroplane-noise campaign, Sydney's Sonic Soldiers, aka Laurie's Alarm Clock (named after the Minister for Transport) visit the homes of various senior politicians

OLYMPIC GAMES ABORIGINAL TENT EMBASSY
SYDNEY 2000

Aunty Isabel Coe hands out gum leaves during a welcoming ceremony at the Aboriginal Tent Embassy set up in Victoria Park during the Olympic Games to protest the continuing dispossession of Indigenous people.

Photographer: Mark Cunningham

S11 (WEF BLOCKADE)
MELBOURNE, 2001

From September 11-13, 2000, tens of thousands of demonstrators
blockaded the World Economic Forum at Melbourne's Crown Casino,
calling for global justice rather than elitist, profit-driven "globalisation."
The range of protest activities was as diverse as the people who
engaged in them and included mass picketing of the venue, a union rally,
impromptu hip-hop performances, copious graffiti, a march through the
central city, an occupation of the *Herald Sun* headquarters, the trapping of
the WA Premier in his car and much, much more.

Photographers: Jacqui Brown and Lou Smith

at 6:00am to give them a little taste of what others are suffering. With the help of 4,800 watt rock'n'roll bins driven by a 3,000 watt amplifier, the group plays them numbers by the Screaming Jets as well as other Oz rock classics. While their slogan is "Share The Peace ... Not The Noise ... Close Sydney Airport," the protesters are inevitably set upon by pissed-off neighbours.

MELBOURNE, 2001

Angry at the Carlton Football Club's involvement with the corporate giant, activists unfurl a banner reading "Nike sweatshops give us the blues" during a game at Princes Park.

CANBERRA, 2001

As protesters, in defence of the Aboriginal Tent Embassy, converge on Parliament House one Indigenous activist announces that the House's inhabitants are all Survivor-style "voted off the island."

MELBOURNE, 2001

Members of the group QUEER (Queers United to Eradicate Economic Rationalism) stage a die-in and chant "George Pell, go to hell!" distracting worshippers during the conservative Archbishop's Easter address.

SYDNEY, 2001

An "invasion" by 50 Greenpeace protesters, some dressed as barrels of nuclear waste, exposes the lax security at the Lucas Heights nuclear reactor. It takes police four hours to remove the demonstrators, who hang banners from buildings and scale a weather tower as well as a building housing nuclear material.

MELBOURNE, 2001

During a thunderstorm, activists evade security and scale the roof of the Maribyrnong Detention Centre to drop banners reading "Close These Hell Holes" and "Free The Refugees".

SYDNEY, 2001

Following the eviction of the Sydney Broadway Squats by the South Sydney Council, former residents and their supporters keep the pressure up. One squatter recalls a particularly frenzied protest action on Australia Day as follows:

South Sydney residents received an invitation from South Sydney Council to join Mayor John Fowler and councillors in a Centenary of Federation Cricket Match. Not many attended the game at Sydney Park on Sunday 21st ... well, not to play cricket. Shortly after the catered, ratepayer-funded lunch, with the Mayor's XI batting and the General Manager's XI bowling, there was an eruption onto the cricket field with three oversized inflatable yoga balls by the General Manglers versus Mayhem, who were celebrating the SquatSpace Commemoration of Invasion Soccer Match.

The council greeted the soccer interventionists with profanity, pushing over players, running off with the game balls and booting them off the field. Soccer star Minnie Temple was attempting the rescue of one of the balls when she was accosted by the Mayor, who threw his glass of bubbly in her face and grabbed her by the arms, yelling, "Get outta here," until she demanded he stop assaulting her.

Meanwhile, amid council shouts of, "You need a D.A. to play here," and, "Look at your hair and your clothes," Tony Spanos of the Council-plagued Graffiti Hall of Fame was drop-tackled by cricketers as he attempted to hold the cricket wickets ransom for the safe return of the soccer balls. But alas, the inflatable balls fell victim to the sharp end of the retrieved wickets as overheated council folk speared them. The ball deflation brought forward the presentation of the giant cardboard trophy bearing the words "Awarded to the Mayor, John Fowler, on the occasion of the Commemoration of Invasion for the short sheeting (blanketing) of homelessness in SSCC, harassment of street workers, closure of the Graffiti Hall of Fame, sustained campaigning against the Broadway Squats and the Aboriginal Tent Embassy and Outstanding Development in the field of Development." The Mayor thanked the presenters but would not accept the trophy.

MELBOURNE, 2001

Anti-sweatshop activists burn a naughty Nike-wearing puppet on the tram tracks of Collins Street before following this up with a mass burning of Nike shoes.

SYDNEY, 2001

Following the killing of a security guard in a Melbourne Family Planning clinic, Right to Life NSW receives a visit from a few hundred angry feminists chanting, "Right to Life, your name's a lie. You don't care if women die." While some women wear stickers reading, "I've had an abortion and I'm not a criminal," others spill paint on the footpath leaving red handprints as a reminder of, and memorial to, all women who have died because of unsafe abortions.

MELBOURNE, 2001

Responding to the news that children imprisoned at the Woomera Detention Centre have been banned from flying kites they have made out of plastic bags, 30 people turn out at the Maribyrnong Detention Centre to fly their own creations in solidarity.

AUSTRALIA, 2001

In response to an email claiming that, "If there are enough people in the country, about 10,000, who put down the same religion, it becomes a fully recognised and legal religion," over 70,000 Australians claim Jedi as their religion in the national census. Whilst the Australian Bureau of Statistics initially claims that they will not recognise Star Wars-related responses, the unprecedented number of worshippers forces them to both release the figures and engage in further analysis of the age, background and locality of the 0.37% of Australians subscribing to the Jedi cause.

SYDNEY, 2001

One participant at a union blockade of the NSW Parliament recalls:

All day we rallied outside to try and to stop the politicians from going into Parliament to vote against workers' compensation rights. Afterwards I put up some posters about it in the early hours of the morning. In order to glue one onto an overhead sign outside the office of a Labor MP who had crossed the picket line I had to stand on a wheelie bin. While in the process of doing so a police car pulled up with one of the cops inside shouting out, "Hey are you the one who's been putting up the posters all over the area?" With the evidence in hand I could hardly bullshit my way out of it so I said, "Yeah, I suppose I am." To which the police officer replied, "Keep up the good work mate, we support you all the way." He then drove off and left me to finish covering that scab's window with super-glued posters.

SQUATFEST
SYDNEY, 2001 ONWARDS

With Sydney's Tropfest burgeoning into a massive corporate spectacle, squatters and artivists have hosted their own short film festivals since 2001. Held on the same day and time as their wealthier counterpart, Squatfest has been hosted in reclaimed venues such as the Broadway Squats, the Midnight Star Social Centre, the Sydney Park Brickworks, the Sydney Dental Hospital and under the grandstand in Erskineville. Its film programmes have also toured to Newcastle, Melbourne, Perth, and Indonesia.

Photographs courtesy of Keg De Souza and Squatfest.

MELBOURNE, 2001

During the court case concerning two S11 demonstrators who stripped nude to protest against corporate globalisation, a third woman strips outside the Magistrates Court, asking why nudity is considered a crime when global poverty is not.

SYDNEY, 2001

Greenpeace activists expose lax security at Australia's Lucas Heights nuclear reactor by invading the site, climbing the reactor and dropping a banner reading, "Nuclear. Never Safe!"

MELBOURNE, 2001

As part of Fairwear's campaign against the exploitation of outworkers an army of elves invade the David Jones city store to vainly search for clothes bearing the "No Sweat" label. Passing shoppers are also treated to an assortment of "sweat-free" Christmas carols.

SYDNEY, 2001

Interrupting the inauguration of conservative Archbishop George Pell, scores of queers stage a die-in complete with coffins, wreaths, and chalked body marks to demonstrate the results of religious homophobia. The protest is broken up violently by the police and ends with protesters singing the Darth Vader theme to every passing cop.

ALICE SPRINGS, 2002

During a large protest at the Pine Gap US military facility, four anti-war activists decide to do a nude run through the site. After walking all night, avoiding police patrols and navigating the NT desert, the activists strip off and paint slogans on each other's bodies. They wait until a patrol has passed, leap across the fence and run into the base—all within sight of the beefy police presence. After ten minutes of madly dashing through the desert they become lost, and are unable to figure out why the police aren't chasing them. After some further investigation, they discover that they have jumped the wrong fence, and have been running around naked outside of the base. To make matters worse the male members of the group have "Penises for peace," sunburnt into their chests and the women, "Cunts against cunts."

SYDNEY, 2002

In a bizarre promotional effort, the Federal Government's nuclear agency ANSTO decides to hold a competition asking school kids to name its proposed second nuclear reactor at Lucas Heights. Greenpeace and other anti-nuclear campaigners get in on the act coming up with such choice titles as Leukemia Heights, Melting Moments, Lupus Blights and ANSTO's Ashes.

MELBOURNE, 2002

After a colleague has her pay cut for the crime of having more than three personal items on her desk, 40 of her colleagues at an Australia Post call centre flood their desks with photos and nick-knacks.

SOUTH AUSTRALIA, 2002

At least 58 asylum seekers at the Woomera Detention Centre sew their lips together in protest at their ill-treatment and silencing by the Federal Government.

MELBOURNE, 2002

After fooling the producers of Australia's top rating current affairs TV shows into producing programs 'revealing' the activities of a phalanx of masked welfare rorting, sewer dwelling activists The Dole Army release the following statement:

Last night the big guns of Tabloid TV ran competing stories on the fictional group the "Dole Army". They claimed to expose gangs of jobless militants inhabiting Melbourne's drains, surfacing only to scavenge food from bins – and organising through the internet.

Today Tonight reporter Norm Beaman's introductory voiceover began: "If it wasn't true, it would almost be comical." It wasn't true and the joke's on you, Norm. These ridiculous stories of sewer dwellers would have more accurately described the journalists themselves. "We approached them with exactly the kind of story they love and they lapped it up like dogs," said The Dole Army's Emma Goldman. "They enjoy nothing more than victimising the poor and unemployed. We did it to avenge the Paxtons [a family persecuted by the tabloid media].

We also wanted to publicise our website, www.

dolearmy.org", added Kool Keith. "And it's worked – the website has received literally thousands of hits since the stories went to air last night. That's thousands of unemployed people now better equipped to deal with the inhuman Centrelink bureaucracy – and we'd like to thank these TV shows for helping us get the message out. Not to mention the $1,000 Today Tonight paid us which will help keep The Dole Army website alive."

The shamelessly ratings-driven bully tactics of these two programs are well known. A Current Affair (ACA) were publicly embarrassed by their hatchet job on the Paxton kids, the Robert Bogucki "Banana chunder blunder", and most tragically, by Benny Mendoza, a repairman who committed suicide after ACA accused him of poor workmanship.

(ACA host) Mike Munro is not known for his honesty, but the following closing comment surprised even us. "Let me assure you that we did not pay anyone from that courageous and charming pack back in the Dole Army." We'll give Mike the benefit of the count and assume the producers neglected to mention the 30 blank digital videotapes (worth $360) they gave us in exchange for a video of masked figures pretending to play Cluedo in a tunnel, and the $2000 they offered us to deny Today Tonight a chance at the follow-up story.

Today Tonight (TT) is also no stranger to the invented story paraded as fact – the infamous "Majorca Skase Chase" was mocked up in the theatrical district of Barcelona. True to form while shooting the Dole Army expose, the TT crew happily colluded in setting up a fake drain dwelling in an above-ground brick factory.

DARWIN, 2002

In response to racist attacks on Muslim women, Avigail Abarbanel, President of the Australian National Network of Counsellors, organises National Headscarf Day in which thousands show solidarity with Muslim people by adopting their head wear.

CANBERRA, 2002

While an on-ground demonstration distracts police, three Greenpeace protesters climb the Parliament House flagpole to unfurl a massive banner reading "Ratify Kyoto Now."

UNREAL ESTATE, NEWCASTLE, 2002

During the This Is Not Art festival activists from SquatSpace highlighted the large number of disused properties going to waste in Newcastle via an unconventional advertising campaign entitled unReal Estate. Utilising postcards and a property board featuring a number of empties, the group lured in hundreds of shoppers in the Hunter Street Mall. Although the artists were condemned by developers and real estate agents, they received the support of Newcastle Mayor John Tate who stated, "I would like to think that people didn't have to squat, that is not reality but it is a goal."

Photographs courtesy of www.squatspace.com

Abandoned
unREAL ESTATE

DIAMOND IN THE ROUGH!

This gem of a building located in the gothic precinct of West Newcastle is the jewel in the crown of the city's empties. Classic post-art-deco styling up top, grungy poster wall on street level, and, out the back, a fully secluded nature space to call your own. This one was hewn from the same blood sweat and tears as Newcastle itself, and you, too, may have to carve out your own way - note that the owner has removed half the rear staircase!

Hunter Street; Newcastle West

Don't Let Houses Rot! ™

http://squat.net/shac
squatspace@yahoo.com

WOOMERA, 2002

1,000 people protest over Easter in opposition to the mandatory detention of refugees, and in solidarity with those protesting inside. During the protest fences were torn down and a number of refugees escaped. Festival of Freedom, Woomera Detention Centre, South Australia.

Photographer: Tom Sevil

ANTI-WAR ACTIONS
SYDNEY 2000s

Top: Advertising billboard located on top of the old grain silos overlooking Anzac Bridge is revised to read "Skyy Blue So Baghdad" and "democracy – we deliver". Christmas, 2004.

Photographer: Dean Sewell.

Bottom: "You're just another spare part" Billboard alteration, Sydney.

Courtesy of Mutiny Collective.

Opposite Page: Placards and banners. Sydney peace protests, 2002-03.

Photographer: moz.net.nz

STREET ART & POETRY,

2004-2005

Stencilled billboard collage. The word "terrorist" is repeated over and over, emulating tabloid newsprint. The billboard backing this one, facing the other direction, was for army recruitment. Princes Highway, Tempe, Sydney, 2005.

Courtesy of Ned Sevil and Anwyn Crawford.

"BIT BY BIT THE CITY BEWILDERS US" painted beside busy overpass near entrance to Pyrmont Bridge, Sydney, 2004.

Courtesy of Ned Sevil and Anwyn Crawford.

HUMAN ALPHABET PROTESTS,

2000s

Women take part in the Disrobe to Disarm action spelling No War with their naked bodies. Leichhardt Football Oval Sydney, 2003. All work to make such a large-scale event possible was donated, including cherry pickers, helicopters and security. Widespread media was garnered including interviews broadcast on CNN and Al Jazeera.

Photographer: Peter Carrette
(ICON IMAGES)

Together 1,027 people make up a whale on Bondi Beach to bring attention to the plight of the Australian Humpback whale and the more than 1,000 whales now being threatened by Japanese whalers. Sydney, 2007.

Photographer: Peter Carrette
(ICON IMAGES)

MELBOURNE, 2002

The mainstream media go mental over a flag-burning kit sold at alternative bookshops containing a US flag and a pack of matches along with detailed instructions on their use. Despite the fact that there is a beer can clearly shown on the cover, humourless hacks haplessly attempt to portray the kit as a dastardly attempt to smear Australia's Islamic community.

SYDNEY, 2002

Amidst a range of groups planning more conventional forms of action, the Spin The Bottle Bloc announces it will host a "mass action" version of the popular teen kissing game as a protest against the WTO's Mini-Ministerial meeting in Homebush. Unfortunately, then-Police Minister Michael Costa misunderstands the group's call to "turn up the heat until every kiss becomes a molotov," proudly announcing in parliament that he has "decoded" this violent plan. Police then confiscate the group's rickety, oversized bottle prop before a single activist is able to lock lips.

Undeterred, the Bloc organises a protest a few days later to demand their democratic right to pash. Outside State Parliament, the group cheerfully practise what they preach, as well as dedicating a rendition of Tony Basil's '80s hit *Mickey* to the Police Minister — Oh Mickey, what a pity you don't understand etc. Meanwhile, a handful of dedicated Spin The Bottle cadre touch tonsils in the public gallery, declaiming against state repression, only to be placed under "parliamentary house arrest" (which they escape by calmly walking away).

BYRON BAY, 2002

In protest against the increasing Americanisation of Australian law and culture locals hold an Independence From America Day carnival on July 4th replete with a burning Bush and a dance through the streets to the local courthouse.

MELBOURNE, 2002

Vividly demonstrating the consequences of the continuing bombing of Iraq, the Medical Association for the Prevention of War and the Federation of Community Legal Centres pile up volunteers in body bags outside the British Consulate-General's office.

MELBOURNE, 2002

Nude protesters from the organisation Free Bodies are set upon by picnicking Italian war veterans whilst hosting a protest BBQ for the right to go naked. Despite the activists having been beaten and their video equipment smashed they find the police are only interested in charging them with indecent exposure.

SYDNEY, 2002

Three women who strip off, lie down on US flags and cover themselves in fake blood in front of the US consulate are arrested during anti-World Trade Organisation protests.

MELBOURNE, 2003

After a high school student is ordered by the principal of Strathmore Secondary College to change out of a T-shirt reading "Nobody Knows I'm A Lesbian", her fellow students turn up to school wearing shirts reading "Nobody Knows I'm Bulimic", "Nobody Knows I'm Pregnant", and "Nobody Knows I'm On Steroids".

SYDNEY, 2004

Armed only with hundreds of plastic toy soldiers, anti-war activists close down the offices of the Worley Group for two hours in a protest against the company's role in the exploitation of Iraq.

AUSTRALIA, 2004

In a televised Big Brother eviction like no other, contestant Merlin Luck, whose own family came to Australia as asylum seekers, uses the program to silently protest against the treatment of those now fleeing danger by taping his mouth shut and holding up a sign reading "Free The Refugees."

SYDNEY, 2004

A protest flotilla, calling for an end to the war in Iraq, moors itself offshore from Prime Minister John Howard's residence at Kirribilli House.

MELBOURNE, 2004

During an anti-Howard rally in Federation Square one angry and intoxicated young man throws his half-full coffee mug of cheap plonk at the PM, splashing him with wine and only just missing him with the cup. The man is immediately arrested by police and put into a waiting police car. Luckily for him, the car is unlocked and he escapes when a fellow Howard hater opens the rear door on the other side of the car to where the police are standing.

SYDNEY, 2004

Five hecklers interrupt and halt a speech given by Defence Minister Robert Hill at the inaugural conference of the *Australian Defence Magazine* by singing *The Grand Old Duke Of York* and in their own words, "generally acting crazy".

MELBOURNE, 2004

About 60 anti-war activists dressed in cowboy outfits prepare to storm the Kellogg Brown & Root office in Melbourne declaring that it is "High Noon for Haliburton [KBR's parent company]". Unfortunately when they reach the foyer they discover a sign informing them that the company has moved. Undeterred, the activists occupy the offices of ANZ (also profiteering in Iraq) on the next floor instead.

LAUNCESTON, 2004

A 49-year-old man narrowly avoids a jail sentence after placing PM Howard under citizen's arrest during the 2004 Federal Election campaign. Approaching Howard as he left his car to enter a hotel, Barry Jessup no doubt had numerous charges running through his mind but settled on Australia's illegal occupation of Iraq, grabbing the PM by his coat sleeve to announce, "I arrest you for crimes against humanity." Jessup is dragged away and charged with disorderly conduct, eventually receiving a 12-month good behaviour bond.

CANBERRA, 2004

The day before the Federal election a group of 40 people storm the Australian head office of Kellogg Brown & Root in opposition to the company's involvement in the Iraq war. To their great surprise, when they burst into the office

SYDNEY HARBOUR ACTIONS,

2003-2005

Greenpeace activists attach themselves to the *HMAS Sydney* as it departs for the Gulf in 2003. The ship was stopped in the middle of Sydney Harbour by activists placing wires across its path. Legislation was introduced soon after restricting the distance protesters could be to naval vessels. The action also led to the formation of water-borne anti-terror squads.

Photographer: Dean Sewell

The maiden voyage of the *Spirit Of Tasmania*, a car-carrying ferry that operates from Sydney to Launceston saw a huge banner draped over the vessel's side. Six months of logistical legwork was put in to achieve this. The ferry stopped in the middle of the harbour to remove protesters. Sydney, 2005.

Photographer: Dean Sewell.

they discover the KBR executives watching an internal film on how to deal with protesters. The activists never discover the extent of what was on the film, however the KBR executives deal with them by calling the police, who subsequently shower them with pepper spray.

MELBOURNE, 2005

After visiting American anti-war activist Scott Parkin is arrested by Federal Police and deported by the Government on the grounds of "bad character", a group of fifty activists attempt to push their way into the Federal Police Headquarters with suitcases requesting that they also be deported, as if Scott is of bad character, they must be too.

SYDNEY, 2005

70 people take part in a backwards march to highlight the similar steps taken by the NSW ALP government in spruiking dirty energy sources like uranium and coal.

MELBOURNE, 2005

Cleaning workers place three toilet bowls outside the Stock Exchange and hand out "hygiene kits" to brokers to help them practise their skills, as workers claim they no longer have time to clean bathrooms properly due to cuts in pay and hours.

SYDNEY, 2005

Pell's Angels descend on St Mary's Cathedral carrying banners reading, "Queerupting the Church Campaign Of Hate" and "Hating Love Is Not Christian," after the Catholic Cardinal George Pell publicly criticises his 19-year-old lesbian cousin for "the path she has chosen".

NORTHERN TERRITORY, 2005

Four members of Christians Against ALL Terrorism become the first-ever Australians to be arrested under the Defence (Special Undertakings) Act of 1952 after a Citizen's Weapons Inspection of the US spy base at Pine Gap causes it to be locked down for six hours. Two of the team enter the base undetected and take photos of themselves on the roof of a building before being arrested, while the others wander

around the base for an hour before being caught cutting through an inner fence. After a judge awards only minor fines for trespass against them, rather than the heavy sentences the Federal Government had been seeking under the Act, the Commonwealth Director of Public Prosecutions appeals. However, following jail time for the non-payment of the fines and a further appeal of their own, the four are finally acquitted of the "crime" of bringing to light the base's role in the Iraq war.

SYDNEY, 2005

Green activists dump a pile of coal on the steps of Parliament as part of April 1st "Fossil Fools" Day actions.

MELBOURNE, 2005

A sharp-eyed public transport rider tips off the media to the fact that the Federal Government has been doing its bit to encourage terrorism by including a web address containing information on bomb-making as part of its National Security Information Campaign billboards. When contacted about why they hadn't used a dummy site, the Attorney-General's office lamely replies, "It needed to be included so people would be aware of that kind of behaviour."

MELBOURNE, 2006

In the build-up to the G20 protests guerrilla gardeners from Melbourne and interstate create a new vegetable garden in the Floral Clock opposite the National Gallery of Victoria featuring a large floral display reading "STOP G20".

SYDNEY, 2006

During an occupation of Boeing's head offices, activists superglue anti-war propaganda to the walls.

MELBOURNE, 2006

When a group of young anarchists from a local squatted social centre hear that a unionist is going to be fired from his position as a swimming instructor for trying to agitate around conditions they enrol in his classes to end the pretence that his work is being cancelled on the basis of unpopularity.

CANBERRA, 2006

Greens Senator Kerry Nettle faces condemnation from PM Howard after wearing a T-shirt to Parliament reading, "[Anti-abortion Catholic Health Minister] Mr Abbott get your rosaries off my ovaries". She responds, "It's not the T-shirt that needs changing, it's the Health Minister's attitude, which we are seeing increasingly and is about bringing fundamentalist religious views into the Parliament."

SYDNEY, 2006

Guerrilla gardeners plant potatoes, tomatoes, cucumbers and various herbs for community consumption in a park in Redfern.

MELBOURNE, 2007

The day before the large and militant G20 mobilisation in Melbourne, a Collingwood squat that activists are using for interstate accommodation and a conference is stormed in an incredible show of force by police. Dinner has just finished cooking so, after the eviction, the seventy or so activists present simply set up on the footpath in front of the squat and, completely surrounded by police, hold a dinner party. During festivities a leotard-wearing activist entertains the crowd by doing an interpretive dance, in and around the legs of the nervous officers, to the sounds of Survivor's *Eye Of The Tiger* playing on a car radio.

MELBOURNE, 2006

On the first day of protests against the meeting of the G20, demonstrators fan out across the city to take part in actions against companies and organisations involved in the ongoing occupation of Iraq. One crew takes over the offices of the Tenix Corporation for a brief period, debating workers, tossing glitter, and supergluing toy soldiers to various surfaces before moving on to the army recruitment offices where they put up "I Don't Know Mate, I Just Work here" stickers. An attempt by the staff to evict the occupiers via the building's lift fails after security helpfully turns off all the elevators. The protesters eventually make it out of the building without arrest after a fire alarm is set off, allowing them to blend in with others exiting via the stairs.

ON THE STREET, 2000s Clockwise spiral from top left: TV stencil by VEXTA. Photographer: Lonely Radio • "I must tread the Earth carefully" stencil by Beat Street Lewis and Civil. Photographer: Lonely Radio • Paste-up by Miso, Heffernan Lane, 2008. photo courtesy Miso. • Woman stencil by A1one, visiting street artist from Iran. Photographer: Helen Richardson • "It's never as bad as it seems." discarded arm-chair stencil. Photographer: Lonely Radio • War Pig character by ITCH. Photographer: Helen Richardson • Anon stencil. Photographer: Peter Chen • Al Stark street drawing. Photographer: Peter Chen **Centre:** "Money Is Not Your God", RiDL, Sydney. Photographer: Anon • Kissing skeletons by VEXTA. Photographer: Helen Richardson • PHIBS spray-can character. Photographer: Helen Richardson

CRITICAL MASS, 2000s

Since 1992 hundreds of cities around the world have seen cyclists take to the streets en masse to reclaim the right to ride without fear. The first Australian events took place in Melbourne and Sydney in 1995 and have since spread to thirteen towns and capitals. Each ride typically takes place on the last Friday of the month and sees between 50 and 1,000 cyclists assert that they are "traffic too!"

BAXTER DETENTION CENTRE PROTEST

PORT AUGUSTA, 2005

A paramilitary policeman crunches a kite flown by pro-refugee protesters in solidarity with imprisoned children who had previously had their own creations, made out of plastic bags, confiscated by detention centre guards. Both the 2003 and 2005 Baxter Detention Centre protests saw renegade kite flyers arrested for petty offences against air traffic regulations.

Photographer: Mark Cunningham

OPPOSITE PAGE: Top to bottom, left to right: Critical Mass, Melbourne, 2003. Photographer: moz.net.nz • Sydney Harbour Bridge ride, Sydney, 2003. Photographer: moz.net.nz • Anti-Forbes Global CEO conference ride, Sydney, 2005 Photographer: moz.net.nz • Critical Mass, 2004. Photographer: Geoffmo • Photographer: Damon Rao • Photographer: Damon Rao • Tall bike, Sydney, 2001. Photographer: moz.net.nz •

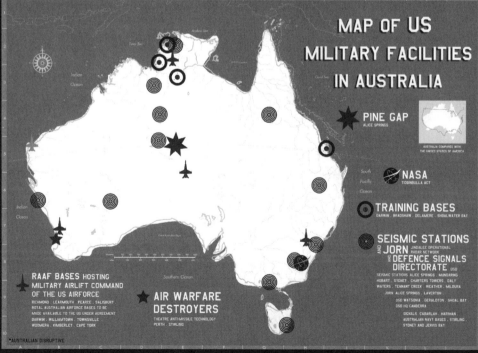

POLITICAL MAPS OF AUSTRALIA

2000s

There are many maps of Australia, here are two that offer different perspectives.

Top: Produced by the Anti Nuclear Alliance of Western Australia in July 2001 with information compiled by SEA-US. Courtesy: australianmap.net

Bottom: Produced in 2007 for distribution at the Sydney APEC meeting with information supplied by the Australian Anti-Bases Coalition. As part of its expansion in the Pacific the US government has stationed marines in Darwin since 2012 and proposed locating a Drone base on the Cocos Islands. Design by Australian Disruptive.

Higher resolution versions available at:

howtomaketroubleandinfluenceeople.org

Protests against the dredging of Port Phillip Bay. Melbourne, 2006-08. Photographer: Tanya Fry

ANTI-FORBES GLOBAL CEO CONFERENCE PROTESTS, SYDNEY, 2005

Over two days in August 2005 protesters gather in Sydney to demonstrate against a meeting of 350 of the world's richest business leaders. Taking part in rallies, a Critical Mass bike ride and other actions demonstrators force the conference organisers to move their official opening party from the Opera House and bring joy to corporate nasties across the CBD. All photographs: moz.net.nz

CITIZENS'
INSPECTION TEAM
PINE GAP, ALICE SPRINGS,
NORTHERN TERRITORY 2005

Four members of a Citizen's Inspection Team, Christians Against All Terrorism, enter the remote Pine Gap spy base on December 9th 2005 to highlight its connection to state terror and condemn its critical role in providing communication links for the US war machine. During the action, activists Jim Dowling and Adele Goldie wander the base undetected for two hours and photograph themselves on the roof a building before being arrested. Their colleagues, Bryan Law and Donna Mulhearn, also enter the base for over an hour before being caught cutting through its last inner fence. The security breaches see the base shut down for five hours with 600 employees denied access as their cars queue up for kilometres outside.

Despite receiving permission from the traditional Aboriginal owners to enter the site, the pacifists are all charged with counts related to trespass and damaging government property. They later become the first people to be sentenced under the Defence Special Undertakings Act of 1952 and are fined a total of $3,000. All serve up to two weeks in prison after they refuse to pay their fines. Following a concerted legal campaign the foursome are acquitted of their convictions in 2008 after the Northern Territory Court of Criminal Appeal unanimously rules that they have suffered a miscarriage of justice.

Photographs courtesy of pinegap6.livejournal.com

STOLENWEALTH GAMES
MELBOURNE, 2006

A national Indigenous convergence and gathering of supporters called the Stolenwealth Games is held in Melbourne during the period of the Commonwealth Games, March 15th–26th, 2006. Camp Sovereignty is declared a few hundred metres from Government House in Kings Domain. During this period, hundreds of protesters engaged in dialogue with visitors and tourists and held a series of actions and rallies around the city.

OPPOSITE: Top to bottom, left to right: Wayne Thorpe and Paul Spearim (2 Black 2 Strong). Photographer: Jacqui Brown • Isabel Coe talks at the Sacred Fire. Camp Sovereignty, Kings Domain, Melbourne, 2006. Photographer: Tom Sevil • Mick Edwards and Jungala Coombs. Photographer: Jacqui Brown • Aletha Penrith engages in street theatre on Parliament steps during the march through the city. Photographer: Jacqui Brown • Marji Thorpe, Robbie Thorpe and Targen on the first day of Camp Sovereignty welcoming everyone to the fire. Photographer: Tom Sevil • Police escort kids to welcome the Queen with gum leaves. Photographer: Tom Sevil • Wayne Thorpe at Sacred Fire. Photographer: Jacqui Brown • Elders speak at the Melbourne Museum inviting Queen Elizabeth to some "Sovereign-Tea". Photographer: Jacqui Brown • Rose Gillman and Lisa McLachlan (Respect our Land) take to the streets. Photographer: Jacqui Brown • Isabel Coe, Jenny Munro, David Dryden • Paul Spearim, Lionel Fogarty and others burn the Australian flag out the front of the Melbourne Museum where the Queen was having lunch. Photographer: Jacqui Brown • Camp Sovereignty Dancers - Bart Willoughby, Andrew Clarke, Paul Spearim. Photographer: Jacqui Brown

THIS PAGE Robbie Corowa. Photographer: Jacqui Brown • Six-foot high wooden letters spelling STOLENWEALTH GAMES are held during the Moomba Parade by people on the footbridge over the Yarra between Southbank and Flinders Street Station. Photographer: Tom Sevil. Organised by ANTaR Vic and Megan Evans. • Tennisha Ellis, Robert Corowa, Michael Penrith hold banner. Photographer: Jacqui Brown • Monica Morgan speaks to a rally. Photographer: Jacqui Brown • Uncle Max (Budgetti Man) carries coals of Sacred Fire. Photographer: Jacqui Brown

Following the occupations, the protesters move on to demonstrate outside a variety of ANZ offices. Although the bank has already done their job for them by closing all of its city branches in anticipation of such protests, the opportunity is taken to highlight its role in Iraq, and also hassle other war profiteers.

As the day goes on, 100 people occupy the Orica Corporation's chemical services department, protesting its involvement with Barrick's Lake Cowal Gold Project. Having handed over a document for Chris Avramopoulos, Orica's General Manager for mining chemicals, the protest disperses. Meanwhile Melbourne's shoppers are treated to the spectacle of Radical Cheerleaders spruiking upcoming events.

The second day of the meeting sees the action move to the sealed-off area around the Hyatt Hotel, with police removing a Christian embassy for the poor at around 3:20am. A rally held later in the day sees cross-dressing Tranny Cops lampoon riot police, while G20 lollipop ladies and gentlemen call for an end to neo-liberalism. Members of the Arterial Bloc, wearing white overalls and face masks in the style of the Italian Tute Bianche, get into fisticuffs with the police, charging barricades and trashing a police truck. Later on in the evening the party poopers in blue decide to soothe their bruised egos by mashing up a crowd and removing people dressed as endangered species from a Pink Cadillac parked outside Parliament.

The following day sees police reprisals continue with one man, who hadn't even been at the protest, being kidnapped off the street and held for around two and a half hours by plainclothes police who assault him and refuse to tell him who they are or why he is being driven around in an unmarked van. Given carte blanche by the State government to carry on however they see fit, the police go on to snatch other people from the streets before laying into a group of protesters gathered outside the Melbourne Museum.

NEWCASTLE, 2006

Declaring the area a Climate Disaster Zone, members of Rising Tide set up road blocks into the Carrington coal terminal, stopping vehicles to warn them of the climate-related dangers that lie ahead.

AUSTRALIA, 2006

During a national day of action targeting pronuclear industry consultants Parsons Brinckerhoff the company's offices are occupied in Melbourne and Sydney, with activists offering staff freshly baked "yellowcake". In Newcastle would-be occupiers engage in a "radioactive" green jelly fight, hang banners and slip leaflets under the locked doors of the company's office, while in Brisbane up to forty police keep activists at bay before being led on a goose chase around the city.

MELBOURNE, 2006

The Prime Minister's office and the Australian Federal Police have the satirical website johnhowardpm.org shut down by Yahoo and domain registration body Melbourne IT for supposedly looking like a site set up to "phish" people's personal information. Site creator and veteran protester and underground magazine publisher Richard Neville later states that:

> It was like being struck on the head with a hammer when [Yahoo] told me that the site was taken down after phone calls from the Prime Minister's department. For a Prime Minister's Secretary to be involved in this sort of thing is bizarre. What are they so paranoid about? To suggest that I was trying to violate the property rights of the Prime Minister's website is ridiculous. Every link in [a satirical apology speech for the war in Iraq displayed on the site] takes the reader to information contradicting everything Howard had said and still says about Iraq. Anybody who believes this action was taken solely because of the similarity between the two sites may as well believe in fairies. I can't pretend to know how this all works but the atmosphere these people [Yahoo] are now operating in is one of paranoia. What would have happened to them if they had left the site up? After a phone call from the PM's department and from three federal police I guess they got the message.

SYDNEY, 2007

The Guerilla Energy Efficiency Gang exchange incandescent lightbulbs for energy efficient ones at a housing development near the Eastern Distributor.

BEGA, 2007

During a visit by Prime Minister John Howard, an anti-woodchip activist blocks the southbound lane of the Princes Highway for two hours by chaining himself to a logging truck stopped at a traffic light. The PM is heckled during a speech at the local RSL club by another man dressed only in speedos, a hat and swimming goggles, who shouts, "What are you doing about global warming? There is no snow, there is no snow."

MELBOURNE, 2007

During a speech given by the Immigration Minister Kevin Andrews at the Hotel Sofitel anti-racist protesters hand out their own version of the Federal Government's citizenship test:

The Australian citizenship test is:

> A) *Played on Boxing Day*
> B) *A cynical attempt by the Australian Government to show they can filter out international terrorists and not workers with low level English*
> C) *Free with every pot and parma*
> D) *A good idea*

Australia's first Prime Minister Edmund Barton famously said:

> A) *"The doctrine of the equality of man was never intended to apply to the equality of the Englishman and the Chinaman"*
> B) *"Why must they insist on calling me Toby Tosspot!"*
> C) *"I just don't know about letting Queensland join."*
> D) *"You know what I think Australia needs? Big things. Heaps and heaps of big things. I mean I'm talking giant prawns and sheep and bananas and rocking horses. Ah ha gentlemen."*

The past two hundred years of Australia's history are:

> A) *A specialised narrative that if told right gets you on the ABC board*
> B) *An unfinished war*
> C) *Super chillaxed, like one big bar-b-que*
> D) *Not something we really need to think about*

PO Box 143 Heidelburg VIC 3084

If you want this payment to continue...

- **Grovel humbly** whenever you contact us
- **Whinge** as pathetically and impotently as possible when we totally fuck you over, and then accept it as fatalistically as death and taxes
- If someone tells you that John Howard didn't leave home until he has 32 (when he moved in with his wife) and thus has no idea what it's like to live independently, keep it to yourself
- **Vote Liberal** at the next election (or vote for whoever you like; no matter who you vote for, Centrelink is always here—just like the police)
- Repeat the following to yourself ten times daily: "The fact that I'm poor is because I'm a genetically inferior mongoloid pleb of questionable intelligence and moral integrity and has nothing at all to do with any supposed contradictions inherent within capitalism."

Ms. Petunia K. Second-Class Citizen
123 Your Street
EVERYTOWN VIC 3086

Payment of 300,000 times your allowance was given to a multinational corporation through tax breaks, subsidies and other incentives to stop them moving to Indonesia on April 28 2003.

⟳ Centrelink
giving you the option to do what we tell you to, or else

Application for payment of The Spirit of Resistance Needs a Jump-Start Allowance

The questions are for the period:

The rest of your natural born life

1. Did you go through the phone book about five minutes before filling out this form?

Yes ☐
Come on! ☐
No. I made everything up ☐
No. I used a copy of Beat and said I was looking for bar jobs ☐ → Proceed to Q.2

2. If you worked cash in hand over the period, are you dumb enough to tell us?

Hell no. ☐ → Proceed to Q.3

3. Did you get out of bed before 11.00am at least once over the period?

Yes ☐   No ☐ → Proceed to Q.4

If yes, why? ....

4. Did you write "if voting changed anything they would make it illegal" or "John Howard is proof that God would have a sense of humour, if he existed" on at least three (3) surfaces during the period?

Yes ☐   No ☐

If no, what do you think you will be doing if Howard is re-elected for another term?

Living in a cardboard box ☐
Living in a fallout shelter ☐
Hiding in the mountains shooting at soldiers ☐
Running suicide bombing missions against US roadblocks in Kingsbury ☐ → Proceed to Q.5

5. Did you do a bullshit training course or work for the dole project over the period?

Yes ☐   No ☐ → Proceed to Q.6

If yes, how many does that make now? ....

6. Did you watch a daytime talk show such as Jerry Springer, Oprah or Ricki Lake over the period?

Yes ☐   No ☐ → Proceed to Q.7

If yes, which ones? 1. ....
2. ....
3. ....

Which do you prefer? ....

List at least two (2) topics discussed.
Topic 1.
Show ....
Subject ....
Interesting Points Raised ....
Topic 2.
Show ....
Subject ....
Interesting Points Raised ....

7. You must let us know if any of the following happened to you over the period.

You didn't get to bed until 4am ☐
You didn't get out of bed until 4pm ☐
A parent asked you what you plan to do with your life ☐
Your answer pissed them off ☐
You had an argument with a relative who works 60 hours a week, is a divorcee and has high blood pressure ☐
You couldn't afford to go to a restaurant with your partner ☐
Your partner felt sorry for you and paid for the meal ☐
A politician on TV gave you the shits ☐
You sat by the kerb outside a Centrelink office weeping while posing for a cliche "unemployed" photo ☐
You had no money for milk and had to put water on your breakfast cereal ☐
You had no money for food and had to put your groceries down the front of your trousers ☐
You began plotting what to do to the Centrelink office come the revolution (eg. turn it into a homeless shelter) ☐

The half-price bread you bought had blue dots on it ☐
The day before your payment came through, you had three meals of boiled rice and tomato sauce, again ☐
The phone got cut off, again ☐
You hocked your CD's, again ☐

8. Declaration and signature

I declare that I am pulling the wool wherever possible and that I will make a sincere effort to fob off any attempts to get me a non-unionised, shitfully-paid job flipping hamburgers for ten dollars an hour three hours at a time when it takes me 45 minutes to get there over a hot stove in the middle of summer without an air extraction system in some fucking fast food joint. I declare that I'd rather slowly sink into squalor over a six to twelve month period on $370 a fortnight and engage in continuous warfare with the Centrelink bureaucracy than submit to the misery and degradation of wage labour or having any dealings whatsoever with any sorry excuses for human beings like my last three bosses ever again blah blah. I declare that I haven't read the small print and that I need my dole by tomorrow because I owe half of it already.

Your Signature .... **Date** ....../....../......

Please write your phone number below if we can call you at home. It's not that we'll use it, because we probably won't. It's just about making another hurdle for you to jump over.

(..........) ....

- Centrelink may make plenty of empty threats about checking up on the information you supply. What they won't tell you is that they're way too understaffed to do anything of the sort, and that there's no way they can check up on you if you say you went to somewhere like a supermarket, where people go and ask for work all the time. Generally speaking, as long as you give them real phone numbers, there will be enough reasonable doubt to get you out of any shit on the extremely thin likelihood that they do.
- You may get out of a particularly shithouse job and back onto the dole without an Employment Separation Certificate by taking less shifts at work and telling Centrelink that you're not getting enough work (for whatever reason–the poor state of the economy, etc). You can get a partial payment and then wean yourself out of your job altogether, and tell Centrelink that you're being paid when you aren't for a few weeks. Remember to fuck shit up at work before you go (watch Fight Club again for inspiration).
- Some Work for the Dole providers will exit you if you earn over $60 a fortnight. Find out which ones do, and sign up with them. Then get a real job mowing your neighbours lawns and get out of six months of useless crap.
- More information is available on the web at www.dolearmy.org.

OFFICE
USE
ONLY

KILL THE POOR 666

A few official-looking boxes to make you think we're writing things about you
....../....../......

Hopeless case ☐   Arrived late ☐
Badly dressed ☐   Has a new tattoo ☐

Top to bottom, left to right:
Centrelink parody. Melbourne, 2003. Anonymous • Patch. Sydney, 2007. Artist unknown • Poster. Melbourne, 2000. Artist unknown • Poster. Melbourne, 2000. Artist unknown • Poster, Tasmania, 2000s. *Black Sheep*. Artist unknown

The First Annual Most Boring Photo Competition

First prize $50

Send:

Most boring photo
Return address
$1 entrance fee

A copy of the winning photo will be sent to all entrants.

SEND ENTRIES TO: The First Annual Most Boring Photo Competition
348 St Georges rd
Thornbury
Victoria 3071
Australia

note: Photos sent in will not be returned.
Judges decision is final.

Date: Friday 19th May 2000

Don't be a thicky, take a sicky!

It's good for you:

Whether you work in a high-stress office or a factory filled with toxic chemicals, most jobs today are a health hazard. Having a day off will help your body recover. *A sicky a day keeps the doctor away!*

It's good for your family:

Most of us work hard so we can afford to buy the things we think our families need. But by spending so much time at work, we forget that the most important thing in any family is love. *The family that wags together, stays together.*

It's good for the economy:

When you stay away from your job for a day, you create the opportunity for the employment of temporary workers. If you use this time to take your family to the beach or to the cricket, the money you spend is also creating more jobs for Australians. *Take a day off work, and help get this country working again!*

Written and authorised by Howard Beazley on behalf of the Disenfranchised Workers Union. PO Box 187 Leichhardt NSW 2040

FALSE GODS

BURN FAST

FOREST BLOCKADES
TASMANIA, 2006 ONWARDS

Since 2006 the Still Wild Still Threatened (SWST) campaign for Tasmania's Southern Forests has engaged in a series of actions to protect the Styx, Weld, and Upper Florentine old-growth forests. Strategies have included occupations, blockades, trespassing into proscribed logging areas, the launching of a "Weld Angel" atop a tripod and the building of the Weld Ark, a massive road blocking "pirate ship." Photographs courtesy of Huon.org (right) and film stills taken (above) from *In Defence of Ancient Forests*, Abnormal Productions, 2007.

WORKCHOICES PROTEST
MELBOURNE, 2007

15,000 people protest against the Federal Government's industrial relations laws, and the use of the Australian Building and Construction Commission to attack the nation's most successful and militant unions.

Photographer: Rodney Dekker

TAXI DRIVER BLOCKADE
MELBOURNE, 2008

Taxi drivers block Flinders Street for the entire day to demand legislation that would protect them from assaults and to prosecute fare evaders, 11 August 2008. Sick of government, police and industry indifference, the protesters bring central Melbourne's peak-hour traffic to a standstill. The protest continues through the night and into the next day, forcing the issue of racist violence against immigrants into the spotlight. Under pressure, the Victorian Government hurriedly introduces new safety measures, and quietly orders the police and council to rescind a number of the fines placed on taxis used in the blockade.

Photographer: Rodney Dekker

CLIMATE CAMP
NEWCASTLE, 2008

In July 2008 1,600 people came together for five days to oppose the continuing reliance of the Australian economy on burning and exporting carbon-emitting fossil fuels. Amidst discussions and workshops around climate change, protesters engaged in various actions including locking on to a coal loader, protesting outside the NSW Treasurer's office and holding a mass blockade that shut down the movement of coal by train for the best part of a day.

Top to bottom, left to right: Radical Cheerleaders. Photographer: Allan Milnes • Five minutes to midnight, human clock. Photographer: Ben Baker • Polar Bear. Photographer: Allan Milnes • Coal is Over. Photographer: Allan Milnes • Pete Gray and Bridie McGinte are arrested after crossing police lines to occupy and sit on a coal train that was taking coal for export to China and beyond.

HAZELWOOD COAL-FIRED POWER STATION
LATROBE VALLEY, 2008-2009

Top: The affinity group of "The Ministry of Energy, Resources & Silly Walks" outside Hazelwood power station. Hundreds of people gathered on September 13th 2009 to place a "Community Decommission Order" on the 45-year-old power station.

Photographer: Louise Morris

Bottom: Banner drop, lock-on and occupation at Hazelwood Power Station, 2008. Hazelwood pumps an average of 17 million tons of greenhouse gases into the atmosphere every year. The power station was due to be closed in 2009, but was given a 30-year lease of life by the Victorian ALP.

Photographer: Rahima Hayes

www.switchoffhazelwood.org

OPPOSITE: Top to bottom, left to right: Radical Cheerleaders. Photographer: Allan Milnes • Five minutes to midnight, human clock. Photographer: Ben Baker • Polar Bear. Photographer: Allan Milnes • Coal is Over. Photographer: Allan Milnes • Nobbys Beach banner. Photographer: Allan Milnes • Pete Gray and Bridie McGinte are arrested after crossing police lines to occupy and sit on a coal train that was taking coal for export to China and beyond. Photographer: Sam Taylor

Immigration Minister Kevin Andrews' comments about cutting African refugee numbers were:

A) *A sensitive well-measured response to the death of a young man*
B) *Based on the UN refugee agency advice*
C) *An unusual example of the Liberals using race politics in the lead up to the election*
D) *Strange because we don't let Africans into Oztralia — do we?*

Apartheid was first introduced in:

A) *Australia with the Aboriginals Protection and Restriction of the Sale of Opium Act 1897 (Qld)*
B) *South Africa in 1913 with the Land Act*
C) *2005 Cronulla*
D) *2007 Northern Territory*

The 72 Tamil and 7 Burmese Refugees currently incarcerated on Nauru show that:

A) *We have come a long way since Edmund Barton*
B) *We are a compassionate and flexible county*
C) *It helps to be a white Zimbabwean farmer if you're seeking asylum in Australia*
D) *Anybody want some zinc cream?*

Any and all able to successfully complete the test are rewarded with a Vegemite sandwich and offered zinc cream in case they are in need of a change of skin colour.

GEELONG, 2007

Anti-logging activists are charged under anti-terrorism provisions in the Maritime Transport Security Act after they scale fences at the Geelong docks to lock on to a conveyor belt delivering woodchips to ships.

NSW, 2007

A satirical website (www.miningnsw.com.au) reading, "Rising sea levels: Brought to you by mining," is created by Rising Tide Newcastle to parody the NSW Minerals Council's "Life: Brought to you by mining," campaign. The site is forced to move offshore after the group receives legal threats over copyright violations.

MELBOURNE, 2007

Ten activists from Animal Liberation Victoria, wearing white body suits and carrying signs reading "Ban Whaling", pour fake blood over themselves in the offices of the Japanese Consulate.

SYDNEY, 2007

Pro-choice activists successfully impede a procession of anti-abortionists to a Salisbury Rd Family Planning clinic by getting in front of them and marching incredibly slowly. Police attempts to shove the velocity-challenged marchers out of the way are foiled with the result that the sickly-titled Helpers Of God's Precious Infants are delayed by an hour and a half. With their hire bus threatening to leave, the anti-choice group only get to spend a short time outside the clinic before being bussed back to wherever they came from.

NSW, 2007

Over the Easter long weekend environmentalists converge on Lake Cowal in support of the Wiradjuri traditional owners' campaign against a polluting gold mine which wastes 16 million litres of water a day. During the weekend's actions, protesters occupy the offices of mine operator Barrick Gold, hold a corroboree at the mine's gates and enjoy a drag show with some "miners" miming to Britney Spears' 'Toxic'.

NEWCASTLE, 2007

Over 100 protesters against impending climate chaos participate in a flotilla of kayaks, canoes and small boats attempting to block the movement of coal along the city harbour's main shipping channel.

CANBERRA, 2007

Having previously attempted to arrest Attorney-General Philip Ruddock for war crimes, activist Peter McGregor interjects during Parliamentary proceedings to declare, "Point of order, Mr Speaker. I have a Warrant for the arrest of John Howard, Alexander Downer and Brendan Nelson as war criminals." Clearly getting the wrong man, police arrest McGregor, charging him with "unlawful entry on enclosed lands."

SYDNEY, 2007

Laughter reigns in court when two members of the Tranny Cops (originally an abbreviation of transit cops, Sydney's notoriously violent and undertrained train ticket inspectors), a group of anarchist queer genderfuckers who lampoon riot police, face court on charges of impersonating police at a protest against US Vice-President Dick Cheney. When the Magistrate David Heilpern is presented with the Tranny Cops group's outfits, which feature an anarchy symbol and the words "Cop It Sweet", he begins to giggle. When a witness, Asia-Pacific Economic Forum [APEC] Security Command's Sergeant Ian Franke, admits that the group's sideburns, moustaches and goatees were clearly made of ink, the prosecution's case further unravels. More laughter greets his description of the Tranny Cops' cop routines as including, "placing their thumbs inside their belts and rocking back and forth in a heel-toe manner". Heilpern finally dismisses the case after no one outside of the police force can be produced to vouch for the fact that the Tranny Cops were directing traffic away from the protest. Summing up his decision, the magistrate declares that there is a "Village People-style defence" for wearing a police uniform, citing the Sisters Of Perpetual Indulgence as another example of the legitimate lampooning of authority.

NEWCASTLE, 2007

Grassroots climate-change action group Rising Tide blockade coal trains en route to the world's biggest coal export port at Kooragang Island in Newcastle Harbour.

SYDNEY, 2007

100 detainees at the Villawood Detention Centre form a human barricade to prevent the deportation of a Chinese refugee belonging to the Falun Gong sect.

NEWCASTLE, 2007

Hanging a banner reading, "APEC Fuels Climate Chaos" five protesters lock onto coal loading equipment at the Carrington terminal, shutting down coal train movements and machinery for over two hours.

VICTORIA, 2007

As part of a protest against the Asia-Pacific Economic Cooperation (APEC) meeting in Sydney, activists from Real Action On Climate Change enter the Loy Yang power station in Gippsland's La Trobe valley at 5am. Locking themselves onto a coal conveyor,

STREET CROSS STITCH
MELBOURNE, 2008 ONWARDS

Engaging in "seriously seditious stitching", the Melbourne Revolutionary Craft Circle, and other radical cross stitchers, have brought together militant crafties to share their individual work and communally create banners and other pieces targeting the speculators and property moguls of inner Western Melbourne.

Photographs courtesy of Rayna Fahey (www.radicalcrossstitch.com) and Lou Smith.

they overburden the conveyor belt and shut down production at Victoria's biggest coal user for five hours.

NORTHERN TERRITORY, 2007

After the Federal Government announces its plans to further encroach on Aboriginal autonomy and land rights under the cover of an "intervention" against sexual abuse, locals at the Willowra community post a sign at their gates reading, "Please Feel Free 2 Take Over." Other signs placed around the community protest against the proposed use of troops to patrol Aboriginal areas by renaming the Youth Centre as an Army Recruitment office, offering up open areas for tank angle-parking and a helipad, and warning that termite mounds are, in fact, "Pointy Land Mines."

NEWCASTLE, 2007

12 Greenpeace activists are arrested during the time of the APEC conference for painting "Australia Pushing Export Coal" on the side of the coal ship *Endeavour*.

MELBOURNE, 2008

After a Year 8 student at Collingwood College is threatened with suspension for wearing a T-shirt reading "Free Tibet" to his Chinese Language class, two of his classmates respond by putting signs around their necks reading "Free Tibet, Free Michael."

MELBOURNE, 2009

Former *Overland* editor Katherine Wilson makes a mockery of Aboriginal-genocide-denier and right-wing commentator Keith Windschuttle's claims to objectivity and belief in the strict use of empirical evidence when she successfully submits a fake article littered with errors to the right-wing journal *Quadrant*. Taking a shot at Windschuttle's career-building penchant for sifting through the footnotes of those he disagrees with, in order to find minor errors "proving" that everything they have argued is a fabrication, Wilson crafts an article that conforms to the *Quadrant* editor's own biases. Writing as "biotechnologist Dr Sharon Gould",

she submits a piece entitled *Scare Campaigns and Science Reporting* claiming that researchers at the CSIRO have abandoned plans to commercialise varieties of wheat, mosquitoes and cows that have "been engineered with human genes" due to "perceived ethical issues in the public and media understanding." Despite the inclusion of false footnotes and a number of clues, such as a reference in the opening sentence to the infamous Alan Sokal hoax (in which the US academic successfully sent an article filled with nonsense to a post-modernist journal), Windschuttle happily accepts the piece informing the author that, "I really like the article. You bring together some very important considerations about scientific method, the media, politics and morality that I know our readers would find illuminating."

On the day of *Quadrant*'s release the hoax is exposed by on-line magazine *Crikey*, who reveal that not only does the article "rely on false science, logical leaps, outrageous claims and a mixture of genuine and bogus footnotes," but that Windschuttle had not even bothered to do a check on Gould's academic bonafides. Had he run even a basic web search he would have discovered that Wilson/Gould had been running a blog, entitled *Diary Of A Hoax*, since November 2007, detailing each step of the project and musing, following the admission of former *Quadrant* editor Paddy McGuinness that he had run an article by neo-Nazi Michael Brander without checking his background, as to whether the magazine's editor would be "as expert a Googler with me."

Following the publication of the article Wilson posts the following message to her blog:[28]

> For pity's sake, *Quadrant* fell for my ham-fisted ruse! At least with the Sokal hoax, Alan Sokal was a bona fide physics professor. So it's understandable that a journal editor might unquestioningly publish his nonsense. But so neatly did my essay conform with reactionary ideology that *Quadrant*, it seems, didn't even check the putative author's credentials. Nor it seems did they get the piece peer-reviewed. Nor did they check the "facts"; nor the footnotes. Nor were they alerted by the clues … still, now my experiment has worked, I'm not sure how I feel about it. Do I feel schadenfreude? Not really. I

feel ambivalent. I'm almost embarrassed for you, Windschuttle … I didn't do this to be unkind to you personally. This experiment wasn't designed with ill-intent, but to uncover hypocrisy in knowledge-claims, and also spark public debate about standards of truth when anything is claimed in the name of "science".

In responding to the prank Windschuttle unwittingly hammers its point home, claiming to *The Age* that it is a fraud rather than a hoax since "a real hoax is something that exposes people's ignorance of a topic and laughs at them for their pretension."

MELBOURNE, 2009

Proving that location is everything, graffiti reading "Can this be the wall we put the coal barons up against?" goes up on a North Fitzroy residence that previously played host to "Detain Howard. Give us boredom protection."

AUSTRALIA, 2010

In response to moves by the Federal government to impose some of the harshest censorship of the Internet in the world, hacker group Anonymous launches Operation Titstorm. During the attack a number of government websites, including that of Parliament House, are shut down, the PM's website is plastered in porn and key political figures receive "a shitstorm of porn email, fax spam, black faxes and prank phone calls" focusing on "small-breasted porn, cartoon porn and female ejaculation, the 3 types banned so far." Ten days later further attacks are carried out under the banner of "Operation Freeweb".

AUSTRALIA, 2011

As part of international events against rape and victimisation thousands dress up and take to the streets in Slutwalks held across the nation. Brisbane sees traffic halted as one speaker tells the crowd, "I don't care if you are the bastard child of Paris Hilton and Voldemort and your full-time job is a stripper and you are the only girl for miles – you still don't deserve to be assaulted or raped." In Melbourne a photo booth is set up for the costumed whilst a myriad of placards and banners, including "A Dress Is Not A Yes" and "I Might Be Asking For It, But Not From You" greet city shoppers.

SEA SHEPHERD
GREAT SOUTHERN SEAS,
2008-09

Sea Shepherd crew member Laurens De Groot hurls a bottle of butyric acid (rotten butter) at Japanese harpoon whaling ship, the *Yushin Maru No. 1*, as the Sea Shepherd helicopter flies overhead. The Yushin used water cannons to keep Sea Shepherd boats at bay in New Zealand territorial waters north of the Ross Sea off Antarctica on Monday, Feb. 2. 2009. Sea Shepherd engaged the ship, along with two other vessels from the Japanese whaling fleet - the *Yushin Maru No. 3* and factory vessel, the *Nisshin Maru*, as part of Operation Musashi, its 2008-2009 campaign to end what it deems to be illegal whaling operations in Antarctic waters. (Photo by Adam Lau/Sea Shepherd Conservation Society) • The Steve Irwin sails past an iceberg in the Southern Ocean on Monday, Dec. 29, 2008. (Photo by Adam Lau/Sea Shepherd Conservation Society) • 2009-02-06 Steve Irwin collides with *Yushin Maru No. 3*.

OCCUPY MOVEMENT
AUSTRALIA, 2011-12

Responding to the global call to take part in actions regarding the unequal distribution of power and wealth, protesters took over city squares and other urban spaces in most major cities and towns around Australia during mid-October 2011. As elsewhere, police and authorities responded by employing council by-laws and trespassing statutes to harass and evict demonstrations and protest camps. Nevertheless Occupiers held out for up to three months, using creative tactics to spread their messages, build community, and reclaim public space. This image is from the Melbourne eviction of Occupy Melbourne from the City Square, 21 October 2011.

Photographer: Jessie Boylan

Despite rain, Sydneysiders rally outside Police headquarters in Surry Hills to recount experiences that show Australian officers can be as sexist as their Canadian counterparts (comments from one of whom originally kicked off the movement). The Adelaide gathering sees chants of, "Yes means Yes, No Means No" ring out across the city, Slutwalk Hobart features a "frilly contingent" and in Perth women march to the sound of Nancy Sinatra's "These Boots Are Made For Walking".

MELBOURNE, 2011

Protesting state government plans to introduce fines for the use of "offensive" language in public places (including sportsgrounds, pubs and private venues), hundreds take part in a series of foul-mouthed rallies. After a swear-in sees expletives ring out across the city, a fuck-walk is held during which placards and T-shirts reading "Rock Like Fuck", "Dang, There I Said It" and "Under Baillieu Free Speech Is A Fucking Lie" are proudly displayed.

MELBOURNE, 2011

To mark the tenth anniversary of the invasion of Afghanistan stickers are plastered around the CBD reading "If you had $21 billion to waste, how would you spend it? On 32,078 jellybeans for every child in Australia OR On ten years of increased military spending and wars in Iraq and Afghanistan?" Similar efforts suggest the money could have been used for a "Trip to Phuket for every man, woman and child in Australia" or for "5 billion scratch tickets and 226 million Quinella bets for [recently disgraced football celebrities] Dean Wallis and Brendan Fevola."

On the actual day of the anniversary free lollies are given out to commuters, as a sample of the peace dividend an end to war would bring. A rally sees the names of all the Australian servicemen, and some of the many Afghanis, killed in the war read out and, despite interference from security guards, a banner reading "Afghanistan, 2001-2011: 30,000 dead and counting" is dropped from a balcony.

SYDNEY, 2011

On New Years Eve anarchists drop 18 banners from five disused buildings in the city centre. Accompanied by a sound-system blasting anti-police tracks, the group drops banners from a recently evicted social centre reading "Visualise Industrial Collapse", "Don't Fuck With Us", "Property Is Theft" and "Fight Back." A construction site owned by banking giant and mining investor ANZ is adorned with the messages "No Jobs On A Dead Planet" and "Can't Drink Gas, Can't Eat Coal", whilst a building directly across from the Australian Federal Police plays host to "All Cops Are Fuckin' Bastards, ACAB" and "2012, A New Year's Revolution: Destroy Capital Before It Destroys Us All."

AUSTRALIA, 2012

During 40th anniversary celebrations held from January 23-26th at the Aboriginal Tent Embassy in Canberra protesters camp out and engage in discussions, protests and cultural events. Following negative comments made by Opposition Leader Tony Abbott on Invasion Day a group of demonstrators make their way to a nearby restaurant where he and PM Julia Gillard are attending an awards ceremony. Surrounding the venue, banging on windows and demanding an audience with the leaders of Australia's major political parties, those assembled are shocked when Federal Police panic and smash their way through the crowd. Whilst being roughly dragged out of the venue by security officers the Prime Minister loses one of her shoes. Before it is returned Indigenous activists offer to exchange it for their land, telling Ms Gillard she can make a "title claim" for it, and consider auctioning it online to raise funds for the Embassy.

Within weeks of the anniversary a second Aboriginal Tent Embassy is set up near the statue of the Indigenous resistance leader Yagan at Matagarup (Heirisson Island) in Perth. Protesting against miserly compensation for wages stolen from Indigenous people in earlier decades, the occupation also rejects moves to extinguish Nyoongar native title over South-Western Australia in return for $1 billion compensation in cash and land. Asserting their sovereignty and demanding a treaty, campers defy a number of eviction attempts stating, "The jails are already chock-a-block full of Aboriginal people, so where are they going to fit us all?" After a final eviction, six weeks after the Embassy was established, sees 70 police, including members of the dog and riot squads, remove the camp protesters begin holding rallies and marches whilst maintaining a presence on the island.

A Brisbane embassy is subsequently launched at Musgrave Park, a traditional gathering place, in March. Drawing supporters from all over Queensland, including a group who set up their own short-term embassy in Moree, the embassy holds cultural events, workshops and film nights before being evicted by over 200 police on May 22nd. With the support of unionists the embassy is rapidly re-established in a corner of the park and the previously recalcitrant Brisbane City Council enters negotiations concerning the establishment of an Indigenous cultural centre.

PERTH, 2012

GLBTI rights supporters throw glitter on those entering an anti-same sex marriage rally. They also attempt to drown out Christian rock with chants of, "One, two, three four, fuck the homophobic law" and "Five, six, seven, eight, How do you know your kids are straight".

MELBOURNE, 2012

Disability activists draw attention to the fact they are denied entrance to 83% of trams by parking electric wheelchairs in front of one on Elizabeth Street for 20 minutes.

CANBERRA, 2012

Indigenous people gather outside the Canberra War Memorial on ANZAC Day to commemorate all those killed by the Crown during Australia's frontier wars.

LISMORE, 2012

Christian fundamentalist Peter Madden's "hate truck" receives an unexpected pit-stop whilst parked in Lismore. After locals chain themselves to the vehicle and let its tyres down, the homophobic billboards it is carrying are blanked out with glitter, love hearts and streamers and revised to read "Equal Rights" and "Love Not Hate."

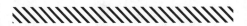

Chimney graffiti commenting on the Commonwealth Bank's "Which Bank?" advertising slogan. At the time the Commonwealth Bank was the largest shareholder in Gunns timber company who were logging old growth forests in Tasmania. Sydney, 2004.

Photographer: Dean Sewell

WHICH BANK TRASHES TASSIES FORESTS.

"
Making Trouble
CONVERSATIONS

Meredith Burgmann

In 1948, the majority of white South Africans voted to fully institutionalise the already harsh racial discrimination that existed in their country. Under the apartheid laws all residents and visitors were classified into racial groups (black, white, coloured, and Indian or Asian) with strict segregation applied to housing, leisure, health, education and social services. Apartheid (meaning "separateness" in Afrikaans) essentially delivered vast privileges to whites while confining Black Africans to fake "homelands" from which their labour could be drawn when required.

Right from the beginning South Africans of all backgrounds resisted with strikes, demonstrations and other forms of mass defiance. Anti-apartheid groups were also set up internationally, although strong opposition did not occur until the 1960s, when a variety of groups began focusing on ending their countries' economic, diplomatic and sporting ties with the South African regime.

In Australia it was the sporting link that proved to be the most contentious and, following the example of their British counterparts, Australian anti-apartheid activists began to disrupt a number of events from 1969 onwards. The peak of this activity came in 1971 when a six-week tour of Australia by the South African Springbok rugby team was thrown into complete chaos. From the city capitals to the country the South Africans were abused in the street, harassed in their hotels and disrupted on the field. In the following interview veteran activist and former President of the Legislative Council of NSW MEREDITH BURGMANN describes her role and that of the Sydney-based Anti-Apartheid Movement (AAM) in ending Australia's ties to apartheid.

Tell us about your political background and how you got involved in the Anti-Apartheid Movement?

Well, totally typically, I arrived at university in 1966 and got confronted with Vietnam. I was fairly conservative but immediately got involved with Vietnam and became radicalised. Towards the end of 1969, a meeting was called in Sydney and the AAM was set up. The co-convenors were Peter McGregor, me, and Dennis Freney. It was in the days of collective activity and anti-hierarchical structure and it worked very well because we all got on.

The main focus was around the universities, although we worked with the radical trade unions, particularly the waterside workers and the seamen and of course the builders' labourers. The NSW Builders Labourers Federation (BLF) under Jack Mundey and Joe Owens and Bob Pringle were very involved.

How did sports come to be such a big focus for anti-apartheid activity?

It was there, is the answer. There had been a call for sporting boycotts by the African National Congress and it was a very easy way to demonstrate opposition. And frankly, racially selected all-white teams coming out here was pretty offensive, and even quite conservative people were a bit confronted by it. So it was the Anti-Apartheid Movement being sensible about its best target, really.

What other groups were involved in the Stop The Tours activities?

Well, at the time in Sydney there was the South African Defence and Aid Fund (SADAF), which had been set up by lawyers and expatriate South Africans to raise money for the families of political prisoners. That was the main South African group and that was set up around the

Brinks — John and Margaret Brink.

Then Campaign Against Racism In Sport (CARIS) was set up about the same time as we set up the Anti-Apartheid Movement, a group called CARIS — mainly run by John Myrtle, who was also a personal friend, so that worked well, too. CARIS knew everything it was possible to know about sporting teams, and was part of that Dennis Brutus [South African poet and anti-apartheid activist] push to isolate South African sport.

The three groups were really quite complementary in that CARIS produced most of the material and all the good arguments about sport, and that's where we got all our information from, in terms of the unfairness of the sporting activities and evidence that racism was happening. They didn't believe in direct action, but they would hand out leaflets at the games and we would try to disrupt the games. But they never disapproved of us. Well, they never condemned us. And it was quite good, because the media would go to them for the serious stuff.

We always said that we were a direct action, non-violent movement. We made it very clear we didn't approve of anything that would hurt anyone. But we also made it clear that that didn't mean we wouldn't be involved in sabotage, and we said that whole thing about how there's no such thing as a dead door or a wounded window.

I always believe in multi-pronged approaches. Because the authorities are never going to give in to a bunch of wackos, but in the end, it's the bunch of wackos who create the situation where they have to give in to the serious people. Also the authorities prefer to look as if they're giving in to serious discussion and argument, rather than the fact they can't control the situation.

How did you pull off AAM's first anti-sports action at the Drummoyne swimming competition in 1969 and was anyone arrested for it?

Until I read my ASIO file last year I thought we'd got away with that, but the police obviously believed it was us. We were very inspired by what Peter Hain [anti-apartheid activist and later UK Labour Minister] had been doing in Britain with the 1969–70 rugby tour, where they had got onto the ground, and those pictures where you see them sitting on the goal posts and things. That had inspired us, so we decided we had to have some direct action activity.

They were choosing a swimming team to go to South Africa — I remember Shane Gould was swimming — and we decided to disrupt it. It was actually much, much easier than we had imagined. I mean, everything worked! We put black dye into paper bags and we found a road that looked down over the Drummoyne swimming pool, where the trials were taking place. We just lobbed the paper bags into the swimming pool, and they had to stop the races. Shane Gould complained that she couldn't see the end of the pool. It actually worked. We were absolutely amazed!

We were pursued back to Balmain, where we hid in the toilets of the Forth & Clyde Hotel. Two of us were actually picked up — I think Jeremy Gilling and Peter Landau were picked up and questioned by police — but no-one was charged out of it. There was quite a lot of publicity for that, and that was our first sort of guerrilla moment. We were very pleased with that.

What actions did you take after that?

We needed to build up to the Springbok rugby players who were coming in the middle of '71. Because we knew we probably couldn't stop the footballers, our main target was the cricket tour which was coming at the end of 1971. From the end of 1969 and through 1970 we demonstrated against South African tennis players, women basketballers and surf lifesavers. With the basketballers there was a demo of about 20 of us, but the Nazis came and broke us up, so there was sort of a riot at the airport. There were quite a number of arrests — of our people, of course.

I'd forgotten about that until I read my ASIO file, and I kept looking at a list of people at the demonstration, and I kept thinking, "I don't know these names," and I suddenly realised that half the names were Nazis. The police just listed us all together; they made no distinction between the anti-apartheid activists and the Nazis.

Later on we threw ourselves onto the basketball court and things like that. Throwing ourselves onto courts was fairly standard.

By the time the lifesavers came we had significant numbers at our demonstrations, and that was really exciting for us. I can still remember saying to a Special Branch guy, "Just you wait, when the footballers come there'll be 500 of us at the demonstrations." And of course there were, like, 20,000 or something. But I was excited at the thought of 500 turning up.

With the surfers, I reckon there were probably 200 or 300 at the demonstration at Coogee. That was one of the first times I got arrested because the four of us, four girls, were able to lie down in front of the surf lifesavers. They just marched over us. They didn't miss a beat. Nevertheless that was the first moment that I realised we had something going and there were going to be significant numbers at the football.

We'd also achieved the support of the Sutherland Shire, which had refused to let the lifesavers compete at Cronulla. It was the first time an official body had actually refused the South Africans anything, in sporting terms. It was very significant, and it was totally ideological, because the president of the Shire was Arthur Gietzelt. He was later a left-wing Labor senator, but as President of Sutherland Shire he said, "No, they're white South Africans, racially selected, and they can't have our beach, full stop". Later his home was bombed and the front room was destroyed. It affected his hearing, and he wore a hearing aid from then on.

When we went down to Wollongong the anti-surfer demo went really well, too. That was when Jim Roxburgh came down and spoke at the rally. He was one of the seven internationals who came out against the Springbok tour. Some of them had retired, but some of them actually refused to play and lost their careers because of it. It was sort of led by

Anthony Abrahams, he tended to be the spokesperson, and there was also Jim Roxburgh, Paul Darveniza, Terry Forman, Barry MacDonald, Bruce Tafe, and Jim Boyce. They were fantastic. Very important morally, and also in terms of making people be a bit anxious about it.

The other thing I remember about the Wollongong rally was that our loudspeaker broke down and we didn't know what we'd do and Merv Nixon, who was the secretary of the South Coast Trades and Labour Council said, "That's all right, dear, I'll fix that." He went over to the police and borrowed their bullhorn and brought it back. I said, "How did you do that, Merv?" He said, "Oh, love, this is a union town." It made me realise Wollongong really was different.

What was the response of the players and audiences like?

Things could get pretty intense. For example, another thing we did in that period was go out to football matches and hold up signs. This was mainly at the trial matches, when they were choosing the teams for the rugby. I remember one game where we were chased by one of the players, and he tried to run us down in his car.

People just kept saying, "You can't muck around with our sport, keep sport and politics separate," all that sort of rubbish. Most of them had no idea what it was all about. The media, of course, attacked us all the time and there was no sympathy towards us at all. However, although they supported the white tours, they also began reporting on the true story of apartheid because they wanted to appear non-racist. It was quite interesting. They were having to print stuff that was anti-apartheid even though they were opposing us. I'm sure the media would like to think they opposed the all-white tours, but they didn't.

What sort of support did you receive when the Springboks actually arrived in 1971?

Once they got here the trade union movement and even the churches came out. The trade union movement put bans on and wouldn't transport the Springboks around, so they had to hire their own airplanes and transport. They also put bans on supplies and the like to the hotels where the players were staying. They actually made the hotel go broke in Sydney.

Tell us about your involvement in the protests at the first test in Sydney?

I'd been travelling about a bit with the protests in the other cities, but because rugby is a NSW- and Queensland-based game the stakes were very high at that first game in Sydney. There were four matches at the Sydney Cricket Ground (SCG). The first one's the one that everyone remembers, and a huge crowd, some estimate it at 20,000, turned up. There were smoke bombs thrown and chanting and total chaos, it looked like something out of a movie.

It was also the one where only five people were able to get onto the field. By this stage Denis Freney had restraining orders against

him so he wasn't allowed within 100 yards of the cricket ground. I'd also been arrested every time I sort of set foot outside a match so I got disguised as a middle-aged Afrikaner. There were four of us including my sister Verity. We borrowed member's tickets and we got right down the front in the members' area. For the first half of the game we talked to each other in what we considered were South African accents, and chatted to the police who were standing in front of us. There was a policeman about every three feet. We chatted away and supported the South Africans. We had a steel esky [cooler] with us, and we actually asked the police to move aside so we could see better, and by the beginning of the second half they actually did.

About five minutes after the beginning of the second half we used the esky as a bit of a leg-up and jumped over the fence to run onto the field. I had always assumed we would be caught within a few yards, but the police were so flat-footed. They were obviously very surprised at these middle-aged Afrikaners running onto the field. We actually all got into the middle of the field and Verity, in fact, got the ball, and kicked it. *The Bulletin* called it the best kick of the season. I just didn't know what to do, so I got myself right in amongst the players and lay down. No-one else knew what to do, either, because it had not occurred to us that we would actually all get into the middle, so we all just lay down. Then the police eventually arrived and they dragged me off. They let the others walk, but they dragged me off. It was very painful. They dragged me right around the edge, and the sporting fans all came down and sort of spat on me and things as I was dragged around the edge. They were really angry.

The fantastic thing was that it actually stopped the game. I think we were the only people to stop the game. Africans listening to it in South Africa have told me since how exciting it was for them to listen to that happening on the radio. It was, in retrospect, a very proud moment. At the time I didn't think of it as anything terribly huge, but I think in the scheme of things it was pretty important.

Now, the other guy that got on is a wonderful story. A big, ambling, huge guy who played rugby league for Sydney Uni called Dave Hughes dressed himself up in footy gear, and just ran on, and they thought he was, like, twelfth man or something. They just let him run on. And then suddenly someone said, "Hey, this guy isn't meant to be on the field," and the police went, "Oh," and dragged him away. He was the only other person to get on the field.

What other activities happened around the games in Sydney?

One of the funny things was that the Squire Inn Motel, which is where the Springboks stayed for five or six weeks, was located about 100 yards from a house in Eveleigh St where a bunch of radical Aboriginal activists lived. It was just by accident. Most of the Aboriginal activists did not live in Bondi, but Paul Coe, Gary Williams, Gary Foley, Norma Ingram and Lyn Thompson, all of whom were key activists at the time, all lived there or stayed there a lot.

A lot of our activities took place out of that house. At one point they built a rocket launcher in their back yard, and one night they launched a rocket. I'm sure it didn't arrive at the Squire Inn Motel, but that was an ongoing project for many days. There was also a car park opposite the Squire Inn Motel. That was terrific because we would head there each evening to yell and scream and throw things.

There were lots and lots of other terribly convoluted ways in which people were proposing to stop the games. I remember one involved trying to get tacks, carpet tacks, onto the ground. There was a bit of a debate about whether this would hurt the players, but nobody seemed to care very much. Everyone was more paranoid about "How would you get them into the game?" and so they were going to be hidden in cream cheese sandwiches or something. Crazy stuff.

Everyone had their own particular scheme. One bloke had a model aeroplane that was going to zoom around and drop smoke bombs or something. Fred Hollows, of course [an ophthalmologist who set up a number of initiatives to assist Indigenous Australians and others with eye care], ended up with wire-cutters and was arrested for trying to cut the barbed-wire fence. There was also the famous occasion of Bob Pringle and Johnny Phillips cutting down the goal posts the night before the game. That was a wonderful occasion.

The scheme we got involved with was to get a greased pig onto the field, but that meant we had to get the greased pig into the area. We went and bought the pig, and it was huge, of course. Pigs are huge when they sell them. We had to disguise it as a baby in a pram. I remember Franny Letters giving the pig a bath to make it smell better. We had a vet who was going to give it a sedative so it didn't get too stressed. This was all happening in the back of a van, and I remember the vet trying to sedate the pig and eventually the pig got away. It was last seen hurtling down Darghan St, Glebe.

In the end it was the smoke bombs that were most effective. They were simply marine distress flares, which would put up a wonderful pink or grey smoke. Our house in Darghan St, Glebe, which had turned into the headquarters of the Stop The Tours campaign, was actually one house up from a marine chandler's. So everyone, as they dropped in to see us, would also drop into the shop and buy a few smoke flares. They weren't hard to buy or anything, you just had to pretend to be a bit of a yachtie and away you would go. Everyone was well stocked.

What was your involvement outside of Sydney, because anti-apartheid protesters caused total chaos wherever the Springboks went, except for in Queensland where the Premier, Joh Bjelke-Petersen, called a State of Emergency?

I was arrested five times during the actual rugby tour. One of those occurred at Manuka Oval in Canberra, and that was for doing nothing. I really fought that case and was found guilty, but then won on appeal.

We also went to Orange, which is a fairly small country town where they were playing a game. That was extraordinary, that was high-noon stuff. A friend of mine who was a lawyer got arrested for just sitting on

a park bench while waiting for the game to start. When the people at the game got arrested I went to bail them out, and they wouldn't let me. They said I was of bad character. Then we got Dick Buchhorn, who was a Catholic priest, to bail them out, but they wouldn't let him bail them out because they said he was a bad character as well. So he rang up the local Catholic priest and they wouldn't let *him* bail them out. This is the local Catholic priest, who hadn't even been at the game. In the end we got the local Member of Parliament in and they decided he was of good enough character to pay the bail.

By the end of all that I was exhausted! When they went up to Brisbane, I remember going to bed for a few weeks, just to recover so we could have a final onslaught when they came back to Sydney.

You also had to deal with the courts, didn't you?

I made the mistake of facing court before they'd left Australia. I think they were up in Brisbane when I went to court. That was crazy because it was in the heat of everything, and of course I was going to get made an example. The magistrate — he was the deputy magistrate, a bloke called Bruce Brown — gave me two months' jail. Just straight off. No option for a fine or anything, just two months' jail. It was considered extraordinary at the time and it still is extraordinary that a simple demonstration offence could get a jail sentence. I appealed. The other three who'd invaded the ground at the first match got good behaviour bonds, but I got a jail sentence because I was considered to have been a bad influence on them. They were younger than me. I was 22, and my sister was 17. I was considered to have led her astray.

All in all, the cases arising from the tour went on for about another two years. I was in America in 1973 and they said they'd extradite me if I didn't come home. So it went on for two years.

I was in prison for a couple of days while the lawyers were all fighting, but I was eventually given a suspended sentence. I did get arrested on a number of occasions after that, but they never brought up the issue. It was sort of like they'd lost the papers. And you could tell why, because to put me in jail for two months would have made me a martyr.

Did you receive much harassment from the pro-apartheid lobby during this time?

The Nazis were very active. They threw a brick through my window and wrote "Red Rat" over my house, which we later changed to "Fred Rat" because it sounded more friendly. I got knocked unconscious once, by the Skull, who was a huge guy and one of their leaders.
We also had problems with the white Rhodesians; I got hit by one of them when we went to disrupt their meetings.

What was your role in convincing Don Bradman [legendary batsman and Cricket Australia Chairman] to place a ban on Australian cricket games with South Africa?

I was in correspondence with him as he'd written to me before the

Verity Burgmann, Meredith Burgmann and Janice Jones hold up play at the SCG, Sydney, 1971.
Courtesy Meredith Burgmann.

footballers arrived, asking, "Why are you doing this?" Peter McGregor and others wrote to him too and we all thrashed out the issues.

When he announced that the cricketers were not coming, he actually made a wonderful statement where he said that until South African cricketers are chosen on a nonracial basis, and until the system of apartheid is finished, Australia will not play against South Africa. It's a really, really great statement. He and the Cricket Board probably gave in because they realised they couldn't protect the cricket, because a cricket game's obviously much more vulnerable than a football game, but officially he gave in to the principled argument. However, if we hadn't disrupted the rugby matches, the 1971 cricket tour would never have been called off. It was as simple as that.

We couldn't believe how successful we'd been. It really was an absolute success, to have Bradman come out and make that statement. After that and the chaos at the rugby no other white-selected

teams were game to tour the country and we just had to deal with a few individuals, like the silly golfer Gary Player. We felt justified in continually demonstrating against him because he'd written an autobiography where he'd basically supported apartheid, but claimed he wasn't a racist. This was in an era when Papwe Segolum, the great African golfer, won the South African Open one year and had to accept the prize trophy through the window because he wasn't allowed into the club house. On one occasion, in order to show what a good non-racist he was, Player actually brought a black caddy with him, not understanding the significance of it all.

As a result I made Gary Player's life a misery. I was arrested on many occasions. Golf matches were very easy to disrupt. You just had to yell out as they were doing an important putt. Mind you, golfing crowds were the worst and there was a famous occasion when Robert Tickner and I both got arrested at a Gary Player

Above: Graffiti on the entrance to the South African embassy, Canberra, 1971. **Right:** Having put South African golfer Gary Player off his putt Meredith Burgmann and Robert Tickner are arrested by plainclothes police at the Royal Sydney Golf Club, Sydney, 1974. **Far Right:** Meredith Burgmann speaking at a Stop The Tours meeting in Glebe, Sydney, 1971. **Opposite:** Stop The Tours Campaign meeting, Sydney, 1971. **Opposite Bottom left and right:** Demonstration outside the South African Airways building in Elizabeth Street, Sydney, 1970. All photographs courtesy of Meredith Burgmann.

demonstration, and the head of Special Branch had to protect us from the rabid hordes that were furious with us.

But the Gleneagles Agreement, basically it stopped all sporting contact, which was really good, although most of it had stopped before then. As I say, after '71, I don't think there were any racially-selected teams that arrived in Australia.

How did you deal with the criticism throughout this period that the Anti-Apartheid Movement was ignoring racism and issues of colonialism within Australia?

That was the favourite argument of our opposition and the media would always say, "What about your own backyard?" And we'd say, "Well, we're involved in those issues, too."

The young Aboriginal activists were also totally involved in the anti-apartheid stuff. There was a famous picture of Billy Craigie and Paul Coe wearing the Springbok jerseys because the captain of the Springbok team had said, "A black man will never wear the Springbok jersey." They were given to them by the seven anti-

apartheid footballers who'd picked them up on tours of South Africa. It was all very symbolic.

How did the focus of the anti-apartheid campaign change after the sporting tours ended?

We had endless vigils outside South African Airways for some time, but once the sporting ties were largely cut we began to go after Australian companies who were involved in economic dealings with South Africa. We had quite a successful campaign against John West and protested outside their offices and also placed stickers reading "Made with black blood" on their items and others in shops, like South African wine.

As the 1970s went on we sort of morphed into an organisation called the Southern Africa Liberation Centre. We kept up the consumer boycotts and demonstrations against South Africa Airways but we also became more of a support group for the liberation movements, especially in Zimbabwe and Mozambique and Angola. It became very Southern-Africa-based.

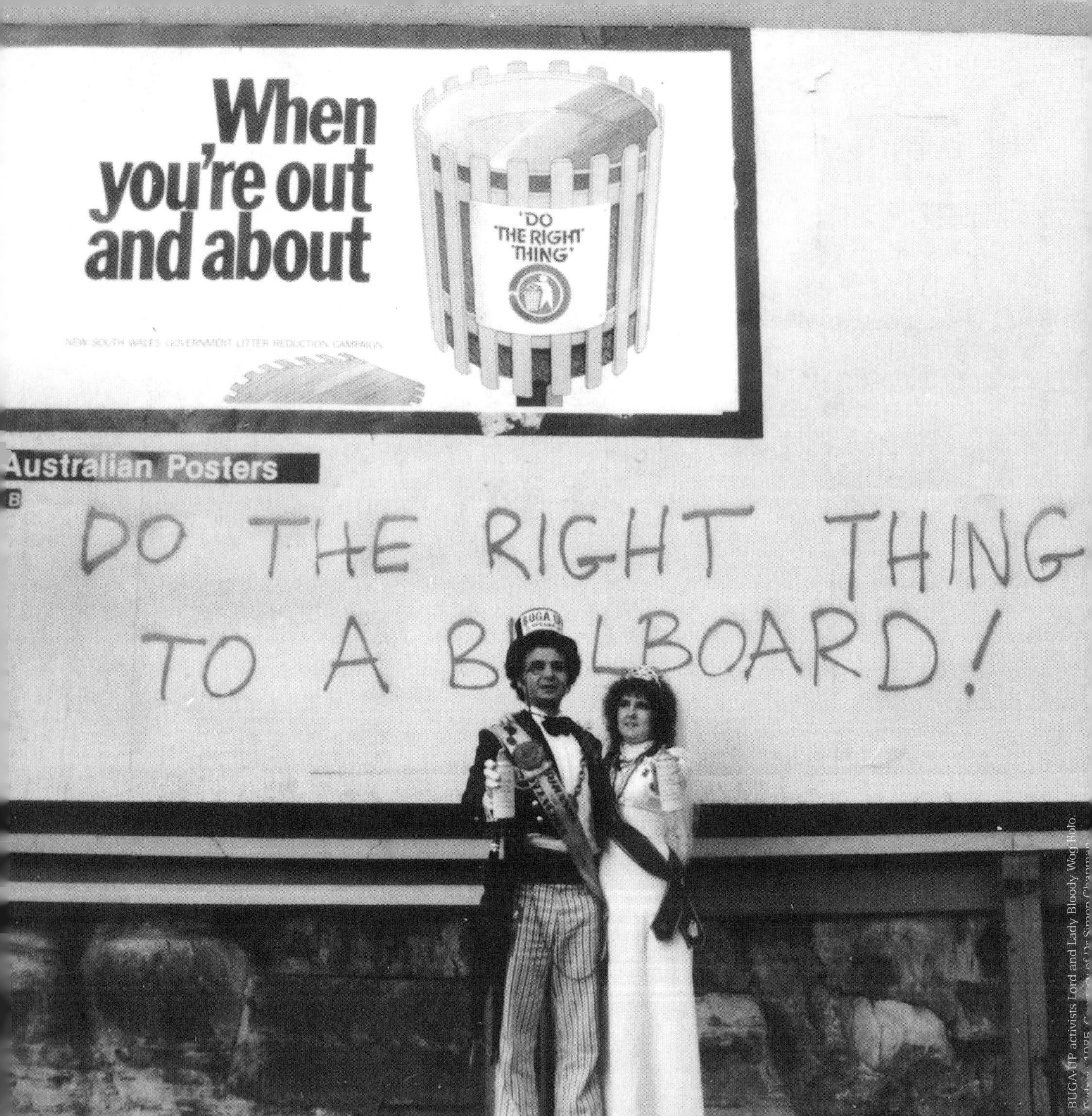

When you're out and about
'DO THE RIGHT THING'
NEW SOUTH WALES GOVERNMENT LITTER REDUCTION CAMPAIGN
Australian Posters
DO THE RIGHT THING TO A BILLBOARD!
BUGA UP

BUGA-UP activists Lord and Lady Bloody Wog Rolo.
Sydney, 1985. Courtesy of Dr Simon Chapman

BUGA-UP

Formed in 1979, BILLBOARD UTILISING GRAFFITISTS AGAINST UNHEALTHY PROMOTIONS (BUGA-UP) rapidly made its mark on hoardings around the nation. By cleverly revising advertising slogans and disrupting tobacco-sponsored events, the group revealed the true cost of tobacco and alcohol company deception. Having racked up numerous fines and arrests over its 16-year existence BUGA-UP formally wound up in 1994 as Federal and State Governments finally began to tighten up regulations governing the advertising of alcohol and tobacco. In the following interview graffitist TOFU recalls his part in the group's early adventures.

How did you first get involved with Sydney BUGA-UP?

The first billboard I saw that BUGA-UP had done was one featuring five newsreaders where someone had written across the bottom, "Five blind mice". That got me interested in the whole process. Shortly after, I passed by a local hall that had a meeting board up about a presentation by BUGA-UP and I went in. I got interested and decided to, not exactly join the group because you couldn't join the group, but get involved. You just turned up and helped with the billboards.

Soon after the meeting I went out with three other members. We generally just sat around in the car, parked near some billboards and discussed what we were going to do. Some people who'd done it before had pretty good ideas. You could get your own line across if you wanted to. Once that was decided, we'd get out and there would be one or two lookouts and maybe up to three working on various bits of the billboard, because they were pretty big. The easiest ones were on the railway stations as they have quite big billboards on a lot of the train stations in Sydney. One night I think we must have done 20, all along the railway line, from station to station, just following on. That was all pretty trouble-free because there was no surveillance in those days, no CCTV or anything like that.

In the time that you were involved, did you have an idea of how many other people there were revising billboards?

I was aware of a core of about 12 or so people, but there were probably up to about 20. We didn't know the full extent of our numbers because people would often just do it by themselves. Generally we only met people on the run. We had a couple of workshops where we made extension rods and things like that, but that still only involved five or six people. There were about four or five people who were the original instigators or the beginners of the organisation and it expanded from there.

No-one knew everyone involved and there were lots of individuals and teams doing their own thing. The principle was that if you did a billboard on your own you could sign it BUGA-UP and that meant you were part of BUGA-UP. It was a very loose, informal kind of arrangement, deliberately so because of legal reasons.

Which companies did BUGA-UP mainly target?

People went after various targets, but it was generally cigarettes or alcohol. I only did the cigarette- and alcohol-related ones. Some people were pretty obsessive about doing whatever billboard they could find.

A lot of the cigarette advertising was on government property as the railways had a lot of billboards. I think up to about 50% of the advertising on billboards for cigarettes was on government property. It seemed like a crazy idea that the government would be promoting, or helping to promote, addictive things.

BUGA-UP was very loose though, there was no great prospectus or aims or principles written down. It was really based on an objection to using public space for these products and an attempt to break up the images and values that the advertising was trying to project. They were using a lot of glamour images for cigarettes. Alcohol had already changed a bit and I think they'd even brought in some sort of regulation. They sometimes just had the bottles or the cans and a clever caption. It was a challenge to work out new words to parody those. With tobacco they were still using luxury yachts and beautiful blonde people.

While your main agenda was clearly to subvert and alter the messages that the billboards carried, were you also trying to waste the companies' money?

Partly that. The aim was to force the stuff off the billboards. The chances were pretty small, however, of making it uneconomical for them, because the cigarette industry had been taken off TV. So they had plenty of money to play with.

How many billboards were changed on a regular basis?

Quite a few along the railways because even individuals would do up to a dozen a night, maybe once a week. When you put together all the different individuals and groups there were probably at least 50 getting changed a week.

How long would they stay up?

Varying times. The ones on the railways were the best because they took months to fix them. As a big bureaucracy they didn't really care that much. They would often stay up for several weeks. On private land generally they would have someone up there the next day, or within a couple of days.

What time of the day would you normally go and do the actions?

Normally late afternoon up until midnight. Generally the consensus was that after 10pm it was a bit harder because the police were more alert. More police were about and you were more conspicuous. The first time I got caught it was after 12 o'clock.

Would you dress up to make it appear that you worked for the billboard companies or did you just go out and do it?

I think some did get into character, but I didn't do that. I basically turned up with a bag of spray cans and just started doing it. You kept looking about to make sure that there was no-one making themselves too obvious. When there was a group, probably four or five of us would go out in a car, and someone would keep a lookout. Generally people

didn't use disguise, as far as I know. There were some daytime actions where they made it quite public for the media.

How long would it take to do a billboard, roughly?

Probably not more than five minutes. Possibly only three minutes. It was all pretty quick. If you had more than one person doing it, then one would write the BUGA-UP thing, someone else would do a couple of words here and a couple of words up the top. Speed was of the essence, really.

What was the connection of BUGA-UP to MOP-UP (Movement Opposed to Unhealthy Promotions)?

There were, I think, one or two people in BUGA-UP who were also in MOP-UP. MOP-UP was mainly involved in the legal and medical side of fighting this kind of advertising in the courts. They used more conventional methods in fighting the companies.

But BUGA-UP captured the public's imagination ...

Yes, BUGA-UP was more public. Obviously it was pretty hard to get publicity for the opponents of tobacco and alcohol advertising when the companies involved had big budgets and the ear of the media. However, once our messages were up on the billboards all the commuters saw them and people liked them. Anything to break up that monotony of commuting, I guess.

There was quite a lot of positive feedback and generally not much resistance from people who saw us whilst we were actually changing them. There was one case where there was a newsagency which had a billboard above it that had been paint-bombed a few times. We were doing some billboards across the road on railway land when we saw the guy. He had seen us and we figured that he was calling the cops so we all scattered. We waited about half an hour and then came back just in time to see the police pull up. It wasn't good timing.

How did the police react?

Although there were five of us and two of them it was all very peaceful. They took us back to the station and fingerprinted us. When it came to court, the original witness couldn't actually determine who had done the spray on the billboard so the case was dismissed.

Many of the magistrates were pretty anti public disorder, but some of them liked the idea. The magistrate I got for that case was not a very happy guy. He said something like, "If you want to do something for society, why don't you go and join the Lions Club or Rotary?" He just didn't like the idea that what we were doing was illegal. The charge was "malicious injury to a billboard", which was the heavier of the charges that they had available as it made it a criminal case.

Generally the police themselves would only act if they got a complaint from a member of the public. In another case concerning me there was a young trainee cop who was with his sergeant when they

BUGA-UP billboard revisions. Sydney, 1980s. Courtesy of Dr Simon Chapman.

BUGA-UP billboard revisions. Sydney, 1980s. Courtesy of Dr Simon Chapman.

drove past and caught me at it. That was one I was doing on my own. He later apologised and told me that he had to say something because he would have been in trouble himself if the sergeant had seen me and he hadn't said anything.

When I went to court I was charged with wilful defacement, which was a civil offence. I didn't get a fine because it was a first offence. I didn't contest the fact that I'd done it, but I did contest the compensation costs with the company. I had seen an ad in the paper looking to hire someone to fix billboards at one point and I rang up to find out how much they were going to pay them so I could use that in my defence. I was able to get the costs down to half what they wanted because I knew how much they were paying their staff. That was a pretty good result.

One of the guys involved in BUGA-UP was a photographer who was also involved in silk-screen printing. You could let him know where the billboards you'd done were and he'd photograph them for you. It was really handy when you went to Court because you'd have a record in case they tried to say that you had done more damage than you did. They might try to say that you had done some paint bombing, as well as the lettering and that wouldn't have been as clear a message, I think, because the paint bombing could be seen as just vandalism.

As time went on they began to use the heavier charges against people. I think they felt a bit threatened by the whole movement. I had heard that Melbourne had introduced fines of up to $2,000 whereas Sydney was still around $150–$200 at that time.

Were people getting arrested a lot?

You heard of the occasional arrest. One guy was a continual offender and he used to do at least one billboard a day. He'd carry a bucket and some spray cans wherever he went. He was a regular arrestee, but generally there was not more than one arrest a month. There was a fighting fund which would pay half your fines as long as you signed BUGA-UP on the billboard.

How did the advertising industry react?

I think they mainly tried to play it down. Sometimes they would just paste white paper over the message and it would be clear that it had been altered. After a while they moved the captions to the top of the billboards so that it was harder to alter them. Generally, up until then, they had been at the bottom. So that made it a bit harder as we had to get our extension rods out.

Tell us about the use of the extension rods?

Well, they were a bit of a design challenge. You could buy an extension rod, I guess they were for professional painters, but they were quite expensive. I had this idea that we should find a cheap way to make one. We started off with a broom stick, some angle brackets and some wire and managed to create a prototype that just about anyone could put together with things you could buy from the local hardware shop.

You had to adjust the way you did things. You held the extension rod sideways to the billboard. The rod had a roll-on deodorant attached to it to keep the can a particular distance from the surface so that you could control the horizontal movement. That took away a lot of waving the stick about so you had a much more consistent spray angle on the billboard. It worked pretty well.

Did the advertising industry also move the advertisements to less accessible spots?

Where they could they did, but there were still lots on the ground. Some moved up a bit. They were still accessible, but higher than they used to be. Some of them were moved to the tops of buildings. I remember seeing a photo in the paper of some BUGA-UP people who did those sorts of jobs and used paint rollers. They probably only did that once or twice.

Did they have to scale the building?

No, they had access through the building. They were wearing white boilersuits as if they were workers. They only had to change a couple of words to change the meaning of the billboard completely. Paint bombing was a much better method for the high ones.

How would people do that?

The people I knew generally used paint-filled eggs. They were pretty good. You could get a pretty decent throw with those. Other people used balloons, but they weren't as easy. I heard about one guy who had adapted the back of a panel van so that he could open the doors to use a catapult that was attached there. He could hit quite high billboards with this method. He was a very good aim and used quite large paint bombs.

How much of a role do you think that BUGA-UP played in getting tobacco advertising eventually banned and alcohol advertising restricted?

I think we mainly affected public awareness. Not just with tobacco and alcohol, but generally with making people more aware of how the advertising industry was attempting to manipulate them, the images that they were using, and the role of consumerism in all of that. I think BUGA-UP's actions helped break down all that stuff.

For more information on BUGA-UP visit www.bugaup.org and tobacco.health.usyd.edu.au websites.

Making Trouble: CONVERSATION #3

John Safran

In 1997 ABC TV launched *Race Around The World*, a program in which eight young Australians were sent off to a variety of locations to shoot and edit ten four-minute documentary films over a 100-day period. During the series, 19-year-old Melburnian John Safran emerged as the audience favourite due to his propensity for performing pranks including placing a voodoo curse on a former girlfriend and streaking through the streets of Jerusalem wearing only a St Kilda football scarf.

Despite coming last in the judges' poll Safran won the popular vote and with it the opportunity to shoot two pilot programs for the ABC. The making of *John Safran: Master Chef* and *John Safran: Media Tycoon* earned the ire of the government broadcaster, however, particularly due to the satirist's decision to engage in a tabloid-style confrontation with Channel 9 media star Ray Martin. Exiled from television for a brief period Safran continued to work in community radio and cracked the music charts with an ARIA-nominated caricature of Baz Luhrmann's *Everybody's Free (To Wear Sunscreen)* in 1998.

Following a brief run with Channel 7's *The Late Report* Safran produced two series of largely documentary-based material, *John Safran's Music Jamboree* in 2002 and *John Safran vs God* in 2004, as well as a talk show, *Speaking In Tongues*, in 2005. These programs perhaps best exemplify Safran's approach, with him generally subverting, sending-up and questioning the beliefs of a whole range of individuals, organisations and subcultures including those of his largely inner-city, leftie following. In the following interview John discusses the various stunts he has been involved in as well as the ups and downs of a career in the entertainment industry.

Were you a prankster as a teenager, and if not, what put you on the path to using pranks in your work?

No, not at all. I'm constantly embarrassed in real life. I wouldn't do a prank if I wasn't filming it or whatever, I don't think.

When I look back at *Race Around the World*, where I first started doing pranks, I can't quite figure out why I did them. That was before the Ali G stuff, and I hadn't seen Michael Moore. So in retrospect I'm confused as to why it even occurred to me to do that.

There was this one book that was out when I was at uni called *RE/Search Pranks!*, and it had this thing about how pranks were applied to making social commentary. Also things like Abbie Hoffman's *Steal This Book*, I read that in uni. But again, I wasn't reading them and going, "I'm going to do this!" It was more like they went into my brain somehow, and when I bumped into *Race* and I found myself thinking, "I want to do comedy, and I want to do a documentary that's not really a documentary at all," so it just seemed to come together.

The only other thing I remember is just before I went on *Race* there was this friend of a friend we went out on a camping trip with, and he was just obsessed with doing pranks. I was quite confused by it, but took it in. He'd want to do things like buy wood-panel wallpaper and then cut it up and put it on the side of cars to make them look like station wagons from the 1970s and stuff.

The story behind me getting onto *Race* was that I had to do an audition where you sent in a tape of a little mini-documentary, and I did one about drinking my own urine. That wasn't really a prank, but it was weird. My first few stories on *Race*, we had to file one every ten days from around the world, weren't even prankish. It was still me trying to figure it out. Then somehow it all came together at about Story Four, where I put a voodoo curse on a former girlfriend. Then it just seemed to gel and I thought, "This is what I'm meant to do. I'm meant to do this stuff where I superimpose comedy, but in the real world."

What were some of your favourite trips during the series?

The whole thing was just utterly crazy. I couldn't even process that I was doing it, because I'd never used a camera before, I'd never been on TV and I'd never even thought of going on TV. This was not only pre-YouTube, but pretty much pre-internet. Not totally, but the whole thing of DIY media wasn't everywhere. I don't know, I was really confused the whole time. I sort of went crazier and crazier as it went on.

I remember when I streaked through Jerusalem for a story on trying to use the power of Jewish prayer to affect the outcome of a football match back in Melbourne. I was streaking through Jerusalem, and that was just something I would never have normally done. Not only would I never have done a prank, but something like that, where you're naked, just so wasn't me. That's how mad I went. But it came together and I got this confidence even though it was kooky.

My favourite segment was when you had a plan to prowl around the Japanese subway system after hours, but got locked into a small area and wound up making a doco about what you do when you're trapped without a story. I thought you managed to turn that around quite well?

That made me wince for years, that story. That was my opening documentary for the show. Maybe if it was buried in the middle, like, "John does all of this, then he does this story that's slightly different," it would have been okay. But to open with the whole, "Oh, I fucked up the story and had to make up a story out of nothing," was pretty painful.

Tell us about sneaking into Disneyland, and the plaques that you put up?

I was reading an exposé of the Disney empire. Again, because it was pre-internet, all that stuff seemed far more exciting. Information like that wasn't as easily accessible, so it was exciting to discover some book in a bookshop that showed the dark side of Disney. It talked about how Walt Disney, before the Nazis did all their really bad stuff, but they were still formed as a political party, was a member of the American Nazi Party.

So one of the things I did in Disneyland was to go to the Walt Disney Museum where they've got all these gold plaques telling you about the things Walt Disney did over his lifetime. I had my own made up, and I stuck them in there. It took a couple of days before they noticed them. There was one about the Nazis, and one about how he dobbed in fellow artists to the [anti-communist] House Un-American Activities Committee.

As a result of winning the viewers' poll for *Race Around The World* you got to make two pilots for the ABC. Given that the programs pushed the boundaries on a number of fronts, did you expect that a series would come of it, or did you figure you'd just have as much fun as possible before they canned you?

I definitely thought a program would come out of it, but it didn't. Again, it was just half making it up as I went along, and half instinct, and lots of confusion. It was pretty crazy to make, on all sorts of levels. For example, with the pranking/subversive genre, it was impossible to find anyone at the ABC who could get it. There weren't enough reference points for them. You couldn't say, "It's like *The Chaser* or Michael Moore," or whatever at that point. I'd be lumped together with some ABC producer, and I'd be wanting to do a prank at McDonald's, and he'd be like, "Oh, yeah, so we'll get some actors to play the security guards and they'll throw you out." I'd then have to say, "No, no. We won't get actors. We're actually going to go in there and do it." No one there could understand what I was getting at.

There were all sorts of things like that. I'd be in the Comedy Department, where they shoot sitcoms and that sort of thing, and I would need a crew that could stay out with me all night as I might need a camera locked on the outside of a nightclub, or something like that. It was like, "Well, there's not a crew that do that, because this is the Comedy Department." Everything was hell. While shooting those pilots, I had to shoot a kind of parallel show to the official show, just to get what I wanted. For example, the famous Ray Martin footage was actually shot — not all of it, but most of it — by my friend. I was sleeping on her floor while I was in Sydney, going, "I'm not getting what I want, can you come with me to Ray Martin's house tomorrow?" And she just did.

I was also uninformed about what the motivations of different people would be. I was like, "Surely they want a fun show and surely this is all good. Why wouldn't they want young people going out there and blah, blah, blah?" It took me a while to realise there were other agendas going on. That shooting something without the crew they assign you with is like a hand grenade. I just didn't get it at the time because I was like, "Why wouldn't they just want a cool show?" I wasn't as across things as I am now.

Even nowadays, however, when I shoot things I still have to go off and do what the station doesn't officially want, or tell them, "Oh, that's what you say now, but actually I'm going to be in more trouble if I bring back something that's not shocking or not funny." So I listen to everyone's complaints in-house, from the TV station or whatever, and then for my own good, but also for their good, go ahead and do what I want to do. I listen, and if they've got something handy to say I'll take it on board, but there's a lot of wanting it both ways. A lot of, "John, do your shocking thing, but don't break any rules."

With me I think it's a bit odd because a lot of what makes my stuff work is that it's idiosyncratic. I'll talk a lot about religion and then I'll talk a lot about my upbringing and my Jewish education, how that's affected me, and putting all that personal stuff in seems to add up to the stuff everyone likes. But if you're working for some stations, they're just like, "Well, no-one knows who the Mormons are, why can't you just do something about Shane Warne?" However it just doesn't work like that. Unless I'm involved in the story and I believe in it and it's personal and it's about the stuff I'm interested in, then it just never seems to come out quite as funny as it does when I'm going more with instinct.

The most famous segment of the ABC pilot was where you confronted Ray Martin, Australian media icon and the then host of tabloid TV program *A Current Affair (ACA)*. What was amazing was that he and his wife reacted in exactly the same way as every person his show had ever hijacked did in getting aggressive, trying to pull off your [*ACA* reporter] Mike Munro mask, pushing the camera out of the way, etc. Talk us through what happened and the involvement of Shane Paxton?

For those who don't remember Shane Paxton's family were featured on *ACA*. They were this iconic family in the late '90s who were featured on several episodes of *ACA* in which the show tried to prove they were dole bludgers and unemployed slackers. They were set up in various ways and received a lot of harassment as a result.

As part of the pilot on how the media works I turned up to Ray's house with Shane Paxton, as the official timekeeper, and said I was going to see how late Ray got out of bed and finally headed for work. We shot it over two days. The first day we went there and were just hanging outside on his lawns, waiting for him to come out, and he didn't appear.

The weird thing was that when I did get to confront him Ray took it pretty seriously. I accused him of being slack for loafing around in bed till 11 o'clock and he felt like he needed to justify himself. He's going, "Listen, John, I stay very late at work," and he started talking about his hours and stuff. And I'm thinking, "Man, I'm just joking and mocking your show. I'm not really calling you slack." But he couldn't handle it; he took it as a personal affront.

How could I have predicted he would lay his hands on me and start wrestling? I don't quite know what I was thinking, but I guess I expected that, "Oh, it'll be sort of funny. We'll be at his doorway and he'll say, 'What, what?' and be confused, something like that." It wasn't like, "Let's see if we can get Ray Martin to punch me."

Had he been smart he would have just gone, "Oh, very clever, now go away"?

I guess so. I'm kind of in two minds about it, or in three minds, actually. On this theoretical level, considering his show, he just frigging deserved it and someone needed to satirise how current affairs programs treated people back then. Then on a human level, I just think, "Well, I probably would have reacted the same way to someone confronting me outside my home." But then that's the point. His show goes and winds people up, and then when they react in that way, they're judged as guilty. But really, if you wind people up in the right way, they'll always go crazy. And demonstrating the point to full effect, we did it to Ray Martin and he just went crazy, like all his guests. It's like, "That guy put his hands on the lens, he must be guilty." Well, Ray Martin did exactly the same thing.

I heard behind the scenes that he was really shocked and upset by it, and I just thought, "Jesus, chill out." I didn't really have it in for him on some personal level, and I didn't think he acted wrongly. The whole point of the story was to show that that was how people would naturally act under that kind of pressure.

At the start I was cool with him, because he'd be bagging me in the media, but he'd at least be telling the truth. He never said anything in the media that wasn't the truth, it was just his spin on it. However, with lots of people who weren't there and who hadn't seen the pilot it became this Chinese Whispers thing, where I followed his children home from school and all this stuff. Which just wasn't true. Even going through his recycling bins, it was just that we were waiting out there for hours, and then I went through his bins to shoot this thing, that ended up on the cutting room floor because it wasn't funny, where I'm going "Oh, I see here in his recycling bin he has all these *TV Weeks*. Must be filling out his own Logie forms." It wasn't like I was trying to find his tax returns or anything like that.

Recently, however, I heard him in the media, and he was crapping on about how much he loved *The Chaser*. When questioned he tried to make some distinction between when the *Chaser* team jump someone and when I jumped him, which for some reason means he's not a hypocrite for liking *The Chaser*, but still having it in for me after, what, ten years or something?

During the confrontation Ray Martin talks about having made a call to personal friend Roger Grant, then Head of Corporate Affairs for the ABC, about what you were doing. What effect do you think that had in preventing the pilot from ever being released?

It's really hard to tell, and again, why wouldn't he do that? I have more of a problem with the ABC caving in to him than him trying to get at me. He claims that all he did was complain, and that he didn't make any big dramatic threat or whatever. I think the ABC just took the path of least resistance, which was to bury the pilot. And again, because it was before the internet, things could actually be buried. I think these days the ABC would be cognisant enough to know that you can't really hide anything. But back then you actually could try to bury things.

Nevertheless someone at the ABC, who knows, in the edit suite or whatever, started dubbing it, and then handed it to friends, and it got distributed all around Melbourne and then all around the country. It was around the same time as the Pamela Anderson sex tape that was doing the rounds.

Again, I was just a bit confused about the whole thing. Like, what can you say if a TV network's saying, "We're not playing it because we don't think it's good enough." There's not much you can say back to that. Even though you secretly suspect it's not the truth.

Although the programs are now available via YouTube and other places on the internet, Channel 9 and the ABC initially did all they could to stop the pilots from being made available. Did their legal action forcing the University of Queensland to shut down Robert Whyte's website for carrying links to the pilots affect you personally at all?

All this was out of my hands. I still don't quite know how to upload things. The ABC were sort of implying that I was doing all this sneaky stuff behind their backs, but it just wasn't true. People got their hands on the pilot and it was broadcast at different universities. It was broadcast on public radio. The ABC were just utterly confused by it all, because it was a bit unprecedented, and as I keep saying this was this pre-internet era where the people at the top were quite used to being able to stop things, and they were confused by the fact that they no longer could.

Following your brief time at the ABC you went on to work at Melbourne community radio station 3RRR. Tell us about the satirical version of Baz Luhrmann's *Everybody's Free (To Wear Sunscreen)* which you released while you were there.

Luhrmann's song hadn't been released yet, but it was being played a little bit on Triple J. I just heard it once and had this gut instinct that it was going to become iconic and really take off. So I went and found a music record guy who knew the ins and outs of the industry, and we recorded this parody of Baz Luhrmann's sunscreen song called *Not the Sunscreen Song*.

The original had all this high-faluting lecturing about, "Hey kids, you're about to graduate," and then gave a list of inspiring things you could do. And I released a sarcastic, negative one, which is about all the bad things you could do like, "Wear sunscreen, but only if it's that coconut oil that gives you cancer," and, "Shoplift as often as you can. Shopping centres factor shoplifting into their prices so if you don't do it, it's like they're getting money for free."

As soon as Baz's song started getting a lot of airplay we were able to put our version out. From what I hear, from Baz's people behind the scenes, that's what really confused him or hurt his feelings a bit. "How did they turn it over that fast? I'm releasing this song, and I was hoping it would be really inspiring and everyone was going to go, 'Baz, you've really inspired me,' and then some sarcastic bastard's just released a sarcastic version five minutes after mine's been put on the shelves."

How did your version go with the public?

It got to number 20 on whatever the regular, mainstream, non-cheat's charts are and sold over 20,000 copies. However someone in a record store told me it was because Baz's version only came out on the full-length CD and you couldn't buy it as a single. "People come in here and they want to buy it, and then they don't want to buy a whole album so they just end up buying yours." So I think I got a few sales like that.

Most people took it the right way. It did feature on two current affairs shows where they tried to hype it up as this outrage or whatever. I had a pot shot at Adelaide in the song, saying, "Never go to Adelaide, it's a hole," which referenced a lyric in the original. So a couple of Adelaide politicians got angry, and that's how it all got put on the current affairs shows. They were making out that kids were listening to the lyrics of my song and trying to follow each and every thing. They also said that rival gangs in Adelaide were trying to outdo each other with the instructions from the song. I wasn't offended, it just made it more lively or more fun or something. I'm not quite sure how any modern person would listen to it and not take it as a piss-take. I wasn't feeling all this moral guilt or whatever.

You'd already had some experience with songwriting for jingles, hadn't you?

When I was working as a copywriter, jingles were considered the lowest of the low. Everyone who was a copywriter and working in an ad agency wanted to work on the beautifully photographed, black and white, arthouse Toyota commercial or something. Then there was the dregs, doing the radio ads or writing the jingles. For some reason I thought it was cool writing the jingles, so I'd get together with this musician, Chris Copping. I would sing into a dictaphone. I don't know anything about music; I've never studied a musical instrument or whatever. I'd just work out the lyrics and sing like an idiot in to a dictaphone, or to him live, and then this musician would work it all out. Then it would come back. I found that really fun.

I did one for Sea World on the Gold Coast, which was actually played all over the speakers whenever people were there. What else? In advertising, there's just so much stuff that the average person doesn't even notice. Like if you look at a newspaper, there's like a hundred ads, or a thousand. One of the ads is the big dramatic one that grabs your eye, but there's all this other stuff to do. Lots of the jingles were things people would never have heard of, like there were these children's playpen park ones, and Plants Plus Warehouse. It was all that kind of stuff.

John Safran attempts to join the Ku Klux Klan, 2004. Courtesy John Safran.

How did the 2002 SBS *Music Jamboree* series come about? There was a bit of a gap between doing the ABC pilot and doing that, wasn't there?

Yeah, between them I did a few segments for this show on Channel 7 called *The Late Report*, but that just sort of ... no-one was quite hitting their stride. The only interesting thing with that is I did get to do a story where we raided a McDonald's. I dressed up as Ronald McDonald and tried to do an alternative Ronald McDonald show. Channel 7 wouldn't play it, but they were honest, they just said, "Listen, we can't wake up on Wednesday morning after this and have our major Olympic sponsor in our ear saying, 'Why the hell did you run that?'" That was refreshing after my experience at the ABC where everyone was just bullshitting you around, and trying to have it both ways, like, "Hey, we're the management that is crushing your dreams, but on top of it, we want to look like we're the underdogs and the good guys, so we're gonna lie to you." That story ended up getting played on a show on Channel 4 in Britain called *Disinformation* and I did a couple of other things for them, also.

With *Music Jamboree* on SBS, it was just that the right people had seen my pilot, and said, "Try to come up with another show idea." I pitched them a book show, but they didn't think much of that. With the whole music show thing, it seemed like everyone could get their head around it. There was this woman called Glenys Rowe, who was the boss of SBS Independent. She and [producer] Debbie Lee just said "Do it." They really took a bit of a risk, because SBS in itself doesn't have huge bucketloads of money, and within that, SBS Independent has even less money, or at least did then. So by commissioning my show they weren't commissioning other things, and they were taking a risk. People would have said to them, "Why the hell did you do that?" if it hadn't have worked.

I guess that show was interesting for me to film because I didn't quite know what it was going to turn out to be. It was a bit like going on *Race* again — it evolved as we went. I started off and my pitch was, "It's going to be like *Video Hits* if *Video Hits* was hosted by Stuart Littlemore from *Media Watch*." That was the pitch that got it up. But when we started doing it, it became more theatrical. We did this one thing where I was dressing up like a prince and I thought, "That's pretty fun." So we just started writing more and more things where I had to wear ridiculous outfits and get thrown into the real world. It just seemed colourful and created good energy.

It was also that show where I simulated *Footloose*, but at my old school. This is a really religious school where we didn't have any end-of-year school dances or anything, and we weren't allowed to mingle with the girls' school. I made these parallels between my life and the story in *Footloose*, where Kevin Bacon's character went to a school where dancing was banned, and then he fought the establishment and went back to the priest that ran the school and said, "In the Bible, in Ecclesiastes, it says about how King David danced before the Lord." He

does this dramatic thing in *Footloose*, arguing the case for dancing and wins over his priest. So I went back to my school, to the Rabbi, and I used all the arguments and quotes that Kevin Bacon used in *Footloose* to try to convince him that dancing was okay. When that failed we went and danced *Footloose* — me in my '80s gear and some girls in their '80s gear — on the schoolgrounds. And that was ... that was fun!

Have you been invited back to the school since?

I live just around the corner from the school, and it's really hard. Usually when I'm actually doing one of my pranks everyone gets shirty and really annoyed by it. However when they see the final product it usually doesn't seem as malicious and, as soon as it doesn't seem malicious, people are a bit forgiving. For example I did this thing on my show *John Safran vs God* where I went to see the Ku Klux Klan and tried to join even though I'm Jewish. I actually read on the internet this thing where these skinheads were discussing it on a message board. One skinhead piped in, "I was there that day when he did that. He came in, we thought he was a serious reporter, and then blah, blah, blah." Then he said, "Having said that, when I saw the thing on YouTube, I thought it was pretty funny." You can even get forgiveness from the KKK, as long as your thing doesn't look too malicious.

The other prank from the *Music Jamboree* series that I really enjoyed was the Steve Price ecstasy pills one, where you got a fluoro-clad raver to deliver pills bearing the 3AW logo to the Melbourne shock jock. I think with that one there were some parallels to the prank you later did with Sheikh Omar Bakri as the two of them, a little bit like the current affairs people we were talking about earlier, live in this reality where children do go out and follow John Safran's songs, or where there really are 3AW logo pills, or where some anodyne Australian talk show host really does hate Muslims. I think that's an interesting dynamic, finding these people whose take on reality is somewhat skewed and then playing up to their inanities?

There was a bit of good luck with the Steve Price thing because I was working at 3RRR at the time. I was on the radio and, absolutely without thinking about it, made some offhand comment about Steve Price because he was going on about ecstasy. I made a comment about how someone should press up some 3AW ecstasy tablets because he was going on and on about what all the different logos meant on ecstasy tablets. He picked up on it and made it into this big thing for his afternoon show because he's always looking for some drama. So that was fortunate that that happened.

We went into his mind where he thinks that someone listening to me on 3RRR, and hearing me say, "Press up some 3AW ecstasy tablets," would actually follow through with that. It was just playing into his fantasies. We got a whole heap of people from the office to ring him up and say they had been at parties and had seen 3AW ecstasy tablets. He was getting more and more excited as it went on. Then we delivered these funny tablets to 3AW and he ranted on for a while before we exposed the whole thing on the TV show. Apparently he threatened some legal action, but it never came to anything.

In 2004 you returned with the program *John Safran Versus God*. What made you decide to focus on religion?

It was a combination of a sincere interest in the topic, and also me thinking that because it's such a serious topic everyone could get their head around that concept on some archetypal level. It presented itself as a really good, overarching theme for a comedy show. It was also after 9/11, and all my inner-city leftie friends didn't seem to get that outside of Fitzroy and outside of East St Kilda, religion's just so important to a billion Indians and the Timorese, and most of America. I mean, it's all changed now, but it seemed to me at the time that they didn't realise that we haven't reached this period of secular enlightenment where everyone's thinking like we're thinking. People who don't have a religious belief, out of the six billion people in the world, are a real minority. I found that interesting, too.

What was it like making *John Safran Versus God*?

I just can't believe what a fortunate but absolutely kooky life I have. Like, we were flying around the world, we were spending two days in Japan in a Buddhist temple and then we get on a plane and fly to spend two days in Arizona having peyote and then we get on another plane, etc.

It's also weird because it's not like you're there as a tourist. You don't have time for anything, but to get the footage. You have to pre-plan what the arc of the story is to within an inch of its life, because usually when people shoot documentaries they'll be bumbling around for a year or something. Or at least a week! And we somehow have to get something funny and exciting in one and a half days at a Buddhist temple or whatever. So we'll plot out on paper what we think the story arc is going to be. Then you get there and you have to adjust for whatever the circumstances are, because how you plan it out in your head isn't necessarily how it's going to go down on the day. Usually the thing that's making me happy is when the story's working because that's usually the big stress. "Oh my God, we've flown out all the way over here and this story isn't funny." That's my biggest fear. My biggest fear isn't that the guy from the KKK is going to beat me up.

So you have all these counterintuitive thoughts in your head. When I was drinking this peyote, this hallucinogen that Indigenous Americans drink to have a spiritual experience, I was drinking it for ten hours slowly, following the instructions, and it just wasn't working. Then finally I vomited. I just vomited and vomited and vomited, and the whole time I'm thinking, "Thank God I'm vomiting, something's happening." So the vomiting for everyone else would have been the

John Safran in the US, 2004. Courtesy John Safran.

worst bit, but I was just thankful that something was happening.

So the most relaxed times I have on these things is when I realise that a story's going to work. I went and met this exorcist dude Bob Larsen, I think it was in Arizona. We walked in there and within one minute he was just the most charismatic, offensive person, who spoke in these fantastic over-the-top soundbites, and was totally unaware of how offensive he was. I thought, "Oh my God, this is just going to work." So we hung out with this exorcist for four days. We actually changed the schedule a bit because we were going to only do two days, but then we found out he was going to do some exorcisms in front of a crowd in Oklahoma.

That was this real relaxing four days away because it was like, "Not only is this going to be an okay story, but we're going to be able to spread it out over an episode," while all the other stories would only last five to seven minutes.

How did your own exorcism at the hands of Bob Larsen come about?

The thing I remember was that when I met him he sat me down and said, "John, these are other shows I've been on." There was some show that had this British woman that had come to hang out with him and I was like, "God, this woman's doing what I'm doing. People will think I've watched her show and copied it." My heart sank, but then I realised that she had just hung around on the borders, and that's when I said to myself, "Screw it, if I do this I have to get right deep into it and have an exorcism and be the centre of it and all that." It was like some weird sense of competition, not wanting anyone to be able to say, "John just did what that other woman did."

The exorcism was interesting because I remember that when I was watching the series a friend who was receiving hypnotherapy pointed out that Larsen was using all these basic hypnotic techniques?

It was kind of hard to tell. Everyone had all these theories, like someone said he might have put something in my drink. But I don't really think he did that, unless he was really clever. So yeah, it was like hypnotism or exorcism because he just lulled me into it. The thing we had to crunch down was how long it took for him to get me into that state. He'd take ten minutes to get me into the state. He'd touch me and say these things. Obviously people who are into hypnotism think it's all hypnotism, and the Christians say, "John, you see, you see?"

Generally Christians really liked the show. Again, you'd expect Christians to hate my show, but for some reason they just didn't. It's more the opposite. Now there's Christians who've put that up on the internet and badge it with their own church thing, as if this is somehow proving that their church is right, using my footage to advertise their churches.

And did you feel exorcised?

Well, it was kind of calming at the end. We had to leave just before he was going to baptise me in the hotel swimming pool. We'd already gone two days over and he was asking, "John, will you come now and be baptised in this swimming pool?" Due to a combination of me having been baptised on *Race Around The World* and the fact that we'd have to delay the flight again and that we already had him rambling on for four whole days, we decided we didn't need anything more. So I never went through with the baptism. Maybe that would have been the thing that would have finally got the demons out of me.

Tell us about the fatwa that you got placed on talk show host Rove, which I notice is part of his official bio now?

I did that because I was once bumped from his show. He was going to have me on, but then he bumped me. On my religion show I was talking up the concept of fatwas and talking about how there was this guy in the UK, Sheikh Omar Bakri, who was famous for throwing fatwas on everyone. Some guy would come out with a gay-themed play and, bang, the old fatwa. Salman Rushdie gets a fatwa even when the fatwa gets taken off him in Iran. Just throwing fatwas everywhere. I wondered, "Is it really that easy to get a fatwa out of him?" So because Rove had bumped me from his show I decided to use him as my guinea pig. I threw together all this falsified evidence

that he'd insulted Islam and went to Sheik Omar Bakri and yes, he put a fatwa on Rove. It worked!

Were you worried that Sheikh Omar Bakri would cotton on to what you were doing, because you got more and more ridiculous as the segment went on, claiming that Rove had done ads saying, "Forget halal, get some pork on your fork", and so on?

It's a bit easier overseas than in Australia because in Australia there's something about my voice where I sound sarcastic. But overseas, because of the Australian accent, that becomes the thing that hits everyone's head. People just take you seriously, for some reason. I find it easier to do these things overseas.

The only thing I usually regret when I shoot these things is when I mildly chicken out or something. Then I just go, "God, how could I, I had that chance and blah, blah, blah." With him he took ages to track down and he had all these minders and it was this nightmare to finally get to him. We tried getting the fatwa one way, and then asked, "Can we meet up again tomorrow?" because we wanted to have another opportunity. He said yes, but we could never get him again, so we had to deal with the footage that we had. Which was fine because we'd gotten a fatwa, but I always have that in my head now when I go out. If you actually get someone in the room, get all that you can, because there's not going to be a second chance.

How much did SBS change the final segment?

There were two sets of changes. There was one thing that we did that involved this other cleric, Sheikh Abu Hamza, who talked about how he thought Rove should be beheaded. When we filmed it there hadn't been all the beheadings yet in Iraq. It just seemed funny because it seemed so fanciful, like, "Oh my God, no-one's been beheaded since the French Revolution." Then when people started getting beheaded in Iraq, the context was different. It wasn't funny anymore.

The other thing was that we had to demonstrate to the television audience that the fatwa had been taken off Rove, that we'd fessed up. SBS were worried that it only takes one lunatic to be watching and to actually think that there's a fatwa on Rove and chase after him or whatever. So we had to cut it to make it obvious that we'd fessed up to Sheikh Omar Bakri at the end, and that he'd taken the fatwa off.

When we were first showing the footage to SBS, they were like, "What the hell? You've got these two Sheikhs to put a fatwa on Rove?" I was saying, "Oh, don't worry, these guys are just clowns. They're like rent-a-quote." It's a bit like in Australia, if you want some outrage you get [former Returned Services League President] Bruce Ruxton on the line, and he'll say what you need for your story. I just said, "Don't worry about it, they're nothing, they're just clowns, no one in the Muslim community takes them seriously." Then after we edited the story Abu Hamza gets arrested on terrorism charges, and the other one flees the UK. SBS didn't really believe my reassurances after that.

How did your connection with the left-wing priest Father Bob Maguire came about?

Two guys, business acquaintances, had separately told me, "John, you've just got to go to this church in South Melbourne. There's this guy there and he's crazy." Both of them had only been there because they'd taken their mothers or been there for a christening or something. It happened to be around the corner from the production company I was working for at the time, so I just innocently wandered in and sat at the back during a weekday afternoon mass. He immediately spotted me and started doing his schtick. But then he just does his schtick all the time, to this three-quarters empty church, it doesn't matter who turns up. I thought, "This guy's pretty funny," and we filmed a story with him.

It was the one odd story in *Versus God* because all the other stories didn't work unless I was the protagonist. As soon as we decided to concentrate on some other person, for some reason, it didn't work. But it worked with him being the protagonist and screaming at me the whole time.

We then went on to do a show together on JJJ where we just blabbed at each other. Then someone came up with the bright idea that we should do it on television, but I don't think *Speaking In Tongues* was my most successful foray into television. We'd blab on about religion, but ultimately we were just behind a desk and on TV that kind of dynamic doesn't work as well.

Did you have any success with the matchmaking segments?

We had a zero strike rate. We focused on these little religious groups where there's an expectation on the person to marry someone who's also in their group, but because they're living in Australia there's not that many Zoroastrians or Baha'is or whatever. Each person gave their pitch and then people could contact the show and set up a date. Sadly the most successful thing we got, and we couldn't even put this on TV, was from an ex-girlfriend of one of them who wrote this long rant email explaining why we shouldn't set him up with anyone.

In 2008 you shot a pilot for *About Life* in the US. How did that go?

A lot of it didn't work because the producers wanted to force me to do things that weren't really funny. They had me going around shoving a microphone in people's face and trying to make them look stupid and the problem was that, for the most part, Americans weren't as stupid as they wanted them to be. Nevertheless, two and a half months in Los Angeles was crazy and fun.

One of the more successful stories we did was about marketing the army, because in America, the way they market the army is much more full-on than in Australia. In Australia there'll be some fairly generic-looking ad they run in the evening and at family times saying, "Maybe you want to join the Australian Army," with shots of tanks and stuff like that. But in America they'll have some hip-hop thing and it's really literal, like, "Hey, you're young, you're a kid, you're into hip-hop, you'll also like the army." It's quite odd as an outsider to see it. They had one ad where these two kids are playing this video game with two soldiers, and the soldiers turn to the kids and say, "Hey kids, you're good at this, but how would you do it in the real world?" It's advertising saying that kids who are into PlayStation should join the army.

Anyway, we did one story about trying to market the army to kids. We showed the ads that were trying to appeal to the hip-hop generation, and then said, "Rather than going for the hip-hop kids, why don't they go for other musical genres? Why don't they go for kids into goth and kids into emo?" Then we did an ad trying to get emo kids to join the army and we went to the army, to this marketing guy, and he said he liked it. And then we did a research group with emos, and they all hated it.

Finally, with your work do you primarily see yourself as an entertainer, or do you see yourself as having some sort of wider role in trying to get people to think?

It's always hard to unpack these things and to tell exactly what percentage of what you're doing is narcissism, because you like being stroked or because you're trying to make up for being ignored when you were a child, and what percentage is you trying to do a slightly good thing because it feels nice to feel like you're contributing something. A lot of it is entertainment, but whenever I'm in an environment, I always feel like it's really handy if there's someone there who's saying slightly cheeky things, or saying slightly inappropriate things — I don't know, it seems healthy. It's healthy for a community and a society. You need those sorts of things to be flowing through the media landscape because it just de-stresses things a bit.

For information on John's latest doings visit www.johnsafran.com

Dave Burgess

In 2002 and 2003, tens of millions of people across the world took part in demonstrations against the United States' launching of a second Gulf War against Iraq. On February 14th the largest protest in human history took place, with rallies occurring in approximately 800 cities. In Australia, up to one million people took part in demonstrations calling on the Federal Government to withdraw from the "Coalition of the Willing".

Predictably enough, the Howard, Blair and Bush governments pushed ahead with their war plans and although huge rallies continued to be held, an increasing sense of futility overcame the global anti-war movement. One small light in the gloom occurred on the day on which the first bombs fell, 18th March 2003, when two activists climbed the sails of the Sydney Opera House to paint the words NO WAR in bright red paint. In the following interview DAVE BURGESS explains why he and his friend, Will Saunders, felt compelled to take such action and what happened to the pair following their deed.

What is your involvement in the social justice movement and what were you involved in before the action?

In the lead-up to doing the Opera House I'd had fifteen years' experience in social change movements, whether it be for the environment or human rights issues. So I guess there was no ignorance of what we were doing, as such. I'd been through a number of campaigns, primarily involving forest protection, in Australia, Papua New Guinea and in Africa. I'd also campaigned around human rights issues concerning Bougainville, and also in Africa with the oil drilling in the Ogoni region of Nigeria.

How did you come up with the idea to paint NO WAR on the Opera House? What was the impetus for this action and why that particular target?

I don't think that the justice system ever fully believed us, but it came about very haphazardly. It began with Will telling me that he had a tin of paint which he wanted to paint an anti-war message with somewhere. I guess I didn't want to be involved in just another bit of political graffiti down some back alley. He asked where the most

effective place to put it would be. I jokingly said, "Well, the most effective place would be on the sail of the Sydney Opera House." Almost to my horror, I guess, I saw him scientifically calculating the possibilities. I said, "Go away and think about it. Ring me if you're serious." Two weeks later I got a phone call.

Had he mapped out how to do it? What were the logistics involved?

No-one had planned anything. I lived outside Sydney. So I had to get myself into the city and go and have a look at the building. I guess the logistics first got planned at a pub on a photo of the Opera House which was on a cigarette machine. We could roughly plot an angle which might be possible to climb up, from the photos. It then involved Will having a look and thinking about what we needed. All in all, it took three days of careful planning, with a couple of days' delay from rain.

How did you go about getting up there? Was it hard to scale the building?

The first 15 metres out of the 67 were the hardest. It involved a pretty serious incline, also a drop off to one side. So it was a case of getting as much momentum up that first bit and then flattening out onto the

Painting NO WAR on the Opera House. Sydney, 2003. Photographer unknown

surface and crawling sideways for a few metres to get onto a gutter where there was a foothold. But we decided that it was possible and reasonably safe and we decided to go from there.

So you just climbed it. You didn't use any equipment?

No. No equipment whatsoever. When looking at the building I put one cautious sandshoe on the tiles and I decided I needed something better. I purchased a pair of Dunlop Volleys and they held on very well.

I'd heard there'd been a recent banner drop off the Opera House and that security had been beefed up in response, were there many security guards around?

No. In fact, one of the reasons for looking at the building before we did the action was to see what the security was like. I went back to Will and said, "It's not an issue. So long as we walk directly towards where we

want to go to there won't be a problem." Once on the building there wasn't actually much that security could do. They certainly weren't going to chase us up the tiles and we had some access to the roof.

At the hairy point on the climb this voice below me said, "Come down now mate." I was fully focused on not falling off. I remember just looking over my shoulder and saying, "I just might so don't talk to me," then I just kept going.

In fact, what we found out later was that there was a dispute between the security at the Opera House and their employer. Numbers had actually been cut despite a major State Election promise that security would be beefed up to provide the best protection on any building in Australia.

I guess your experience put a lie to that. The timing of the action was quite important, wasn't it?

We ended up doing it just as George Bush was addressing the American people on television, in the same 25-minute window. That was a fluke on our part. We postponed it for two days running — one because we thought we might need some shoes with a better grip, and two because of a rain event. So it was just random that we happened to go up there that day. It carried a lot of heat beyond what we had thought about or what we were really concerned about. The State election was just four days away so it was quite delicate timing in New South Wales politics to be doing that kind of thing, but our main game was to get a message to the world that Australians were against the war, not to play domestic politics. So we went ahead.

What sort of paint did you use?

It was paving paint, which is paint that you apply to concrete and other surfaces. I didn't know too much about it scientifically. Will said, "I've got some paint which is used for hard, concrete surfaces," and I replied, "That sounds like the right paint." It was a mix of choosing the right paint for the surface and a hippyish, amateurish decision.

I think I gathered the full consequences of it when I was reading someone's blogspot and the words said, "Oh, my God, they used paving paint." A lot was made of it during the trial. Also we had tested acrylic paint on tiles before the action and it hadn't particularly adhered well so we did have our reasons ...

You didn't want dripping-blood letters that would quickly disappear?

That's right.

How did the police react? Did they take very long to arrive?

The first thing I did was type a big note in probably 64-point font saying, "Give us a call," and put my mobile phone number on it. I made it clear that we had no intention to be violent or to do anything but paint the message. I left that down at the bottom with a friend who handed it to the first policeman who arrived. I got a call from the police maybe 15 minutes after we'd started.

The first question he asked was, "Why did you give me your number?" and I said, "Just so we can communicate and make sure nothing bad happens. You guys are paranoid at the moment." He said, "But you're peace protesters aren't you?" And I said, "Yeah ... that's good." From that point there was, I hesitate to say it, a pretty good working relationship between us. There was a good communication going. He said, "Don't come down. We'll come to you." And I said, "That suits us fine because we're just gonna keep on painting until you get here."

By the time the rescue squad got up there they had to use one of the hatchways further down the roof because we had padlocked and shut the two at the top. That never came out in court.

It bought you some time obviously?

Yes. It was essential. By the time they were coming up I had taken it off and put it back in my bag. The first words they said were, "It's water-based, isn't it?" I just shook my head and they said, "Oh, you are in trouble."

By then we were all very tired from climbing and painting. We took a minute to look at the view and then we headed down inside the sail.

How did the Opera House staff react?

It was quite spontaneous. While coming down through the sail with the police there was a moment where we actually crossed the Concert Hall catwalk and the full sounds of an orchestral rehearsal hit us. I turned round to the policeman behind me and said, "Oh, that's lovely," and he nodded.

By the time we'd got down to the paddy wagons a number of Opera House staff and a number of the orchestra had stood in a line by the paddy wagon. They applauded us in. That was done behind closed doors. The reaction publicly from the Opera House management was a lot more hostile and we found it a lot more difficult to engage with them as the court case progressed. The police were very easy to talk frankly to, whereas the Opera House was quite difficult.

How long did the slogan actually stay up?

Initially, rather than remove it, they added an additional layer of white paint to it to prevent it from drying. There was a big report produced about the clean up. It did appear that the initial reasons for covering the message in white was not to remove it, but to cover it up whilst they came up with a plan to remove it. We weren't allowed near the building so we weren't allowed to go and see what was happening as it was being removed, but I've seen various photos of the paint running down the sail as they applied high-pressure hoses to it. However, there are also references in the report to it being there two weeks later. For four hours it was quite readable.

Being in the centre of Sydney gave the graffiti a lot of visibility. Then, of course, you got a lot of national and international coverage in the media about it?

I'm often asked about what we wanted to achieve and really the most important thing was that we wanted the message to be seen on a building that was immediately recognisable as Australian, and for it to be seen by a Middle Eastern audience. The Australian Government had just joined part of a coalition that was about to go and attack another country for reasons that were untrue and fraudulent. The real motivation wasn't stated truthfully until [then Defence Minister] Brendan Nelson admitted in 2007 that securing oil supplies was a major factor. The most important thing was that those people in the countries directly affected saw it.

The action also had a whole lot of other impacts. One of the things was the disbelief from some that we'd have done that to what was seen by some as a holy monument. At the same time, the paint washed off. What's a holy monument in Australia compared with the treasures, apart from the human life, that were destroyed in Iraq? There was a bit of a challenge there for people to deal with. Even though that wasn't the intention I think it was good that that element was there.

What sort of support did you receive immediately after the action? Were either of you at risk of losing your jobs or anything like that?

Will was at immediate risk of deportation. Because I was working in the environment movement and engaging with politicians, I'd almost immediately made my position untenable. As far as his work went Will got great support from work, including the support his colleagues gave him at the trial. I also received good support from my colleagues although I was unable to continue in the position I was in. As far as support from other sources, friends, unknown people and others, it was great, but not always predictable as to where it would or would not come from.

Did you receive any harassment from people? Outside the media and so forth?

There were numerous threats, some of which were serious, others not. Various letters. Someone sent our email addresses around American military bases and that led to a flood of crazy emails. The key thing was to try and not be bothered by them and not reply. I guess occasionally someone would recognise you during the time it was going to court and we were on television a bit. Most often those interactions were really good. Occasionally it was threatening. Overall we received a positive reaction.

When you faced court the prosecution's position was that what you had done was an act of malicious damage. How did you respond to that?

We defended ourselves in court on the grounds of self-defence, which was probably a suicidal thing to do as far as the law goes, but it also seemed to be the correct thing to do. If you read it that way and took international law into account then you are committing an act of self-defence if you are trying to prevent criminal trespass on your or other people's land. It also applies if you are attempting to prevent injury or death to yourself or others, damage to your or other people's property and a couple of other clauses.

We certainly believed that with a bucket of paint and a brush we were trying to do that. The situation was desperate. Interestingly, with running a defence like that, you have to prove a link between what would be your victim — in this case the Opera House — and the issue. Previously there had been an action in the 1970s during one of the Springbok Tours when a man went to the Sydney Cricket Ground and chopped down the goal posts with a chain saw. He won his case on the grounds that he was able to prove a nexus between the goal posts at the SCG and the apartheid regime in South Africa. Unfortunately

we couldn't prove that there was a nexus between the war in Iraq and the Opera House. So it's a fine line. But we felt it was worth saying that this was the only building that was going to carry that message and everyone who saw it would instantly know where it was.

Funnily enough the question of whether the Opera House was going to get up and attack anybody was raised.

You weren't allowed to present that defence the first time around, were you?

That's right. The jury was sent out of the room while it was debated whether we were allowed to present it. So it was a bit confusing when the jury came back into the room as we continued to plead not guilty, but then had to say that we had no defence case. Later on, in the Supreme Court, the Appeal judges ruled that it was not a valid defence and didn't need to be heard.

It seems a bit bizarre that one of the Supreme Court judges claimed that your defence was tantamount to justifying any act of terrorism?

Yeah. I thought that was pretty harsh, in many ways, given that we had gone out of our way to let the police have our phone number and to explain to them that there was nothing more sinister than what they could already see. But I guess that if we had succeeded then the legal system would have had to have dealt with just about every activist using the same defence to get off for things they'd done and the legal system couldn't have that!

What sort of protests happened around the court cases?

There were numerous rallies that the Stop the War Coalition in Sydney held for us. They were very supportive and were probably the key element in making sure that we weren't forgotten and were assisted throughout the whole process. They usually conducted rallies outside the court on the major days of the case.

A lot of other people also backed us publicly. Most notably the former Defence Minister, Bill Morrison, and Andrew Wilkie, who had just left his job in the Office of National Assessment because of the hypocrisy he felt Australia was indulging in by taking part in the Iraq War. He and Bill Morrison spoke up on our behalf, which interestingly went totally unreported.

There were also spontaneous things. On the day of our appeal a big billboard on Victoria Road, one of the main arteries into Sydney, was graffitied. It was a Channel 9 News one and it had the News crew, with the Opera House and the city skyline in the background. Someone wrote No War on it on the day we got sent back to jail.

Following the loss of the court case you wound up having to spend time in weekend detention. How difficult was that and how did the other prisoners respond to you guys being in there?

We were put in a special category and were there with [corrupt businessman] Rene Rivkin on weekend detention. It was called RAMP,

Above: Chanel 9 billboard defaced on the eve of Will and Dave being sentenced for writing on the sails of the Opera House (the real one).
Anzac Bridge, Rozelle, Sydney 2005. Photographer: Dean Sewell

which is Risk Assessment Management Program. It's applied when you are considered a risk prisoner. In our case that was on the basis of media exposure.

There was a fair bit of intrigue. Certainly when I arrived everyone knew we were coming. We were in separate jails, mainly because of where we lived. I lived in the Hunter Valley and Will lived in Sydney.

There were people waiting to hit you with a verbal barrage to see how you reacted. The first night I was in there I went to watch television for a bit and I came back and my sheets had been strung up in the shape of the sail of the Opera House with No War written on them, in tomato sauce. I took that as a compliment and went on from there. Like in the outside world there were those who were for and against the action. Generally we had a good laugh about it. Once the gates are closed there you are all in the same boat.

Were you shocked by the amount of compensation you had to pay?

Yes, we were a bit. We figured it would be high. We understood that it did require abseilers and a fair bit of logistical work getting it off. At the same time, it did come off. We were concerned that they had added another material over the top of what we'd done. They were seemingly more intent on hiding the message that was there rather than removing the paint in the most efficient way.

At the same time, the victim does have the right to determine how to respond to the crime against them. I was actually disappointed with the way that compensation claim was dealt with in court. If we'd been allowed to discuss it a bit more I think it would have been considered in more lenient terms. There did seem to be some awfully huge costings in there.

The total was $151,000. Initially it was $166,000, including GST, until we pointed out to the court that the Opera House, being a government body, doesn't pay GST. That was very quickly withdrawn. $15,000 was taken off, like that. That was probably indicative of how the Opera House behaved as far as the clean-up bill was concerned.

How did you go about raising the money? I know you made some snow domes and postcards and other interesting items?

The money was raised by everything from a person on the pension sending us $5 right through to creating our own versions of awfully tacky Opera House souvenirs. We had art shows and benefit concerts. Slowly it all came together via a combination of things that would rarely be in a handbook of fundraising! It really spoke volumes for how people responded to that action, with their hearts.

You asked before about where I wanted that action to be effective. In some ways the most amazing thing was when people came up to us and said, "You made me happy on what was a really sad day." Many

Left: Dave Burgess addresses the media after being sentenced to weekend detention, Sydney, 2004. Photographer: moz.net.nz
Right: Will Saunders at the fence outside the Opera House, Anti-Forbes Protest, 2005. Photographer: Matt Steer

people responded in that way. It was almost like a last insane little piece of defiance against an inevitable disaster.

I guess the remarkable thing about the various merchandise was that it helped keep the message rolling on, long after the action?

Yeah. It was funny with the snow domes because numerous examples went into the Opera House itself without anyone admitting that they'd got one. I believe that there are snow domes in about 40 countries now.

What happened in 2006 when you were forced to sue the police in order to get your brushes and paint can back?

Just when we thought it was all over we received a notice that the police had applied to destroy our paint brushes and pot on the grounds that we might sell them and make a profit. In one sense we might have just let them do it, but in another sense, it was like a red rag to a bull. They had done everything else to us that they could and now they wanted to destroy our paint pot too!

We applied to have it back. After a series of bungles over getting the date right we finally went to court early in 2006, and the police applied to have it destroyed. We were armed with letters from a couple of museums asking what would happen if you destroyed the Eureka Flag

or Ned Kelly's armour or some other rebellious relic? They pointed out that it wouldn't be a very interesting country.

After an adjournment we found that the Police Prosecutor had been replaced by a Department of Public Prosecutions lawyer so they were obviously taking it very seriously. Will spoke well and made a very clear case for giving us the pot back. We were prepared to make an assurance that we were not going to profit from it and we thought we could find a home for it so that it could, at least, live on as some small part of protest history in Australia.

Interestingly there were two paint pots. I had put mine in the rubbish and the paint brush in a juice bottle! Another one had been auctioned off, but it was an imposter pot. We knew nothing about it. It was auctioned for some cause, somewhere down the south coast of New South Wales. It definitely wasn't *the* pot. The pot is safe and we think we have finally found a home for it.

So they did return it?

Oh yes. We won. It was quite an incredible thing. After all that defeat of not stopping the war, of losing a court case and then an appeal case only to see the final battle won with us asserting the right of the paint pot to exist.

Chas Licciardello is arrested after The Chaser team breach the $170 million Asia-Pacific Economic Cooperation (APEC) Forum security zone in a fake motorcade. Despite being some of the most famous entertainers in the country, with Chas dressed up as Osama Bin Laden and members of the group wearing mocked-up security badges reading "Chaser's War" and "It's pretty obvious this isn't a real pass", the comedians' use of fancy cars bearing Canadian flags fools armed police into waving them through two separate checkpoints. In the end the group are allowed further into the "Red Zone" than they had expected and have to force themselves on the police, with Licciardello hopping out of his car to complain, as Bin Laden, about not being invited to the conference. Sydney, 2007. Courtesy of *The Chaser*.

The Chaser

THE CHASER TEAM FIRST CAME TOGETHER in 1999 through their involvement in a satirical newspaper before being approached by the ABC's Andrew Denton to produce a program tackling the 2001 election. *The Election Chaser* spoofed the ABC's regular election coverage and ambushed a number of politicians in the process. With the show proving popular, the team satirised news networks with *CNNNN* from 2003, revisited *The Election Chaser* in 2004 and launched the AFI Award winning *The Chaser's War On Everything* in 2006, before going on to haunt politicians once again in 2007 with *The Chaser Decides*.

Although the members of *The Chaser* claim to have no particular political agenda their brand of humour has nevertheless proved to be highly subversive in poking fun at a variety of authority figures. Having emerged during the Howard era the team has certainly had no lack of cruel and imbecilic policies and politicians to choose from. Their ability to crash events from the Asia-Pacific Economic Cooperation (APEC) forum to Family First and Alexander Downer's election parties has won them both high ratings and the ire of conservative politicians and media commentators. In the following interview CHRIS TAYLOR discusses the team's origins, modus operandi and most famous stunts.

What forms of creative protest or acts of civil disobedience have inspired you and the methods you use on *The Chaser*? Were you, or other members of the team, involved in media pranks and creative political protest before you became involved in *The Chaser*?

No, we're probably much less politicised than people think. A couple of the guys have been members of a political party, and were doubtless involved in protest campaigns during their uni days, but most of us don't have a background in this kind of thing. We're actually quite shy, introspective types by nature, so the pranks don't come naturally at all. We kind of adopt a different persona when we have to film them, in much the same way as a character actor would. And we only really do it because there's an onus on us to create comedy for a television show. We'd never do it in our spare time, or just as a hobby in the absence of cameras. And it would certainly be wrong to say we've been inspired by political protests or acts of civil disobedience. Our main influence has largely been other comedians — people like Chris Morris, Michael Moore, John Safran and Sacha Baron Cohen. I think we only drifted down the path of stunt-based comedy because of our limitations as comic actors. And shows like *TV Nation*, *The Awful Truth* and *Brass Eye* showed us that you could create quite interesting comedy by interacting with real people in the real world.

How did *The Chaser* team come together?

Most of the team worked on student newspapers together at Sydney University. They had such a fun time doing it that, after graduation, they decided to start up their very own newspaper called *The Chaser*. The original four editors were Charles Firth, Julian

Morrow, Dominic Knight and Craig Reucassel. Andrew, Chas and I contributed the odd piece here and there, along with a handful of other great writers and cartoonists. It was mostly a labour of love and was never intended to become a full-time career. We all had proper day jobs, or were still finishing degrees, so when the TV and radio offers came along it was only the most reckless of us who opted to put everything on hold and give it a go.

Tell us more about *The Chaser* newspaper. Was there much of a market for a satirical newspaper in Australia?

No, not really. It was a very niche publication, and sadly it never turned a profit. In fact we ran it at a loss for about five years before it eventually folded. I think Australia's population is too small to sustain a paper like that. Many other people have tried and failed, just as we have. The other big problem was our website. We published a lot of content on the site for free, believing it would help promote the newspaper, but what we found was that most people were getting a sufficient fix from the website, they didn't feel obliged to fork out for the print edition. At *The Chaser's* peak, I think the site was getting quite a lot of hits — it was certainly the kind of site that bored office workers would surf during their lunch hour — but we never really found a way to turn all those hits into revenue. It's a great shame. I've always been a huge fan of magazines like *Private Eye* and *The Onion*, and it's a pity that we can't produce a similar publication in Australia.

How did you get hold of John Howard's phone number and why did you decide to print it on the cover of the paper? What kind of response did you get from his office and from the media? What was his answering machine message?

We printed Howard's home telephone number just after all the anti-war marches. Thousands and thousands of people had taken to the streets to oppose the Iraq war, but Howard was unswayed by their pleas. In our view, he was defying what the majority of Australians wanted. So we published the headline, "Howard ignores the people — so call him at home on (02) 9922 6189". We got the number from Howard's own daughter, Melanie. She was at Sydney University at the same time we were. Some of us had worked with her on one of the Law Revues. She was the producer and she gave everyone her home number at Kirribilli House in case we needed to contact her. So we'd been sitting on the number for about six years before we eventually published it. It was a pretty slack thing to do, and not a particularly funny joke, but I suppose it had an endearing impudence about it. I think we tried to defend it in the media by saying that an invasion of privacy isn't nearly as bad as an invasion of a country. Janette copped the lion's share of the calls but, from memory, the number was disconnected and changed within about two hours. We never heard from Howard's office, but we did have a visit from the Federal Police, who merely wanted to know how we got the number. We said they should talk to Melanie Howard about that.

How did the TV show come about? What were some of your favourite pranks, and which politicians did you have the most fun with on the show? Over the years who has been scariest to deal with — Bill Heffernan or Mark Latham?

The TV show came about after Andrew Denton picked up a copy of our newspaper, and saw an irreverence that he thought had been missing from Australian comedy. He got in touch with us, offering himself as a producer for any television ideas we might have down the track. We were incredibly flattered and overwhelmed, but we put our heads together and came up with the format idea that eventually became *The Election Chaser*, covering the 2001 Federal Election. It was a pretty rough and ready debut, but the ABC obviously saw enough potential in it to invite us back to make further programs.

Funnily enough, the pranks are probably my least favourite component of the show. I always prefer the more scripted, polished sketches such as the *CNX News Slam* or *The Chaser Affair* sketches in *CNNNN*; or sketches like *Cats: The Movie, Hill$ong* or the *Horse Flu Handicap* in the *War* series; and also the crit and review pieces like the one Chas and I did about *The Secret*. I think too many of the pranks in recent times have fallen into borderline *Candid Camera* territory, which is something we've all vowed to avoid in the future. The best stunts are always the ones that make some kind of point, or expose something interesting, such as the Race Card, Al Kyder or the Trojan Horse.

Most of the politicians we've confronted have been pretty good sports about it, with the singular exception of Tony Abbott, who's reliably humourless every time. We actually prefer it when they don't play along. People like Vanstone, Latham and Rudd always tried a bit too hard to be chummy. Interestingly, people like Garrett and Turnbull seem less comfortable with us — although, to be fair, they both have to endure more ambushes than most simply because they live in the same city where we make the show. The minor backbencher pollies are always the best, because they haven't had the same level of media training. In *CNNNN* Craig interviewed the Liberal senator Judith Troeth about a hoax leadership challenge, which she took to be real, and she more or less goes to pieces trying to explain her position. And in our first election series, Bill Heffernan threatened to smack Charles Firth in the head after a fairly ugly standoff in the tallyroom on election night. Sadly those kinds of moments are a lot rarer these days, since the pollies are now all worded up about how to deal with us.

What are your thoughts on how best the media can be used as a tool for social change more broadly?

I think the introduction of the internet has been incredibly valuable. The internet's made the media much more democratic. Anyone can now create their own website or start a blog with the potential to reach millions of people, whereas in the past all editorial content and opinion was in the hands of a few wealthy magnates. Websites like

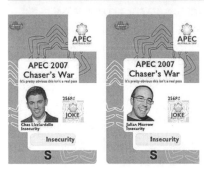

Top: Chris Taylor addresses the media following their release. Photographer: Damian Cronin. **Middle:** Chris Taylor, on a pantomime horse, offers the APEC police contingent some assistance. Despite being ordered by police to remove his outfit for inspection no charges of impersonating police were laid. Sydney, 2007. Photographer: Damian Cronin. **Bottom:** APEC 2007 *Chaser's War* "Insecurity" passes.

GetUp and MoveOn.org have redefined political activism, and have been substantially more effective at reaching people than old-fashioned forms of protest like street marches or rallies. Even something as simple as the Free Hugs clip on YouTube has demonstrated the power of the web to spread a humanist message. Mainstream contributions like Michael Moore's films or Al Gore's documentary will always have their place, but I think we'll increasingly find that grassroots content that originates on the internet will play a bigger role in setting the agenda.

Tell us how the rivalry with *Today Tonight* and Anna Coren came about? It seems as though you continued the tradition of *Frontline* in reducing the credibility of such programs to nil?

I don't think the rivalry between the two shows is real. It's mostly a bit of show business, and a fairly cosy arrangement, since both shows benefit by feeding off each other. Anna Coren herself has always been a great sport, and a very willing participant whenever we've barged in with the cameras. Her predecessor Naomi Robson was a lot harder to pin down. The only real fly in the ointment is *Today Tonight's* executive producer Craig McPherson, who I think genuinely dislikes us, and takes our jibes at his program very personally. He detained Chas and Andrew in his office once and apparently screamed at them so hard that they feared he was going to have a heart attack. He's obviously quite an intense character. But the rest of the staff there are mostly very nice, and often even ring us up with suggestions for segments.

The key to many a good prank is deception, the art of showing that appearances are not everything. Have you all become masters of disguise?

Not really. We actually use disguises very rarely. Julian put one on to get into, of all things, a conference about identity theft. And I think Chas used one to get into the Liberal Party's election night function. But usually they're not necessary. And they're never a great look — you always end up looking like Tony Mokbel in that bad wig.

Your masterful hoax and general all-round disruptions of APEC gained *The Chaser* international notoriety and much support from the community at large. Firstly, why the target? What were the logistics of such an operation? What happened with the arrest and the subsequent court case? How about the Government and media response?

The APEC stunt was one of those days when you just get lucky. The odds of getting into the official APEC restricted zones were extremely slim, but we were all determined to give it a crack. The massive security measures had been a big news story, as well as a major inconvenience to Sydneysiders, so we thought it might be interesting to see how tight the security really was. We came up with a couple of ideas to try to gain access to the restricted areas: one was to "accidentally" drift into the restricted water zone on a pool pony; the other was to try to drive in by pretending to be one of the official motorcades attending the conference. We actually got the idea, ironically enough, from an expert security officer who had visited our offices ahead of the summit warning us not to try anything. "You won't get in," he assured us. "You'll be barred at every gate. The only people getting through those checkpoints are motorcades." That was the light-bulb moment. An hour later we were on the phone booking three black limousines and some motorbikes. We added the comic idea that the motorcade actually belonged to Osama bin Laden, who wanted to add his voice to the APEC discussions on terror. Never in our wildest dreams did we think it would actually work. But sure enough, due to several strokes of good fortune, we were let through two checkpoints, and could have gone all the way to the Opera House had we not voluntarily turned ourselves around. Apparently the day beforehand John Howard had complained about his own motorcade suffering several delays at checkpoints, so the next day the police were issued with new orders not to hold up any motorcades. I think that new rule was the reason we succeeded so easily.

The shoot itself involved many days of planning, and countless high-level meetings at the ABC, discussing every possible contingency, as well as our legal responsibilities. But all the planning in the world can't always prepare you for the chaos and unpredictability of a location shoot. The ABC had strictly advised us not to enter the illegal "red zone". The fact that we ended up in the heart of the red zone was partly due to confusion about where the boundaries were, and partly because the police were so insistently waving us into it. The footage shows Julian Morrow making every effort to turn the motorcade around once he's realised how far they've got, but not before making sure we had the comic pay-off of Osama getting out of the car.

Once the police wised up to the stunt, they arrested 11 people and detained them in a holding cell for most of the day. They were all charged for entering a restricted area, but about six months later the charges were dropped when the DPP concluded that the chances of a conviction were slim. They felt that we'd be able to successfully argue that we had the tacit permission of police to enter the illegal zone.

I don't think there was any serious political fallout. The NSW Police Minister was huffing and puffing a bit, mostly because his department had so much egg on its face, but higher up people such as Alexander Downer and even the White House itself acknowledged it to be a bit of harmless fun. As for the media, I think they were just grateful that something interesting had happened at APEC. The rest of the summit had been a fairly dry affair, so the motorcade breach became the one story that they all latched on to. Perhaps it's a slightly sad reflection on our media, and on the state of political commentary, that it was much easier to sell a story about something that happened outside of the summit, rather than something that happened inside it.

The set of *The Chaser*.

Were you surprised at the effect of the APEC hoax and the level of support you received, as there's always a risk that you could misjudge community opinion?

I think community opinion was pretty split down the middle. Talkback callers were almost universally against us and most op ed pieces were running the line that we'd been hugely irresponsible, even if we had inadvertently highlighted shortcomings in the security. We were copping it from the police, the media and our own bosses. It wasn't until a few days later when I got on the bus to go to work and all the passengers suddenly broke out into applause that I realised some people were on our side. Despite the legal headache that the stunt became, it was actually very good for us on the whole. More people started watching the show. International networks took an interest. And, most usefully of all, I think it restored our reputation as a team that was still capable of pulling off a big public stunt, rather than just those limp *Candid Camera*-style pratfalls. It helped give the show a bit of a credibility boost.

Sadly the much wider effect of the APEC stunt is that it's compelled governments to draft even more ludicrous and draconian laws to prevent a repeat incident. The "annoyance laws" that were passed ahead of World Youth Day were a completely over-the-top attempt by the NSW Government to criminalise any behaviour that had the potential to embarrass them. Thank god that some sane judges on the Federal Court later agreed to overturn them.

Tell us about some of the pranks you did during John Winston Howard's walks? Do you think another pollie will allow themselves to be such an easy target?

Whatever you think about John Howard's policies, we actually loved him because he was such a publicly accessible Prime Minister. He went for a walk every morning without fail. Craig usually had the job of hounding him. He hounded him in a giant worm suit; he hounded him wielding an axe and a chainsaw; he even hounded him in a Delorean car dressed as the Doc from *Back to the Future*. The best one of all was during the 2004 election when Howard said that if ever fell under a bus then Peter Costello would be his natural successor. So we hired a big bus and dressed it up as the Succession Express and tried to run the Prime Minister over on his morning walk. It was quite a difficult logistical exercise and, as with APEC, we were blessed with quite a bit of good luck in our attempts to get the bus so close to Howard. Sadly Kevin Rudd doesn't go for morning walks, so he's a bit more elusive. In fact during the 2007 election campaign Rudd and his staff were much more uncooperative, and sometimes even aggressive, when it came to dealing with *The Chaser*. They did everything they could to keep us at bay, whereas Howard's team generally accepted us as part and parcel of the campaign circus.

And more generally have politicians changed the way they do public appearances, not just to avoid *The Chaser*, but also various protesters? Do you think this was evident in the reaction of the Logies security team and Dick Cheney's security to your presence and pranks?

I can't speak for protesters, since that's a different ball game altogether. The *Chaser* team belongs to the media, we're not subversive activists. We produce a television show on the national broadcaster, and yet even *The Chaser* finds it impossible to attend certain events these days. When people like Condoleezza Rice and Dick Cheney visited Australia, we not only had our formal requests for accreditation denied, but they also issued all security personnel with our headshots and strict instructions to do whatever was necessary to keep us out. It's a similar story at a lot of corporate events as well. We've been ejected from Telstra press conferences, even when we're officially accredited to be there. The Logies ceremony in 2007 was ridiculous. Channel 9 had assigned a massive security guard to specifically stand over our table all night, and when Craig and I eventually tried to film something we were pounced on and frogmarched out of the event. Earlier when we arrived, security officers held us in arm locks, pushed us against the wall and frisked us after we spilled fake cocaine all over the red carpet. The Liberal MP Christopher Pyne once even tried to ban us from attending press conferences at Parliament House. All of this adds up to a pretty drastic overreaction—after all, we're just a comedy show. Sure, we can be a bit annoying at times, but it's always done with good humour and minimal disruption wherever possible. At press conferences, for instance, we always let the journalists ask their questions first before carrying out our own gag. These more recent measures to squeeze us out altogether are a pretty extreme development, and a bit of a worry for a country that supposedly enjoys the right to free speech.

And finally, do you think that the popularity of *The Chaser* show can be attributed to the fact that Australians are a "bunch of larrikins"? Or is this just a popular myth and in reality Australians just love to "watch a bunch of larrikins"?

I think Australians have a great knack for taking the piss. Most of us have an irreverent streak and a healthy disrespect and distrust of authority. In some countries they take up arms when their leadership lets them down, whereas in Australia we're quite happy just to take the piss instead. It's the default position for many Australians, but it doesn't necessarily travel across to the professional sphere. We actually have very few professional larrikins and shit-stirrers in Australia. John Safran is one. Several editorial cartoonists probably qualify. But I can't think of too many others. There are traces of it in the *Chaser* team I suppose, but it's only one strand of our act. We were slightly bemused to read letters in the paper lamenting our absence at World Youth Day, as if the *Chaser* team somehow had an exclusive monopoly on the disruption of big events. Our response was, where were all the other piss-takers? Why should larrikinism be quarantined to only one group in the country? We weren't on air at the time of WYD so there was no point doing anything if we didn't have a program to broadcast it on. But what was everyone else's excuse? I think if piss-taking was as healthy in this country as we like to think, then there'd be ten Chaser teams, not one. Or ten John Safrans, not one. So, yeah, to some extent I think it is a bit of a myth.

www.abc.net.au/tv/chaser
www.thechaser.com.au

Making Trouble: CONVERSATION #6

John Howard Ladies' Auxiliary Fan Club

DURING HIS 12-YEAR REIGN as Prime Minister John Howard proved to be a cunning politician able to spin almost any situation to his advantage by appealing to the most selfish and bigoted aspects of the Australian character. Although Howard had tried and failed to use anti-Asian and anti-Aboriginal racism to win the 1987 election, he successfully exploited and created crises around national security, terrorism and refugees from his 1996 victory onwards to shore up conservative support and divide the ALP opposition. Along the way he also cut Medicare and social services, colluded in attempts to smash the Maritime Union of Australia, continued the ALP's flogging off of government-owned property, introduced the Goods and Services Tax and decimated civil liberties and workers' rights. Although Howard's agenda was largely designed to increase the power and wealth of his corporate backers, much of it also stemmed from his socially conservative dream of resurrecting the supposedly "relaxed and comfortable" Australia of the 1950s, in which women were consigned to the kitchen and nary a non-white face could be seen.

Unsurprisingly, many of those targeted by the Howard regime refused to quietly submit, and a wide-ranging series of protests and actions followed the Coalition's every policy turn. Disruptions of public appearances rarely fazed the PM, although on occasion he could become apoplectic, such as when Indigenous representatives turned their backs on him en masse during the 1997 Reconciliation Convention. Amongst the groups haunting Howard until the bitter end, when even the stripping of Aboriginal rights under the "Intervention" and wholesale union-bashing failed to save his political skin, were the John Howard Ladies' Auxiliary Fan Club. In the following interview, ZELDA GRIMSHAW and LIZ CONOR talk about their joy at wiping the smile off the PM's face.

Who was involved in the John Howard Ladies' Auxiliary Fan Club?

Zelda Grimshaw: Well, Liz and I were the ringleaders. Liz played the character Bea Wight and I was Bea Wright. There was also Jasmine Salomon who was Bea Rich and Bridget Cloonan who was Bea Strait. Rocky Humphrey (Bea Marshall, camera) and Carla Van Laar (Bea Sterling, driver) made up the rest of the team. All are mothers based in Melbourne.

Liz Conor: Our husbands were Mr Ernest Leigh White and Mr Christian Wright. Then there was Mr Phil T Rich and Mr Ben D Strait. Poor Mrs Strait never got to speak very much because her husband didn't like her speaking in public. So she had quite a silent role in the campaign. We thought it was quite important that the quartet reflect the key pillars of Howardism — being white, right, rich and straight.

Photographer: Rocky (aka. B. Marshall)

When did the Fan Club start out?

Zelda: It began during the 2004 election campaign. It was actually an idea presented to us by another well-known radical stirrer, Linda Memery. She thought it would be great to chase after John Howard wearing 1950s housewives' outfits whilst bearing his pipe and slippers. Unfortunately during that election campaign the closest we got was 50 metres away as we got stuck behind a cyclone fence.

Liz: For the 2004 campaign we had to do a lot of very intricate and delicate espionage to find out where Mr Howard would be. Eventually we found out that he and Kim Beazley flew from the Tenix hangar which is in a paddock outside Sunbury. We all went over there in our fabulous frocks and chased his car across the paddock. None of the guys who worked at the hangar could believe it. They were right out

in the middle of nowhere. We had to go to Tullamarine airport first to try and work out where this hangar was. We were wandering around asking all of the people who worked there — the security guys. They were all very helpful.

Tell us about the outfits you wore?

Zelda: We were channelling the Queen. We thought that was appropriate as Howard had taken us back to 1952, or at least wanted to. So the look was the Queen. She still wears gloves and hats and has a little dinky handbag. So it was the hats and the white gloves and the 1950s floral, frumpy, housewifey frocks, and little buckled patent shoes. Always panty hose. Always pearls. And very bad coloured make-up!

Liz: We were blue in 2004, but we went pink in 2007 because we found these four remarkable hats — just amazingly bad hats. Once we had the hats, it was like, "Now we're onto something." We had to find the frocks to match the hats.

Zelda: That year it took an amazing search. The whole costume hunt was a long journey. To get vintage frocks like that for under $200 is pretty difficult. For the record we were completely self-funded, self-motivated, self-organised. Nobody put us up to it. We kept getting asked who put us up to it. Our motives were quite pure — pure hatred of Mr Howard! We hated his guts. We wanted him gone.

Liz: So back in 2004, when we were wandering around asking the security guards where the hangar was they were so helpful because we were so ladylike and so beautifully dressed. We were so charming that they were really quite helpful.

What did you do during the period between the two elections?

Zelda: Liz and I really began to develop the characters. We did a lot of that on Community Radio 3CR as part of a show we do on mothering issues. Then we did a few public appearances. Our first public one in the 2007 election year was on Australia Day, known to the black arm bandits as Survival Day. We launched our White Blindfold Campaign on a tram. We did a Tram Overboard quiz, organised by the arts activist group Boatpeople.org. It was a satirical, "patriotic" Australian history quiz.

Liz: We asked, "What is the correct use of an Australian flag? Is it to promote social cohesion in the south-west suburbs of Sydney?" Those sorts of questions.

Zelda: We did that in character and we launched our White Blindfold Campaign. Under that anybody who knew anything about Indigenous history or had studied the Humanities was a black arm bandit. We produced these little origami white blindfolds which we handed out to the passengers and we said, "Now, this is the official John Howard view of history. What happens with the white blindfold is that you put it on and you can't see a thing. It completely whites out everything. All you can see is white."

How did people respond to that?

Zelda: They laughed. I was concerned on two fronts the first time we did a public appearance. On the one hand I was concerned that the Howard lovers might lose it and have a go at us, but on the other I was also concerned that people who weren't native English speakers or who weren't politically astute enough wouldn't realize that we were taking the piss.

Liz: There is that line between being offensive and taking the piss out of people who are offensive. And it's hard for people to sometimes draw that line.

Zelda: I was happily wrong on both counts. The Howard lovers still enjoyed the humour and the non-Anglo people on the tram were the first to laugh.

Liz: And they knew all the answers. Particularly a nine-year-old boy of Indian descent.

Zelda: He knew all the cricket scores. He knew Weary Dunlop. He knew Steve Irwin. He knew all the history. He had Australian values that I don't even have, lots of them.

So what happened when the election was called?

Zelda: Having done a few more public appearances and developed our characters we called in Mrs Bea Rich and Mrs Bea Strait. We then went on standby as it was really difficult to find Johnny. He kept his cards really close to his chest. The media didn't even know where he was going.

Liz: It's the same for Rudd. It's just become standard now. Even when you are travelling in the media pack you don't know where you are going. You are put on a bus. You are told what time you are to be on the bus and then you are taken to an undisclosed destination. That's how you go through the campaign. So that made getting to him very difficult. Again, we had to use very delicate and intricate espionage. We had to have people in unexpected places looking out, just in case he stayed in that hotel.

Zelda: But as ladies, of course, we can't reveal our sources.

What happened when you met up with him for the first time in 2007?

Liz: We got word early in the morning.

Zelda: It wasn't the first time we'd had a five o'clock start! We'd had a few false starts before that.

Liz: We met up at my place and frocked up and so on. We were rushing and still getting dressed in the car. Then we got to his hotel and there were the media packs so we knew that we were in the right place.

Zelda: That was where we got our best coverage. The media had never seen us before. Howard hadn't actually turned up yet and here we were all dressed up. We walked through the foyer of the hotel asking, "Where's Johnny? Where is he? We're the John Howard Ladies' Auxiliary Fan Club." We got to introduce ourselves to the media and present all of our material. We said, "We are the John Howard Ladies'

Auxiliary Fan Club. We've made some electoral Viagra for Mr Howard, scientific name 'xenophobia'. The idea is that you get the populace to swallow as much as possible — that gets him his hard elections." They loved that. "Mr Howard, you've got a very hard election coming up. You need this electoral Viagra."

Zelda: Yeah. He'd been flagging in the polls. Going a bit soft.

Liz: Our outstanding member had been going soft on us. We wanted to give it support and succour, didn't we?

Zelda: Mrs Rich had the Race Card. This was right at the start of the campaign. We were still thinking that that was the card he was going to play because that's what he'd won every other election on. He'd already tried it with the Intervention, Dr Haneef and the Sudanese boy who had been beaten. We had Mrs Rich running after him saying, "Don't forget your Race Card, Johnny. We know you've been trying, but keep playing it. It might work yet."

Liz: I had a lovely plate of home-baked yellow cake so there was a whole line in there about what a wonderful source of energy it was, how it stays in the system for 300,000 years, goes to eternity glowing in the dark, etc. I gave a spiel about how my husband and I had found a huge uranium deposit in Brighton. We were going to get Mr Howard to send the Diggers in to dig up all the uranium and then we could export it to Iran and North Korea and so on.

Zelda: We had a whole stable of gags that we were trotting out. It was wonderful to actually catch him a bit later that morning at the Tan [a running track in Melbourne's Royal Botanical Gardens]. He saw us standing outside the Shrine waiting and his car went to an entry further down. We had a black 4WD and a lovely driver so we piled in the 4WD and we got to him before anyone else was there.

Liz: He really did a second take when he looked at us. I was saying, "Would you like some yellowcake, Mr Howard?" He looked at us and smiled as though all his dreams had come at once. He smiled. He was happy, just for one split second, and then he realised — "Electoral Viagra" — that we were evil.

Zelda: You can see it on the YouTube clip. He turns around and he looks almost happy. Then it clicks over in his mind, "Hang on ... they're not 70." Then he starts sticking his headphones back on and storms off.

Liz: When we suggested that it might be a hard election for him and, for his age, it might be difficult to get such a hard election on, well, he took offence really. After that we couldn't get anywhere near him. His minders kept saying, "I've warned you once," and elbowing us aside.

Zelda: However, if we hadn't been in pink hats and white gloves we would have got rougher treatment than we did.

What actions were you involved in after that?

Liz: Once people knew about us they wanted to help. We went out to Bulleen Plaza to intercept Kevin Andrews [the then Minister for

Immigration and Citizenship] who was campaigning there. I had my nine-year-old daughter in handcuffs. I handed her over to him because she had been found on a bridge without a bridging visa.

We waited a long time for Andrews to show up. We were sitting inside the shopping centre and this lady rushed in and said, "Mr Andrews is outside." People really wanted to help. They loved it.

Zelda: We also went to the Melbourne Cup. We campaigned at the Melbourne Cup because after we caught Johnny at the Tan, the following day he didn't do his public walk. Instead he did his walk on the race track at Flemington so that people like us couldn't get to him.

At the time that area was an equine flu exclusion zone. Johnny either had to become a temporary horse for the day to get to walk there or somehow he got this special license to breach the exclusion zone. So we ladies decided that Johnny must be running in the Cup. Johnny must be training. So we went along to the Cup to bet on Johnny. We figured that £500 each way on Johnny was a good bet because he's sure to either get a win or a place. We went and tried to place a bet, but we were told, to our dismay, that Johnny wasn't running.

We thought it might be a good place to play the Race Card as well so we went up to the place where the winning horse comes out. There are always cameras there. There were security fences everywhere, but I realized that they were done up with wing nuts and just started unscrewing them. The next thing I knew an elderly lady standing next to me started helping me and then this Aussie blokey–bloke-looking fellow came along and said, "Are you ladies having trouble? I'll give youse a hand." He lifted the fence up for us.

They helped us get in and then several people cheered us. There were other people booing us as well and saying, "Get out, get out." While we were inside the exclusion zone with our pink fluffy hats and our floral frocks and our white gloves we were waving the Race Card around. The security stopped us getting to the podium and then the police came and escorted us out. They were saying "It's a $5,000 fine for breaching the exclusion zone," but we replied saying "But Johnny did it and we're his fan club. He's asked us to be here."

Liz: We also said, "We were thrown over the fence by those dreadful communists and frightful feminists. They've thrown us over the fence!" They couldn't work out how we got in there because we'd put the fence back.

Zelda: They were not that bright. Anyway, they escorted us out. I was thinking, "Okay, this is it. We'll be in the station for hours. There'll be a $5,000 fine. We're going to have to fundraise, blah, blah, blah." In case of arrest we had one person who was not going to be arrestable who had contact numbers and so on. However the police just walked us out and said, "Okay, don't come back."

Liz: They were cross and they gave us a lecture. They took our names and numbers, but if we had been wearing normal clothes I'm sure we would have been in the back of the divvy van.

Didn't you make an appearance at a teachers' rally as well?

Zelda: Yes. We were at the Vodaphone Arena for the teachers' strike. There was something like 10,000 of them. It was so nice. Because we'd been campaigning in all of these potentially hostile places with Johnny's people, like Bulleen Shopping Plaza, the Sofitel and at the Melbourne Cup. It was nice to be with people who understood our jokes — all of them!

Liz: Calling them all communist scum was one of the best moments I've ever had. When we realised that we were actually addressing a bunch of striking teachers, not a Scotch College Old Boys' gathering, we decided to detonate these explosives. They turned out to be the wrong type of explosives for the purpose.

Zelda: We had pink princess Christmas crackers strapped to our fronts because we were waging a holy war against the unions and the working class. We weren't terrorists. We were government operatives, of course, because we were on the right side. At one point we popped our pink Christmas crackers to make the ultimate sacrifice for Johnny.

What happened when you tried to get at John Howard the next time?

Zelda: It was a few days after the Cup when he was addressing the Institute of Public Affairs [a right-wing policy think tank] at the Sofitel Hotel. There was a group of protesters out the front, but we were able to drive straight past them and past a police barricade. When we dropped our car off at the valet parking they asked, "Where are you staying?"

Liz: We said, "We're staying with Mr Howard, in Howard's suite. We are his ladies." They just kind of went, "Ooohhh."

Zelda: So we got through the second layer of security. There was a third layer of security up the stairs, but they just thought, "Oh, they look cute." So there we were, just milling around, with Howard's people for a good half hour offering them, in fact forcing them, to take the xenophobia pills. We had different colours for different types of fear. "Are you afraid of Muslims, dear? No? Okay then, you're going to have a white one and that will make you afraid of Muslims. Vote for Johnny." We had some pink ones for gay people, purple ones for feminists and women in general, and red ones for communists and unionists.

Liz: The IPA people just laughed. Some of them had their photos taken with us, especially the elderly gentlemen. They loved having the attention paid to them. The nostalgia ...

Zelda: Eventually the security at the Sofitel got quite cross and made us stand in one place until the police came and ushered us out.

How did you avoid being arrested in these situations?

Zelda: I think the key to it was that we were seen as performers rather than protesters. It really put us in a different category and meant we had an entirely different relation to the police to what I had ever had before. I literally put my arms around the police and said, "Give us a lift, you lovely boy, won't you?"

Liz: We charmed them. "Look at the boys in blue. Look at the lady in that uniform. Doesn't she look just divine. If only they had black leather gloves to go with them."

Zelda: We really flirted with them. Outrageously. With the Australian Federal Police who weren't in uniform we were shocked and horrified and said, "This is just dreadful. We've got this huge budget surplus. Why aren't they giving you proper black double-fronted serge uniforms? Hitler managed to even put children in uniforms. Can't we manage to give our Federal Police agents some uniforms?"

Liz: They were laughing. The police enjoyed it, the security guards enjoyed it, but they still did their jobs.

Zelda: What all that taught me was that with a pink fluffy hat you can go anywhere. Being seen as performers rather than protesters got us access to a lot of media as well as places we might not have gotten access to otherwise.

At the same time it helped that we were four small white women. We were very non-threatening. If we had been large black men they might well have carried us away, but as four small white women, even strapped with "explosives", we were welcomed in.

Another thing I learnt was to keep your props really camera-friendly. At the Tan our Election Viagra bottle was round and its label couldn't be read on camera. So that's a tip – keep your props big, bold and camera-friendly.

Tell us about your election day trip to NSW.

Zelda: Our final encounter with Johnny as PM was on the morning of the election outside the gates of Kirribilli House. We all flew up and we were there to greet him at 6am on his last day as PM. You can't imagine how delighted he was to see us. He stepped out of Kirribilli House and there we were, the John Howard Ladies' Auxiliary Fan Club waiting for him with a brand new bottom — a new seat, because we had heard that he was going to lose his seat. So we were there. We'd made this great, white, prosthetic bum and we were there, holding it up, saying, "It's all right Johnny. If you lose your seat, we'll be right behind you. And look, we've got a new bottom for you!"

We chased him down the street with that. And Liz and Jasmine, who were Bea Wright and Bea Rich, were on either side of him in each ear, the entire time. I kid you not. His last morning walk as PM was hell. The image of him as he came out of Kirribilli House and saw the four of us, standing there smiling and doing the Queen's wave and holding out his bottom will stay with me for quite a long time.

One of the great things about having a group like the John Howard Ladies' Auxiliary was that we were very flexible. We had these characters that could respond to anything. When he started attacking the workers and running those ads saying, "The unions are coming back," we asked, "Where have the unionists been darling? Haven't they all been locked up in Guantanamo Bay? That's where they should be, shouldn't they?"

Liz: So we hounded him about that. I'd have to say that Jasmine and I stayed with him all the way around and he really did look cowed. At times I felt for him, but then I thought about the suicide rate of Aboriginal youth and the psychological collapse of refugee children who'd been detained for years and years. Then I thought, "No, you've got this coming, you bastard!"

Did you script most of what you did or ad lib?

Zelda: It was all ad libbing. We would write ideas as they occurred to us and they would sort of permeate through us, but when you're live you really can't be reading off a script.

Liz: It was a kind of a mix of a stable of gags we were running and adding to all the time. Things just came up. It evolved constantly. We were in character 90% of the time. Because we were in those ridiculous clothes we just kept coming out with things. As we went along we got a sense of who owned what jokes. We tended to speak the jokes we made up ourselves and we were able to run routines much better as we'd had practice.

Zelda: You never knew when it was going to happen, so the fact that Liz and I had done a year of this on radio made it so much easier. The parody stuff really worked, it was like a shot in the arm for people. The Left was so depressed with bad news and tired out from fighting and hating Johnny. There was some relief in just coming out and saying what the Liberals believed in, which wasn't being said in the media. We were showing that Howard's "dog whistle" was actually calling on people's racism and homophobia, or their fear of welfare recipients. To bring that to light we went around saying that we wanted to send all the single mothers to forced labour camps receiving a hundred strokes a day, and that we wanted to send all the unionists to Guantanamo Bay and abolish wages for workers. That we wanted to get all the uranium out from under the Aboriginal children and wash them until they're white.

Liz: It was foul what we were saying.

Zelda: By taking what the Right really meant and making it ridiculous we were able to put their agenda out in the open as well as have a laugh, and make political points at the same time.

Liz: I've never had so much fun — it was a hoot.

So where are the Ladies now?

Zelda: I'm afraid the John Howard Ladies have died and gone to hell. We've realised that now that Johnny has lost his election, he's never going to have another one. As a result we've gone over to the other side. But one way or another, we'll be back!

www.youtube.com/user/joholafaclub

Making Trouble: CONVERSATION #7

Pauline Pantsdown

When the Liberal Party dumped Pauline Hanson for making racist remarks during her 1996 election campaign, little did they know that the decision would come to haunt them, and the rest of Australian society, for years. Still listed on ballot papers as the Liberal Party candidate, Hanson subsequently won the seat of Oxley and joined the House of Representatives as an independent. After giving her famous speech in Parliament on 10 September 1996, in which she harked back to the White Australia policies of the 1950s, she was catapulted to celebrity status. While left-wing independent Phil Cleary, the Greens and other minor parties were starved of media oxygen, Hanson's defiantly ignorant racism received massive coverage.

During 1996 and 1997 Hanson toured the country touting the idea of a new party with the support of elements in the corporate sector who, while wary of the effect of her anti-Asian rhetoric on Australia's trade partnerships, saw her anti-Aboriginal rhetoric as an opportunity to counter growing support for Native Title rights. One Nation predictably fared best in conservative Queensland, winning 25% of the vote and 11 seats in the 1998 State Election. The party soon unravelled, however, over the autocratic rule of Hanson and her two key advisors, David Oldfield (who was to win a NSW upper house seat in 1999) and David Ettridge. Hanson lost her seat in 1998 after an electoral redistribution and failed to win the neighbouring seat of Blair in that year's election. Although One Nation gained one senator in Len Harris the party was on a slide and Hanson subsequently failed to win a senate spot in the 2001 election.

Hanson's attempt to exert total control over her party also saw her sentenced to prison in 2003 when it came to light that One Nation had defrauded the Australian Electoral Commission by claiming that it had the requisite number of members to register as a political party. In actuality under the Party's dictatorial structure it had only three official members (Hanson, Oldfield and Ettridge) with the rest of the Party relegated to supporter status. Unable to pay back the $498,637 that One Nation had received in electoral funding, Hanson and Ettridge spent time in prison for electoral fraud and dishonestly obtaining property, before being freed on

appeal. After a period of languishing in the "Where Are They Now?" bracket, Hanson bizarrely reinvented herself as a member of the D-List in 2004 by appearing on Channel 7's *Dancing With The Stars* program and an ad for donuts.

Although One Nation only lasted a few short years the Party's rise had a deep impact on Australian politics. John Howard, who had tried and failed to whip up fears of an "Asian Invasion" in 1988, skilfully exploited the racist elements of Hansonism to divide the Australian electorate and shore up his support from the far right. A host of policies which bashed Indigenous and non-Anglo Australians followed.

Both One Nation and the policies it was able to push into the mainstream rarely went unchallenged. Hanson's barnstorming tours during 1996 and 1997 were dogged by large and rowdy protests and leading members of One Nation were often subject to abuse from members of the public. Among a series of satirical songs targeting Hanson came a particularly successful effort from sound artist Simon Hunt, who wittily collaged Hanson's interviews and statements to create the underground radio hit *Backdoor Man*. Moves by Hanson and her supporters to suppress the song soon backfired as court action only spurred Hunt on to create a new song, *I Don't Like It*. Alongside the single and a film clip Hunt also publicly launched the drag queen character Pauline Pantsdown, who successfully parodied and dogged the bigoted politician by running in the 2001 election.

You have a background in sound production, haven't you?

Yes, sound is what I've done mostly. Pauline Pantsdown was really an intersection of a whole lot of different things I'd done. I'd done some performing work, some sound work, some cut-up work and also a few political things. The direct lineage of the Pauline stuff was that each year at Mardi Gras there had been a club called Club Bent which was more the weirdo, arty side of the parade and I'd done an annual cut-up for that, taking some sort of text and performing to it. One year it had been all these personal ads people leave about themselves on phoneline chat things. So there were boys and girls doing drag performances to these personal ads. *Backdoor Man* was initially part of one of these performances.

Tell us about the action you did targeting Fred Nile in 1989?

Nile did an anti-gay march on Oxford Street to coincide with the Mardi Gras. For those who don't know him, Nile is a Christian crusader who has a seat in NSW Parliament and who has basically built his career on being anti-gay. He faded away for a while, but in recent years has significantly shifted his focus to an anti-Muslim stance.

It was a pretty spectacular day as I'd been involved with the counter-protest. We were worried no-one would turn up, but in the end there were ten times as many gays and lesbians there as there were fundamentalists. We really gave it back to them, but in a good-natured way, chanting things like, "2 4 6 8, are you sure your priest is straight?" (Laughs) I did a cut-up of Nile speaking on behalf of all his lesbian friends and saying how much he enjoyed their company. We broadcast it through some speakers onto Oxford Street.

How was that received?

People loved that one. We had it going through a few ghetto blasters as well. The initial plan was different though. Fred ended his march at Taylor Square, which is the heart of Sydney's gay community. I'd been there earlier in the day with some friends and the plan had been to swap the channels on his P.A. while he was speaking so that my cut-up would come out instead of his speech. I had a very romantic idea of how easy that would be to do, but they had some big, burly, muscular Christian bouncers around the mixing desk. (Laughs)

How did Nile's supporters react?

They'd stop and say it was unfair. (Laughs) It didn't appeal to their sense of fair play, while doing an anti-gay march obviously did.

A number of years later you wound up with an underground hit on your hands with *Backdoor Man*. How did that come about?

Well initially I did it in 1997 at Club Bent and then I did a performance at a night run by Vanessa Wagner who was on *Celebrity Big Brother*. He's openly HIV-positive and does a lot of charity work and has been on TV ads and stuff. He was doing a dance party and we gave the track to Triple J as a way of promoting it all. The song immediately provoked

a huge response and was the number one request by that night and remained so for the next ten days. It was never properly released because Hanson stepped in and sued for defamation.

Backdoor Man is a clever piece that works on many levels. It has the obvious double entendres, but also goes deeper in replacing her racial supremacy with gay supremacy?

I was primarily just having fun with it, but if you break it down I was also trying to show how ridiculous her ideas were by mimicking her style of argument. It doesn't mention racism at any stage, but it subtly undermines her politics. Everyone knew her issues, but the idea was to reflect back the stupidity of her arguments. In the end though it means different things to different people. For a lot of people it's just that song where Pauline Hanson talks about taking it up the arse. (Laughs)

Effectively though, that is what the best pranks do. They parody something on the surface level, but also go a bit deeper to give people something to chew on?

I was trying to replicate what some political cartoons do. It is a very simple medium, but some cartoons can really drive home an issue.

Would it be true to say that you hadn't envisaged taking on the whole Pantsdown personality until the court case?

I wasn't intending for it all to last for a few years, that's for sure. When I dressed up as her for the initial performance it was my first time in drag because she was a woman and if I wanted to send her up then I had to get into drag.

With the court case there was an irony involved because despite all the media hype she received, she was always going on about other people denying her freedom of speech?

She's a mountain of contradictions and the sad thing was that at the time even those on the supposed left of the media had a grudging respect for her. They'd say, "Well at least she's shown up most politicians for what they are, she's a salt of the earth type, etc." When you look at where she ended up with loads of money unaccounted for and the electoral fraud and so forth you see she was just a typical politician. She fell into everything she ever railed against.

So, what happened with the defamation case?

Well, after the song had been on air for about six days she threatened the ABC with defamation, but they laughed that off and put in on high rotation. (Laughs) Then she got a temporary injunction to hold it off the air and that remained in place until 2003 when the ABC reached some sort of undisclosed settlement with her. The ABC did various challenges, but it stayed off the air. People could still download it from various websites and

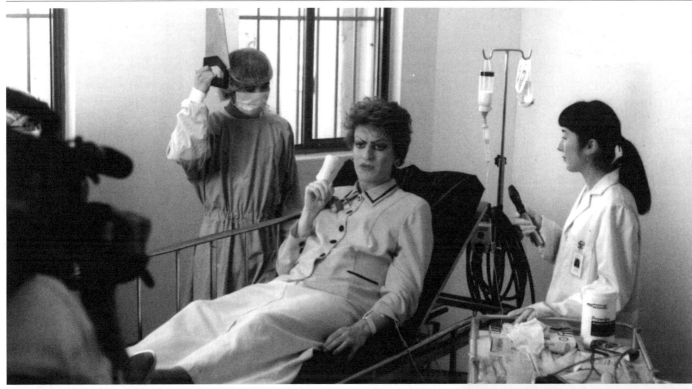

Top and Right: Pauline Pantsdown on the campaign trail. Sydney, 2001.
Centre: Electoral material, 2001. **Bottom:** Pauline Pantsdown confronts One Nation member of NSW Legislative Council David Oldfield, 2001. All photographs courtesy of Simon Hunt.

Vote 1
Pauline Pantsdown for NSW Senate

Vote 2 JASON YAT-SEN LI
(Unity: Say No to Hanson)

or 2 ADEN RIDGEWAY
(Australian Democrats)

Keep Astraya Beautiful
Number all 69 squares
Put David Oldfield last

Vote 1
Pauline Pantsdown
for NSW Senate

Clean up the Racist Rubbish

Written by Pauline Pantsdown.
Authorised and printed by Owen Trembath,
1st Flr, 10 Ward Ave, Kings Cross, NSW 2011.

file sharing networks though. It was illegal to distribute it, but perfectly legal to listen to.

How did you get around these legal problems when you came to doing the second cut-up track, *I Don't Like It*?

The way I got around it was to get several legal opinions. I'm fortunate in that I'm the only person in my family who isn't a lawyer. Also my father works directly in this area of law and is considered to be pretty much Australia's defamation expert. Most of the *Backdoor Man* case was fought around interpretations of stuff my father had done, so it was pretty ironic really. So I ran lyrics past my family and other people and my manager, who was a lawyer. So there were lawyers everywhere basically.

Her writ of defamation against *Backdoor Man* is quite a good read because they take the song literally. It says things along the lines of, "The song imputes that the plaintiff engages in unnatural sexual practices including anal sex with members of the Ku Klux Klan." There are two pages of that sort of stuff and it's quite hilarious. I'm thinking of reading it aloud as a performance some time. With *I Don't Like It*, the underlying meaning that can be drawn is that I'm calling her a racist, while with *Backdoor Man* the literal meaning is that I'm calling her a homosexual. She could fight me on that, but she wouldn't have dared to take me to court over the racism stuff because I would have had a field day proving that she was one.

With *I Don't Like It* things were obviously more planned out with the CD release, video clip and electoral campaign?

The *Backdoor Man* thing had been a bit of a shock. Most of the political work I had done before had been around censorship and gay issues, but what struck me about this was that it had reached a much wider public. There was a six-month build up. I'd decided I was going to become a pop star and have my fifteen minutes of fame and get into the same media as her to have ten-year-olds hear the song, have the kids of One Nation supporters hear the song. So I tried to make it as commercial as possible. I tried to make the music repetitive and poppy and used the standard formula with a few guitars in it for commercial radio.

The way I feel I can best give a political message is to sit down and talk things over with individuals, but you don't reach many people that way. With the song I wanted to reach as many people as I could, so half the words are silly and don't mean anything, but the other half is fairly incisive. I also wanted to parody her pop star image. I met a lot of her die-hard supporters while I was chasing her around the country and most of them didn't know what her real policies were. It was just a cult of personality thing.

What was involved in putting the film clip together?

That only cost $500, but I had to draw on every favour I ever had in the film industry. A whole bunch of friends contributed by shooting it, editing it, getting a nightclub for free, etc. It basically involved Pauline

Pantsdown cavorting around with masses of gay Asian dancers and also sent up her Channel Nine "I have been murdered" video. There were direct quotes from Madonna's *Ray Of Light*, which was in the charts at the time, and it also had Chinese subtitles.

There was a lot of goodwill around that and indeed the whole thing. *I Don't Like It* was a fully independent production. If a magazine wanted a photograph I had to send it out. Our distributor's main job was to distribute plastic security casings for CDs to all the major chains so we'd just stick a box of *I Don't Like It* singles along with those.

As part of all this you ran for the NSW senate against One Nation adviser David Oldfield. What were some of the highlights of that?

I had to change my name legally to Pauline Pantsdown six months before the election. The whole thing was fairly crazy and hectic. One memorable moment was being at Triple J. I'd just been interviewed and they were starting to interview Oldfield. I had a huge dossier including stupid quotes from One Nation on just about any subject and I was able to feed this information to the producers. As a result the interviewer just flattened Oldfield.

Their slogan during that election was "Equality For All Australians" so the interviewer asked Oldfield about his views on gay marriage. While he was waffling on about his gay friends I was able to pass on information about the author of their gun policy who had once put out a bumpersticker that said, "Under God's laws the only right Gays have is the right to die." When they threw that at him he wound up leaving in a huff. Obviously he knew about it, but no-one in the media had actually cornered him on it.

The only time I faced Hanson directly was at the Mortdale Bowling Club. I was hiding in the back of a car and she pulled up with Oldfield and I leapt out and asked, "Mrs Hanson, can you please explain your racist policies to all Australians?" She bolted and ran into the club, leaving myself and the entire media scrum waiting for her to return. After an hour and a half she came out and her bodyguard did a bit of a number on me, pushing me aside and kneeing my cinematographer in the back. However we did manage to get me and her into one frame.

A week after that the ABC had their appeal in Brisbane against the banning of *Backdoor Man*. I wasn't going to go there, but everyone rang up to say that she was going to turn up despite it being the day before the election. So I raced up and did my make-up on the plane really badly, only to miss her by about a minute-and-a-half. She'd done her press conference and jumped into her car as my taxi pulled up. I jumped out and gave my statement on exactly the same spot.

Do you think your campaign and single contributed much to her losing her seat in that election?

I think One Nation pretty much did themselves in, in the end. By trying to replace the National Party they overreached themselves and fell apart badly. The day after the election the Liberal candidate who beat her in her seat in part attributed his win to what we did by saying that, "We just focused on local issues while she just seemed to be out there battling Pauline Pantsdown and running a three-ring circus". My intention had been to show her up as an empty pop star by being one myself. Her die-hard supporters would have been solidified by the fact that I was a city poofter who was making fun of her. With everyone else I think it helped distract her from the real issues that she wanted to rail on about.

Certainly there were stories of record shops putting on the song when she visited shopping malls and kids quoting it at her?

Yeah, her voice was heard more on my song than out of her mouth during that campaign. (Laughs)

At the end of it all you did a big performance at the Sleaze Ball, didn't you?

Mardi Gras coincided with the election night that year, and for a couple of years there had been this giant Pauline Hanson puppet used during the parades. One year it was chasing Aboriginal and Asian people who had fish and chips on their heads down the street and the next it was dressed in a brand new Chinese cheongsam dress, hitting me on the head with a legal writ whilst I sang *Backdoor Man*. For 1998 they cut the head off with a big angle grinder.

Using the head we did a big production number of *I Don't Like It* with 20 Pauline dancers. At the beginning I came up on this mechanical stage which wrapped around the Pauline head. Then at the very end they exploded the head, some six or seven hours after she'd conceded defeat. It was a wild moment as the head exploded in front of 15,000 or more people all on drugs at 10am in the morning.

At times it must have been difficult to parody Hanson because she and One Nation did some ridiculous things. At one point she released a post-assassination address to the nation in case someone knocked her off, and at another her official support group published a book that warned of a future Australian Republic under the rule of an Indo-Chinese Lesbian Cyborg President?

One time I wrote a thing for the ABC in the build-up to the court cases as they'd asked me to describe my intentions in doing the songs. In the piece I talked about satirising her in the same way that the left-wing in Germany had satirised Hitler. During the Weimar Republic they wrote a lot about how Hitler was impossible to satirise since his politics were so over the top. So within the Berlin underground night club scene they would dress up as Hitler and have him talk about topics completely unrelated to race and German nationalism — stuff like shopping. Like Hanson, Hitler was a bit of an outsider with his weird Austrian accent and similarly Hanson spoke quite differently to most politicians. So I liked the idea of almost ignoring the substance of what was being said and sending up the style to reflect back into the substance.

I'd tried for about six months before *Backdoor Man* to reverse some of her policies by saying stuff like, "Australia is in danger of being swamped by Caucasians," but it just wasn't funny. Her own stuff was funnier. (Laughs)

Did you get much coverage in Asia? She built up quite a reputation in the region and often the only mention Australia would get at the time would be in relation to her?

There was a week or so when I was the international joke story, the bizarre thing tacked on the end of the news. I had a lot of AAP and Reuters reporters interviewing me and in the Malaysian *New Straits Times* there was a great photo of me singing to children in Martin Place.

Did the single sell well?

It nearly got a Gold Record (35,000 sales) which was crazy. It was a real struggle to keep up with it all as it was happening so fast. In all it was a six-week period in the run up to the election.

Did you encounter any aggro from her supporters during that time?

Not directly. They weren't really a violent bunch. I think I had overestimated how old most of her supporters were. They were of an average age of late forties and fifties, and struck me more as the people who at school had always been the last to be picked for the basketball team and they were getting off on the social thing they had with each other. It was the most rebellious thing any of them had ever done. The only time I ever had any violence against me was at the Homebake Festival where 16-year-old homophobic boys threw bottles at me.

Despite Hanson losing that election, and her party collapsing due to their own amateurishness in many ways, they were successful in restoring open racism to the mainstream of political life.

Howard basically hid behind her and then picked up all her voters by making the appropriate noises. Once she'd lost her populist power there was a space to encourage tolerance, but instead they spread One Nation out on toast and ate it.

You did a parody on Howard as well didn't you?

Whilst I haven't done any cut-up in recent times, I did do a treatment of Howard around the time of the 2000 Olympics called "I'm Sorry". It disappeared without a trace, though, when Triple J refused to play it. It made me realise what a narrow path *I Don't Like It* had trod, as it required Triple J to break it first for commercial radio. With the Howard one a particular Triple J DJ took offense and spoke against it at a number of programming meetings. It had a very good film clip where a make-up artist was able to make me look like John Howard although we had to stretch the image out sideways to get the shape right. (Laughs)

Kevin Buzzacott

Since the 1970s a significant number of Australians have opposed uranium mining in seeking to break their country's involvement in a nuclear industry that is prone to accidents, facilitates the creation of weapons of mass destruction and ultimately results in carcinogenic waste. Indigenous Australians in the Northern Territory and South Australia have largely borne the brunt of the nuclear cycle from exposure to weapons testing at Maralinga in the 1950s through to attempts to force waste dumps and new mines upon their lands today. Although some Aboriginal people have supported involvement in the nuclear industry, largely on the basis of desperately-needed royalties, others have been at the forefront of the anti-nuclear movement, leading successful campaigns against mining at Jabiluka and against the construction of a waste dump at Coober Pedy during the 1990s and 2000s.

One prominent anti-uranium and land rights activist is Arabunna man UNCLE KEVIN BUZZACOTT. A key figure in the opposition to the South Australian Olympic Dam mine and the nuclear industry in general, Uncle Kevin has engaged in a series of campaigns taking the issues of dispossession and Aboriginal sovereignty directly to State and Federal Governments and the corporations they serve. In the following interview he outlines a number of the creative actions he has taken part in, from serving eviction notices on Western Mining Corporation through to engaging in Peace Walks thousands of kilometres long.

How did you and the Keepers Of Lake Eyre group come to set up the Arabunna Going Home Camp in 1999 in opposition to Western Mining Corporation's plans to expand the Olympic Dam uranium mine?

I've been at this game of calling for justice and peace for 30, maybe 40 years, but what really got me going was when Western Mining Corporation (WMC) set up the Olympic Dam mine. They started doing deals with the Government on pastoral leases. So they did deals with S. Kidman & Co. and took up one of their cattle stations, Stuart's Creek Station, which is on Arabunna land. Because of our native title and ongoing land rights campaigning, we've been fighting for these places for a long time. Stuart's Creek is a very special, sacred place for us, and we've been trying to get it back for a long time.

I thought that just before they bought that place I'd go and protest and camp on it. Also, it is on that station, on the shores of the Lake Eyre, where WMC started taking the sacred water out of the Lake Eyre Basin [millions of litres per day since 1982]. That was where they started sucking the first life blood out of us. That is where they put their first big bore down, right on the shores of the lake.

That was a real kick in the guts for me and really got me going. I weighed it all up and I said to the mob, "I need some help out here. We'll set up camp and contest WMC." There were a lot of levels involved with fighting the mine, but making the camp was like

The Lizard's Revenge protest saw hundreds gather in outback South Australia in 2012 to oppose the expansion of multinational corporation BHP's Olympic Dam uranium mine at Roxby Downs. Actions at the site included a zombie walk, Breakfast Not Bombs blockade, a cricket match on the access road, and a march to the "Gates of Hell". The expansion has since been put on hold due to falling commodity prices. This photo shows Arabunna Elder Uncle Kevin Buzzacott with a Lizard car based on Kalta, a sacred sleepy Lizard who lives beneath the area. Sadly police banned the car from approaching the mine site.

Photographer: Jessie Boylan

Photographer: Joel Catchlove

reclaiming the land or making a statement.

We had a lot of tourists that came to visit, and were interested in finding out what was going on. Thousands of people came through the camp. We had flyers at an information tent, and free tea and coffee; we set up a lot of things. People who came across us on a trip to the desert and Lake Eyre learnt about the issues and were concerned about what was going on. When they talked with us they were upset about what was going on. Nobody knew about it, and that was one of the reasons in my mind why that was happening out in the desert.

We blocked off the whole highway there — Oodnadatta Track – and stopped all sorts of people from coming and going. We still had intruders, but we stopped them for a little while and had a yarn with them about what we were doing and why. We did actions on the pipeline and also at Roxby Downs Station, right near Olympic Dam.

We tried to negotiate with the mining people, to sit down and talk with them. They came and talked with us, but on their terms, not on ours.

During one of the camps, this one or a later one, I served them with an eviction notice demanding they shut down the operations and start compensating and resourcing us to maintain and heal the damage that they had caused. It was a big thing, and it really put a lot of pressure on them.

How did they respond to the eviction notice?

They just kept sticking to their guns about the Government's mining policies, that they did the right thing and that I was the one trespassing on their land. They claimed that the campsite on Stuart's Creek on the shores of Lake Eyre was their country. According to them I was the one at fault, the one doing the wrong thing. That went on and on.

Uncle Kevin Buzzacott and supporters outside the Supreme Court. Canberra, 2005. Photographer: Chris Littlejohn

Roxstop protest outside BHP Annual General Meeting, Melbourne, 2008. Photograph courtesy of Friends of the Earth Melbourne.

The judge was a pastor in the Lutheran Church, and I asked him to stand down because I believed he had a conflict of interests as his church was a shareholder in the WMC. When he refused to do so I told him to get stuffed, walked out and went straight down to Government House to start a protest. I took flags, banners, and whatever things I had.

While I was talking to the media I was confronted by the cops. I looked over the road and saw a patch of grass and thought, "Bugger it, I'll make camp and a fire here." I ended up calling it Genocide Corner, and renamed Adelaide the City of Genocide. It was on the intersection of King William Street and North Terrace [one of the main intersections in the city] so loads of people were passing by. Four ceremonial fires for peace were lit, and after 21 days the Adelaide City Council and 50 police came down and arrested me for failing to cease to loiter. It was one of those laws they hadn't used in a long time, but they used it to clear away all my stuff and my supporters. One of the court conditions was that I was not able to walk within the vicinity of Genocide Corner. I was of a mind just to walk straight back there, but I had the peace walk from Lake Eyre to Sydney coming up so I had to let that one go.

Since then there have been vigils and meetings held at Genocide Corner. It was a real wake-up for Adelaide, and this is the sort of thing you have to do get your message across.

Tell us about the court case you brought against WMC's owner Hugh Morgan and the cases you brought against Alexander Downer (Federal Foreign Affairs Minister), Robert Hill (Federal Environment Minister) and the Commonwealth Government?

I realised I had to go down to the cities and tell people what was going on. There's nothing wrong with sitting out in the desert and talking with the old dingoes and crows and flies, they're the best, but the population is in the city. I've met lots of good people, but there are a lot who keep harbouring these criminals, like BHP and WMC, who are killing the land.

I did a court action against Hugh Morgan, who was the head of WMC. I charged Hugh Morgan with genocide, trying to flush him out and some of the shareholders. Hugh Morgan is based in Victoria. People in Melbourne deserve to live in a good place, they don't need to live with these criminals and warmongers.

Another court action I did was one I brought against Alexander Downer and Senator Robert Hill for stopping Lake Eyre from becoming a World Heritage site. The case was thrown out of court, and I think one of the main things there was that I wasn't fully equipped and resourced to take this mob on.

After the Going Home camp was destroyed by WMC in December 1999 you travelled to Adelaide. Why did you decide to set up camp at Genocide Corner?

I had to go to Adelaide for the court case against Hugh Morgan, and when I was there the charges against Hugh Morgan were dismissed.

In June 2000 you started a peace walk from Lake Eyre to Sydney which lasted 87 days and involved carrying a sacred fire as an alternative to the Olympic torch. What sort of response did you receive along the way?

We walked for months, for 3,000 kilometres, and all sorts of people from all walks of life joined us. We were carrying the fire for peace and justice. I made sure that we went through lots of different Aboriginal communities. I got a lot of support, but the Government also pressured a lot of people not to support me by threatening their jobs and funding. Each place we went to, people took us through their land and we respected each mob.

There were all types of pressure put on people along the way. The cops were nasty and threatened some of the walkers with guns and everything. I visited all the jails along the way from Broken Hill to Dubbo and Bathurst. It was sad to see so many young brothers confined and locked up.

We went to Canberra and met up with the Tent Embassy mob. A couple of politicians came to meet us and then we all went to Government House to present the Governor-General with a document of peace and justice. When we arrived in Sydney for the Olympic Games the Tent Embassy mob had already set up a camp [in Victoria Park], so we joined up with them. We did all sorts of things. We did a re-enactment at the beach where Captain Cook came in. We re-enacted the bad way in which he came with guns and all that and then the next day we did how they should have come.

All the media was there for the Olympics and they all came down and talked with us. We couldn't get to any of the places where the Games were happening because of the police and security, but we held ceremonies and met up with lots of people.

When did you first get involved in the Aboriginal Tent Embassy in Canberra?

I first visited them in the 1980s. I knew about it in the 1970s, but we didn't have phones and computers and all that back then and we were stuck out in the desert so we couldn't really make contact. Over the years I've visited for rallies and lit the Fire for Justice in 1998.

The Embassy is important to defend because it's a sacred place. It was set up as a platform for Aboriginal people to come to put their issues up. There are gatherings and meetings there and no matter what the issues are — mining, deaths in custody, whatever — the Embassy is there as a platform. It's not supported by the Government and it's pretty rough living there without a toilet and showers and all that. There aren't many people holding the place right now, but it will stay. The Government doesn't like it as it's sitting right under their nose, but when it comes to the crunch people will turn up in their hundreds to defend it, as they've done before, so the Government can't do much about it.

In 2002 you reclaimed the Arabunna Emu and Kangaroo totems from the Australian Coat of Arms hanging outside Parliament House, Canberra. Why did you take this action and what was the result of the court case that came out of it years later?

I had watched the Federal Police arresting our people at the Tent Embassy and other places. They all wore these caps with the Emu and Kangaroo emblem on them. I knew how sacred these animals were to us and I had talked with old people about how the Government was misusing them while they locked us up and treated us like dirt. On the 30th anniversary of the Embassy I told everyone that I had a plan and that they should join me with their cameras. We went up to Parliament and I climbed up one of the pillars and grabbed the Coat Of Arms and walked off with it. It was in broad daylight and I said: "I'm not stealing this, I'm reclaiming it and taking back the use of our sacred animals."

Years later [in 2005] when I was visiting Canberra the cops came down to the Tent Embassy with a summons for theft and defacing government property and so on. During the court case I questioned their authority and jurisdiction over me and over this land. I talked to the jury about the imposition of foreign laws upon our people and the theft of our lands and got a 12-month suspended sentence with good behaviour.

How did the 2004 Peace Pilgrimage from the Olympic Dam Uranium Mine to Hiroshima, Japan come about?

During the first walk and then in Sydney we met people from all over and that got everything going. Aboriginal nations from Queensland were saying there should be a walk up the coast to show the world

the things they were suffering. Then some people made contact with people in Hiroshima to have a walk from the uranium mine in Roxby to where the bomb was dropped in order to show how all these things are linked. Aboriginal people, Japanese monks, all sorts of people were involved. It started at Roxby and then went to Canberra and then an aeroplane took us to Japan where we walked all over the country. We visited Nagasaki and Hiroshima and met a lot of people who were kids when the bombs were falling. We did talks and took part in a huge ceremony on the anniversary of the bomb being dropped. There were people everywhere and lanterns lit and people crying, it was full on.

In 2006 you came to Melbourne for the Stolenwealth games. Tell us about what happened during those protests and your involvement in them?

After the court case I came down to Melbourne where Robbie Thorpe and others were setting up a camp in Kings Domain during the Commonwealth, or Stolenwealth, Games. We had hundreds of people camping and visiting. We also had all sorts of hassles from the cops and council and everyone else, but we stayed put and proved our point.

When the Games came we had rallies and big marches and ceremonies and I talked about the need for justice and the need for white Australia to respect our cultural values and to stop the destruction of our sacred sites and our country.

In 2008 you visited Melbourne again and got to speak at the BHP Shareholders Annual General Meeting. What happened there?

BHP have taken over WMC. They now own Olympic Dam and want to make it bigger. Myself and others who want to stop the mine got to be proxies for shareholders, they gave us tickets and we got to go inside on their behalf. I got to speak and I told the people there about the damage they are doing and that they need to stop it immediately.

Aboriginal people have lived here for more than 40,000 years and cared for this country, but now its being turned into a sick and evil place. Myself, and others around this country, were born to be peacemakers. We mustn't be frightened to educate others and fight, but not in a warlike way, to protect the earth and let everything run free. I don't want to shoot or bomb the people from BHP and the others who are destroying this country because two wrongs don't make a right. I think if I can help them to wake up to what they are doing then that will be punishment enough.

Deborah Kelly

Over the best part of three decades, artist Deborah Kelly has used her work to challenge prevailing beliefs around racism, sexuality and religion with humour and profundity. Working alone and in collaboration with others, Kelly has utilised billboards, projections and the broad-scale distribution of posters, postcards and stickers to engage, and at time enrage, a wide cross-section of the community. In the following interview she discusses a number of projects including Hey, hetero!, Boat-people.org, and the Rile Nile Home Kraft Kit.

How did you first get involved in using your artwork to present subversive messages?

When I was a teenager I was in love with Goya, Grosz and Daumier, and as a Catholic schoolgirl I was a first-person witness to systemic injustice. Putting two and two together I started drawing to articulate what I saw and the drawings kind of turned into cartoons. Then at Monash Uni I was, by magic, invited to be the *Lot's Wife* [student newspaper] cartoonist, and so I had to start really thinking about public address. My cartoons also wound up in newsletters, newspapers and magazines. Sybylla Feminist Press published a lot of them as cards and posters. Looking back, those ones are from a feminism far, far away!

What other political activities were you involved in during that time?

At that time I was involved in women's anti-ANZAC Day protest organising, the women's Pine Gap protest camp of 1983, the fight against the national ID card and the development of local independent media in Fitzroy — stuff like that. I was a peripheral member of a group called FUGM, the Feminist Urban Guerrilla Movement, which was primarily a grandly-named graffiti gang which was ace. Friends and I also set up a social events collective called the Caviar Club that we ran for 10 years. We believed that a thriving movement needed a rich cultural life, so that's what we were trying to help build — we were taking [pioneering anarchist] Emma Goldman literally. She said, "If I can't dance, I don't want to be part of your revolution."

In 1997 you and Liz Conor came up with the idea of wearing and selling black armbands as a way of both showing grief for the mistreatment of Indigenous Australians and as a rebuke and pisstake of John Howard's refusal to say sorry to the Stolen Generations. How did you distribute these and how many wound up being sold?

The armbands were Liz's idea, I was just the artist. But watching the idea catch fire, as coverage went national and you started seeing people wearing them on the streets, that changed my life, and how I think about art in public. 25,000 of the armbands were sold, mainly through The Body Shop, who supported the project.

What specifically inspired you to create the Escaped Refugees Welcome Here poster in 2001?

In early 2001, I heard the anthropologist Dr Ghassan Hage say he wished he could stick a sign in his window inviting the people who had just escaped from the Villawood Detention Centre to hide at his place. I thought, "everyone wants that sign," so I ran home and made it as a simple little PDF. I sent it to Ghassan, and he and I then sent it to everyone we'd ever met. I have no idea how many went up, but I did count about 25 websites from which you could download it, at one stage.

2001 was a busy year for you because you also created the Hey, hetero! project. How did the Hey, hetero! series of billboards and bus shelter advertisements come about and where did they appear?

Hey, hetero! was a consequence of living under the endless grinding duress of heteropatriarchy. It was a development from a 1997 project called It's Great To Be Straight, which was a series of fake magazine ads for the many benefits and privileges of heterosexuality. I'm a terribly gullible audience member, even with my own work — I convinced myself with those works so thoroughly that I had to go back to the idea, make it better, fiercer, funnier and more beautiful, and find a bigger audience for it. I honestly thought that the edifices supporting the domination of heterosexuality over other life forms would crack, would even begin to crumble, in the face of Hey, hetero!

My producer Su Goldfish, the Sydney Gay and Lesbian Mardi Gras Festival and lots of friends helped get together the financial and logistical support the project needed for it to appear in the bus shelters and on billboards. Local councils helped, the bus shelter company helped and the wonderful photographer Tina Fiveash and the beautiful models all helped.

Hey, hetero! got so much attention around the country that it was big news, at least big queer news or I should say big queer art news (laughs) because there's a bit of a shortage of queer art, especially in public. There was some official resistance, and hate mail, and public homophobia and talkback radio nastiness, etc, and the project saw lots of arguments in the streets, and a barrage of calls to the anti-discrimination board on the grounds that to acknowledge queer families is to damage straight ones ... but that's what the artwork was actually for, I guess. Now it's online, in textbooks — sociology, not art! — and has a kind of ongoing life. Which is great, I guess, but I wish it had helped smash said hetero-hegemony at least a bloody bit.

Who is involved in Boat-people.org and when and how did the group first come together?

After all the fuss about Hey, hetero! I was asked to speak at various events. In October 2001, I was invited to give a keynote at a conference called TILT. I'd recently moved to Sydney and was looking for collaborators. Having the authority of the microphone gave me the opportunity to say, in relation to the manipulation of the truth that was being so effectively broadcast by the Howard regime, "Who would like to work together on talking back to this stuff? Isn't it driving you all crazy? Who is tired of shouting at their bloody television on their own?" Because I certainly was.

Out of that, a group of people came together which now includes Safdar Ahmed, Zehra Ahmed, Stephanie Carrick, Dave Gravina, Katie Hepworth, myself, Enda Murray, Pip Shea, Sumugan Sivanesan and sometimes Jamil Yamani, and our friends and partners who help when we need them.

Remember that at this time, the 2001 election campaign was on, and it was the most overt race-based election in living memory. John Howard repeatedly called asylum seekers various pejorative names, especially "boat people". At TILT, an Indigenous speaker, Rebecca Bear-Wingfield, kept referring to the non-Indigenous people present as "boat people". That was very resonant and startling, so the first work we made ran with that.

The first thing we did together was to project an image of a First Fleet tall ship with the words Boat People onto the Opera House. It went so well and we were so thrilled that it gave us the energy to continue with many more actions.

I'm a terrible chicken myself, but the other people were bold and brave, and we egged each other on. We got a projector and a small generator, which fitted into two handbags. We all promised each other that we wouldn't tell anyone what we were up to, but of course each person secretly told a few friends, who told a few more friends. When we turned up, all dressed in black like cat burglars and pretending not to know each other, we found more than 100 people waiting for us (laughs). It looked pretty weird because what were 100 people doing milling around the Opera House in the middle of the night?

We razzed up the little generator and plugged in the 35mm projector and popped the slide in and suddenly there was a 10 by 15 metre billboard, made of light, projected onto the sails of the Opera House. It had a poetic resonance with the sails and all. Everyone had been very good in staying quiet, but when it went up it was so beautiful and surprising that we all started screaming. This was before the No War graffiti action so there wasn't much security about and it was only all the screaming that tipped them off. They ambled up in their red-faced, puffed-out security guard way and didn't quite know how to react. They started out by saying that this was a public space, but we replied, "Well, we *are* the public." After a bit of friendly debate we agreed to disperse because we had plenty of video and photos by then.

Boat-people.org's next action didn't quite go so smoothly did it?

The sheer pleasure of talking back to the Government meant that we got quite intoxicated and so we kept doing actions. We decided to do the Opera House again and figured the best way to get around the security was to hire a ferry and project from the harbour. On the day however, Good Friday, loads of asylum seekers broke out of the

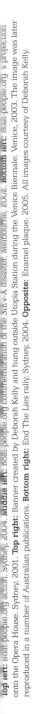
Top left: Boat-people.org action. Sydney, 2004. **Middle left:** boat-people.org commemoration of the SIEV-X disaster. Melbourne, 2002. **Bottom left:** Boat-people.org's projection onto the Opera House. Sydney, 2001. **Top right:** Banner created by Deborah Kelly and hung outside Utopia Station during the Venice Biennale. Venice, 2003. The image was later reproduced in a number of Australian publications. **Bottom right:** End The Lies rally. Sydney, 2004. **Opposite:** Enamel plaque. Sydney, 2005. All images courtesy of Deborah Kelly.

Nuclear power will solve global warming *and* feed all the world's children

BOAT PEOPLE

Woomera detention centre during a big pro-refugee protest. I was so excited about that, that when Radio National rang me for an interview I blabbed about what we had planned for that night. Unbelievable, but true. As a result the Sydney Harbour Foreshore Authority got onto the Federal Police. The Harbour Police then had all their Easter leave cancelled to deal with us. By the time we got to the ferry, a big delegation of Federal Police had already come on board and terrified

the captain. They'd told him, and this wasn't strictly true, that if he allowed us to project from the ferry he would lose his licence, and naturally enough he wasn't prepared to risk that.

We went ahead with the ferry trip and about 150 people came. We had refugee rappers and other performers and food and it was kind of a fabulous night, but I spent most of it feeling miserable. Everywhere that we went we were surrounded by police boats. It was total overkill. We had hired this super projection rig, but the most we could get away with was to project this image of Jesus with his heart wrapped in barbed wire with the word Refugee underneath, onto some cliffs and an abandoned warship. That was okay, but what we'd wanted to do was to project it onto the sails of the Opera House in order to really, really shit the Christians in government who had locked up asylum seekers. After all, Jesus himself was a Middle Eastern refugee from the tyrant Herod, as their book exhorts: "I was a stranger, and you took me in," Matthew, 25:35.

After the action I sent the image to a few friends and it was passed on to the Brotherhood of St Laurence, who decided to use it for their big refugee campaign. They turned it into a giant merchandising opportunity; it appeared on postcards, T-shirts, badges, a gigantic banner and the cover of magazines. Which was great. I loved that it had so many broadcast vectors. While I'm interested in preaching to the converted, because I am one of the converted and I need to feel that I belong to a culture that is rich and delightful and clever and going somewhere, I also want to make transgressive or dissident ideas available to people more generally.

In October 2001 the group was also involved in a Melbourne commemoration for the 353 asylum seekers who drowned in the Java Sea while travelling to Australia on a vessel that came to be known as the SIEV-X (suspected illegal entry vessel x). There was a lot of conjecture around the incident, which the Howard Government used to further bash refugees, and a Government committee later concluded that "…it [was] extraordinary that a major human disaster could occur in the vicinity of a theatre of intensive Australian operations and remain undetected until three days after the event, without any concern being raised within intelligence and decision making circles." How did Boatpeople.org come to be involved in reacting to this?

Katie Hepworth, a member of the group, went over to Western Australia for a protest at a detention camp and on the bus she made friends with a 16-year-old Iraqi refugee, Hassan. She talked about what our group was doing and he suggested we might be able to help commemorate the SIEV-X disaster because he'd lost 16 little cousins and the Government was refusing to release any of the names of the people who had died. The Government said it was for privacy reasons, but it was obviously about dehumanising them. Hassan wanted Australians to know that the dead were children, women and men with faces and names. He provided us with photos and the kids' names and we put together a work that would allow people to mourn their passing and to mourn them as actual individuals, not just numbers. Some of the organisational side got a bit complicated, but in the end we made slides out of the photos and personal details and invited people to come to the banks of the Yarra all dressed in white and we projected these images onto them. It was very sad and very beautiful, in the end.

In 2008 we did a similar projection for the fifth anniversary of the invasion of Iraq where we projected an animation of the names of Iraqi civilians killed in the war onto people again dressed in white, as living screens. We were trying to build a link with the early anti-Iraq War actions that were called Not In Our Name, using the names of civilians like us, who didn't consent and who, like us, were implicated against their will.

On a formal level, I like the fact that projections are ephemeral and

Hey, hetero! Project. Sydney, 2001. Courtesy Deborah Kelly.

that they allow you to create a really complex artwork without having to stand there with 17 stencils. Some of the first public art I made in the early '80s was graffiti for Hiroshima Day, made with a series of life-sized, multi-colour complicated stencils that involved a lot of standing around, which made you very vulnerable to arrest. Projections are so much more portable and you can get them into places where you can't get graffiti or posters. I also love that they are made of light, and that you can make the images really huge.

Fred Nile campaigned in 2002 to ban schoolgirls from wearing the hijab to school, on the basis that they were breaking unity with "mainstream Australia." Other right-wing politicians also called for a total ban on all women wearing the hijab because they could supposedly hide bombs. In response, you produced the Rile Nile Home Kraft Kit. What was the kit made up of and how did you go about distributing the 6,000 sheets you had printed?

The kit was just a little piece of paper — you had to add glue, matchboxes, scissors, and your own energy, to make it work. Each one had six images on it of the Virgin Mary with the words "Veiled Woman" and "Danger: 50 Concealed Incendiary Devices," which were designed to be stuck on matchboxes. Brave friends snuck into newsagencies and slipped the kit into the pages of women's magazines. It was designed to look kind of like a recipe card, so it wouldn't be too big a surprise to find. Mainly I just gave them out and sent them to people in the post and by email.

I have no idea how many were made up, but I did meet quite a lot of people who were absolutely astonished when they found the little made-up matchboxes about the place. Inspired by merchandising queen and friend Sylvia Tai, I sold some made-up versions as anti-terror fridge-magnet matchboxes. They went incredibly well and

we sold enough to help cover the production costs of the Temporary Protection Visa Legal Guide in English and Arabic.

Tell us about the actions that Boat-people.org were involved in around the 2004 election?

Liberal Senator Brandis had called PM John Howard a "lying rodent" over the Children Overboard Affair [in which, just prior to the 2001 election, the Government falsely claimed that refugees on a sinking ship had thrown their children into the sea in order to force Australia to give them asylum]. We decided to bring that rodent metaphor to life and every Thursday we would go into the Pitt St Mall in central Sydney dressed in the style of Young Liberals. Only these Young Liberals had two metre long, slinky rat's tails and their heads were wrapped in the Australian flag. It probably makes less sense now, but in that moment those metaphors were very legible. Because there was so much media around those issues and motifs people immediately understood what we were on about.

The election stuff was quite a challenge because although the group includes visual artists, a film maker, musicians and web people none of us are performance artists or actors. Our original plan was to get a series of images shown around the CBD, but in order to do that we had to dress neatly in suits and play certain roles. It was all a bit weird when we wrapped our heads up in Australian flags, but also it was a bit of a relief not to have to look at each other looking so bloody stupid.

On one of the Thursdays we hung out Howard's dirty washing. We made these humungous undies and big socks and hung them on a giant line. We then projected a video onto them with a hip hop soundtrack featuring samples of John Howard's actual voice lying about refugees and the Iraq War. We handed out How To Vote cards, with the Liberal "L" filled with the American flag rather than the Australian one, which told you just to Vote 1 for George Bush, meaning that a vote for the Liberals was really a vote for the Bush agenda. We also had helium balloons made up with an image printed on them of John Howard with his pants on fire. Whenever we brought them out we were mobbed by kids.

Generally, the public reaction to what we were doing was so enthusiastic that I really thought the Liberals would lose that election. In retrospect maybe the shoppers were just glad of the free entertainment. Occasionally people would get angry and I remember one particular man who came up and started viciously kicking my tail as if it was really going to hurt me.

What led Boat-people.org to brew its own *Best We Forget* beer in 2006 in order to make political points about the history wars of the Howard era?

I think that every single Boat-people.org meeting has involved drinking beer. We were discussing the history wars [which involved a series of right-wing commentators denying the existence of genocide against

Since 2005 you've been working on the *Beware Of The God* project. It's been a pretty big effort given that it has involved projecting the words "Beware Of The God" onto clouds as well as producing a series of postcards, dossiers, metal plaques, screensavers and more. What inspired this project and what was the role of the Museum of Contemporary Art (MCA) in getting it off the ground?

The rise of politically-active monotheistic fundamentalists across the world was the inspiration. The project started off very small — I had no idea how I could ever get it off the ground. But on the very day I despaired of it coming to life, the MCA rang to ask what I was up to, and if they could help. *If they could help!* So I wrote them a megalomaniac proposal containing all of my wildest dreams, and they made every single dream, however barking mad, come true. They pulled together a series of great sponsorship deals, and a very small cash budget, most of which they recouped through selling the metal plaques in the MCA shop.

Avant Card sponsored the 40,000 sticker postcards, printing and distributing them, and the people who own the 42 video billboards in the Sydney train stations sponsored my little animated video which was shown on each one every ten minutes for ten weeks. The website was cheap to set up as it was done on blog infrastructure, although it's more like a magazine, I think. Pip Shea set it up for me and the wonderful researcher Chloe Martin provided the information for the dossiers on politicians and their links to religious organisations. She also researched the newsletters, which I then edited and designed as downloadable resources.

Through the video being shown at train stations over 1,000 people contacted me through the website, mainly interested in the information, or wanting to argue about the project's premise. It was super interesting and social. At its height about 15,000 unique visitors were coming to the site every month and lots of people downloaded the resources, the posters and dossiers, and wrote in asking for stickers. I posted them anywhere in the world. I still do!

The projections onto clouds are the part that many people best recognised as "Art", but I consider the whole project as one work of art. The projections were pretty spectacular and well documented. I don't know if the MCA copped flak as a consequence, they didn't tell me. I got some, and some vague threats, but my main problem, besides the ongoing activities of the fundamentalists themselves, is spambots.

Indigenous Australians] and were looking for a way to complicate the discourse, or to put it in plain English, fuck with things. One of the questions we were trying to get to the bottom of was about why Australians were so willing to just forget the past and simply get drunk. Out of that, the idea of making our own beer featuring limericks and satirical labels just suggested itself. We created some postcards out of the labels, but it cost a lot to do the beer properly so we only distributed a few hundred through some events that also featured satirical quizzes on Australian history.

For details on Deborah's current work visit:
www.forget2forget.net
www.boat-people.org
www.bewareofthegod.com

Grevillea

Although the range of options for protest activity extend as far as the human imagination, all too often those seeking change opt for the same old tired methods of gathering petitions, marching around the block and lobbying politicians. Even when activists engage in more theatrical endeavours many of their performances are clichéd and didactic efforts aimed at telling people what to think rather than encouraging them to think for themselves. One group who attempted to inject some vitality into the political life of their city during the late 1980s and early 1990s was the Western Australia-based Grevillea. In the following interview Mar discusses how the group applied a dynamic and creative perspective to approaching issues such as militarism, pollution and international solidarity.

When did Grevillea first come together?

It was during the late 1980s. It started out, as the best things do, by accident. There was one of the regular US war fleet visits happening in Fremantle. During the 1980s we would get visits about four times a year. These involved battle fleets composed of an aircraft carrier, a battleship, three or four destroyer escorts and often a submarine as well, which meant that at any one time there could be anywhere between seven and ten thousand American sailors in town. For us, it felt as though we were living in an occupied city. For mainstream Perth, it was a cultural celebration. That was really distasteful.

There had been a long series of demonstrations with varying degrees of success in response to the visits. In particular, a group I was involved with, War Resisters Fremantle, had done a lot of actions against them. On this occasion an anarchist rang around to friends saying she wanted to get some sort of specifically anarchist response together.

About eight people turned up to the meeting and the general mood was one of wanting to do something creative and wanting to do something quite different from what had been the run of the mill responses to the warship visits. War Resisters Fremantle and other people doing stuff in relation to the warship visits were not happy that the primary response to warship visits was to worry about nuclear weapons. We saw nuclear weapons as just the extreme manifestation of something that was horrible from start to stop — it was a side issue to the military occupation of our city.

What we decided was to do something which emphasised the military aspect of the warship visits rather than the nuclear. There was a march already organised by an anti-nuclear organisation, either PND (People for Nuclear Disarmament) or FPND (Fremantle People for Nuclear Disarmament). These were a regular thing and for the most part were stupid, boring affairs. We were used to, as a part of our political life, attending activities like demonstrations and going home feeling worse about ourselves and the world than when we had turned up. You got to the point where people preferred to do nothing rather than do what was on offer from the mainstream organisations because you felt all the energy was being taken out of you.

So we wanted to do something where not only would we provoke a more creative response from other people, but where we would energise ourselves, empower ourselves. That can sound very vague and touchy-feely, but there's a huge difference in going home from a demonstration where at the very least you have affirmed your collective opposition to what was going on, rather than just going along and feeling like you're making some token flag-waving effort that anyone could safely ignore.

With this in mind we decided to put together a piece of theatre. We decided that we would stop the demonstration as it was going through the busiest part of Fremantle. One of the people who turned up to the meeting could walk on tall stilts. We decided that she would be the person who would halt the demonstration by striding out in front of it and yelling, "Stop." At that point the rest of us would attack the demonstration.

Operation Baby Jesus. Perth, c. 1990. Courtesy of Nigel Livesey.

We wanted to do a few things at once. We wanted to ridicule the military, so we got some costumes together and dressed up as military clowns. We put on silly make-up. We all wore one sort or another of a military jacket or shirt, with clown pants. For weapons we used domestic things like frying pans as machine guns. We ran around the crowd doing the most mad laughter we could while yelling, "Join the army. It's fantastic in the army. Join the army. It's fantastic in the army." We pretended to shoot people and we'd arranged with some friends in the crowd that when that happened they would fall over "dead".

On the day, thankfully, there were enough people in the crowd who were awake to what was going on. Everyone, three or four hundred people, just fell down dead in the road outside the café strip in Fremantle. After a while of that we gathered together at the front of the march and led it down onto the wharf where the warships were. We had a great time and it got a good response from people.

Following the success of that action was there a decision to formalise things more?

Yes. We were very pleased as the action had done what we had set out to do and had done something extra. It brought people together who didn't know each other or who only vaguely knew one another, into a cohesive little group that was very keen to do more of this sort of stuff.

It sort of emerged that we were the Fremantle Anarchist Street Theatre Group. This was actually misleading as only half the group were living in Fremantle, only half the group were anarchists and only half of what we did was street theatre. We were always called that as we only gave ourselves a name (Grevillea) just before we broke up.

What sort of approach did the group employ?

As I mentioned, we weren't a street theatre group as such. What we were about was creative intervention, which meant that we were looking at creative, artistic, positive ways of addressing issues with humour and energy. Most street theatre is didactic, preachy and obvious, and we wanted to get away from that. Some of our actions were straightforward and had an obvious meaning, but many of them were designed so that they had multiple meanings. The point was to not limit ourselves to the accepted political, cultural forms.

What sort of actions did the group do once you started meeting regularly?

I can't remember the exact order of the things that we did after that, but we did a lot of things around the issues that were important for us. So, for instance, I remember that we did a very large painting, about five metres square, with a picture of the earth and stuff about various important rainforest issues that were going on at the time. This focused, in particular, on the destruction of the culture of the Penan people in Borneo by logging activities, and celebrated their resistance to that. They weren't going to win, and that was clear to them all along, but they set up fantastic blockades that went on for years.

To highlight all that we did this painting and glued it to the footpath in the Perth Cultural Centre, with a little rope barrier around it. It stayed there for a whole weekend and thousands of people would have walked past it.

A piece like that is clever in that most people would just assume that it was meant to be there.

The thing you need to think through with each of these activities is, "How do you do this in a way that makes it look as though it does belong? How do you give it its own air of legitimacy?" The way to do this sort of thing is to act as though you have a right to do it, because people get caught when they are acting nervously, or as if they shouldn't be there. What's even better is if you not only behave as if you have a right to do it, but as if it's your job. If you look bored, then everyone will assume that you're supposed to be there.

Grevillea was involved in one action where we were almost certain to be observed while doing it. We printed up a whole lot of stickers to put up the night before another war fleet visit, that said things like, "No credit to US sailors", "US sailors not welcome here", and so on. We literally stuck them on the front door of *every* shop in Fremantle.

Chilean solidarity action, Perth, c1990. Courtesy of Mar.

You're not going to do that and not be seen. So how can you do it? There were eight or twelve of us involved and we just went out in male/female pairs, holding hands. What can be less suspicious than a man and a woman with their arms around each other in a shop doorway? If anybody stopped to look you could just start kissing. No one was caught and the stickers went up without a problem.

Was there a public response to the stickers?

The Chamber of Commerce was a bit on the upset side. Various business people said it was a disgrace.

You did some other actions around the Art Gallery didn't you?

Yes. One of the members of the group, who was a keen surfer, said that he really wanted to do something about plastic waste because he was dealing with it on a daily basis. Every beach he went to had plastic waste washed up on it. We made a very large sculpture, about five metres tall, about eight metres long and about three metres wide. It was a fantastical creature that was part-dragon, part-dinosaur and part-machine monster with five heads. It was constructed entirely out of plastic waste and we installed that in the Art Gallery pond. We did it at 5 o'clock on a Friday when any of the arts bureaucrats who would be likely to call the police had gone home. There were just a few people hanging around when we stuck it in the pond. It took quite a while because the thing had to be transported in parts. It was huge. Each of the heads had to be put on separately and it had legs that had to be tied on, but was it fun installing it!

We made an information leaflet to explain what it was about and they were left on a stand made out of plastic milk cartons. The creature stayed there for ten days in one of the busiest places in Perth for pedestrian traffic. The other point about using the Art Gallery pond was to respond to the hijacking of art by a very squeaky clean Art Gallery.

So by using this location you were able to generate multiple meanings out of the one action?

Yes. By making a monster out of plastic waste we were making a statement about plastic waste; by putting it in the Art Gallery pond we were making a statement about the Art Gallery; and by doing it without permission we were making a statement about claiming public space.

Tell us about the action in which a Grevillea member got to lecture Perth's elite about the Chilean junta?

That didn't even start out as an action, but it showed what's possible when you have this creative approach in mind. I wasn't there, but some members of the group had turned up for a protest against an opening at the Art Gallery of Western Australia that involved one of Alan Bond's Van Gogh paintings. Bond [a high profile magnate at the time] had just bought into the Chilean telephone exchange, which the Pinochet regime was using to bug people whom they later tortured.

All the "nice" people were standing around with their drinks when this woman noticed that the microphone was unattended. She got up as if she was one of the intended speakers and said, "Ladies and gentlemen, welcome to the Art Gallery of Western Australia. While you are sipping on your chardonnays, I hope you are very happy with the idea that the money that is funding this event is coming from the torture of dissidents in Chile."

At that point people sort of realised that, "Ah, this isn't what we came to hear." Nice people don't like being reminded that their wealth is being supported by the torture of dissidents. She was escorted out of the building, but she'd made her point. It was great.

While the spontaneous approach worked that time we tended to discuss every action beforehand and at great length, if necessary. We'd focus on what the action was for. We'd also discuss what our attitude to the media would be. Most radicals don't do nearly enough of this, this actual thinking it through. We would ask ourselves if we wanted media coverage and, if so, what kind?

Another action the group did concerning Chile illustrated the need to organise our handling of the media. We did an action outside a concert that Alan Bond had organised which was supposedly raising money for street kids. It lost money and was a stupid publicity stunt. It was at Subiaco Oval, the main football ground in Perth.

One of our members was interviewed by a Channel 9 reporter. Alan Bond owned the channel at the time as well as the Swan Brewery, so he had people's drinking and viewing habits well under control. The reporter asked, "Are you saying that Alan Bond shouldn't organise this concert?" and our member said, "No. We're here to talk about Chile and Alan Bond's connection with the torture and the massacre of the dissidents in Chile, in which Alan Bond is closely implicated." The reporter kept asking the question, again and again and again, until the member started a sentence with "Yes". That was all that went to air. "Are you saying that Alan Bond should not have organised this concert?" "Yes."

We took that as an important lesson in dealing with the media. When dealing with journalists you only speak in single sentences that can stand alone and still get your message across.

You targeted Alan Bond on a number of occasions. Why?

He owned the bloody town. When he went to jail some people said, "Of course, we all supported Alan Bond back in the '80s." That was bullshit. Anybody who opposed Alan Bond wasn't going to get in the newspapers at the time because Alan Bond owned the newspapers. I thought he was a disgusting creep and a thief, but it wasn't possible to say so, even in the alternative media. To say it publicly left you open to the defamation laws. Now I can call him a thief in public because he has been convicted of thieving, but it was obvious that what he was up to involved large-scale deception and the asset-stripping of companies. It was as plain as day. Everybody knew it, so it was important to try and do something to disrupt the smooth flow of everyone's cash into Alan Bond's pockets.

At one point the two women who'd been there at the start of Grevillea said, "Wouldn't it be funny if LILAC came out in support of Alan Bond?" There was a group in Queensland called LILAC — Ladies In League Against Communism. It was a sub-group of the [quasi-fascist] League of Rights. So we did that. We set up this organisation in Perth — Ladies In Line Against Communism — and we held a number of public events in support of Alan Bond.

Now, obviously, if you've got an organisation which is called Ladies In Line Against Communism and it's being run by a group which is fifty-fifty men and women, which Grevillea was, then you have to set up a Men's Auxiliary. Which was a very nice take on the sexism of the Ladies' Auxiliaries at bowling clubs and so forth. We found lilac-coloured dresses of various sorts and the men all dressed up in the daggiest clothes we could find.

The first thing we did was to hold a cake stall to raise money for Alan Bond, which was closed down by the Health Department of the City of Perth. It was hilarious and got us a fair bit of coverage.

Alan Bond was actually crying poor at the time, wasn't he?

Yes. His creditors were suing him to try and get some of their money back, to which Alan Bond's response was, "No chance, and by the way, I haven't got any." So we tried to raise money for him. We held a cake stall and then we held a press conference in response to the banning of the cake stall. It was very, very funny because a reporter from Channel 7 turned up — he was the only person who turned up — and he'd come along thinking we were for real. He didn't realise that it was a prank. He had worked out how many lamingtons we'd have to sell to pay Alan Bond's debts. He said to us, "Do you realise how many lamingtons you'd have to sell?" When we started answering him he realised what we were up to and played along with it beautifully.

He also gave us a wonderful tip. He said, "If you want to do something and get it on the telly, then do it on a Tuesday." We didn't know this at the time, but the news does work in a quite rigid weekly cycle. On Friday and Saturday the news is all sport with five minutes of headlines. Tuesday there's no sport around and Parliament hasn't sat since Friday. Business is just waking up from the weekend. So news directors on Tuesdays are actually scrabbling around for something interesting to stick on the news. With this in mind we organised our big events for Tuesdays from then on in.

We had a Walk For Wealth, which was a gag on Community Aid Abroad's Walk Against Want. The Ladies In Line Against Communism managed to drag in a dozen friends of the group so there were about twenty ladies marching, with the Men's Auxiliary lamely tagging along behind. We marched from the Stock Exchange to the Alan Bond Tower. It's now the Bankwest Tower. At the time it was the largest office tower in Perth and it had the Bond Corporation on the top two or three floors.

Being the restrained and dignified people that the Ladies In Line Against Communism were, that march only went for about 150 metres. We then got into the foyer of the Bond Corporation offices. You know when people win lottery prizes and they have those huge cheques? Well, we made up a huge cheque, made out to Alan Bond, for $15 or something which was supposed to be the proceeds of the cake stall. He had just had to sell *Irises*, which was the Van Gogh painting he had bought for lots of money. So we gave him a painting called *Viruses* to replace it. I found this really bad, sub-science fiction doodle in an op shop and we turned it upside-down and added some bits to it and signed it with something silly.

The security guards panicked when we got to the building. They didn't know what to do and it took us a long time to negotiate getting in. As it was, they agreed to let us into the building. Every TV station in Perth was there except, incidentally, the ABC. A friend of the group had written a version of *God Save The Queen*, which, of course, is the favourite song of Ladies In Line Against Communism. We sang *God Save Our Billionaires* in a rousing chorus and then two of the group were allowed up to the offices to deliver the painting and the cheque.

What was the official response from Bond's people?

Somehow they had got hold of one of the postal addresses that the group used and the painting turned up a few days later. They didn't send back the cheque. It had a note that said, "We received this painting and a 'cheque'. We thank you for your efforts on behalf of the Bond Corporation, but we think we'll solve our own financial problems."

Despite all the gags some of the media appear to have been taken in. Looking back at the coverage the line seemed to be, "Are they right-wing loonies or are they left-wing loonies? We know that they're loonies but we don't know what kind"?

Some people were onto it straightaway. When we were in the Bond Tower singing *God Save Our Billionaires*, I recognised that one of the TV journalists was someone I'd been at uni with. He casually sidled over to me and, out of the corner of his mouth, said, "This is brilliant, Mar." He thought it was hilarious. People at a distance, though, didn't know what to do with the whole thing and we sent out a lot of press releases

as background for this.

The spokeswoman for the group was Elizabeth Lean. She was the wife of Terry Lean, who was a character one of the other members of the group had invented during an earlier mock election campaign. Elizabeth Lean did a whole lot of radio interviews, all around the country. Some people just wanted a very basic thing and some knew what she was up to straightaway.

There was a really hilarious interview with this woman from ABC Darwin who had a reputation for being a bit of a hard-head. She was quite radical, as well, apparently. She arranged for this interview with Elizabeth Lean and started out thinking that LILAC was for real. She started really getting into Elizabeth, who had all these lines prepared. Elizabeth just worked on the principle that if you are asked a question that you don't know how to answer, don't answer it. Say what you came to say, anyway. After the first couple of answers the interviewer realised what was going on, but it was already live to air and it was too late to change her tack. She gritted her teeth and went on with the interview for another few minutes. We later heard through the grapevine that when she turned the microphone off she shouted, "Bastards! Bastards! Bastards!" because she'd been had.

We also made national TV. Channel 7 and Channel 10 loved it because it was a way of having a go at Channel 9's owner. We thought that the ABC would enjoy this and were sending stuff to the ABC newsroom, but we didn't get any bites back. Someone in the ABC newsroom was sabotaging it because the letters and press releases that we sent to a journalist who was a friend of a friend never got to him. I don't know whether they didn't believe it was a joke and hated it, or did realise that it was a joke and hated it.

Tell us about the election campaign for Elizabeth's husband Terry Lean?

We'd always wanted to run a fake election campaign. There have been a couple of prank election campaigns in Perth. A guy called Michael Crossing ran in the Perth electorate in the mid-1980s for the League of Experimental Psychiatry. He promised to increase Perth's rainfall by 10% and to build the Narrows Dam. For people not familiar with Perth, the city is on a river with a bend that passes through a narrows with a freeway bridge over it. If you dammed it, you would basically flood Perth. He promised to be a loving electoral father to all his electoral children, and got about 300 votes. Later on Alex Manfrin ran a campaign in Perth in about 1994 for CFC (Citizens For Corruption) and got more votes than the Democratic Socialist Party did.

In 1990 we did our own campaign for Terry Lean. We looked at the legalities and the person who was going to be the main Terry Lean decided he didn't want to change his name by deed poll. Since that meant that he couldn't run officially we decided to make him the unofficial candidate.

We made a whole lot of posters with ambiguous political slogans on them and held a couple of rallies in the street. These were run like most election rallies, but with everything not quite right. We

Action in response to New Zealand's deportation and the subsequent freeing of the French state-terrorists responsible for bombing the *Rainbow Warrior.* Perth, 1986. Photograph courtesy of Mar.

developed a style of doing things like that. Where what appeared on the surface to be an ordinary election campaign forced people to go, "Did he really say that?" By doing something that appeared just slightly off, you forced people to think.

Similarly, if you looked at the posters that were put up all around Fremantle saying, "Vote for Terry Lean", you might have noted that, while the person on each poster wore the same hat and shirt and tie, there were twelve different faces. We were playing with the form and having a lot of fun.

We also did a similar thing called Project Baby Jesus. Two of us dressed up as street preachers and did all this ridiculous street preaching stuff. A lot of people really couldn't tell if we were for real or not, even though we were wearing the most obvious wigs.

How did you go about deciding who you were going to target and how you were going to do an action?

It was very ad hoc, but once an idea was presented and agreed on as a group project, it was discussed in great detail. With each activity that we did we discussed what it was for. Sometimes what we were doing was as much directed at our fellow demonstrators as at the media crews. Other times we did stuff that was intended to be just pieces of TV footage.

There was a peace march held when the French secret agents who destroyed the *Rainbow Warrior* and killed Fernando Pereira, were released back into French custody. Four or five of us dressed up in wetsuits with flippers and snorkels and wore various things that

indicated we were French. We sat in deck chairs and the rest of the group waited on us hand and foot. It was a visual tableau designed to get ten seconds of TV coverage and that's what it got.

In the build-up to the 1991 Gulf War I was involved in some other street theatre, but Grevillea decided to intervene in the official protests, to change it from being just another boring, ritualised march. The anarchists' response to demonstrations for many years had been to object to the way that the police would hurry up the marches. For years we did that by just staying up the back and walking as slowly as possible. The police would overtake us and say, "If you don't move we'll arrest you," but they never did.

At one of the biggest anti-Gulf War demonstrations a few of us talked about doing the opposite. We went up the front and walked really, really slowly. As well as that, we got a chant going of "Politicians to the Front." Going right back to the First World War, radicals in the peace movement have pointed out who does the actual fighting in wars and we did the same. The IWW had a slogan, "Let the bosses fight the bosses' wars."

So we got up to the front of the march and we were astounded. Half a dozen of us had started this chant. We didn't expect it to take off, but thousands of people started chanting, "politicians to the front," for half the march. One of the speakers, as happens at far too many of these things, was a Labor politician. He was the first to speak and it had really shaken him. He got out, "You've just heard people chanting 'politicians to the front', and I'm a politician and I agree that we shouldn't do this." He muffled through his speech. A couple of weeks later he resigned from the Labor Party, which was a really great thing. I thought that it was an indication that we'd had some sort of impact, although it may have been unrelated.

Over the group's history what do you think the response of the public and the broader Left was to its activities?

I think we had a good impact on a lot of people, and even if we had no impact on anyone else, we did have a good impact on each other. We got significant media coverage across the country for LILAC and got significant media coverage for some of our other actions. I think we also had some impact on people who were otherwise used to very ordinary political demonstrations. I think people started looking at doing more creative things to make their point. We were part of politicising more elements of the contemporary arts in Perth as well. Whether we were just part of this trend or whether we were just pushing it along, people responded in seeing that there was a better way of doing things than just having marches and listening to boring speeches.

NUNS 4 SAFE SEX

PRIESTS 4 ABORTION RIGHTS

www.socialist-alliance.o

Members of the Holy Orders distribute condoms.
Sydney, 2008. Photographer: Alex Bainbridge

Making Trouble: CONVERSATION #11 "

No To Pope Coalition

The hierarchy of the Catholic Church, along with all the other religious denominations, has long played a divisive and oppressive role in Australian society. Despite providing some level of succour to those persecuted by the colonial Protestant establishment, the Church's leaders have inculcated homophobia and sexism for centuries and worked against the efforts of those within its ranks to create a more equitable society. While the Australian laity includes a strong core of Catholics committed to social justice, the highest ranks of the Church have followed the rightwards trajectory of the Vatican in recent decades in condemning contraception, reproductive science and free sexuality. Along with a number of other religious bodies the Catholic Church has also gained increased access to both the pockets and ears of Australian Governments in recent years, as clearly demonstrated by the financial and political support given to the 2008 World Youth Day (WYD) Papal visit. In the following interview, No To Pope Coalition spokesperson Rachel Evans discusses how opponents of the Vatican's bigotry managed to overcome a series of anti-protest regulations to assert their right to "annoy".

Tell us how the No To Pope Coalition came together, and who the groups involved were?

Well, Community Action Against Homophobia (CAAH), which is a group based in Sydney, had a discussion around May 2008 about protesting the Pope. Particularly the young members of CAAH, the 19-year-olds, the 17-year-olds, were saying that all of their friends, their queer friends, were noting that the Pope was in town for July and that we should rally and protest the Pope's homophobia. We called a meeting for a No To Pope Coalition—we didn't quite know what the name would be, but we came up with that one in late May, early June. And then from then on it was bigger than Ben Hur, and different groups signed on.

The first groups to sign on were CAAH, Socialist Alliance and the Raelians and then others like the Sudanese Human Rights Association.

We got an international organisation at the end called Italian NoVat, which is "No Vatican", as they saw our press within the European media and rang us to sign on to the No To Pope Coalition as well. We ended up getting about 16 to 17 organisations signing on to the Coalition, within a month, month and a half, which was really good as we didn't have a lot of lead-in time.

We settled very quickly on the politics of the No To Pope Coalition, which was saying No to the Pope's homophobia, his anti-woman stance, and also his anti-contraception, anti-condom stance.

You also came with came up with the slogan "The Pope is wrong ... "

"... Put a condom on!" "The Pope can have his own party, but he should pay his own way," was another slogan that got a little bit of coverage. I guess the other thing that was pretty exciting in the early stages was seeing the different groups come on board, and the different ideas come on board. So for example, one person came in and suggested that we should have a massive same-sex sex education documentary projected onto Saint Mary's Cathedral at the beginning of the Pope's visit. We thought that maybe *Brokeback Mountain* being screened in the middle of the night on Saint Mary's Cathedral would have been a goer also, but in the end it got a bit technically difficult, so we did other stuff instead.

I guess the thing that really exploded the campaign was the decision by the NSW Government to pass the World Youth Day (WYD) regulations. What did this regulation allow the NSW police force and others to do, in terms of dealing with conduct considered to cause "annoyance" or "inconvenience" to participants in a WYD event?

What happened was, the No To Pope Coalition put our Notice of Intent [to protest] in on Friday 25th of June at 3pm. And then on that Friday, three hours later, the State Government in NSW passed this Annoyance law. So it was very clearly designed to stop protests going ahead. We looked at the fine details on that Friday and Saturday, when the information came out about it, and it included a $5,500 fine for annoying the Pope or annoying a pilgrim. Now, a pilgrim was defined as anyone — a Catholic youth, a Catholic elderly, a Catholic adult — who came to visit the Pope. So you could get a $5,500 fine for annoying any one of the up to 200,000 pilgrims that were in Sydney's CBD and around the city, within those two and a half, three weeks.

We were a bit shocked to see such intense regulations come down, but were also quite aware of the power of the Christian Right in Sydney and Australia in general. The Christian Right, of course, get very obsessed about things like abortion and marriage rights and civil unions and they have managed to win their demands from State Labor Governments and Labor and Liberal Federal governments. We pinpointed the fact that Archbishop George Pell, who was one of the key organisers of the Pope's visit, has a very close relationship with the Labor Party in NSW. As a result Pell had to come out and explicitly say, "I did not ask the State Government to introduce these regulations, and they [protesters] have a right to do whatever they want, but they shouldn't be extreme in what they do." Thanks to all the backlash even George Pell had to come out and back-pedal and say these things.

The regulations were really severe, and in all of my time as a protester, which stems back to 1991, I have never seen such an horrendous monetary disincentive for protesting. $5,500 is a lot of money! But the thing that was also outrageous was that it was so vague. How do you define "annoying"? A whole lot of civil libertarians came on to the campaign in a way that they hadn't before the Annoyance laws. We challenged the laws in the courts, with the NSW Council for Civil Liberties doing a whole lot of pro bono legal work for us. Myself, and Amber Pike went to court and challenged the State law. Fortunately we won and repealed the annoyance section of the WYD laws so that was really fantastic.

What areas were covered by the regulations, and what sort of items were people to be prevented from handing out?

Well, the No To Pope Coalition had decided to hand out condoms to pilgrims and young people who were around. We'd also decided to hand out coathangers to illustrate the fact that backyard abortions were killing women across the world, because of course, the Pope has a policy of condemning abortion. He says that abortion is a threat to world peace. He also condemns contraception. He says that contraception and pre-marital sex are a sin, and so of course for women who have an unwanted pregnancy, this can condemn them to death, because backyard abortions kill up to 85,000 women across the world every year.

We wanted to hand out these things and we also wanted to sell T-shirts. These things were very much under threat from the Annoyance laws. The other thing that we found out later, through the court case, was that you couldn't sell anything, even a bottle of water or a sandwich to a pilgrim if you hadn't signed onto the WYD Corporation. McDonald's had signed on, of course, and Sarah Lee had signed on, and *The Daily Telegraph* had signed on so they could sell things to pilgrims, but if you were just someone trying to hand out something it was illegal. Even handing out water was a bit of a grey area. The actual regulations were quite thick and hearty, even though they had supposedly been gotten together within a three-hour period, and hadn't passed through State Parliament, but via an executive component of the State Parliament. The situation was quite anti-democratic on a whole range of levels.

This was a pretty intense regulation, and of course, it led to our defence lawyers in the courts saying, "It's so vague, how dare you introduce these regulations with minimal public debate," and so on. But the thing that we were most concerned about, and of course the civil libertarians were most concerned about, was that we couldn't protest. Having a $5,500 fine for protesting set a really dangerous precedent in NSW. It is bad enough already in NSW as we have this thing called Notice of Intent where you have to lodge your intent to rally with the police seven days prior to an event. If you don't do that then they can wrap you all up and stick you in the clinker.

Because of all that it was really good that we had the victory in the courts, and it really blew the issue open to the world media in a way that we hadn't envisaged. The State Government really overstepped the mark. With every single international media outlet in Sydney and looking for interesting angles we were able to get on the news pretty much every second day. We did ten Alternative Commandments one day, for example.

What we some other ways that you responded to the regulations?

We encouraged people to produce annoying T-shirts and held an Annoying Fashion Show outside State Parliament about a week before our court date. "The Pope is wrong, put a condom on!" was generally the No To Pope Coalition's T-shirt slogan, but other good ones included,

Top to bottom, left to right: Giant condoms at the No To Pope Coalition Rally. Sydney, 2008. Photographer: Alex Bainbridge ●
A Tranny cop and a nun take part in the giant Same Sex Kiss-In. Sydney, 2008. Courtesy of www.greenleft.org.au ● A No To Pope
pilgrim. Sydney, 2008. Photographer: Jack Pam ● "Gay is the new black". Sydney, 2008. Photographer: Allan Milnes

"Pope go homo," "No God no guilt," and "$5,500 — A small amount to pay for annoying Catholics." There was also a really nice one, which was "This T-shirt is annoying" followed by a list of all the Labor State Government officials. I wore that one with extra glee.

The regulations affected skateboarders as well, which wasn't something that was really widely known. So the skateboard community, particularly online, produced all of these incredibly beautiful T-shirts. One of them was Jesus Christ on a cross, except the cross was made out of skateboards.

We also handed out a few thousand condoms throughout the course of the campaign. Interestingly, in 2000 there was a WYD in Rome, and after the event all of the young people got to sleep together under the stars, in tents and so on. When the cleaners came through there were thousands of used condoms littered about the place. Which is fantastic to see. It is really good to see young people, Catholics particularly, having safe sex. It's what we're promoting and we did our bit to help things along by handing out as many condoms as possible.

You also mailed out condoms to the WYD pilgrims at hundreds of schools around Sydney. How did you know where to send them?

There were a couple of activists who got online and found out all of that information, and we sent a package to all of the schools. We knew there were official Government organisations and HIV/AIDS research associations that had tried to give the pilgrims, as part of their pilgrim package, condoms and information about safe sex. We had a number of calls from these people who weren't prepared to go on the record, but who supported our campaign.

What was the Court's final ruling and how much did it actually restrain the police from being able to prevent the campaign, or the march, from doing what it wanted to do?

The ruling struck down the annoyance sections of the regulations. Mind you, there were other sections that still remained. Two or three days after the ruling we had one of the final No To Pope Coalition meetings, and we had to put in another Notice of Intent. The police came in and said, "We're not going to give you the right to go ahead. We're not going to sign off on your Notice of Intent because we're worried you're going to do something offensive, or you'll offend a pilgrim." The police then went on a bender for about three days to stress us out over the question of offending someone. But in the end, the Council for Civil Liberties again came down and said, "Well, we can go to the Supreme Court," which is what the Stop Bush Coalition had to do during the APEC protests. So they went to the Supreme Court, and the Supreme Court kind of ruled in their favour and that was fantastic. The police ended up backing down and they behaved themselves reasonably well on the day of the rally. The fact that we had about 20 to 30 lawyers taking photos and observing them probably helped.

Nevertheless they did engage in other forms of harassment and just before the court rulings we had activists being visited by police at their homes, and intimidated in that fashion. Another wing of the campaign, which we started to talk about later in the piece, was the Broken Rites organisation from Melbourne who campaign for justice for the people who've experienced sexual assault at the hands of Catholic priests. They were also being harassed by the police, but like us they refused to back down.

Despite these manoeuvres the thing that we did all along was speak really clearly to the media about the issues that we were raising, showing them that we weren't anti-pilgrim and that we had real, serious issues that we were contending with. As a result we had the ear of the Australian population and a hell of a lot of support. We had Catholics ringing up to say, "We're going to the WYD celebrations, but we support you and we're embarrassed at what's happening."

We'd reached quite far and wide and had a lot of support. That's really the basis of the success of a campaign, the support that you get on the ground. We were pretty confident that we'd get good numbers at the rally and we ended up doing that, so that was really good, too.

How did the rally itself go in the end?

It was really successful and I think it emboldened people in saying, "we can stand up to authority and get away with it." There were about 1,500 to 2,000 people there. People were wearing the most incredible costumes with the greatest array of annoying T-shirts that you could see. It was a really, really vibrant rally and the march afterwards passed through the pilgrims. There was a sea of pilgrims marching to Randwick Racecourse to stay overnight and the police had to stop them all to let us through to a park where we chanted, "The Pope is wrong, put a condom on," and "Gay is great," for a couple of hours until we marched back for a mass same-sex snog. That was put all over the media, which was fantastic to see.

With the march we decided to follow the Gay and Lesbian Mardi Gras route. Of course, Mardi Gras has up to a million people involved in it every year in Australia, and Sydney is the gay Mecca of Asia. There was a conscious decision to start at Taylor Square, which was the site of the first Mardi Gras uprising in this country in 1978, where a whole lot of people got bashed for coming out of the closet to have a street party.

Other than the same-sex kiss-in you also had a Jesus look-alike competition, didn't you? Did any of the contestants look much like Jesus?

Yeah. One drag performer, who's fantastic, came down from Lismore with the beard. He's kind of drag, anti-drag, and very political, and he won. The other thing is we had a T-shirt competition, and the T-shirt that won was "Mary was a virgin if you don't count anal".

What other actions happened around Australia?

Perth, Brisbane, Melbourne, Adelaide and Lismore all had events either during or before WYD including same-sex kiss-ins, rallies and T-shirt parades. In Brisbane, where there were official WYD events as well, demonstrators were manhandled by a number of police who didn't want annoying placards anywhere near the pilgrims. But generally, the protests across the country went off very well, and were well received by passers-by and pilgrims.

Overall it seems that while the Government's threat to civil liberties was real, it was also a bit of a miscalculation on their part, because it generated a lot of public outrage and increased media interest in everything you did. Just how much media coverage did the campaign get in the end?

We did heaps of interviews with media from across Australia and part of the reason for that was that The *Daily Telegraph* had signed on to the WYD regulation board, which meant they were the only official media present. As a result of that competition, we had Channel 10, Channel 9, *The Sydney Morning Herald* and others saying something that we don't usually hear from the corporate press in this country, which was, "You have a right to protest and this is an attack on civil liberties." Because their "civil liberties" had also been violated by the regulations and the agreements that WYD and the State Government had come up with.

We got a really good inning, as well as internationally, with the

Rachel Evans speaks at the No To Pope Coalition Rally. Sydney, 2008. Photographer: Alex Bainbridge

campaign being reported all over Europe, the U.S. and New Zealand. Pope Benedict is a German, so the German press interviewed us incessantly. We got on Al Jazeera as well, which was absolutely brilliant. We were wearing "The Pope is wrong, put a condom on!" T-shirts, and they got beamed all over the Middle East.

What effect do you think all this media profile had on the way WYD and the Pope himself operated?

Naturally enough the media did not engage in a huge amount of discussion around the politics of what we were saying. Nevertheless the Vatican has a media unit and we had debates with them on radio, which was really good. The main line of argument from the Vatican's media unit was that condoms actually aren't protecting people from

HIV/AIDS. They are absolutely obsessed about this, and they have a document which says that condoms have holes in them and are only 70% effective against HIV/AIDS. We really started to hone in and make sure that they weren't able to get away with such distortion and disinformation and lies.

Interestingly, the Pope only came out and made reference to reproductive technologies being evil. Within all of his speeches in Sydney and around Australia, he only mentioned that. He didn't say that contraception is a sin, which he's said before. He didn't say that homosexuality is a threat to world peace, and homosexuality is an objective disorder. We thought we did pretty well in putting him on the backfoot in that regard.

Vote 1️⃣
The Network Against Prohibition's

(From left)
Rob Inder-Smith,
Stuart Highway
and Gary Meyerhoff

Chan Ward   LORD MAYOR   Lyons Ward

For DARWIN CITY COUNCIL
Saturday, May 29, 2004

Photographs by VIVIAN RAJALA

Smoke up for human rights
12pm RAINTREE PARK
EVERY SECOND Saturday
OF THE MONTH
STANDING UP FOR YOUR RIGHTS!

FREE FOOD, MUSIC, and JOINTS

PROTESTING AGAINST NEW GOVERNMENT LEGISLATION.

JUNKIES, DRUNKIES, LOSERS & TOKERS LETS BUST SOME! POLICE

Drug Premises Orders

Web: NAP http://napnt.tripod.com Email: napnt@yahoo.com Phone: 0415 16 2525

COMMUNITY SMOKE UP
for human rights

**Free food, music, smoko and BBQ
& the amazing, ever expanding 1.6 metre joint**

Every 2nd Saturday of the month (August 10, Oct 12, Nov 9, Dec 14...)
in Raintree Park (opposite old Woolies in the city) Proudly brought to you by NAP and PARIAH
For more info ring 0415 16 2525 http://napnt.tripod.com www.country-liberal-party.com

COMMUNITY SMOKE-IN FOR HUMAN RIGHTS

When? Midday, Saturday, September 9, 2006
Where? Raintree Park, city
Help the Network Against Prohibition oppose the War on Drugs. NAP will provide food and entertainment and there will be an open microphone for people who want to say a few words. NAP came about because of the Martin Labor Government's draconian and widely discredited "Drug House" Legislation. This absurd law was copied from the United States which for the two-million-plus people incarcerated in its jails, is not the "land of the free".
Nor is it the home of the brave with the cowards in government drawing the world further into a spiral of unending war. The War on Drugs is part of that.
End the war on Drugs. Show your support at NAP's 29th Smoke-in

Network Against Prohibition — NT Chapter

Email hq@napnt.org
Web www.napnt.org

F.T.P.

24th NAP Community Smoke-In For Human Rights

Saturday 10th September '05, 12 noon.

**Raintree Park (Woolworths end of Smith St. Mall)
Darwin city**   info: 0406 199 268

All Welcome!! Come along and tell the NT Govt. where to stick its stupid Drug House laws!! BYOD   www.napnt.org

---

Network Against Prohibition http://napnt.tripod.com

Thankyou for coming to today's community smoke-in "Smoke-up for Human Rights", we are *here* to stand up for our human rights and to defend against attacks on our civil liberties.

Due to the brutal attack by the NT Police at the first community smoke-in, we felt that it was important to have some ideas about how we will handle that situation if it occurs today.

It is important to note that NAP is an organization that employs non-violent direct action. We do not fight with the Police, nor do we choose to antagonise them.

The Police always make the first move.

First of all, if you are arrested:
DO NOT Resist Arrest. Try not to wave your arms around. Going limp when arrested isn't necessarily resisting so try it.
DO NOT be abusive or disorderly.
DO NOT Answer any questions except to give your name and address. You do not have to tell them your Date of Birth or place of employment.
DO NOT give or sign a statement. Once they have your name and address you should remain silent, or answer all of their questions with "No Comment" or "I do not wish to answer that question."
DO NOT plead guilty or anything until you have spoken to a lawyer.
DO ask the Police for a telephone so you can contact a lawyer. Normally if you have no money, you will have to ask for bail so that you can see a lawyer at NT Legal AID or NAALAS on Monday.
DO ask for bail. If refused, ask police to telephone a magistrate to apply for bail.

If someone else is arrested at the Smoke-in, *people could sit around the police vans to prevent them leaving and/or attach themselves to the person being arrested.* We sincerely hope that this does not need to happen but any blatant attacks on our right to freedom of speech needs to be defended.

HAVE A FUN AFTERNOON ☺
The following legal services can help you on Monday if you have any hassles. If you have money, look in the phone book and get yourself a lawyer on the weekend.

North Australian Aboriginal Legal Aid Service   89815266
NT Legal Aid   89993000
Darwin Community Legal Service   89821111
Police Professional responsibilities unit   89223339

The *Network Against Prohibition* brings you it's 27th, commemorative

Smoke-in for human rights

When? Midday, Saturday, May 13, 2006
Where? Raintree Park, Darwin CBD
What is being? An appetite for food and a good time, plus personal smoko.

Come along and celebrate with NAP as we remember the infamous Parliament Invasion of four years ago.

Don't know what the Parliament Invasion was? Never heard of the LA Job? Come along and be part of the flashback, as we relive the wild antics of a bunch of renegade human rights activists who changed the way NT politicians think . . . err, would you believe the security arrangements at Parliament House?
All will be made clear by the NAP, Darwin's revolutionary drug law-reform group. People with a grievance, or simply with something to say about politics, the War on Drugs and especially, Clare Martin's Drug House legislation, are invited to make use of our open mike. As well, there will be a *free* sausage sizzle and *free* entertainment.
Be there or be square

DIE!! MORTEEN ADDICT SCUM!!

FRY COP

Brought to you by NAP and PARIAH
Oppose the NT Drug Laws!

6th Smoke Up for Human Rights!
**Saturday 12th October – High noon
Raintree Park – Opp old Woolies in City**

Featuring live local bands, free bbq, politics and the giant community hookah. Volunteers welcome!

For further information contact 0415 16 2525 or email napnt@yahoo.com

www.napnt.org

SUPPORT MARK AT NAP'S 24th COMMUNITY SMOKE-IN FOR HUMAN RIGHTS

SATURDAY, 10th SEPTEMBER. 12NOON IN RAINTREE PARK, DARWIN CITY

FOR MORE INFO CALL 0415 16 2525 OR EMAIL hq@napnt.org

Network Against Prohibition

Drug prohibition first began in Australia during the first half of the 20th century, when anti-Chinese racism and the lobbying efforts of the Temperance Movement saw the possession and use of opium, cocaine, marijuana and heroin all made illegal. In the years that followed new drugs such as LSD and ecstasy enjoyed brief periods of legality before they too joined the list of prohibited items.

Despite the abject failure of prohibition to prevent drug use, with 38.1% of Australians admitting to consuming illicit drugs in the 2007 National Drug Strategy Household Survey, an estimated $2 billion continues to be spent annually in a futile attempt to prevent the public from ingesting the substances they clearly desire. The continuing illegality of drugs has seen tens of thousands of Australians dragged through the courts for possession while the fortunes of organised crime continue to grow. Those who do suffer from addictions are forced to beg or steal to satisfy their habits, while policies that would minimise the health issues associated with addiction are blocked on the grounds that they might encourage drug use.

For a brief period during the 1990s it appeared that prohibition might be in decline as a number of states made moves towards decriminalisation and the downgrading of offences relating to marijuana and other drugs. This trend proved to be short lived as a hysterical media campaign saw the Federal Government block state and local governments from implementing harm minimisation policies such as heroin trials and the establishment of safe injecting rooms.

In 2002 a number of Territorians established the Network Against Prohibition (NAP) to oppose an anti-drug-user campaign initiated by the Northern Territory ALP. In the following interview STUART HIGHWAY discusses how the Napatistas used a mixture of direct action, humour and grassroots campaigning to challenge the continuing War On Drugs.

When was the Network Against Prohibition (NAP) founded and what were the group's initial aims?

It started in early 2002 when a group of people came together, most of them seasoned activists. We were specifically concerned about the War on Drugs as a violation of people's human rights. What prompted it, in Darwin, was that the Northern Territory Government was bringing in draconian new Drug House legislation and we could see that these measures would impact primarily on people who were poor, Indigenous and young — the same people who normally get targeted by the police anyway.

We were fed up with going through the usual channels — writing letters to the politicians and holding tokenistic rallies and demonstrations. They don't achieve much, if anything. We wanted to take it a step further and up the ante a bit with direct action, occupations of offices, and things like that.

How do the Drug House laws work?

If the police are called to any premises three times and they have a "reasonable" suspicion that someone there is under the influence of something illicit, or if they find drugs or people dealing drugs there, then they can declare those premises a Drug House. Once they've achieved that then they're allowed to raid the place as many times as they like, as often as they like, without a warrant. Anyone within 200 metres of the premises can be strip searched and cavity searched. It's ridiculous when you think about it. People just have to be near to some place. They might have nothing to do with drugs, they might hate drugs, and yet they can be strip searched by the police.

With the Drug House itself, they can put a 1.2 metre high green notice on the front door displaying all these rules and you aren't allowed to tamper with that sign. One thing that we achieved with our campaign against these laws was to keep those green signs to a minimum.

On the other hand, in 2002 you were allowed to have two cannabis plants in the NT for personal use. A lot of people didn't know their rights so we also wanted to show people what the facts were.

Beyond that we wanted to illustrate how the laws against drugs are actually worse than the drugs themselves in terms of the harm that they do to the community. We are all paying for the War On Drugs. We're all paying for incarcerating people for drug offences and for the cost of law enforcement. We're all paying in that the War On Drugs prevents our society from dealing with drug abuse as a medical rather than a criminal problem.

You started off with a protest outside the Department of Justice in March 2002 where five people were arrested. They were the first of many arrests for the Napatistas, weren't they?

Yeah. The original idea was to occupy the building, but when we got there it was obvious that we weren't going to be able to do that because the police were already there. We had issued a media release and perhaps one of the radio stations had notified them. Instead we marched down to the building and sat down in front of the line of police. It turned out to be a good thing because it was lunch time and there were lots of workers around. We had a megaphone and saucepans and whistles and made quite a racket.

We thought that we'd just do this for half an hour, or something. We wanted to get arrested to draw publicity to our cause. It was looking like the police weren't going to do anything, but then just as we were about to finish they said "If you don't move in five minutes you'll be arrested for trespass." We thought "Great," and it made it worth staying another five minutes. We all got charged with catch-all offences, things like unreasonably causing substantial annoyance and making undue noise.

We beat those charges later on in court because the magistrate ruled that what we were doing wasn't unreasonable. We did cause a substantial disturbance, but it wasn't unreasonable in the context of a supposedly democratic system. He said, "It's all part of democracy. We've got to expect a bit of inconvenience and a bit of noise now and then. We need people to question the system and to make a fuss about laws and things." That surprised us a bit, but it was good.

What happened at the first Smoke-In you held, in 2002?

The plan was to meet in Raintree Park in the middle of Darwin, but the police were determined to put a stop to it before it could begin. They came after one of our spokespeople, Gary Meyerhoff. They strip searched him and told him that if he went back to the park he'd be arrested. He went back there and when he began to speak the police moved in to do just that. However the crowd had other ideas and tried to stop him from being arrested. It was like a tug of war with people holding on to his body and wrestling. There was a huddle and people linked arms around it and started chanting, "NT police state, we do not appreciate." Then a second ring formed around the first. The police tried to break through the inner ring, but when they looked up they were surrounded by another.

They managed to arrest five people eventually, but it was a big struggle and people were giving them hell. In the long run though people were freaked out by the police violence. 100 or 200 people came to the first Smoke-In, but we never got as many people after that.

After that first Smoke-In you continued to hold them on a roughly monthly basis. Tell us about the V-8 Super Joint?

That was a giant joint that appeared at most of the Smoke-Ins. It started off at one metre, but then we added another 20cm at each Smoke-In. It became difficult to keep it alight. We used legal herbs like Damiana to fill it up. We tried to keep it as an open question as to whether there were actually any illegal drugs, like cannabis, at the Smoke-Ins as we wanted to keep the police confused. They tried to seize all these drugs at the first Smoke-In, but when it came out that there were no illegal drugs there they looked like fools. After that they backed off and left us alone for a few months because they thought it was just a symbolic thing.

After a while however they realised that people were smoking the real thing and during the sixth Smoke-In they made trouble again. At most of the Smoke-Ins, we did about 30 of them all up, we had no trouble. The police left us alone because they didn't want to give us the extra publicity.

The sixth one turned into a bit of a riot and some of us got jailed for that. The police came in and seized this community hookah. We'd stopped using the giant joints by that stage because they'd gotten too long and unmanageable. So we had this community hookah instead. It was an office water bubbler. It was turned upside down and had holes in it with plastic tubes coming out and we had the green vegetable matter on the top in a cone. People would come together and suck these tubes.

Generally everyone would have a good time, but on 12 October 2002 the police moved in and seized the hookah and took it away. There was a tug of war. The four uniformed police who were there were outnumbered and they freaked out and called for back-up. People resented them spoiling our party and one of the police vehicles got damaged.

I think it was probably a set-up because the Lord Mayor of Darwin was there that day with a photographer and a journalist, which was surprising because normally we couldn't get any media to come. They wanted to crack down on us and teach us a lesson, but it kind of backfired on them as they couldn't find anyone who had actually been doing anything illegal. Instead they just grabbed a few people who were closest to hand.

We continued to do Smoke-Ins after that. After 2002 we scaled it back to every second month. The police backed off again as they thought that if they ignored us we would go away. But we didn't. We kept it up.

What happened with the International Darwin Syringe Festival?

In the middle of the year during the dry season we have the Festival of Darwin and the Darwin Fringe Festival. We decided to take the piss out of that and promote needle exchanges and harm minimisation through the International Darwin Syringe Festival. We had a Syringe Art Gallery, Syringe Olympics, a NAP needle exchange, drug culture films, etc, on our Festival program. I don't think that there had ever been anything like this before.

Two women climbed up on this building at the edge the CBD at 4am and they painted an advertisement for the International Syringe Festival on a giant billboard. We put up thousands of posters and of course it got people's backs up. It got so well known that the Lord Mayor of Darwin had to state publicly, "I won't be attending the Darwin Syringe Festival." It was pretty funny that he had to deny that he was attending the festival because we wouldn't have expected to see him there.

Another provocative action NAP was part of involved turning up to a police conference with pigs' heads on a platter?

That was at the Darwin Central Hotel. Some activists presented a pig's head on a platter to the Police Minister and had their photo taken. Two women also had pigs' heads on sticks. The police couldn't really do anything as we weren't breaking any laws.

NAP was also doing grassroots work with drug users weren't you?

Yes, we had NAP House. We conducted an underground needle exchange and helped minimise drug-related harm in the community. That ran on donations and people's hard work. Because we didn't receive Government funding we were free to criticise Government policies whereas other services have to be a lot more careful about what they say.

What happened with the Tent Embassy outside Parliament?

We were inspired by the Aboriginal Tent Embassy and thought we'd set up a Drug Users' Embassy on the lawns outside Parliament House. On May Day some of us broke away from the May Day march and set up camp. We weren't sure how it was going to go, but the police left us

Network Against Prohibition activists Robert Inder-Smith, Stuart Highway and Gary Meyerhoff, Darwin, 2004. Courtesy of Stuart Highway.

alone for a while and we spent the night there. After about 24 hours there was a violent eviction after the Speaker of the House issued an order for us to leave. A few people chained themselves to the flagpoles, which slowed them down a bit. The police arrested a few people who were unwilling to leave.

A few weeks later you went into Parliament itself, didn't you?

Yes. Since they had evicted us and didn't want to deal with us we decided that we had to go and confront them directly. Eleven of us went and sat in the public gallery whilst they were passing the Drug House legislation. They had a condolence motion for the Queen Mother who had just died and we stayed seated for that. Everyone else stood up and did a minute's silence.

We sat up there for half an hour, watching. I think the politicians were nervous, seeing us up there because they didn't know what we were up to. We made out as if we were leaving for lunch, but we tricked them. Instead of going out we went down to the doors of Parliament. We thought that they might be locked, but they weren't so we just pushed the doors open and walked in. Ten of us went in and nine got charged later under a special law.

The politicians were shocked. It was like a white fella sacred site and they didn't expect that we would go in there and say things directly to them. Gary rang the media and said "We're in Parliament now." They said, "Where are you, in the foyer?" and Gary said "No, we're inside the actual Parliament." He was walking around on the Parliamentary Dispatch table in the centre of the chamber while having this conversation.

We went in there with placards that we'd hidden down our pants. There was a plain clothes cop in there who was assisting with the passage of legislation. Gary Meyerhoff got in the Speaker's chair and this cop grabbed him by the hair and threw him down the steps at the side of the table. It was lucky that he didn't get seriously hurt. Some of the other protesters got on the Parliamentary Dispatch table for their own protection. The security guards didn't dare get on the table. There was one woman amongst us and she got singled out for the worst treatment. She got charged with assault when she was the one who had been assaulted.

The Speaker asked the members to leave the chamber and most of the Labor Party members did. A lot of the opposition stayed behind to enjoy the Government's embarrassment and we talked with them a bit. Nobody got seriously hurt, but there was a bit of rough and tumble. After a while we decided that we had made our point so we left and waited outside. The police came and went inside the building and then they came out and took our names and addresses. We also had our photos taken for the media and chatted with them. We thought we'd gotten away with it because they didn't know what to do with us at first. We didn't realise that there was a special law which carries a maximum penalty of three years jail for "disturbing parliament".

What happened with your court cases?

Eventually seven of us were served with summons to go to Court. We were charged under this law that went back to Olde England, back to the time of Oliver Cromwell. It was a big court case and dragged on for a long time.

Out of the seven, two of us ended up pleading guilty and they got off more lightly than the rest of us. We got convicted, eventually, in June 2003 and were jailed. We received sentences ranging from 21 months, suspended after five months, to 16 months, suspended after four months. We were then bailed for an appeal.

We were out on bail for more than three and a half years after that. We went all the way through the appeal process to the Supreme Court and then the Full Bench of the Supreme Court with three judges. We even tried to get to the High Court of Australia, but they wouldn't let us.

We did various things to cause as much nuisance as possible and attract media attention. We subpoenaed most of the politicians who were present in Parliament on that day. They didn't want to turn up to Court. They were really annoyed about it, but it was their system and they had to obey their own laws.

We didn't have lawyers so we ran the cases ourselves. We got to do the cross-examination and there was a bit of a carnival atmosphere.

They were so annoyed, some of these ministers. They just thought that we were a bunch of rabble, but they had to stand there and be cross-examined by us.

I had a go at the Chief Minister Clare Martin. I said to her, "Look, isn't there an element of hypocrisy in your government's drug policies, given that you have admitted to smoking cannabis when you were young?" She stammered, "Oh, no, this is not hypocrisy," but everyone in the public gallery went "Ohhhhhh…" and it was all covered in the media.

We tried lots of things. At one point we claimed that we were covered under the Geneva Convention as we were prisoners of war in the War On Drugs. Gary Meyerhoff used to wear an army helmet to court and sometimes he'd wear a dress as well. Some of the lawyers tried to suck up to us and say, "We're on your side, really. We used to be militant in the old days when we were young and at university. We protested against the Vietnam War. We understand where you are coming from." But still they were prosecuting us. They weren't on our side.

However brilliant our legal arguments might have or might not have been they couldn't afford to let us win. People were saying that we should have got a lawyer, but I don't think it would have made any difference. By doing it ourselves, it was empowering. We got to speak about our politics and about why we took this action. They give you more leeway if you are unrepresented and instead of arguing on legal points you can argue on moral or political points. So that was good. We could say what motivated us. It was a political trial and they claimed it was not political.

In 2004 NAP held a demonstration outside the Human Rights Art Exhibition which was held, ironically, at the Northern Territory Supreme Court. What did the protest entail?

They held this exhibition each year and we felt it wasn't an appropriate place to have it because in the Supreme Court people have their human rights taken away from them. They get locked up there. It certainly hit us in the face when we heard about it because we'd been dragged through these courts. They were like our second home during these years. We picketed the exhibition opening and handed out leaflets asking amongst other things, "What sort of art do they have in the holding cells downstairs?"

What was the eventual outcome of the court cases regarding the invasion of Parliament?

All of it ended with the handing down of a final sentence on 26th February 2007. Gary Meyerhoff had died in the meantime. The four of us who remained were given the opportunity to apologise to the NT Parliament. I didn't apologise because I didn't feel that I had done anything wrong. One of us did though and she got a lighter sentence—a $500 bond. The rest of us got jail sentences. Two people went to jail for a month, but three days were taken off the sentence of one of them because he had been wrongfully imprisoned in 2004.

I got a jail sentence of six months, but it was fully suspended. We had other conditions placed on us and were not allowed to associate with each other until 2008. In 2002 we had been banned from entering Parliament House for 12 months and they banned us again until 2009.

Tell us about the time you spent in prison from October 2005 to January 2006?

I spent three months inside arising from a case to do with alleged damage to the windscreen of a police vehicle during the sixth Smoke-In. I pleaded not guilty and presented my own case in the Supreme Court. The judge came down hard on me. I made it clear that I saw the police and the Government as the guilty party because had they left us alone that day there wouldn't have been a problem. I said to the jury in Court that they couldn't trust the police evidence. Saying that they were liars probably pissed off the judge as he gave me eight months, suspended after three.

I was in Darwin's Berrimah Jail, which is made up of about 80% Indigenous prisoners. It was sad to see so many people in there who shouldn't have been. People were there because they couldn't afford a decent lawyer, basically. Racism was evident and Aboriginal people seemed to get heavy sentences for things that white people wouldn't even get charged for, certainly not go to jail for.

It's sad too because people seem to accept it as a way of life. Aboriginal people live in shocking conditions a lot of the time with overcrowded housing, inadequate health and education, and a lack of recreational facilities. Prison is just an extension of that and many people just accept it as a fact of life. Despite all that, people do resist sometimes and there's solidarity in there. They stand up against the system and support each other.

There was actually a protest at Berrimah while you were inside, wasn't there?

Yeah. I was in the medium security M Block. One day the prisoners said, "When we go to muster up, for the head count, instead of going into the different exercise yards, we'll all go into the one exercise yard." So we did. People started speaking out and saying, "We've got problems here and we want them dealt with. Every time we go through the proper channels we don't get anywhere. We're fed up with this shit and we want something done. You've got to listen to us and take us seriously."

The issues were simple things like the amount of noise on M block and wanting clean mattress covers and shaving brushes. These were pretty basic issues, but the screws freaked out. In their minds they needed to exercise complete control over our lives at all times. It was such a minor challenge to their authority, but they called it a riot even though we eventually obeyed their orders to go into the other exercise yard. Just because we'd asked for a few things they made out that we'd done this terrible crime. Two guys got shifted up to maximum

security and one guy got moved to Alice Springs, which is 1,500km from Darwin; there are only two prisons in the Territory. In the Darwin media it was reported that it was a riot over food. But food was not on the list and it was a passive protest. It just shows you how the media distorts things.

Tell us about your own protest over urine testing?

One morning in December 2005 they decided to do a drugs test on a whole block in medium security and about half the guys had to submit a urine sample. I refused to do so as part of my opposition to the drug laws of NT. After all, that was why I was in there in the first place. They said, "Right, that's automatically 28 days in the punishment cells," which is the same punishment as for a positive drug reading. These cells have hardly any ventilation and are really hot.

It was difficult, but I had a lot of support from the activist community and from the other Napatistas. In the end it was all right because I prepared myself psychologically. Lots of people from NT, southern Australia and overseas sent me letters and cards, and replying to those kept me busy. I was also doing a lot of reading and exercising so it wasn't too bad. It was an experience and although I don't think it's one that you necessarily want to go through, it was worth it. It gives more credibility to your ideas if you're prepared to stand up and go to prison for them. I felt honoured, in a way, that I had this chance to make a stand and that people were backing me up.

For more information on the Network Against Prohibition visit www.napnt.org

Sister Medusa, Sister Volupta (late
Mother Inferior) and Sister Sit on My
Face. Manly Wharf, Sydney, 1981.
Courtesy of Mother Inferior.

Order of Perpetual Indulgence

The Order of Perpetual Indulgence's humble origins lie in the decision of three gay men to wear nuns' habits to a variety of events in San Francisco throughout 1979. In the autumn of that year, founding members Sister Hysterectoria and Reverend Mother attended the first International Faerie Gathering, drawing further support, with the result that in 1980 the Sisters of Perpetual Indulgence officially came into being. Fending off abuse from religious zealots and homophobes, the San Franciscan Mother House has gone on to raise over a million dollars for non-profit organisations serving the queer and sex-positive community. Just as importantly they, and the more than 35 other chapters around the world, have continued to "promulgate universal joy and expiate stigmatic guilt" in an attempt to "expose the forces of bigotry, complacency and guilt that chain the human spirit." In the following interview, Mother Abyss of the Order of Perpetual Indulgence, aka Mother Inferior, discusses the founding of the Sydney Order and its work for a variety of political and other causes.

What inspired the founding of the Sydney House of the Order of Perpetual Indulgence?

Sister Mary Medusa came back from America in 1981 having spent some time with the American Sisters of Perpetual Indulgence. As an Australian he had the view that his experience of living with the Sisters and being received as a novice there would be relevant for the situation in Sydney. He was very fired up with the view that the Sisters would offer the Sydney gay community a new spirituality, the centre of which would be the promulgation of universal joy and the expiation of stigmatic guilt. This was very much in tune with what was then the Radical Faerie movement in America, which saw gay men involved with a movement that would connect them to the ancient religions, the ancient focus of spirituality and of association with the Earth.

There was another person at this time who had been going out on his own wearing a habit, for no particular political reason, who then was told, "Oh, well, there's this existing group and there's a person who has come back from America who would like to start a foundation of the Order here in Sydney." This person was rather shocked because the images he had seen of the Sisters of Perpetual Indulgence in San Francisco showed men, in traditional habit, but bearded, and some with makeup. He felt, well, this is rather strange, rather unusual and it's not necessarily something that he would like to be involved with. However, when he met Sister Medusa he agreed to sew the habits for anyone who wanted to join. He then had a change of heart and felt that even though the American Sisters seemed a little bit theatrical and almost drag-queen-like he'd go along with it.

From that meeting of the two came the initial focus. It was a compromise between the strong political side of the Radical Faerie Movement, as represented by the Sisters of Perpetual Indulgence from San Francisco, and a more personal side. From those two Sisters began a movement which attracted two others, Sister Sit On My Face and Sister Gerontophilia Extravaganza.

Their first public experience was simply going on a picnic in habit at Birchgrove at Long Nose Point, which was forever after known as Long Nun Point. That public picnic resulted in a loss of vocation for Sister Gerontophilia Extravaganza because he was so intimidated by the public experience of being in habit that he felt it mightn't be his thing. It's not true that he wanted to wear a lime green habit and was refused permission. That's a myth, an urban myth. If there had been lime green fabric around he could have worn it, but we were conventionally dressed in plain black habits. In fact, they were old Anglican choir cassocks donated by an Anglican friend. Upon those basic double-breasted-type cassocks was built the habit of the Order of Perpetual Indulgence. We initially tried to copy the American Sisters of Perpetual Indulgence with their wimple, but we didn't realise from the photographs that we looked at that the wimple was actually a construction which was attached to the head and stuffed full of sponge to make it rigid. When we tried to copy the heart-shaped wimple we stitched it as two pieces and it collapsed and we looked like two rather sad koala bears.

You mention that one of the Sisters found the public experience difficult. Was that because of other people's reactions?

Yes. You cannot be a Sister of Perpetual Indulgence easily. You have to be prepared to wear your habit in public and to cop whatever comes. That can be confusion, aggression, adulation, people coming up and wanting to confess their lifelong failings to you and to receive absolution, people going into some sort of nun-sex role, all sorts of things. It's unpredictable. If you are not up to that and you're not prepared for that you can be easily intimidated into thinking, "Why am I doing this? This is putting myself in a very public way at risk from unpredictable reactions from people."

It's better when you are in a group, with a large group of Sisters. Then you feel the strength of the Sisters around you. But isolated, in ones and twos and threes, it's unpredictable. There can be wonderful responses and there can be responses of absolute aggression, fury. It's no good trying to explain that we are an Order of gay male nuns. That may exacerbate things even more.

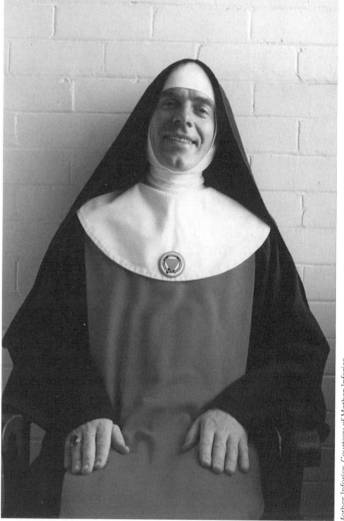

Mother Inferior. Courtesy of Mother Inferior.

In Australia we have opted for a fairly traditional habit. Unlike the Sisters of Perpetual Indulgence in San Francisco, in Paris, in Germany, etc, we have never opted for extravagant habits, makeup, white faces, etc. We look the real thing. We look traditional. This makes our statement a lot easier on some levels, but a lot more complicated on others because maybe people could accept a very dramatic, elaborate, almost Kabuki-like theatrical presentation, with some aspects of the nun's habit. But when you are in something that for all intents and purposes looks like a traditional nun's habit it is much more threatening for people. It's also much more challenging for people. It needs more explanation.

When you say "statement", what sort of statement are you referring to?

The Order has always aimed at being faithful to the original, theological motto of the Order which is, "No more guilt." We are an Order of gay male nuns. Not just an Order of gay nuns or lesbian nuns. We are male nuns so there is a gender statement there. There is a turning upside down of the conventional role. In the past we have had lesbian monks. We have the idea of promulgating a joy that is universal. In other words we celebrate the diversity, the upside-downness of life. We offer a perpetual indulgence which frees people from the guilt that is imposed on them as homosexual people. We do that through consciously wearing our habit.

The Order was established in San Francisco and then it went to Los Angeles, to Australia, to Toronto, to London, to Nottingham, to Edinburgh, to Paris, to Hamburg, and even to Colombia. All around the world you've got this phenomenon of gay male nuns and what holds them together, I think, is the idea of refusing stigmatic guilt. Saying, "People who want to put guilt into the concept, life of being gay need to be exorcised." We used to do exorcisms of stigmatic guilt. In NSW we knelt on the steps of the Parliament and exorcised the demon of homophobia from the Parliament. We exorcised sexism and the oppression of women from the pre-term clinics. We exorcised militarism and excessive nationalism. We had all the ritual elements to be able to exorcise and expel demons. Some people said, "Okay, but you exorcise demons of rising damp, you exorcise demons of excessive mortgages." Yes, we did that too, but our very public role was to exorcise the grander demons that afflicted society.

All of those things, when they are combined, make a kind of theological statement, but they are also a political statement. The San Francisco Sisters were able to go into an environment where fundamentalist Christians were trying to provoke gay people and, by the Sisters' mere presence, completely demoralize them. The humour and the joy and the curiousness and the eccentricity of the Sisters were able to subvert that extreme hostility.

In the same way Sister Third Secret of Fatima would lead Sisters in Sydney to attend "pro-life" rallies. The anti-abortion people would be extremely angry at the presence of the Sisters and would feel demoralised because they couldn't see their statement as being one that was done in isolation of other issues. When we went to the pre-term clinic in Cooper Street years ago, where the anti-abortionists would go and harass the women who were going for pre-term counselling or for actual terminations, we were able to distract and harass the harassers. We were able to say to the women coming, "We are here to remind you of the motto, 'No more guilt'. To remind you that you need to make your decision free of the extreme attitudes of these people who are trying to stop you from making your choice."

Now, those anti-abortionists were very strange people. They were very scary people. But we were there, as much as we could, to try

and distract them from harassing and hurting the women who were going for a pre-term consultation. Regrettably, it became such an issue because all sorts of people got mixed up there, including fascists. It became an absolute melee and it was very difficult for any women to enter for any kind of pre-term counselling. Nevertheless, we made the statement that we wanted to support women in their right to choose — to go and get objective counselling.

We have always said that our very image is at the service of the community. When the fundamentalist Christians would meet, before the Gay and Lesbian Mardi Gras, to pray for rain and to pray for the destruction of Mardi Gras, the Sisters would go and join in the prayer, as much as we could. And, of course, the response of the fundamentalists was that they just felt that they were unable to continue this focus while the Sisters were there.

How has the Order related to the Gay and Lesbian community over the years?

I have to acknowledge that although the Sisterhood promulgates universal and very non-sectarian joy we have been very much inspired and supported by gay people — men and women — coming from the Left of the gay community. People from Gay Solidarity, Gay Liberation, the Gay Liberation Choir, etc have injected into the Order a sense that we have a political role. They have brought a sense of humour, a tremendous sense of humour into the Order and I'm happy to name those Sisters. Sister Third Secret of Fatima, Sister Joy of Man's Desiring, Sister Mary Quant, Sister Mary Tyler Moore, Sister Mary Mary Quite Contrary, Sister Come Dancing, Sister Crème de la Clone, Sister Harry Butler and Sister Mary Any Time. These are all people who brought into the Order a very good political approach so that we were at the service of issues where a gay presence might be useful.

At times we have experienced condemnation from parts of the gay community who didn't like us, who didn't want the Sisters coming to their venues because we were something other than Drag Night on Tuesdays. We were a constant, all-year-round statement. There were those who did not think that our presence assisted the gay community and I think we had some challenging times, making a case to the gay community. There are still a lot of people in the gay community who would think that this is very bad image, that we are wrong, that we are not encouraging any kind of assimilation because we are offending the Church, offending the very essence of a quiet, conformist approach to what it means to be gay.

I think some of these critics would join in the general community's condemnation of the Order where they say, "Look at you, mocking and ridiculing the very women who help to nurse your AIDS people. This is a slap in the face for those wonderful women." In fact, most hospitals are government-funded and the nurses who care for HIV people in the wards don't wear a veil on their heads. It is interesting that the one time we met, formally, a Roman Catholic nun, from the Sisters of the Good Samaritan at Glebe, her only criticism of us was that we seemed to be ridiculing them. They felt that this was unfair because they were on our side. They also disliked the Papacy and its anti-gay pronouncements. They also didn't like the male hierarchy. However, as one of our Sisters said to them, "What would happen if you made your non-conforming views public?" Well, of course, they would be in terrible circumstances. So privately they were supportive of the gay community, but publicly they cannot state what they privately believe.

They didn't understand our statement. They felt that we were mocking and ridiculing nuns as such. When you see the Sisters of Perpetual Indulgence out in the public, however, you wouldn't interpret what they were doing as ridiculing anything. They wear the habit properly. They conduct themselves in the normal manner. They don't lift their skirts and scream. They don't deliberately smoke or drink or carry on in public. Their statement is that they are gay male nuns. It is a strange inversion. On the same level there were lesbian monks. The Sisters have to be judged not on the basis of who they are, but on the basis of what they do. That's the yardstick for judging whether such a group is of value to the community and to the gay community.

What are some of the roles the Order plays in the community?

Over the years people have come to love the Sisters. We've been invited to very intimate, personal moments, such as the naming and christening of children. It's an extraordinary thing for heterosexual parents to do, to say that we want you to come and conduct a ceremony for our children. They have invited their families to attend. For them, this is the baptism, the naming of their children. I've asked them, "Are you sure? Some members of your family may be very upset by this." And they've said, "No, we want to make this statement. We want a world where the Sisters of Perpetual Indulgence and what they stand for are commonplace. A celebration of non-stigmatic joy. A ridding from the world of guilt. The idea of playfulness, of humour, of non-gender-specific living. Of the celebration of diversity." That's why they have asked us to do such an intimate thing for them.

So that's one level where I feel we've had a very good role. We've also been involved in blessing buildings, book launches, art launches and so on. Why do people ask us? Do they think we are a rent-a-crowd? That we're cheap? We don't charge and we are a bit of a laugh, but I think it's because, in many cases, they see us as a very visible part of the gay community. And that is one thing that the Sisters can do. The moment you put a habit on and you go into any public function or even a private function, immediately there is a statement there and the statement is a kind of unapologetic gay presence.

If we go to May Day or Hiroshima Day or any other rally then we are saying, "We are here and we support the issue." There are people who don't want us there, people who say, "Why can't you come in ordinary clothing." Well, the Order's habit is like a badge of identity. If it's worn properly and discreetly, discreetly in the sense that it's worn cleanly and nicely, and we conduct ourselves as what we are, then we make a statement just by our presence. That the gay community is here. These people are gay, because the gay community is the only community with an established order of gay male nuns. Any football team can put on drag or a nun's habit for one night. But year in and year out, here is a group that are regularly there.

How do the Sisters come by their names?

The names are generally chosen by the Sisters themselves. If you don't select a name you risk being named by the other Sisters. They are very sharp. If they think you are a bit of a dill, they will give you a name that sticks. We had a Sister Merry-Go-Round and I think he got his name because he was dizzy, dippy. Other sisters with interesting names have included Sister Monsterio Delicioso Hysterica, Sister Mary Mary Quite Contrary and Sister Rowena, Keeper of the Holy Doily.

Tell us about the work the Order has done around safe sex education?

With this work I think that the Order really has to acknowledge the role of Sister Third Secret of Fatima. He came back from a visit to the Mother House in San Francisco in 1983 and the Mother House was already experiencing, even in its own members, the effects of AIDS. Sister Florence Nightmare was one of the most famous people living with AIDS in 1983. He was called the AIDS Poster Boy because he was a wonderful, beautiful young man living with AIDS. He was also a registered nurse. From the energies and intelligence of the Mother House in San Francisco came a wonderful safe sex pamphlet looking at all the STDs that people have to deal with.

We borrowed from that and in 1985 we had the privilege of being involved in the first safe sex outreach in Sydney. The Sisters were instrumental in providing safe sex demonstrations in the very early days of the virus. Eventually that role was taken over by professional people, but we had a very important role, early on.

We also continued to say that sexuality was good, as a lot of people were terrified and frightened by the sexual act after the AIDS virus appeared. I actually thought that the Order would fold when this dreadful virus appeared, because I thought no-one would be interested in our statement and they would see us as being frivolous, superficial and dismissive of the real health issues related to the virus.

Thankfully I was wrong, as we went to the University and to the Health Colleges and were able, with our habits, to make a very strong statement for educating for safe sex and safe needle use. The health authorities asked the Sisters to spread information and to demonstrate safe needle use. That was a shock to me because I'd never been a needle user, but we had to learn those sorts of things.

How did the Order react to the Papal visit in 1986?

We appeared along the Oxford Street route to both welcome and to remind the Holy Father that gay people were here. We had a wonderful time as many Sisters — probably a dozen — chased Pope John Paul II around Sydney, from place to place. Apparently we gave

a lot of entertainment to the Vatican Press buses which followed the Pope Mobile. His Holiness himself did greet us initially. But then I think Cardinal Clancy advised him that we were not perhaps within the fold so he wasn't so keen on giving us his blessing as he had been initially when he may have thought we were traditional nuns. If he looked closely he would have seen that Sister Harry Butler was sporting a beard.

How has the structure of the Order changed over the years?

Well, it began very, very loosely. There were no minutes kept for the first few years of the Order's life. There were no structured meetings. It was very open. Eventually it tried to model itself on a collective, consensus model which was inspired by the Mother House in San Francisco. Sister Fatima went there to visit the Mother House in 1983 and then Mother Inferior went there and from that community they drew something of the spirit of the first Sisters. It developed in the direction of being non-hierarchical. That's a very difficult way to function because you have to have consensus from everyone. It's a very, very slow and difficult way to make any kind of decisions.

Our first big contentious decision was whether or not to permit women joining the Order to call themselves lesbian nuns. The collective structure came apart very rapidly because a group of Sisters felt it was a clumsy and silly way to make decisions whilst the rest of the Sisters felt that the consensus had to be achieved. So we had our first split in 1992 and that was over the issue of whether women joining the Order should be able to call themselves lesbian nuns or whether they should be required, as they had in the past, to call themselves gay male nuns and if they weren't happy with that to, in fact, go into the branch of the Order that was made up of lesbian monks. This was so that at all times we could maintain the gender reversal of gay male nuns and lesbian monks.

So the decision-making was very intensive and difficult. Some people had the view that the Sisters should have been a very loose, flowing collective. Well, that was perhaps a good idea, but as an open collective we have never closed the doors to membership to anyone. That's how we've had people in our Order who have had all sorts of life problems: kleptomania, alcohol and drug abuse, etc. That had, to some degree, caused problems in the Order because we would be one of the few groups in Sydney who had an open welcome to everyone and tried to accommodate all sorts of people.

We had no membership policies as such. We simply had membership requirements. If you came to the Order you had to serve as a novitiate, with the white veil, while you were on the learning curve. After a suitable time of six months or so you could be professed as a Sister and receive the black veil and be a fully professed Sister of Perpetual Indulgence.

As a result of these simple membership requirements there are conservative Sisters and Liberal Party-voting Sisters and monarchist Sisters! It's a disgrace. They should have their wimples starched rigidly

Mother Inferior at the anti-APEC protest, Sydney, 2007 Photographer: Matt Steer.

for that, because we've always been left-leaning. However, that's what happens when you are an open collective — you get conservatives, monarchists, Liberal Party voters. It's disgusting but what can you do when you are an open collective? We don't have a process of excommunicating or defrocking Sisters easily.

Also, because we had people coming into the Order who had life problems, such as being challenged by a lack of sense of humour, it made things difficult. It forced into a community a group of very varied people. Mother Armageddon To Be A Habit with You, Sister Theresa Bona, Mother Khubler Ross of the Critical Mass of Unconditional Love, Sister Urban Faggott and another Sister, I hope I haven't suppressed his name because he gave us problems, that group felt that other Sisters were not very good at humour and were "tragedies". They saw them as tragedy nuns so they had an independent meeting where they tried to force the Order in a certain direction, to tighten things up a bit.

After things fell apart in the early '90s, you had warring groups. There was a new group formed called the Sisters of Universal Joy who wore beautiful white habits. Those of us in the Sisters of Perpetual Indulgence were left in the same old black drudge. I can understand that it is very difficult for people who are funny, witty and efficient to put up with people who are challenged by such a thing as a sense of humour. We weren't able to maintain a community ultimately.

But there were wonderful days. We've had 150 Sisters through the Order in all the years since 1981. I'm beginning to forget their names but there's a list. I have had wonderful experiences of getting to know people. In our former days young people used to join the Order with tremendous energy and humour. Sister Mary Had a Little Lamb and Shocked the Entire Medical Profession was a lovely nun, with a tremendous wit. When he joined the Order he called himself Sister Jezebel Joystick, Batteries Not Included. He worked in a shop that sold sex objects. One day I looked at him and he looked a bit pale and I said, "Are you OK?" And he said, "I'm tripping Mother. I'm tripping." And I said, "Oh. Is your scapular too long, I've got some safety pins. I can pin up your scapular if you would like. Is that why you're tripping?" And he explained to me what tripping meant. That he had taken some sort of medication that made him very happy. So I learned a lot from the younger Sisters. They were a very varied mob and the sadness of today is that I don't see the younger generation coming to join the Order and I don't see them valuing who we are.

Tell us about the media backlash that the Sisters endured over the 1999 tours of the Opera House?

A person who worked in the Opera House thought he'd done very well to secure a commitment from the Opera House to publicise tours led by Sisters of Perpetual Indulgence, or at least attended by Sisters of Perpetual Indulgence, as tour guides from the Opera House were going to be giving the talks. However, word got to the press that our icon, the Opera House, our national icon, was going to be besmirched and ridiculed and that elderly ladies were going to be frog-marched around by men dressed as nuns. This produced a directive from the Premier's Department to the Ministry for the Arts that the tours be canned. And they were. Sister Mary Mary Quite Contrary took this to the Anti-Discrimination Board, but the nun who initiated the tours in the first place sadly declined to proceed with any case. For a couple of days there were extraordinary newspaper reports in *The Telegraph* and it certainly gave us a lot of publicity. The irony was that when they produced a photograph of the nun who was an employee of the Opera

House they printed the wrong photograph. They printed another nun. We were all highly amused by this in the Order. It was terribly funny.

We laughed some more when the Mardi Gras, in protest at all this, very cheekily suspended a nun from a crane above its official launch. I was glad that that happened. We've had wonderful times. Always challenging. Sometimes boring because you're stuck in the wimple and habit. So long as you're in that habit people are going to treat you as Sisters of Perpetual Indulgence and you're going to have to deal with them. That's why we had to instruct Sisters that, if you're in the habit and you're in a bad mood, get out of the habit, because it's no good being a grumpy nun and being mean to people.

What is your own involvement in the Order nowadays?

These days I go about my life as a gay male nun on my own. I don't go to the meetings any more. I feel after all these years that I don't have the energy to go to these meetings and in a sense it is sad, but then, those Sisters may not feel that they have a lot in common with me. Some Sisters prefer to do things in the gay community. They would bless Gay Pride, but they wouldn't be all that comfortable about going on a rally against the Americans in Iraq. Some Sisters would rather have a house blessing, which we do very well, but they mightn't be so comfortable with going on the May Day Rally.

There's always room for diversity, but unfortunately the diversity hasn't been able to be sustained so we go off and do our own thing. So there's a small group of Sisters and then there are other Sisters who act in a type of freelance way — independent. I guess that's what's got to happen. The disappointment is not seeing anybody, or very few indeed, coming in who are new, young or old, to keep the work of the Order going. And so I wonder what the future of our Order will be.

It's been a rough road because ... well, I always thought that the Sisters would just be a nice little group and I will make habits and won't it be lovely to be a nun, finally? Which was a goal or a dream I'd had all my life. To be a nun. And how can you be a nun if you're not a female? So the Order was tailor-made for those who were called to be nuns, but who were male. And in that sense it's been a wonderful personal experience.

All the same, I'm sad that nobody seems to be gripped by the idea in the way we were in 1981 and 1982. A lot of our wit came from the left-leaning nuns and they were responsible for the Order going in the direction that it did. But even today we can still do small things. It takes quite a bit of energy and commitment to put on your habit and go out in public to a rally because you are a very, very public image of the gay community and you need a lot of personal energy to sustain that. Nevertheless it can be a very simple statement and a very powerful one, even now.

Graffiti Games Organising Committee

Graffiti has been an integral part of Australia's urban landscape ever since the country was first invaded in 1788. From the early scrawlings of convicts through to today's sophisticated murals, the streets have consistently given a public canvas to otherwise marginalised artists and malcontents. Despite being a generally fleeting medium, some early carved pieces, mostly of the "Bazza woz here" variety, still survive on beachfronts around the nation, while others such as a piece dealing with the internal ALP disputes of the 1950s in Melbourne have even been given heritage status.

Despite the increasing regard accorded to stencil and mural work, the majority of government authorities retain the belief that graffiti and street art can and should be entirely eliminated. This position is buoyed by the activities of anti-graffiti bodies such as Residents Against Graffiti Everywhere who, while hardly representative of the wider Australian community (where indifference would appear to be the order of the day), have proven themselves to be highly effective lobbyists. As a result tens of millions of dollars are expended each year in attempts to keep the streets graffiti free.

At the same time, street artists have proven remarkably resilient in the face of criminal charges and the regular removal of their work. Indeed, these factors simply add to the ephemeral and daring nature of the enterprise. While most artists simply toil away, letting their work speak for itself, there have been occasional attempts to challenge the opposition to street art via more high-profile means. In the following interview a member of the GRAFFITI GAMES ORGANISING COMMITTEE (GGOC) discusses how the group sought to resist the Victorian State Government's concerted campaign against street art during the Melbourne 2006 Commonwealth Games (M2006).

What inspired you to organise the Graffiti Games in 2006?

The Graffiti Games concept was basically a response to a highly publicised police crackdown against street artists which involved an anti-graffiti taskforce carrying out numerous raids on houses and placing charges against 48 people. In particular three artists, Stan, Bonez and Renks, who were part of the prolific graffiti crew 70K. One of them was overseas at the time, but the media falsely claimed he'd fled the country. Renks pleaded guilty to charges of vandalising 72 train carriages, a tram, rail bridge, overpass and building during four years of work across the city. Renks was not convicted but ordered to pay a total restitution of $30,000 to V/Line, Yarra Trams and Connex, and perform 250 hours of community service. 70K certainly made train travel a bit more interesting and gave the commuters something to look at other than advertising.

On top of this, 2006 also saw a DVD that was made by 70K banned by the Office of Film and Literature Classification Board for "glamourising illegal activity". A computer game called *Getting Up: Contents Under Pressure* received the same treatment and a push by the South Australian Attorney-General to make it even easier to ban works seen as pro-graffiti was narrowly defeated.

As part of the Victorian State Government's attempt to tidy up Melbourne before the Commonwealth Games it allocated a million dollars for anti-graffiti security teams and a cleaning crew who would buff work on a daily basis. This proved to be more expensive than they'd anticipated so they chucked in an extra $1.2 million just before M2006 began.

Most of the media jumped on the bandwagon with *The Age* and ABC predictably wringing their hands over how to strike a balance between property rights and art, while the *Herald Sun* and the conservative talk back and current affairs shows simply slammed and hyped the "graffiti menace". Even the suburban *Leader* chain of newspapers got in on the act by running a weekly, syndicated column detailing the latest removals and calling for residents and councils to "clean up the streets".

Ironically it was around this time that stencil art was gaining a certain level of international recognition and the city was being touted as one of the premier sites for street art due to the release of a book called *Stencil Graffiti Capital: Melbourne.* In a strong action of solidarity, Banksy wrote an article defending Melbourne's street artists for the UK *Guardian*. The London-based artist argued:

> Witty, playful, often angry, the free rein taken by Melbourne's street artists became about much more than just daubing on a wall. It has drawn in generations of artists, thinkers and tourists to explore and experiment in the city ... Modern street art is the product of a generation tired of growing up with a relentless barrage of logos and images being thrown at their head every day, and much of it is an attempt to pick up these visual rocks and throw them back ... Society's headlong march into bland conformity should not necessarily be welcomed with such open

arms ... The precedent set by Melbourne does not bode well for London in the build-up to the 2012 Olympics.

I'm sure that all this was very annoying for the anti-graffiti mob and it may have influenced the council in sparing a few prominent alleys from being buffed.

The City Of Melbourne declared a "zero tolerance" policy towards street art, didn't they?

Yes. This was particularly galling because in the previous year they'd been in dialogue with artists and policy makers about making some mild reforms. With an issue like street art it's difficult to find a compromise between the people who want to create it and those who want to keep the streets safe for sanctioned "art forms" like advertising. Nevertheless the council commissioned a report that was released in 2005 which basically tried to find a middle way by calling for the decriminalisation of areas like Hosier Lane and Cocker Alley. These had become street art galleries over the previous decade and were popular with tourists and had really made the inner-city culture so vibrant.

As part of this idea of containing street art to certain areas the report advocated the setting up of "maximum tolerance zones" where artists could work undisturbed by either police or council officers. There was widespread support for the policy and even conservative groups like Crime Prevention Victoria and people like Melbourne Police Superintendent Mick Williams came on board.

To my mind the proposal was far from perfect as, while it would have given artists a certain amount of breathing space and made the council look "progressive", it still would have seen harassment occurring in 99% of the city. Nevertheless it was a change from the usual situation in which graffiti was only ever portrayed as a social evil. In the end we never got to see how the proposal would have panned out because, with the Games looming, the council's Community and Culture Committee decided to ignore the report's findings and impose a "zero tolerance" policy — a complete backflip on the hard work that had been done to build communication between the graffiti writers and the council.

How did you and your friends respond to all this?

Basically a few of us got together and discussed how we might turn the situation around. The best way to deal with a bad law is to break it by continuing to do what you were doing anyway. If enough people do so then it's possible to make any law unworkable.

It was clear that while they could curb the amount of graffiti they couldn't stop it altogether. Just slowing things down and removing graffiti for a few months was costing the taxpayers millions of dollars. This was never going to be a sustainable solution to the so-called graffiti problem. We wanted to publicise the need for some realistic, positive, long-term policies as well as celebrate the work that was being created in Melbourne at the time. We also wanted to get up the anti-graffiti lobby

Top left: Train piece posted on the GGOC website. Melbourne, 2006. Anonymous.
Top right: Graffiti Games downloadable stencil. Melbourne, 2006. Courtesy of GGOC website. **Bottom:** Letter from M2006 to the Graffiti Games Organising Committee. Melbourne, 2006. Courtesy of GGOC website.

MELBOURNE 2006 COMMONWEALTH GAMES

MELBOURNE 2006

15 March 2006

Graffiti Games Organising Committee

URGENT

By email:

Dear

Graffiti Games logo and website

It has come to our attention that the Graffiti Games Organising Committee is using the words "Melbourne 2006" and a logo incorporating the official logo of the Melbourne 2006 Commonwealth Games ("Graffiti Games logo") on the website www.graffitigames2006.com ("Graffiti Games website"). The Graffiti Games website also provides stencils of the Graffiti Games logo, with instructions for downloading the stencils and reproducing the Graffiti Games logo with spray paint.

Use of Games logo and references

The term "Melbourne 2006" and the Games logo (and substantially identical or deceptively similar terms and logos) are protected under the *Commonwealth Games Arrangements Act 2001 (Vic)*. Under section 56M of this Act, Games references and logos may only be used for promotional purposes (whether or not for commercial gain) with the express permission of Melbourne 2006 Commonwealth Games Corporation ("M2006"). The Graffiti Games Organising Committee has not obtained permission from M2006 to use Games logos or references on the Graffiti Games website, or in relation to the Graffiti Games logo.

Section 56L of this Act also prohibits conduct which suggests approval or affiliation with the Games or M2006. The use of the words "Melbourne 2006" and the Graffiti Games logo on the Graffiti Games website suggest a formal connection between Graffiti Games Organising Committee and M2006 or the Games which does not exist. This is also likely to constitute misleading and deceptive conduct contrary to the *Trade Practices Act 1974 (Cth)* or equivalent State consumer protection legislation, or passing off.

Copyright

M2006 owns the copyright in the Games logo. Any person who reproduces the Games logo (or a substantial part of the Games logo), or authorises the reproduction of the Games logo (or a substantial part of the Games logo), in Australia without permission of M2006 infringes the copyright in the Games logo under sections 14 and 36 of the *Copyright Act 1968 (Cth)*. The reproduction of the Graffiti Games logo on the Graffiti Games website, and the publication of stencils for people to re-create the Graffiti Games logo with spray paint infringe the copyright in the Games logo owned by M2006.

Action required

In view of the above, M2006 requires Graffiti Games Organising Committee immediately to:

1) remove the Graffiti Games logo from the Graffiti Games website, including removing the downloadable stencils of the Graffiti Games logo;
2) undertake in writing to M2006 that Graffiti Games Organising Committee will not in future make unauthorised use of any intellectual property associated with M2006 or the Games, or authorise others to do so. The undertaking can be given by email to the address:

Your co-operation in this matter would be appreciated. Please comply with the above steps by 5pm on Thursday 16 March 2006, to avoid the need for me to escalate this matter.

If you have any queries, please contact me on

Yours sincerely

Brand Protection Manager

and Government's nose and annoy them as much as possible.

In an attempt to achieve these ends we formed the Graffiti Games Organising Committee or GGOC [a play on the Sydney Olympics' SOCOG]. We put out a press release a few weeks before the Commonwealth Games calling on street artists to defy the council's "cultural cleansing" by competing in the Melbourne 2006 Graffiti Games. We declared the whole of Melbourne a "Maximum Tolerance Zone" and challenged people to create as much new work as possible.

A website was set up so that people could post photographs of street art and vote on works in categories such as Most Seditious Piece, Most Daring Placement, Most Elaborate Stencil Piece, Funniest Slogan, Largest Graffiti Piece and Best Caricature of the Mayor or other City of Melbourne Councillor. The website also had all our press releases, a copy of the City of Melbourne's abandoned graffiti report and various articles about street art. It was all done in the style and colours of the official Commonwealth Games website and included a downloadable stencil of our logo which added spray-cans and paint brushes to the hands of the figures in the M2006 one.

What was the response of the authorities and the media to all this?

With all the hype against graffiti and around the Commonwealth Games in general we thought that the media would lap this up and they did. We received extensive coverage over a couple of weeks with articles and commentary appearing in the three major Melbourne dailies as well as in local, interstate and international newspapers and radio. *The Herald Sun* ran a classic headline with "Graffiti Outrage" and MX made us their cover story.

Predictably, various anti-graffiti spokespeople's opinions dominated the coverage. Victorian Police Minister Tim Holding was desperate to divert attention away from a scandal he was involved in over ALP branch stacking and described us as "mindless, idiotic people — people who are apparently incapable of winning anything other than a pointless vandalism competition". This was from the genius who, as Victorian Water Minister, told people that they shouldn't bother installing water tanks because it doesn't rain all year!

Despite these negative tirades the Graffiti Games website was listed and we got to promote street art as a valuable element of urban culture that should be respected, not obliterated. The number of hits on the site rocketed and the *Sydney Morning Herald* even ran some of our lines such as "Unlike the elitist Commonwealth Games, the Graffiti Games will be open to anyone with a spray can and a good, or bad, idea."

At one point GGOC was threatened with legal action by the organisers of the Commonwealth Games over our logo and downloadable stencil. They strangely believed there was no formal connection between the Graffiti Games Organising Committee and the M2006 or the Games, and that we were promoting misleading and deceptive conduct which apparently is contrary to the Trade Practices Act 1974. The letter contained such useful information as "the reproduction of the Graffiti Games logo on the Graffiti Games website, and the publication of stencils for people to re-create the Graffiti Games logo with spray paint infringe the copyright in the Games logo owned by M2006." It was exciting to see our name so "official" in print.

Rather than enter into protracted legal proceedings over the nature of copyright, parody and "fair-use" we decided to remove the logo, picking up more media coverage in the process.

Why did you use the name Michael Stewart for your press releases?

As some of us were practising street artists we wanted to keep our identities hidden, as getting raided by the police would have put a bit of a dampener on our campaign. We used the name of New York graffiti artist Michael Stewart, who was murdered by police in 1983, to both honour his work and hammer home the point of where "zero tolerance" policies could lead. The journalists who interviewed us caught on quickly, they'd obviously done a web search, and a few of the stories mentioned what had happened to Stewart.

You weren't the only group responding to the negative effects of the Commonwealth Games were you?

No. There is a long tradition of cities being sterilised in the build up to these events and all sorts of Melburnians were suffering from police and government harassment. After doing bugger all for years the State Government miraculously found the funds to provide short-term housing for some homeless people during the Games, but for the most part their response was to move on anyone who failed to shape up to their expectations of happy, shiny shoppers. As we said in our press release, "With street artists and the homeless currently being purged how long can it be until people with less than $100 in their pockets, non-designer tracksuits or crooked teeth also find themselves 'United By The Moment' in being frogmarched to the city limits for fear of cluttering up the view of wealthy tourists?"

The group that was most active during this time was the Indigenous-led Black GST (Genocide to end; Sovereignty acknowledged; Treaty to be made) collective who hosted the Stolenwealth Games protests and Camp Sovereignty. Their main concern was with the continuing dispossession of Indigenous Australians and they saw M2006 as an opportunity to demand a treaty and expose Australian racism to the world. Aboriginal people and their supporters came from all over the country and they held loads of protests and set up Camp Sovereignty in the Kings Domain for 60 days. They published our press releases and supported us through their website, which looked even more like the official M2006 than ours. The M2006 organisers never came after them either for displaying our logo or for their own piss-take.

Another inspiring action was the roving "graffiti wall". A group of people printed large photos of well-known street art galleries onto boards which they then paraded around the city. Since it wasn't illegal the police couldn't do much about it and the group picked up a fair bit of media to boot.

How many people participated in the Graffiti Games?

During the period of the Commonwealth Games, March 15-26, the level of street art appearing in Melbourne inevitably dwindled and what did go up didn't tend to stay up for very long. With a massive security presence in the city and special clean-up squads and a police anti-graffiti taskforce operating this was hardly surprising.

Nevertheless new work continued to appear and our website received around 100 contributions, demonstrating the inability of the council and police to kill off artistic expression entirely. Some of the postings documented older work that had been buffed, but there were plenty of new pieces and some funny accounts of the adventures involved in getting them up.

Due to the high quality of work received GGOC found that we were unable to give the nod to any individual contestants in the various competitive categories declaring instead that in the end both "Melbourne and Graffiti were the winners". The site stayed up for some time, but eventually came down as none of us had the time or know-how to keep dealing with constant spam attacks.

Did the anti-graffiti crackdown continue after the Commonwealth Games were over?

Despite some of the claims that councils and the State Government had made the reality was that due to all the expense involved they were never going to be able to keep this kind of effort up. Although later on in April 2008 the state-wide Graffiti Prevention Act commenced, which included a tough new approach to graffiti. The laws included prison time and huge fines for people caught making graffiti, restrictions on possessing spray cans without lawful excuse, banning the sale of spray cans to people under 18 with large on the spot fines for stores caught, as well as increasing police powers to search people near public transport infrastructure and if they "reasonably suspect" someone. This was disappointing to say the least.

But in Melbourne after the Games they wound down the clean-up squads and police operations fairly quickly and the train corridors and the alleys and the walls that they'd spent millions on cleaning up were redecorated in no time flat. In the end the street artists of Melbourne proved that whatever the authorities might throw at them they are not going away..

An archived version of the Graffiti Games website can be found via a search at pandora.nla.gov.au

Endnotes

1. Fry, E. (ed) *Tom Barker and the I.W.W.*, Australian Society for the Study of Labour History, Canberra, 1965.
2. Ibid.
3. Farrall, L. *The File on Fred*, High Leigh Publishing, Melbourne, 1992.
4. Fry, E. *Tom Barker and the I.W.W.*
5. Ibid.
6. Ibid.
7. Edmonds, R. *In Storm and Struggle: a History of the Communist Party in Newcastle 1920-1940*, Self-published, Newcastle, 1991.
8. Alexander, H. and Griffiths, P. (eds) *A Few Rough Reds: Stories of Rank and File Organising*, Australian Society for the Study of Labour History, Canberra, 2003.
9. Alexander, H. *The Neglected Works of Oscar Zeet*, Self-published, Sydney, 1998.
10. D'Aprano, Z. *Zelda*, Spinifex Press, North Melbourne, 1995.
11. Ibid.
12. Perry, P. F. *The Rise and Fall of Practically Everybody: An Account of Student Political Activity at Monash University, 1965-72*, Self-published, Balaclava, 1973.
13. Pressley, A. *Living in the Seventies: Being Young in Australia in an Extraordinary Decade*, Random House, Milsons Point, 2002. Courtesy of Gary Foley.
14. Perry, P. F. *The Rise and Fall of Practically Everybody*.
15. www.roughreds.com
16. Alexander, H. *The Neglected Works of Oscar Zeet*.
17. Biotic Baking Brigade, *Pie Any Means Necessary: The Biotic Baking Brigade's Cookbook*, AK Press, San Francisco, 2004.
18. Templin, J. *Mardi Gras Memories*, Griffin Press, Adelaide, 1996.
19. O'Reilly, C. *The Revolution Will Not Be Televised: A Campaign for Free Expression in Queensland, 1982-1983*, Jura Books, Sydney, 1986.
20. Ibid.
21. Ibid.
22. Alexander, H. *The Neglected Works of Oscar Zeet*.
23. Ibid.
24. Rogers, N. (ed) *Green Paradigms and the Law*, Southern Cross University Press, Lismore, 1999.
25. Ibid.
26. Ibid.
27. Ibid.
28. hoaxdiary.wordpress.com

We thank the above authors, interviewees and publishers for allowing us to quote from their works.

Shadow play installation of birds made from wire and tin on blank billboard. Hidden during the day and coming to life at night. Victoria Rd, Balmain, Sydney 2005. Photograph courtesy of Ned Sevil and Anwyn Crawford.

Police search and rescue use a 50-metre crane to remove Tony Quoll from a tree-sit at Dingo Creek. Victoria, May 2001.

Sources and further reading

BOOKS AND PAMPHLETS

Action for World Development, *Aboriginal Heroes and Heroines of the Resistance*, AFWD, Melbourne, 1988.

Alexander, H. and Griffiths, P. (eds) *A Few Rough Reds: Stories of Rank and File Organising*, Australian Society for the Study of Labour History, Canberra, 2003.

Alexander, H. *The Neglected Works of Oscar Zeet*, Self-published, Sydney, 1998.

Australian Independence Movement. *Barricade!: The Resident Fight Against the F19 Freeway*, AIM, Melbourne, 1978.

Baker, K. *Mutiny, Terrorism, Riots and Murder: A History of Sedition in Australia and New Zealand*, Rosenberg Publishing Pty Ltd, Dural, 2006.

Barrett, J. *Falling In: Australians and 'Boy Conscription', 1911-1915*, Hale & Iremonger, Sydney, 1979.

Bassett, J. and Gerster, R. *Seizures of Youth: 'The Sixties' and Australia*, Hyland House, Melbourne, 1991.

Bassett, J. and Gerster, R. *Seizures of Youth: 'The Sixties' and Australia*, Hyland House, 1991.

Beasley, M. *The Missos: A History of the Federated Miscellaneous Workers' Union*, Allen & Unwin, St. Leonards, 1996.

Best, A. *The History of the Liquor Trades Union in Victoria*, Federated Liquor and Allied Industries Employees Union of Australia, North Melbourne, 1990.

Bolton, G. *A Fine Country to Starve In*, UWA Press, Nedlands, 1994.

Bramble, T. *Trade Unionism in Australia: A History from Flood to Ebb Tide*, Cambridge University Press, Cambridge, 2008.

Brown, M. *The Black Eureka*, Australasian Book Society, Sydney, 1976.

Brown, N. (ed) *Talking Straight Out: Stories from the Irati Wanti Campaign*, Alapaltaja Press, Coober Pedy, 2005.

Builders Labourers Federation, *The Builders' Labourers Song Book*, Widescope International, Melbourne, 1975.

Burgmann, M. and Burgmann, V. *Green Bans, Red Union: Environmental Activism and the New South Wales Builders Labourers' Federation*, University of New South Wales Press, Sydney, 1998.

Burgmann, V. *Power and Protest: Movements for Change in Australian Society*, Allen & Unwin, Sydney, 1993.

Burgmann, V. *Power, Profit & Protest: Australian Social Movements and Globalisation*, Allen & Unwin, Sydney, 2003.

Cahill, R. and Fitzpatrick, B. *The Seamen's Union of Australia, 1872-1972: A History*, Seamen's Union of Australia, Sydney, 1981.

Cain, F. *The Wobblies at War: A History of the IWW and the Great War in Australia*, Spectrum Publications, Melbourne, 1993.

Cain, F. *The Australian Security Intelligence Organization: An Unofficial History*, Spectrum Publications, Melbourne, 1994.

Cannon, M. *The Human Face of the Great Depression*, Self-published, Melbourne, 1996.

Clark, C.M.H. *Select Documents in Australian History, 1788-1850*, Angus & Robertson, Sydney, 1950.

Cockington, J. *Mondo Weirdo: Australia in the Sixties*, Mandarin, Port Melbourne, 1992.

Cohen, I. *Green Fire*, Angus & Robertson, Sydney, 1997.

Connor, J. *The Australian Frontier Wars, 1788-1838*, UNSW Press, Sydney, 2002.

Constance, T. and Quinlan, M. *A Divided Working Class*, Routledge Press, London, 1988.

Coombes, A. *Sex and Anarchy: The Life and Death of the Sydney Push*, Viking, Ringwood, 1996.

Curthoys, B. and MacDonald, A. *More than a Hat and Glove Brigade: The Story of the Union of Australian Women*, Bookpress, Sydney, 2000.

D'Aprano, Z. *Zelda*, Spinifex Press, North Melbourne, 1995.

Day, B. *Bunji: A Story of the Gwalwa Daraniki Movement*, Aboriginal Studies Press, Canberra, 1994.

Doyle, T. *Green Power: The Environmental Movement in Australia*, UNSW Press, Sydney, 2000.

Draft Resisters Union, *Downdraft: A Draft Resistance Manual*, DRU, Melbourne, 1972.

Dunstan, K. *Ratbags*, Golden Press, Sydney, 1979.

Edmonds, R. *In Storm and Struggle: A History of the Communist Party in Newcastle 1920–1940*, Self-published, Newcastle, 1991.

Elder, B. *Blood on the Wattle: Massacres and Maltreatment of Aboriginal Australians Since 1788*, New Holland, Sydney, 2003.

Evans, L. and Nicholls, P. *Convicts and Colonial Society, 1788-1868*, Macmillan, South Melbourne, 1984.

Evans, R. and Ferrier, C. *Radical Brisbane*, Vulgar Press, Melbourne, 2004.

Fabian, S. *Left-wing Ladies: The Union of Australian Women in Victoria 1950-1998*, Hyland House, Flemington, 2000.

Farrall, L. *The File on Fred*, High Leigh Publishing, Melbourne, 1992.

Fergus, R. and York, B. *The Black Resistance: An Introduction to the History of the Aborigines' Struggle Against British Colonialism*, Widescope, Melbourne, 1977.

Friends of the Earth Australia. *30 Years of Creative Resistance*, Friends of the Earth Australia, Melbourne, 2001

Fox, C. *Fighting Back: The Politics of the Unemployed in Victoria in the Great Depression*, Melbourne University Press, Melbourne, 2000.

Fox, L. *Australians on the Left*, Self-published, Potts Point, 1996.

Fox, L. (ed), *Depression Down Under*, Hale & Iremonger, Sydney, 1989.

Fry, E. (ed) *Tom Barker and the I.W.W.*, Australian Society for the Study of Labour History, Canberra, 1965.

Fry, E. (ed) *Rebels and Radicals*, George Allen & Unwin, Sydney, 1983.

Gibson, R. *My Years in the Communist Party*, International Bookshop, Melbourne, 1966.

Harris, J. *The Bitter Fight: A Pictorial History of the Australian Labor Movement*, University of Queensland Press, St. Lucia, 1970.

Harris, S. *Political Football: The Springbok Tour of Australia, 1971*, Gold Star Publications, Melbourne, 1972.

Hastings, G. *It Can't Happen Here: A Political History of Australian Student Activism*, Students Association of Flinders University, Adelaide, 2003.

Irving, T. and Cahill, R. *Radical Sydney*, UNSW Press, Sydney, 2010.

James, B. *Anarchism and State Violence in Sydney and Melbourne, 1886-1896: An Argument About Australian Labour History*, Self-published, Newcastle East, 1986.

Jenkins, J. *Ego is Not a Dirty Word: The Skyhooks Story*, Kelly & Withers, Fitzroy, 1994.

Johnson, J. *Jack Johnson in the Ring and Out*, Damon Runyon Softcover, Bedfordshire, 1975.

Kearns, B. (ed) *Stepping Out For Peace: A History of CANE and PND (WA)*, PND, Perth, 2004.

Lane, E.H. *From Dawn to Dusk*, William Brooks Publishing, Brisbane, 1939.

Langley, G. *Decade of Dissent*, Allen and Unwin, Sydney, 1992.

Lippmann, L. *Generations of Resistance*, Longman Cheshire, Sydney, 1981.

Lockwood, R. *Ship to Shore*, Hale & Iremonger, Sydney, 1990.

Lowenstein, W. *Under the Hook: Melbourne Waterside Workers Remember Working Lives and Class War*, Bookworkers Press in association with Working Titles, Prahran, 1998.

Lowenstein, W. *Weevils at Work*, Catalyst Press, Melbourne, 1997.

Lowenstein, W. *Weevils in the Flour: An Oral Record of the 1930's Depression in Australia*, Scribe, Melbourne, 1981.

Mann, T. *Tom Mann's Memoirs*, Labour Publishing, London, 1923.

MacDonald, T. (ed). *Changing Australia: The Union Story*, Unions NSW, Sydney, 2005.

McIntyre, I. *Always Look on the Bright Side of Life: The AIDEX '91 Story*, Homebrew Books, Melbourne, 2008.

McIntyre, I. *Disturbing the Peace*, Homebrew Books, Melbourne 2005.